Crime and Its Victims

Crime and Its Victims: International Research and Public Policy Issues

Proceedings of the Fourth International Institute on Victimology (NATO Advanced Research Workshop)

Edited by

Emilio C. Viano
The American University, Washington, DC

HEMISPHERE PUBLISHING CORPORATION
A member of the Taylor & Francis Group
New York Washington Philadelphia London

CRIME AND ITS VICTIMS: International Research and Public Policy Issues

1 2 3 4 5 6 7 8 9 0 BRBR 8 9 8 7 6 5 4 3 2 1 0 9

This book was set in Times Roman by EPS Group. The editors were Carolyn V. Ormes and Christian Milord.
Cover design by Debra Eubanks Riffe.

Braun-Brumfield, Inc. was printer and binder.

Library of Congress Cataloging-in-Publication Data

International Institute on Victimology (4th : 1987 : Ciocco Hotel, Tuscany, Italy)
Crime and its victims : international research and public policy issues : proceedings of the Fourth International Institute on Victimology (NATO Advanced Research Workshop) / edited by Emilio C. Viano.
p. cm.
Includes index.

1. Victims of crimes—Congresses. I. Viano, Emilio. II. Title.
HV6250.2.I56 1987
362.88—dc20 89-34878
CIP

ISBN 0-89116-950-4

The organizer and director of the Fourth International Institute on Victimology, Emilio Viano, and the Institute participants gratefully acknowledge the sponsorship and financial support of the Science Committee and of the Scientific Affairs Division of the North Atlantic Treaty Organization (NATO) under the program of grants for Advanced Research Workshops.

This volume is dedicated—as an expression of gratitude and appreciation—to the sponsors of the Institute, to its outstanding participants and staff, and to all those whose efforts made it possible and successful.

Contents

Contributors

Richard B. Abell, Assistant Attorney General, Office of Justice Programs, Washington, DC, USA

Michael W. Agopian, Associate Professor, Criminal Justice Department, California State University, Long Beach, California, USA

Maria Rosa Almeida, Technical Staff, Office of Studies and Planning, Ministry of Justice, Lisbon, PORTUGAL

Augusto Balloni, Professor, Department of Sociology, University of Bologna, Bologna, ITALY

Patricia Begin, Research Officer, Research Branch, Library of Parliament, Ottawa, Ontario, CANADA

Prabodh Kumar Bhowmick, Dean, Faculty of Science, University of Calcutta, Calcutta, INDIA

Daniel E. Della-Giustina, Professor and Chairman, Safety Studies Department, West Virginia University, Morgantown, West Virginia, USA

Susan S. M. Edwards, Research Fellow, Polytechnic of Central London, London, UK

Thomas Feltes, Assistant Professor, Institute of Criminology, University of Heidelberg, Heidelberg, FEDERAL REPUBLIC OF GERMANY

Robert Freeman-Longo, Director, Sex Offender Treatment Program, Oregon State Hospital, Salem, Oregon, USA

Burt Galaway, Professor, School of Social Work, University of Minnesota, Minneapolis, Minnesota, USA

Eliana Gersão, Director, Research Unit, Centro de Estudos Judiciarios, Ministry of Justice, Lisbon, PORTUGAL

Joseph Giovannoni, Sex Offender Treatment Specialist, Pacific Center for Sexual Health, Honolulu, Hawaii, USA

Frank Henry, Associate Professor, Department of Sociology, McMaster University, Hamilton, Ontario, CANADA

Stanley W. Johnston, Reader in Criminology, Melbourne University, Parkville, Victoria, AUSTRALIA

Irving Kaufman, Professor, School of Social Work, Smith College, Northampton, Massachusetts, USA

Simha Landau, Senior Lecturer, Institute of Criminology, Faculty of Law, Hebrew University, Jerusalem, ISRAEL

Malcolm D. MacLeod, Assistant Professor, Department of Psychology, University of Aberdeen, King's College, Aberdeen, Scotland, UK

Wesley G. Skogan, Professor, Center for Urban Affairs, Northwestern University, Evanston, Illinois, USA

Jacquelien Soetenhorst, Professor, Social Faculty, University of Amsterdam, THE NETHERLANDS

Aglaia Tsitsoura, Head, Division of Crime Problems, Council of Europe, Strasbourg, FRANCE

Emilio C. Viano, Professor, Department of Justice, Law, and Society, School of Public Affairs, The American University and Editor, *Victimology: An International Journal,* Washington, DC, USA

Lenore E. A. Walker, Licensed Psychologist, Walker and Associates, Denver, Colorado, USA

Velma A. Williams, Child Development Associate Training Program, University of Alabama, Tuscaloosa, Alabama, USA

Vergil L. Williams, Professor and Chairman, Department of Criminal Justice, University of Alabama, Tuscaloosa, Alabama, USA

Frans Willem Winkel, Assistant Professor, Department of Social Psychology, Free University, Amsterdam, THE NETHERLANDS

Duygun Yarsuvat, Professor, Faculty of Political Science, University of Istanbul, TURKEY

Preface

VICTIMOLOGY TODAY

Victimology has recently emerged as a scholarly, policy-making, and service-delivery approach that focuses on the unique problems of the victim and of those who surround the victim: witnesses, bystanders, good samaritans, survivors, the family . . .

It certainly took courage and determination for victimologists to have attempted in recent years to bring the victim's needs and reality to the attention of an oblivious, indifferent, and hurried public. The movement has grown considerably. It focused first on sexual assault and child abuse, then on domestic violence. More recently, it has focused on the victimization of the elderly, of parents at the hands of their children, and of the survivors of victims of homicide and on date rape, sexual harassment, and patient abuse by therapists.

The field has also grown internationally, with services being provided in several countries. The growth of victimology was officially recognized on November 29, 1985, when the United Nations General Assembly unanimously adopted resolution 40/34 and the accompanying Declaration of Basic Principles of Justice for Victims of Crime and Abuse of Power.

While victims and witnesses of crime have received the most attention, victimology can and should also be concerned with other types of victims as well, for example, victims of earthquakes, natural disasters, occupational accidents and hazards, dislocation, and famine. In fact, the common denominator of victimological work is *crisis intervention* and the short- and long-term remedies that should be made available to victims.

Victimology has emerged with a wide variety of research, scholarly, and intervention styles. The profession is diverse in its philosophical orientation, substantive concerns, and occupational activities. However, what on the surface may appear to be scattered work is in fact a ferment of ideas and concerns, and the competition among the various views will lead in the end to the emergence of a field that knows where it is going and that has something special to say and to offer to a society racked by crime and violence.

THE FOURTH INTERNATIONAL INSTITUTE ON VICTIMOLOGY

The Fourth International Institute on Victimology (a NATO Advanced Research Workshop) was held in Tuscany, Italy, on August 9–15, 1987, with the objective of bringing together scholars, professionals, and policymakers to

1. conduct a critical overall review of the state of the art in victimology
2. survey the major research efforts on victimization conducted to date
3. identify and inventory major findings in the field
4. develop a comprehensive research strategy and agenda
5. demonstrate how data on victims can be useful to administrators and decisionmakers
6. strengthen international cooperation and communication

The meeting was sponsored and funded by the North Atlantic Treaty Organization (NATO) and by *Victimology: An International Journal.*

In order to achieve the objectives of the meeting, the agenda was designed around the concept of maximum participation and input on the part of all participants. All relevant disciplines and points of view were welcome. A mix of general sessions, paper presentations, and small-group sessions was utilized.

In particular, four task forces were formed to achieve the objectives of the Institute as they relate to four specific areas of victimological theory and research that were listed in the basic preliminary document of the meeting:

1. harm and its causes
2. seeing oneself as a victim
3. claiming the victim status and role
4. receiving society's recognition and possible support

The four task forces worked intensely during the meeting to answer specific questions related to those four areas and to develop appropriate conclusions and recommendations.

THE PROCEEDINGS

The result of the work of the Institute participants is presented here for circulation among the international community of organizations, programs, associations, scholars, professionals, practitioners, and all others whose work and influence can directly affect the unfolding and outcome of those four stages of the victimization process.

The main purpose of this book is to bring together under one cover—and to arrange coherently—many of the best contributions in research, prevention, treatment, and public policy presented at the meeting. The contributions for this volume were selected because their authors were able both to present their own ideas, research, or practical knowledge in an interesting way and to distill the work of others so as to make it accessible.

The book has been divided into seven major parts:

I. Introduction
II. Victimization Dynamics and Interactions
III. The Victim and the Justice System
IV. The Child Victim and Related Issues
V. Sexual Victimization and Offenses

VI. Public Policy
VII. Conclusions and Recommendations

The book has been designed to provide a balance between practical and theoretical issues and concerns. Since the participants in the Institute represented 15 different countries (Australia, Belgium, Canada, Federal Republic of Germany, Greece, India, Israel, Italy, The Netherlands, Norway, Portugal, Spain, Turkey, United Kingdom, United States) and two international organizations (Council of Europe and United Nations), there is a substantial international dimension to this book.

The volume has been carefully designed with the goal of providing not only data about problems but also information; models; and approaches to solutions, prevention, treatment, and the formulation of public policy. It is felt that in this way the book will represent a truly positive contribution to the development of the field. This will also make it more useful and appealing to students preparing for professional careers (e.g., in law, social work, or the mental health fields) and to those already working in the field.

The victim movement holds great promise as a force for genuine change in society's attitudes and patterns of caring for its members. The publication of this volume will help it gain momentum and attain its full potential. It will also ensure that this crucial movement in our social history will become a permanent part of our moral heritage and lead to the creation of a society that is free of violence, exploitation, and victimization.

Emilio C. Viano

Acknowledgments

The organizer and director of the Institute, Emilio Viano, and the participants gratefully acknowledge the generous financial support provided by the Scientific Affairs Division of the North Atlantic Treaty Organization (NATO) under its program of grants for Advanced Research Workshops and the guidance and assistance extended by the NATO staff, especially by the late Dr. Mario di Lullo and by Dr. Craig Sinclair.

They also thank the management and staff of Il Ciocco, a resort hotel in northern Tuscany, and in particular Bruno Giannasi. Their hard work, genuine friendliness, dedication to excellence, and smooth delivery of services greatly contributed to the success of the meeting.

Finally, participants of the Institute acknowledge and thank the staff of *Victimology: An International Journal,* especially Sherry Icenhower, administrative director of the Institute, for their painstaking and diligent work in organizing the meeting and seeing to it that its unfolding would be flawless.

The director of the meeting and editor of this volume, Emilio Viano, thanks all the attendees for their participation in the Institute; for their superb contributions to the discussions; for their willingness to observe a rigorous schedule of work and of formal and informal meetings; and for their cooperation in the production of this book. Particular thanks are extended to the chairs of the task forces, Susan Edwards, Aglaia Tsitsoura, and Lenore Walker (assisted by Christina Antonopoulou), for accepting the invitation to serve, for assuming the burdens of the office, and for faithfully delivering the final product of so many hours of deliberations.

I

INTRODUCTION

1

Victimology Today: Major Issues in Research and Public Policy

Emilio C. Viano
School of Public Affairs, The American University, Washington, D.C.

INTRODUCTION

This chapter examines four major areas of inquiry that can be identified in contemporary victimology. They correspond to four different and complementary stages in the definition of victimization. These stages also constitute a process which confers official victim status on someone if it is carried out to its conclusion. The chapter examines the nature, development, and dynamics of each stage, utilizing a *process approach*. This approach is important because it helps focus research on the question of who will be in each stage, who will move from one stage to the next, and when, how, and why. At the end of the chapter, major questions for research and public policy are raised.

Persons at one stage will have a different perception of their status as "victim" than those at other stages. This will affect their behavior and will influence (or even determine) who will make the transition from one stage to the next and who will not. The process approach also stresses the dynamics of the situation and the impact that social and cultural values and forces have on the determination of who is a "real" victim. Different research and policy questions belong to each stage.

The four stages are as follows:

1. In the first stage, individuals experience harm, injury, or suffering caused by another person or institution.
2. In the second stage, some of these individuals perceive such harm as undeserved, unfair, and unjust, and they therefore perceive themselves as victims.
3. In the third stage, some of these individuals, perceiving themselves as harmed or victimized, attempt to get someone else (e.g., family, friends, helping

Emilio Viano is a professor at the Department of Justice, Law and Society, The American University, Washington, D.C. He is also the editor of *Victimology: An International Journal*. He has been active in the field of victimology and victim-witness services since the early 1970s. He has conducted research and has organized and chaired several national and international congresses and meetings in the field. He has also directed several programs, including the National Victim and Witness Resource Center, and has served as a national and international expert on various projects. He has published various books and articles in victimology and in other fields of justice. Professor Viano can be reached at 2333 North Vernon Street, Arlington, VA 22207.

professionals, or authority figures) to recognize the harm and validate the claim that they have been victimized.

4. Finally, some of these individuals receive validation of their claim to victim status, become "official" victims, and possibly benefit from various types of support, depending on various variables.

For the purposes of our discussion, a *victim* is any individual harmed or damaged by another or by others who perceives him- or herself as harmed, who shares the experience and seeks assistance and redress, and who is recognized as harmed and possibly assisted by public, private, or community agencies.

While the emphasis here is on the individual, note that institutions, corporations, commercial establishments, and groups of people can also be victimized and claim victim status—basically following the same stages.

STAGE 1: HARM AND ITS CAUSES

According to the traditional view, the essential element for victim status is the presence of harm, suffering, or injury caused by a crime. However, some argue that there is no compelling reason to limit the cause of the harm to a criminal act committed by an individual against another. Institutional victimization, abuse of power, collective victimization, and illegal or illegitimate governmental actions should be considered causes of victimization as well. Similarly, not only acts of commission but also acts of omission should be taken into account. Whether victims of natural disasters, war, environmental pollution, the closing of a factory, etc., should be included in this definition is debatable. One could argue that why or how one is harmed is irrelevant, that what counts is being in crisis, injured, harmed, and needing to recover and regain mastery over one's life and surroundings.

One can experience harm without defining oneself as a victim. Many experience considerable harm or suffering, often harm clearly caused by other individuals, without defining themselves as victims. On the contrary, cultural, traditional, or religious beliefs may supply rationalizations leading them to consider themselves responsible for or the cause of what they suffer and to blame themselves and not the actual perpetrators. Domestic violence, sexual assault, and sexual harassment offer classic examples of these rationalizations. The concepts of susceptibility, vulnerability, and life-style are also important tools in approaching this dimension.

Questions

There has been considerable research about the epidemiology of certain crimes, including research on who is killed, or killed the most, in homicides and who gets robbed, burglarized, and sexually assaulted. Groups or categories of people have also been studied to identify what type of harm they may suffer disproportionately. The vulnerability of women, children, and the elderly to certain types of abuse and neglect and the vulnerability of young males to violence have been stressed by this approach.

Moving beyond mere statistics and frequencies, one might next consider why certain segments of the population are harmed in relatively specific ways. One might also ask why patterns of harm can change. For example, the large [illegible] of women entering the work force may create new situations with harm[illegible]tential for them (e.g., an increase in cases of sexual harassment on the job or of robbery or assault while at work or traveling on business). The fact that a group is found to suffer disproportionately in a certain way can lead to new discoveries or perspectives and reveal deeper causes for such victimization.

For example, the victimization of children, women, elderly people, and minorities is better and more realistically understood if we shift away from analyzing what they did, where they were, or how they behaved and instead look at the cultural, social, and economic values supporting a certain view of them which leads to attitudes condoning or actively generating their victimization. Sexism, racism, and ageism were not always acknowledged to exist. Some still deny the existence of these powerful forces and prefer to "blame the victim." Thus, as one can see, changing the focus of the inquiry leads to a very different understanding of what causes certain individuals or groups in society to be subject to harm.

This, in turn, enlightens us about the appropriate strategy for change. In this sense, the Stage 1 analysis provides a strong foundation for preventive efforts. The policy question here is, How do we reduce the amount of harm people encounter, whether or not they consider themselves victims? The analysis also leads us to ask other fundamental questions like, What does an increasing victimization rate mean for a culture? How do our data bear on the meaning of society as a positive and beneficent entity? What fundamental restructuring is needed to stop the victimization? Or are our efforts to be limited to treating the victims without questioning and attacking the processes that generate them? Moreover, it reminds us of the need to look at and understand the "before" of victimization and its gestation, when it still lurks about as an unthematized, unspoken possibility, an undefined fear, a mere turbulence in the sky appearing against the still predominant horizon of safety.

On the other hand, this approach can have its downside too. For example, the possible pitfalls and the potential for trivialization and for "blaming the victim" that are inherent in the "life-style" approach are pretty clear.

Some do not agree that victimology should include these processes, claiming that victimological inquiry should begin only at the level of the victims' awareness and realization of their victimization and, even better, of their willingness to publicly acknowledge and report it.

Others disagree and feel instead that the questions raised during this stage and during the transition to the next stage can generate important research questions and support vigorous and useful research efforts.

STAGE 2: SEEING ONESELF AS A VICTIM

The transition from suffering harm to seeing oneself as a victim is crucial, and it has been neglected, possibly because of the recent emphasis on sociologically oriented macroresearch (e.g., national victimization surveys) versus the more psychologically oriented microapproaches.

One of the major obstacles to recognizing victimization, even on the part of the victim, is often silent public tolerance of it. Such tolerance can result from a system of values, beliefs, mores, and laws that actively support, justify, and legitimize victimization. At times this silent tolerance is enshrined into a formal code of honor and behavior, as in the case of the *omertá* enforced by organized crime. Danilo Dolci, a social reformer who cast his lot in recent years with the exploited and the dispossessed of Sicily, attracted international attention exactly because he defied the silence and openly spoke about organized crime's evil empire. The fact that high prelates and some parish priests in Sicily recently also openly acknowledged the existence and the activities of organized crime caused a sensation—not so much because they revealed something new but because they defied the accepted code of silence and the pretense that nothing was wrong.

The tacit acceptance of victimization can be the result of a "nonconscious ideology," a system of beliefs and attitudes that are implicitly accepted but remain outside conscious awareness because of prevailing stereotypes. It can also be due to the fact that sometimes alternatives are not available, possible, or even imaginable. In order to avoid the surfacing of troubling "cognitive dissonance," the awareness of injustices and prevarications is blotted out and normalcy is restored by legitimizing and incorporating the victimization into the accepted values, mores, and ways of life of a particular society.

Victims themselves are raised to accept and internalize such patterns as "the way things are," at times even supporting them and opposing reform because of intricate social and psychological dynamics. The few who become aware of the abnormal situation and speak up are ignored, ridiculed, silenced, crushed, cast away, declared insane, or driven to insanity.

It often takes drastic social changes like industrialization, urbanization, the growth of educational and career opportunities, and the opening up of life-style alternatives to shake the status quo and bring relevant issues into the open. This in turn educates the victims about their victimization, heightens their awareness, encourages their quest for change and, most of all, leads them to see themselves as victims of an unjust system. The realization that "this should not have happened to me: I did not deserve it or cause it" constitutes the key psychological dynamic in this complex process. The difficulty of accomplishing this stems from the fact that well-ingrained beliefs, values, and social systems must be challenged and changed and that trusted authority and guidance figures must be rejected with no immediate guarantee of ultimate success. This perceived riskiness of the choice is coupled with the awareness that defeat would bring a crushing backlash.

A major reason why people have difficulty in seeing themselves as victims is the novel, threatening, and shattering nature of the experience of being victimized. Normally, an atmosphere of safety and social harmony supports our activities. Being victimized is not a reality normally facing us. If there is any thought of victimization at all, the tendency is to think "I might be—anyone could be" or, more likely, "I know it happens, but it will not happen to me." Prior to its occurrence, victimization is at most an empty possibility which we are not concerned about in normal, routine daily life.

Being victimized is the dawning of a *new configuration of meaning*, and it occurs in lived experience through a developmental process. In the beginning of this process, it presents itself as strange, unfitting, unfamiliar, perhaps problematic and confusing. Even when victimization becomes a lived reality, the disbelief expressed in victims' reports indicates that it is still a relatively empty sort of quasi-reality. It has not been fully articulated, realized, and understood.

This is because the person's previous world of meaning was built on the foundations of safety and social harmony. Now that these foundations are shattered, the victim is delivered to a strange, unfamiliar, shocking, hardly believable new realm outside the usual norms and experiences of life.

Victimization (or at least the first instance of it) is originally surprising, alien, and unpredictable as it tears away the familiar world. Thus, even when it becomes clear to the person that his or her preferred situation is being destroyed by another, what results is a kind of a void which only gradually begins to be understood. The victim has been torn from his or her life and swept into another which is contrary to it, thus emptying the victim's world of its usual meaning.

There are three major components of victimization that make it particularly threatening and difficult to absorb:

1. The victim's ability to control his or her life is lost, and the victim stands helplessly vulnerable, isolated, and immobilized.
2. All helpful and cooperative social support systems have receded and are out of the victim's reach.
3. A predator has invaded the victim's life and destroyed in various degrees the victim's well-being.

Victimization strikes the victim's sphere of ownness. It is not indifferent or trivial matters which are involved here but the victim's personal world or ownmost world, the *eigenwelt*, whose center is the victim and others intimately related to the victim. Thus, the seriousness and profundity of victimization can be measured by questions like these: How close to home did the crime strike? How essentially was the victim's life affected? There are of course variations in seriousness and significance which reflect individual values and idiosyncrasies. For some, their cars or pets may indeed be more important than their spouses or children!

Seeing oneself as a victim and accepting one's victimization is important for another crucial reason: It can be the beginning of the recovery process. Understanding overcomes shock and confusion and opens the way for the struggle to overcome.

Questions

As a general comment, research questions for Stage 2 could be borrowed from the labeling school of criminology, which has developed questions mostly with deviants and criminals in mind. Acknowledging that one is a victim is indeed a process of *self-labeling*.

What are the circumstances in which people react to harm as unfair and requiring redress? What role do significant others and the larger culture play in this process of self-labeling? Is there a critical mass of ideological communication and consensus that makes it possible for victims to "come out," cast aside previous rationalizations, and acknowledge their victimization? What are the major factors that create a climate favorable to the success of this process? What other givens must be in place for such factors to be successful? For example, the factors often cited to explain our awareness of sexual and domestic violence against women do not seem to cause the same changes in non-Western societies, although on the surface these factors exist there as well (e.g., increased education, affluence, communications, travel, work outside the home and related income, etc.). The current resurgence of fundamentalism in most major religions, which directly impacts the level and awareness of victimization of women and children, also poses interesting questions about the dialectics of this process.

Cultural values also influence which forms of harm are readily and clearly accepted as being injurious so that people easily see themselves as having been victimized. For example, interestingly enough, crimes against property are more easily considered clearly injurious to the victims than crimes of violence or physical harm. Psychological harm is even more difficult to identify, attribute, label, and place a valuation on. How do we take into account individual variations in the perception and evaluation of seriousness and harm? Should we strive for a consensus on a general continuum of victimization that would ultimately govern society's recognition and intervention in a standardized and agreed manner? (At one end of this continuum would be trivial losses and at the other would be the extreme form of destruction of someone's world—homicide.)

Harms affecting a large number of people and harms caused by impersonal entities are similarly difficult. When government, business, or trade decisions adversely affect someone's life, does the victim go through the same process of feeling victimized as someone hurt by an attacker? Can we learn anything from studying the similarities and differences in how people react to personally versus impersonally caused harm? And what are the long-term consequences of this apparent indifference to impersonal harm in our society, in which high levels of technology and computer-driven functions will dramatically increase the sense of impersonality and loss of community in the future?

Another related question is, How do we go about perceiving ourselves as victimized by entire societal systems, like racism, sexism, ageism? What factors and dynamics make it possible for our perceptions to coalesce so that we can see patterns of harm that go beyond individual decisions and actions and are instead part of a larger and entrenched system of beliefs and practices?

Stage 2 alerts us to the importance of *public education and consciousness raising* so that people can transcend particular explanations and justifications of victimization and grasp the systemic and widespread nature of the harm affecting them. This should then lead to the development of a sense of outrage and to a decision that something must be done to change the situation—and not just in a particular case but for an entire class of actual or potential victims, which would thus attack the problem at its roots and solve it in a definitive manner.

The importance of public education and consciousness raising is far-reaching. In most Western systems of justice, it is the jury that determines guilt or innocence. If the public has not been reached and educated, the likelihood is small that the jury will be able to understand the dynamics of victimization and to agree with the victim's vision of him- or herself and of the events. While considerable efforts have been recently undertaken to educate people in the criminal justice system about the plight of victims, if the public from which juries are selected is ignored, all these efforts can easily come to naught.

The implications for social policy are clear. Approaching victimization as an individual, discrete situation leads to interventions that are meant to alleviate the discomfort and suffering of victims but do not challenge or attempt to change

(1) the system that is producing and will continue to produce more victims and that will even revictimize again and again those who are healed, and (2) the underlying values that support such a system.

There might even be collusion between the healer and the victimizer in perpetuating the cycle of victimization. The healer might, without challenging the inequity of the system, (1) mold the victim so he or she accepts the unjust situation and (2) change the victim's behavior accordingly so the victim can escape harm at the individual level. This process of acceptance and accommodation ultimately recognizes, legitimizes, and increases the victimizer's power and grip.

Serious questions have been raised by some in recent times about the role of psychology, psychiatry, social work, and counseling vis-à-vis the victim. Should these professions help a person with psychological problems accept the existing social order as a given that should not be challenged? In other words, should they try to improve the "fit" by changing the individual? Or should they be willing and trained to support the individual whose problems stem from an unjust social order and try to reform it to fit the individual?

Even more troubling is the role of other healing professionals (e.g., medical doctors), who may utilize their knowledge and skills to keep a victim alive for further torturing or to determine how far torture can go before jeopardizing the life of the victim (e.g., when the torturer wants to keep the victim alive for further interrogation or abuse). The role of psychiatry has also been criticized when it supports the status quo in certain countries by declaring social reformers and opponents of the power structure to be mentally ill and confining them to psychiatric institutions.

From a policy perspective, we should also ask ourselves whether or not it is always desirable to make people aware of their status as victims if they are not aware of it and have adapted to the injustice and the oppression. Are there circumstances when this may cause more harm than good? How should this process be conducted to minimize additional trauma? What if there are no available remedies, so that the awareness of victimization is useless and actually inflicts additional pain? What if it leads to isolated and fruitless attempts at changing the situation, attempts that will only result in more repression? Is it right to cause dissatisfaction and raise false hopes when one cannot effectively introduce change or guarantee some success?

Some experts believe that people who have been harmed should at least be willing to consider themselves victimized before victimology considers them victimized. Others argue that no stage by itself constitutes the proper focus of victimology. Rather, in their opinion, victimology must focus on the entire process of victimization. The major questions here are, What are the proper and correct borders of victimology? When does someone become the legitimate object of victimological inquiry?

STAGE 3: CLAIMING THE STATUS AND ROLE OF VICTIM

After an individual has recognized an experience as victimization, he or she must still decide what to do about it. Several formal and informal avenues are open to the victim. There is evidence that victims validate their experience and their conclusions with someone they trust—a family member, friend, spouse, neighbor, doctor, or priest—more often than one would think. Such validation strongly influences whether or not they will ultimately notify official agencies of society (e.g., police, consumer protection agencies, professional societies or boards, ombudsmen, etc.).

Many variables affect the victim's decision to publicly report the victimization: the perceived probability of the police finding the culprit; the amount of damage or harm suffered; the relationship with the victimizer and the impact of reporting on it; the obstacles, expense, and time involved in reporting; the perceived complexity of bureaucratic proceedings; the fear of being ridiculed or of retaliation and revenge; the lack of privacy at the initial stages of reporting; and the place of residence (rural dwellers find it even more difficult to report than urban residents).

Social, cultural and psychological factors may stop a victim from publicly claiming the status of victim. This can at times lead to continued victimization, with the victimizer taking advantage of the lack of action on the part of the victim. A basic and pervasive factor giving victims pause is the value placed on winning and on being successful in society. In the eyes of many, a victim is a loser, even though an innocent one. As a result, the victim can pay a high price when acknowledging victimization. This is why, for example, it may be more difficult for males to admit and report their victimization and seek appropriate help.

In societies where setting the limits of sexual activity is strictly the woman's responsibility, fornication a serious crime, and rape no excuse, one can readily understand a victim's reluctance to report a victimizing event. Reporting it could be the equivalent of passing a death sentence on herself, or at least it could seriously jeopardize her own social status, respectability, and desirability in the community and the social status of her family.

In other words, where victim blaming is prevalent and, worst of all, internalized by the victims themselves, the psychological and social price to be paid in reporting may simply be too high. Similarly, the victims' perception or realization that they will not be believed could effectively close all avenues for reporting and seeking redress for an indeterminate period of time and could possibly lead to prolonged victimization. Moreover, the social devaluation consequent to reporting may make the victim an easy target for harassment and further victimization at the hands of the original victimizer or at the hands of others. Examples of this situation include incest, sexual harassment or assault, domestic violence, and elder abuse.

The reluctance to claim the status and role of victim is not confined to individuals. Corporations, businesses, even governments may not report being victimized in order to maintain a certain image or for other practical reasons. For example, a company may not report a virus invasion or a breach of security in its computer system. Instead, it will absorb the losses to avoid bad publicity, which might shake its customers' confidence and adversely affect its ability to function. The acquiescence of small and even large businesses to the extortionist demands of organized crime or of corrupt customs, government, or police officials also reflects many of the same dynamics affecting the willingness of individual victims to acknowledge and claim their role as victim and seek redress.

Questions

What influences the decision to claim the status and role of victim? What influences the choice of whom to report the victimization to (family, friends, acquaintances, police, private or public agencies, rape crisis center, etc.)? Some victims initially limit the disclosure to closer people and then later extend it to outsiders. When reporting to outsiders, some choose to avoid official or law enforcement agencies in favor of community-based, grass roots, or victim-staffed organizations. There is also evidence that many victims prefer to share their victimization and seek the assistance of informal, rather than formal, networks of social support.

What are the reasons why some people do not claim the status and role of victim? What are the psychological and social consequences of such a decision? How can society increase the likelihood of victim reporting? What do victims anticipate or expect, positively or negatively, when they report?

What is the victims' level of satisfaction with those they interact with when they report? Does the existence of reputable treatment and rehabilitation programs for some types of offenders increase the probability of reporting by victims? How do the different operational philosophies of helping organizations affect whether someone claims the role of victim?

How does reporting unfold (in terms of frequency, nature, and degree of willingness to pursue the matter further) once social and cultural changes make it respectable or safe to report a particular type of victimization? Is there a feedback loop which rewards reporting by changing cultural values in favor of the victim, thus making it progressively easier for later victims to report because of the reporting of previous ones? Is reporting truly to the benefit of the victim or is it officially encouraged because it is mostly advantageous to the system?

Claiming the role of victim can be seen as an important step toward recovery. It represents the victim's struggle with victimization. It is an attempt by the victim to reclaim some active control over his or her own life by coming to terms with reality and by moving toward a resolution of the crisis. It is also an attempt to reestablish and strengthen the helpful, peaceful, and cooperative social supports that may have failed the victim at the time of victimization. Finally, it means taking positive action against the predator.

On the other hand, the inability to claim victim status can lead to very negative consequences. Some repeated victims, seeing no way out, commit suicide—a desperate way to finally take "control" of one's own life.

STAGE 4: RECEIVING SOCIETY'S RECOGNITION AND POSSIBLE SUPPORT

Overcoming victimization is an exact reversal of its meaning and cannot be taken for granted. If the social world causing or supporting victimization does not change or continues to be detrimental, if the victim does nothing abut his or her misfortune, or if others remain indifferent and unavailable, victimization deepens. Society and others play a crucial role in the victim's overcoming victimization and forming a newly constituted world. The active help of others restores a sense of trust and harmony in the victim's destroyed sociality and helps the victim make the difficult transition into the new world "after" victimization.

It is vital for the well-being of the victim as an individual and as a member of society that the damage of victimization be overcome and that the crisis generated by it be successfully resolved. Every victim's task and need is to reestablish the world as he or she prefers it and knows it. This involves rising out of immobility and seizing the initiative, ending isolation and establishing contacts and networks, escaping danger and entering into a safe harbor.

This process requires three interrelated elements: active effort, the world's assertion of predictable safety, and active help from others. It is through this process that victimization will appear as avoidable, preventable, and possible to overcome. Society's understanding and recognition of victimization is crucial to the unfolding of this recovery process.

A substantial amount of victimological research has been conducted on (1) the factors affecting the transition from Stage 3 to Stage 4 (i.e., the factors that determine whether a claim to the status of victim is recognized and acted on by society's agents) and (2) the actions of agents offering support, retribution, restitution, and compensation. Research and writing on the victim and the criminal justice system, victim-witness assistance programs, compensation and restitution, treatment for the victim, legal and criminal justice system reform, etc., clearly dominate the field.

Society's reaction and involvement are greatly affected by Stage 3. The increasing number of victims "coming out" reinforces and intensifies public awareness of victimization and contributes to further establishing it as part of the constellation of issues that cannot be ignored and about which something should be done. It also provides firsthand information on the victims, their numbers, the dynamics of victimization, the needs of the victims, and on how to reach them.

Once victims come out and public and professional interest is heightened, the logical next step will be to formulate appropriate public policy and provide related services. Such planning is required to ensure that society will be able to respond adequately and promptly when victims acknowledge and claim their status and seek the recognition and support of the community. It is not unusual for politicians and others in positions of power to give lip service to a legitimate cause in response to pressure but then fail to provide the adequate infrastructure and the means to responsibly address the problem once the intended target population takes them seriously and requests the services. Overpromising and underdelivering would be a serious setback to the resolution of victimization and would ultimately revictimize the victims.

Questions

How society will react to a victim's claim will inevitably depend on various variables linked to status, visibility, and power. What impact do the status of the victim, the type of victimization, its circumstances, the victim's belonging to a specific group (which may be receiving more or less recognition from official agencies depending on its numbers, visibility, and organized strength) have on the probability that the victim's claim will be honored?

The impact of these variables can be quite dramatic. For example, runaways for a long time were considered delinquents. It was only recently that a different view of runaways—the view that many are victims of abuse, neglect, and incest ("throwaways")—has finally begun to be accepted because of the vigorous efforts of skilled advocates and organizers of shelters.

A crucial concept that affects society's recognition is *victim precipitation*. What exactly is victim precipitation? In what ways does it affect the legitimation of the status of victim?

How can we increase the likelihood that public and private agencies, family, friends, and others will respond positively and show support when the victim asks for assistance?

Another important dimension here is what occurs once an agency, particularly an official one, recognizes a victim's claim to being a "real" victim. Does this recognition keep the victim in that role? If not, how exactly is the victim helped to move out of that role and back to "normal"? And what is normal particularly after a serious victimization? Which treatment is appropriate for which type of victim? Also, whose interests are being served when treatment is offered? Should this treatment include reeducating the victim to see the world differently or should those providing assistance accept victims for what they are, even though they may be returning to a world where they will be revictimized?

What can we learn from research in other fields of victimization (natural disasters, accidents, torture, abuse of power, etc.)? How do other types of victims cope with crisis, deal with the forced recognition of their vulnerability, and begin the recovery process?

What are the consequences of being denied victim status? How do people cope and make sense of the rejection of their claim? What impact does such denial have?

At a time of surging and competing claims within the framework of limited resources, how does one ensure that society will respond affirmatively and adequately to the needs of victims? How should society prepare to meet their claims? As for the most appropriate locus for victim services, should they be established in the private or public sector? Should they be in existing agencies or new ones? Should the programs be self-help or professionally controlled?

CONCLUSION

The framework provided here represents a comprehensive and dynamic approach to the understanding of victimization. It is our responsibility to review and evaluate past work in this field and to develop a future agenda that will spur, guide, and support future research and policy intervention.

Struggling with these issues will allow us to approach the attainment of a fuller understanding of the patterns and dynamics of victimization. It will also allow us to create an equitable society with less suffering, violence, and oppression while we respect the individuality and uniqueness of each victim.

BIBLIOGRAPHY

Birkbeck, C. (1983). "Victimology is what victimologists do" but what should they do? *Victimology: An International Journal, 8* (3-4), 270–275.

Burt, M. (1983). A conceptual framework for victimological research. *Victimology: An International Journal, 8* (3-4), 261–269.

Giorgi, A. (1985). *Phenomenology and psychological research*. Pittsburgh, PA: Duquesne University Press.

Viano, E. (1983). Violence, victimization and social change: A sociocultural and public policy analysis. *Victimology: An International Journal, 8* (3-4), 54–79.

II

VICTIMIZATION DYNAMICS AND INTERACTION

2

Crime and Its Victims: Interactory Roles of Victim, Victimizer, and Society

Irving Kaufman
Auburndale, Massachusetts

This chapter is a beginning attempt to look at the complex interaction between victim, victimizer, and the social matrix in which victimization occurs. It is a philosophical treatise designed to stimulate thinking and research. The particular goal is to encourage a closer examination of society's role in preventing or promoting victimization.

Ostensibly the community sets the standards for acceptable and unacceptable behavior. Statements regarding human and civil rights are made. Institutions, religions, moral admonitions, and legal procedures have all arisen in an attempt to further the goals of preventing victimization, protecting the victim, and helping (perhaps) the victimizer. It is my thesis that these well-intentioned objectives are too frequently not realized and that we often behave in ways that promote what we want to prevent. In short, we ensure more victimization.

The degree to which we are failing to protect ourselves is appalling. For example, there is a system of arrest and trial of alleged criminals. A recent study ("Study on Repeated Crime," 1984) revealed that even at the initial stages of the encounter with dangerous crime we make certain there is more crime. The study found that over 61% of the people arrested for serious crimes (e.g., rape and murder) commit additional serious crimes while they are awaiting trial. Recidivism figures vary, but some reports state that up to 90% of individuals who are arrested for a crime repeat criminal activity after serving a jail sentence. It is unclear what the purpose is of trials and jailing. They certainly don't seem to have a major effect on crime.

Such unsuccessful procedures costing millions of dollars not only do not protect us from being victimized but also abuse the victimizers. There has not been any significant attempt to look at what we are doing and why. No business organization engaged in marketing or manufacturing, for example, would or could tolerate such constant failure (see Menninger, *The Crime of Punishment*).

Irving Kaufman, M.D., has been trained in both adult and child psychoanalysis and is in private practice. He also teaches at the Smith College for Social Work. After 25 years, he retired from the Harvard University School of Medicine. He has been a consultant for many social agencies throughout New England on child and family issues, including delinquency, incest, and child abuse. He has written and published extensively on incest, firesetting, crimes of violence, child abuse, and childhood schizophrenia. One of his continuing interests is the role of mental health workers in correctional institutions.

In contrast, when we deal with individuals who are unsuccessful in some way—unable to learn to read or with emotional or physical problems—we ask what is the cause of the problem. We then try to find a way to solve it. We do not ask these questions in relation to the social institutions established to deal with victimization. This perplexing practice suggests to me that there are underlying reasons for the perpetuation of victimization.

Before considering possible reasons for the perpetuation of victimization, let us look at further failures of this process intended for our protection. Recently a woman in Massachusetts repeatedly appealed to the court for protection against her violent husband, who also threatened to kill her ("Wife's Appeal," 1987). Instead of receiving protection, each time she sought help she was verbally abused by the judge, who ordered her out of the court. She was murdered by her husband.

In another case in Boston, the police department assigned to handle domestic violence received a complaint from a woman that the man she was seeing had threatened to kill her ("Domestic Violence," 1987). He repeatedly committed violent and terrifying acts against her and other members of her family. For example, when she did not let him into her apartment, he kicked down the door and assaulted her. On another occasion he threatened her brother with a knife and slashed his automobile tires. She received no help or protection. He finally murdered her and now he is in jail.

The police department said they were too understaffed to begin to effectively handle the large number of cases presented to them. In view of the above case, which unfortunately is not a rare or isolated example, it would seem that we don't value human life and freedom from harassment and terror very much—at least not enough to provide the necessary funding for staff to protect our citizens from such victimization. In reference to the courts and police, what causes us to set up "the foxes to guard the chickens"?

There are many levels of understanding needed to begin to study the phenomena described above. What motivates a victimizer to harass, terrorize, abuse, and even kill a victim? This is not the major focus of this paper, but it is dealt with in previous articles (Kaufman, 1985, 1986), which describe the victimizer as an individual who is attempting to deal with his or her own terror and fear of destruction by terrorizing and destroying others. This brief formulation barely touches on the complexities of the victimizer and what makes him or her tick.

As for the victims, often they are innocent bystanders who were in the wrong place at the wrong time. There is, however, another kind of victim that requires attention. For example, Pizzey (1987) recently described a group of battered women. These battered women repeatedly found themselves in situations where they were repeatedly battered. Such victimization even occurred in shelters that Pizzey directed. Other women in the shelter would also abuse this group of women. It needs to be pointed out that although most women who are battered or victimized do not desire or seek out such abuse, a small group do. We need to question why and try to help them.

The third element that requires understanding—and the major focus of this paper—has already been delineated. This is the vast complex of legal, religious, political, and social systems that create a climate that fails to prevent victimization and in some ways fosters and perpetuates it. Once a victim or victimizer is on the "sticky fly paper" of "the System," attempting to extricate him or her only leads to further despair.

The above process occurs in many ways. For example, a 35-year-old man I am seeing in therapy is receiving Social Security benefits because he is emotionally unable to function adequately. This support maintains him at a subpoverty level, offers him subsidized housing in a slum area, and does not provide adequate funds to pay for medical and psychiatric treatment. If he were to improve his functions as a result of treatment and then attempt to secure even a part-time job to begin to emerge from his quagmire, he would be in danger of losing his housing and would have to pay taxes on all the money he earned. It has been extraordinarily difficult to offer any encouragement to this patient when the social system has arranged to strangle and paralyze him financially while barely keeping him alive. Committing crime might well become his last resort.

In his classic book *Caste and Class in a Southern Town*, Dollard (1957) gave an explanation of the mistreatment of blacks by the ruling whites. He demonstrated that the whites exploited and used the blacks for economic and sexual purposes. It was actually dangerous for a black person not to submit to the sexual demands of a white person. If the black person objected to such mistreatment, he or she would be identified as "uppity" and would be threatened with serious reprisals, as might the family as well.

The second motivation for such exploitation was economic. The blacks were denied social, professional, educational, and occupational opportunities. This relegated them to the most menial, lowest paying, and most insecure and expendable positions on the economic ladder. In a horrible way, sexual victimization, while vicious, heinous, and atrocious, is more comprehensible in its flagrant, gross, and sick way.

While the above account appears to be accurate, the patterns of victimization and the processes of their perpetuation are even more complex. I postulate that such widespread, irrational behavior must have a motivation. The roots of these deeply entrenched ways of operating are more hidden and complex than have been suspected. Understanding will require the resolve to develop a methodology for uncovering their origins in order that we may take the steps to modify them.

All behavior, whether it is societal or individual, is based on a conceptualization or frame of reference which appears correct to the person who possesses it. For example, if you had lived in Salem, Massachusetts, at a certain time and your cows had stopped giving milk, you would have "known" it was the work of a witch. Our current approach is as mystical, archaic, and brutal as the Salem witch trials. If a man robs someone and is arrested and goes to court, he is faced with a tried and true procedure that is almost religious and naively ritualistic. The robed judge is treated like a high priest, and all stand when he or she enters the courtroom. Then there is a ritual based on the assumption that people capable of murder, rape, or theft will certainly be honest and tell the truth. This naive expectation is reinforced by the belief that those who place their hand on the Bible will automatically become honest and admit things that might do great harm to their life, liberty, and pursuit of happiness. Suppose the robber is found "guilty." He may then be punished by incarceration. How this entire process helps the person who has been robbed is a mystery. The idea that the criminal pays a debt to society illustrates another confusion. This mythical concept fails to define who or what this society is or if it really gives a damn. The incarceration may be shortened by "good behavior," which returns the criminal to a hostile, unaccepting social system. It thus becomes extremely difficult for him not to commit some other criminal act. One could say that the only obvious benefactor of this unbelievable procedure is the court, for it guarantees that it will perpetuate itself whether or not what it does is of benefit to anyone else.

Is it sensible to isolate a human being in a prison where he or she may lose up to 20 years of life and be sexually and physically assaulted? When the prisoner comes out of it, it is into an environment and at an age that make coping even more difficult. There are many ways to introduce humanity into our system and into the lives of victimizers. Granted that the public has to be protected and secure, how does locking a person in a cubicle serve any useful purpose? Arsonists could help rebuild burned buildings. There are conservation needs—planting trees to prevent erosion, cleaning up streams, rivers, and harbors, and so on. The policy of putting prisoners to work, while not totally absent from our present approach to criminology, is not as prevalent as it should be. Instead of wasting human life, we could help victimizers do something useful. Training them to function in constructive ways might help their self-esteem and it would certainly be better than vindictively robbing them and the community of what they might have to offer. Who knows? Perhaps people in the future may look back at our system of incarceration as a form of long-term torture, similar to burning teenage girls at the stake.

In short, we need to be ruthlessly honest in scrutinizing how our culture manages victimology, and we especially need to take a very close look at the frame of reference that is the basis of our actions.

Consider for a moment how individuals with mental illness have been handled. We can see that over the course of time there have been many theories leading to different approaches. At one time, the mentally ill were thought to be possessed. We then used incantations, drums, and rattles. It is no more than 100 years ago that the mentally ill were placed in prison cells with criminals and the paupers. In Massachusetts, Dorothea Lynde Dix went into the East Cambridge jail and insisted that incarcerations be classified. Then there were jails for criminals, "lunatic asylums" for the mentally ill, and "poor houses" for paupers. We still place criminals in institutions. Our current deinstitutionalization of the mentally ill has resulted in a shameful subculture of "bag ladies" and frozen bodies on the streets. Being a pauper has always been the most vilified condition, and there is a dearth of facilities and programs to help people out of such a plight. Currently we believe that some mental illness is caused by "bad" chemicals affecting the neuronal synapses, and afflicted individuals are given the benefit of psychopharmacological treatment.

Using a Freudian model, criminal behavior could be viewed as an outbreak of the id, which is in conflict with the superego as established by religion, the culture, and the social-legal system. The ego function is taken over by the therapist, who has to undertake an investigation of the id outbreak (e.g., the beating of a child). The therapist must also take on the executive function of determining what procedures may be indicated.

The above examples are primarily to indicate that all procedures have an explicit or implicit theoretical base. In the past, the commitment of a crime has been considered evidence that the criminal was possessed by a satanic demon, lacked religious faith, had a genetic or chemical imbalance, or had a personality or developmental-emotional deficit. These different theories have resulted in an extraordinary range of rational and irrational approaches. When we do not know the real cause, we grope. There were volumes of books written on the cause, treatment, and prevention of smallpox, a disease which caused terrible epidemics. Now that we know the bacterial cause and can prevent the disease with vaccination, it is a rare occurrence in this country. Before we knew that tuberculosis was caused by the tubercle bacillus, researchers proved without a shadow of doubt that the incidence of tuberculosis was higher among the socially and economically deprived, who lived in crowded housing, drank, and had poor diets. The disease occurred more frequently and was more deadly in certain minority groups. The exact same set of cause-and-effect sequences which applied to tuberculosis were also applied with equal fervor to the incidence of crime and delinquency. We have been blessed with the discovery of the tubercle bacillus and are at a loss because there is no analogous etiologic agent in delinquency. However, we must take heart and ruthlessly and determinedly agree that none of our preconceptions are sacred.

I would strongly urge that in our review of current and historic practices, we try to understand the hidden human needs that underlie the behavior. Do some of us need to feel powerful and superior and thus give ourselves the license to dominate and victimize others?

Do we glorify the victimizer as a Robin Hood or the expresser of our own repressed criminal desires? Do we create the conditions that allow us the double benefit of having our "evil" urges expressed by someone else and of then being able to take a "holier than thou" attitude toward the obviously villainous victimizer.

Why do we fall into using religiouslike procedures, for example, treating people like witches or utilizing the highly ritualized but irrelevant court system— a system that believes that it helps a woman whose husband has been robbed and murdered to place the criminal in a prison. Even more reprehensible is to have no rationale and to place someone in prison with no thought about the victim or the victimizer.

Some further thoughts on the need of society to victimize are contained in an article on Dr. Dane Archer (Wilkes, 1987). Archer believes that "human violence is a product of social forces rather than the result of a biological drive." I agree with this. Archer also gives extremely interesting and valuable information on how our social system operates in relation to violence. For example, despite the fact that it was documented that "homicide rates tended to decline slightly after the death penalty has been abolished," there is increasing pressure to restore the death penalty. The death penalty, rather than a deterrent to violence, seems to encourage it. Archer states that "capital punishment is homicide." He believes that "putting someone to death seems an odd way to teach lessons about the value of human life." According to Archer, murder which occurs in war is followed by an increased incidence of civilian murder.

In this article, Archer illustrates the irrationality of doctors in the United States brutally insisting on radical mastectomies, despite the fact that simple mastectomies, as done in Europe, achieve the same results. The point, as I understand it, is that all forms of brutality, including surgical brutality, have an impact on the populace. This may help answer the question he raised: "Why does the United States have a homicide rate grossly higher than other industrial nations?" The urge to commit homicide or other forms of violence is inherent in most people. Most individuals raised on the principle "Thou shalt not kill" will, when placed in military service and given a weapon, kill, maim, burn, and obey commands to perform other kinds of destruction.

Is this what the Jungians call the "shadow" or the force of evil (Jung, 1944/1953). Freud (1920/1961) talks of the life instinct and the death instinct. If the death instinct is not "tamed," it can become uncontrollably destructive. Over the course of history, it has led people to kill, maim, and brutalize other people. Often, such destruction is done under the religious guise of saving souls, as in the Inquisition. Humans have found many reasons that have allowed them to feel free to perpetrate mass misery and destruction.

If we do not identify this destructive force and find ways to tame it, it will continue to cause individuals or nations to act violently and wreak havoc.

I contend that we must not blindly suppress this evil force for the following reasons. Jung suggested that the culture attempts to repress the awareness of evil. For example, religion focuses only on the "loving God" of the Trinity. Despite the intent, this serves to make evil more powerful. Jung suggested that the fourth member of the family, personified by Satan, should be acknowledged. Jung believes that enlightenment provides a way to deal with this evil force. Pretending it does not exist paradoxically empowers it. I believe this is a partial explanation why we regularly find excuses to adopt procedures which ensure violence and victimization.

The aggressive and destructive drives which lead to violence need an outlet. Awareness of their existence is a first step. Denial or repression tend to lead to violent destructive behavior. Why this is so is not entirely clear.

Another way to understand the unwitting perpetuation of victimization is to view the general society as analogous to a family. Johnson and Szurek (1952) described delinquency as the acting out, by a child, of the family's unconscious need for antisocial behavior. Many people have described behavior in terms of family systems. According to some views, one person might be the designated victim, another the caretaker, another the hopeless failure, another the applauded success, and so on. Analogously, one might view the general community as having needs which get met in similar ways. For example, at a time of crisis a leader may emerge to forge people together (e.g., Joan of Arc or Hitler). If we believe the forces of aggression, or a shadow side, exist in all of us, it may well be that the community behaves in an unconscious, often unreasonable way to ensure that there is expression of these drives. Recently in Massachusetts a man convicted of murder and rape and sentenced to life imprisonment was freed on "furlough" ("Life Sentence," 1987). He went down to another state and committed murder and rape. Such irrational behavior on the part of the authorities occurs frequently enough to wonder what their need is. My theory is that they are unconsciously responding to the force of evil, and we have set it up so that we ensure the perpetuation of such behavior.

Inherent in this process is the issue of power. One way to handle the sense of powerlessness is to become the attacker. There is abundant evidence that individuals who commit child abuse were disproportionately victims of abuse themselves. There is a seething mass of unexpressed destructive impulses within a society which get expressed in various ways. In the past, rape, murder, and pillage were an anticipated part of war. The holocaust is no different from other incidents of mass destruction that have occurred repeatedly over the centuries. The fact that these horrors can and do occur, both individually and nationally, is well known. It is my strong conviction that unless we discover and treat the deeper causes, attempts to prevent destructive acts through prisons, treaties, or nuclear disarmament meetings will not affect the recurring patterns of victimization.

The intent of this chapter is not to give answers but to raise questions for consideration. Nothing is engraved in stone; nothing should be dealt with as inherently sacred. This refers to all our social systems or rituals. Only caring for and loving our fellow human beings is relevant. I hope that in the future serious research is pursued in four areas. First, we need to study victimizers, focusing especially on why they became victimizers. Second, we need to study victims and try to understand why they became victims. Third, we need to study the social system and try to understand how it perpetuates victimization and why it offers insufficient hope or help to victims or victimizers. Finally, we need to study issues of power and powerlessness. I myself intend to focus on (1) studies based on the view that society is analogous to a family, (2) the origins of power in human development, and (3) the circumstances in which power issues lead to victimization.

BIBLIOGRAPHY

Dollard, J. (1957). *Caste and class in a Southern town*. Garden City, NY: Doubleday.

Domestic violence department ignores cries for assistance—Wife murdered. (1987,). *Boston Globe*.

Freud, S. (1961). Speculations on the death instinct. In *Beyond the pleasure principle*. In J. Strachey (Ed. and Trans.), *The standard edition of the complete psychological works of Sigmund Freud* (Vol. 18, pp. 18–24). London: Hogarth Press. (Original work published 1923.)

Johnson, A., & Szurek, S. (1952). The genesis of antisocial acting out in children and adults. *Psychoanalytic Quarterly*, *21*, 322–343.

Jung, C. G. (1953). Good and evil. In *Collected works* (Vol. 12, pp. 20–37, Bollingen series 20, second edition). Princeton, NJ: Princeton University Press. (Original work published in 1944.)

Kaufman, I. (1985). Child abuse—Family victimology. *Victimology—An International Journal*, *10*, 62–71.

Kaufman, I. (1986). *Arson: From creation to destruction*. Paper presented at World Congress of Victimology, Orlando, FL.

Life sentence murderer furloughed—Commits rape and murder. (1987,). *Boston Globe*.

Menninger, K. (1968). *The crime of punishment*. New York, NY: Viking.

Pizzey, E. (1987). *A comparative study of battered women and violence prone women*. Unpublished paper.

Study on repeated crime while awaiting trial. (1987). *Boston Globe*.

Wife's appeal to court for help denied—She is murdered. (1987). *Boston Globe*.

Wilkes, J. (1987). Murder in mind. *Psychology Today*, *21*, 26–32.

3

Family Violence and Violence in Society

Simha F. Landau
Institute of Criminology, Hebrew University of Jerusalem

INTRODUCTION

The subject of this chapter provides an appropriate starting point for dealing with the topic of family violence. As a matter of fact, family violence and violence in society are closely connected for two main reasons. First, the family is the most prevalent social institution. As a result, family violence constitutes, by definition, violence in society.

Second, when there is violence in society, the roots of this violence should be sought within the framework of the family. This does not mean that the family is "responsible" for all types of violence in society (i.e., violent crime, political violence, war, etc.). Obviously, the family is but one of a number of frameworks affecting the behavior of individuals and groups in society. However, it is the family that transmits the norms and values of society to its members; the family serves as the major socialization agency within which the personality of each individual member is formed. Moreover, the norms and values transferred within the family (which serves as the mediator between society and the individual) determine (or at least influence) not only the level of violence "out there" in society at large but also the role division within the family, the relationships between the family members, and their status hierarchy.

For many centuries, women and children occupied quite low positions in this status hierarchy. These low positions made them the "natural" victims of a variety of sanctions, including violence. As a result of this fact among others, the relationship between family violence and violence in society deserves more detailed attention, especially the following three topics:

1. the growing awareness of the problem of family violence and its development from a personal matter into a social problem
2. the extent of family violence and its characteristics in various countries

Simha F. Landau is a senior lecturer of criminology at the Hebrew University of Jerusalem. His main fields of research are violent and aggressive behavior and decision making in the criminal justice system, topics on which he has published extensively in professional journals. Other topics on which he has conducted research and written include offenders' perceptions of their victims and the effects of institutionalization on the time sense of inmates. He also edited a book on criminology in perspective. The author is currently conducting research on police responses to domestic violence as part of a larger project on violence in Israeli society.

3. the issue of transgenerational transmission of violence within the family (the so-called cycle of violence)

At the end of the chapter, a stress-support model for the analysis of violence in society is presented and suggestions are put forward for the application of this model to family violence.

FAMILY VIOLENCE: FROM A PERSONAL MATTER TO A SOCIAL PROBLEM

Family violence as a social problem in the 20th century has become an issue only in relatively recent years. It emerged only in the late 60s and early 70s. This does not mean that this issue was not mentioned or discussed before. However, previously it was mentioned only sporadically and in very specific contexts in various disciplines in the social, behavioral, and medical sciences. A salient example is the study by Wolfgang (1958). In this classic study of patterns of homicide in Philadelphia, Wolfgang reported that 25% of all homicides were within the family. Further, in these homicides, the victims were mostly spouses. Similarly, the phenomenon of family violence was known to professionals and researchers in the fields of social work and psychiatry and to those involved in the treatment of alcoholics and drug addicts.

It is worth mentioning, however, that in the mid-19th century, violence against women and children was recognized as a social problem in England. Public disquiet about it—and awareness that it was on the increase—led in 1853 to the passing of the Act for the Better Prevention and Punishment of Aggravated Assaults Upon Women and Children. This act provided for six-months imprisonment or a 20-pound fine for those convicted of aggravated assault on a female or on a male under the age of 14. In 1878, divorce was made easier by passing the Matrimonial Causes Act, which enabled abused wives to separate from their husbands legally and entitled them to maintenance and the custody of children under age 10. However, these rights were restricted to wives who had not committed adultery (Minchin, 1982).

It should be noted that these two "spots of light" in the legislation of the last century do not truly represent the normative attitudes prevailing then and, to a large extent, even now. The standard view was that a certain degree of violence was acceptable and did not require the intervention of official social agencies. Moreover, family violence has a long-standing tradition of official legitimation. In 1824, the Mississippi Supreme Court was the first of several state supreme courts to grant husbands immunity from assault and battery charges for moderately chastising their wives (Calvert, 1974; Star, 1980). Such official legitimation for family violence can be traced back to English common law, which gave husbands the right to strike their wives with sticks no wider than their thumbs—hence the expression "rule of thumb" (Calvert, 1974; Davidson, 1978).

This normative acceptance of various types of violence within the family means that such violence was not perceived as criminal. Thus, there was no stigma attached to it and no data about it were collected. Consequently, the myth could be maintained that family violence was not a social problem, and no empirical research was conducted on it.

Several social and cultural forces in the late 60s and early 70s helped shift the issue of family violence from being a private matter to being a high-priority social issue. Straus (1974) mentions three main forces:

1. The public at large, as well as social scientists, became more aware of various aspects of violent behavior as a result of the great increase of violence in most Western countries (e.g., political assassinations, international terror, the Vietnam War, etc.).

2. The emergence of the women's movement played an especially important part by uncovering and highlighting the problems of battered wives. The gradual increase of the proportion of women in the labor market and in other social activities outside the family helped them to bring the problem of family violence into the open.

3. The decline of the consensus model of society employed by social scientists and its replacement (by many scholars) by the alternative social conflict model contributed to the exposure of family violence. Within the framework of the conflict model, women are regarded as one of the minority groups which are discriminated against in the existing social order. Dobash and Dobash (1979) consider the patriarchal family structure as the main source of family violence. Their central thesis is that economic and social processes operate to support a family structure that leads to the subordination of women and contributes to the historical pattern of violence directed against women. The shift from the consensus to the conflict model challenges the historical legitimation of the patriarchal family structure and the problems related to it, including family violence.

All the above factors made family violence no longer merely a personal problem but also a social and public problem. Consequently, an important "chain reaction" took place: A criminal stigma was attached to it; data were collected regarding the extent of the problem; social control agencies (e.g., police, courts, etc.) became aware of the problem; social tools and frameworks to cope with the problem were created (e.g., shelters for battered wives, group therapy for victims as well as victimizers, etc.).

THE EXTENT OF FAMILY VIOLENCE

Today there is a consensus that we do not know the real extent of the problem. We can only come up with estimates based on studies and survey data. First, it is worth mentioning that physical punishment of children is used by 84–97% of all parents at some time in their children's lives (Gelles, 1982). However, children who receive physical punishment are not necessarily battered children. Estimates of the number of battered children (i.e., children who are victims of severe violence) in the United States vary between 250,000 to 4.07 million (Gelles, 1982). As for the most severe form of violence, homicide, researchers generally report that intrafamilial homicide accounts for 20–40% of all homicides (Curtis, 1974). Regarding less serious forms of violence, such as assault, the range of estimates is much wider: 11–52% of total assaults are husband-wife assaults (Gelles, 1982).

Levinger (1966) found that 22% of the middle-class and 40% of the working-class applicants for divorce whom he interviewed mentioned "physical violence" as a major complaint. The extent of violence between couples can also be deduced from a survey conducted for the U.S. National Commission on the Causes and Prevention of Violence. In this survey, it was found that one in four men and one in six women stated that they approved of a husband hitting his wife under certain conditions (Stark and McEvoy, 1970). No wonder, therefore, that in a national survey of family violence in the United States, 28% of those surveyed reported marital violence at some point in the marriage (Straus, 1978; Straus, Gelles, & Steinmetz, 1980). One of the main conclusions of this national study is that 3.8% of American women were victims of violence during the 12 months prior to the survey.

In England, some researchers claim that only about 2% of incidents of domestic violence are reported to the police (Moonman, 1987). In their analysis of police records for Glasgow and Edinburgh, Dobash and Dobash provided evidence that the second most common form of violence reported to police in those cities was wife battering, which accounted for some 25% of all recorded violent crime (Moonman, 1987). The Metropolitan Police records for 1979–1984 show a 22% increase in violence against females, a 48% increase in rape, and a 96% increase in robbery from women (Moonman, 1987). It is difficult to ascertain the extent to which these data reflect a real increase in violence against women rather than an increase in the awareness of the public, the police, and the media concerning this problem. However, even without accurate data on the extent of the problem, the social processes and research conducted in the last two decades have succeeded in destroying the myth that family violence is not a social problem. We know today that violence in the family is probably more common than violence in any other social setting.

THE TRANSGENERATIONAL TRANSMISSION OF VIOLENCE WITHIN THE FAMILY

One of the consistent conclusions of family violence studies is that individuals who have experienced violent childhoods are more likely to grow up to become child and spouse batterers than individuals who experienced little or no violence as children (Gelles, 1982). In a national survey of family violence (Straus, 1979; Straus et al., 1980), subjects were asked about their parents' use of physical punishment when the subjects were 13 years old. Those who stated that their mothers had used physical punishment twice or more a year had, as parents, a child abuse rate of 18.5%. The equivalent rate for parents who experienced less physical punishment at age 13 was only 11.8%. It is worth mentioning that physical punishment by fathers had a lesser effect on child abuse rates (16.7% vs. 13.2%). The above survey found that the observation of violence between parents was also related to violence as an adult. Among those who witnessed their fathers hitting their mothers, the rate of child abuse was higher than that among those who grew up with no such violence at home (13.3% vs. 9.7%). Another relevant finding was the relationship between experiencing violence as a teenager and marital violence as reported by subjects: Those reared in the most violent homes had a rate of wife abuse 600 times greater than those reared in the least violent homes.

Violence between spouses was found to be related to violence among children in a recent Israeli study (Pasternak, 1987). This study reported that among children of parents who live together but are in conflict, the rate of violence (51%) is higher than that among children who live with their separated mothers (36.4%) or divorced mothers (32.4%). The lowest rate of violence was found among children whose parents have good relationships with each other (6.4%).

It is worth mentioning, however, that despite the considerable theoretical and empirical support that exists for the hypothesis of transgenerational transference of family violence, some doubts have been raised recently as to the contribution of physical punishment in childhood to violence between couples. This topic was recently investigated in the United States by Knutson and Mehm (in press). This study, conducted on married and unmarried middle-class couples, found the following:

1. Physically coercive and injurious acts are not uncommon in the intimate relationships of middle-class young adults. In one of the samples, 22% of the women indicated they had been physically abused by their spouse or live-in partner. In another sample, the rate was only 11%.
2. There was no association between coercive childhood histories or acrimonious family backgrounds and coercive acts in intimate adult relationships.

These results, according to the authors, cast doubt on the simple notion that coercive childhood experiences yield coercive and violent patterns in intimate adult relationships. This does not mean that such backgrounds are unimportant but merely that they do not account for enough of the variance to make strong inferences regarding causal relationships. These findings suggest that violence between a couple is likely to be determined by other variables and not just the fact that the victim or perpetrator had a punitive or acrimonious childhood. A further analysis of the data of the above study revealed that if *both* members of the couple had acrimonious childhoods, the emergence of coercion in the relationship was predictable.

Without going into the detailed findings of Knutson and Mehm (in press), we should note two important factors:

1. Family violence, like human behavior in general, is not determined by one single causal factor but is the result of a variety of factors that contribute to the emergence and continuity of this type of violence.
2. A full understanding of this phenomenon requires the inclusion of both sides of the violent dyad in the analysis. Including the victim in the analysis should not be seen as evidence that the victim is being viewed as responsible or "guilty" for his or her victimization. The analysis of both sides has both theoretical and practical advantages, since it enables the problem to be better coped with, especially when there is some readiness on the part of the couple to change the situation.

A frequently raised question concerning the transgenerational transmission of violence is whether family violence is evenly distributed among all social classes. This question brings us back to the relationship between family violence and violence in society. Official data on crimes of violence show quite clearly that violence is not evenly distributed; in particular, it is more prevalent in the lower social classes (Landau, 1983; Newman, 1979). In this respect there is a similarity between family violence and violence in society. Official figures on family violence, based on complaints filed with the police and on data from shelters for battered wives and from some studies, indicate that families of low socioeconomic status are much more likely to experience violence than middle- or upper-class families. In spite of these official figures, there is no consensus in the literature about the class distribution of family violence. Early research claimed that social class should not be considered a cause of family violence (Steele and Pollok, 1974). However, later studies, as well as national surveys, have found a relationship between levels of income and family violence (Pelton, 1978; Gelles and Straus, 1985). A note of caution: One should not be too impressed by findings of class differences, for they may be largely due to the fact that poor people are more "visible" to official agencies. Thus, the differences between upper and lower classes regarding family violence might well be smaller than presented in official figures. The higher prevalence of family violence in lower-income families is mainly a result of the fact that these families have less alternative resources with which to deal with stressful situations. Families of higher socioeconomic status can more readily avoid the stigma of being labeled abusers by official agencies (e.g., by getting treatment, by their greater ability to cope with the financial burden of marital separation or divorce, etc.). Apart from the explanation given above, at least part of the class differences regarding both crimes of violence and family violence is due to a greater reliance in the lower classes on physical force (i.e., transgenerational transmission of violence may make some contribution to both these types of violence after all).

A STRESS-SUPPORT MODEL FOR THE ANALYSIS OF FAMILY VIOLENCE

In this section, a suggestion is made regarding the analysis of violence in society and family violence within a common conceptual framework.

A recently developed theoretical model for the analysis of violence in society was proposed by Landau and Beit-Hallahmi (1983). The general starting point of this model is the frustration-aggression hypothesis (Dollard et al., 1939), which was extended from the level of the individual to the level of populations following earlier work along these lines (see, among others, Feierabend and Feierabend, 1966; Henry and Short, 1954; Hovland and Sears, 1940; Lieberson and Silverman, 1965; Ransford, 1968). Unlike previous studies, Landau and Beit-Hallahim (1983) proposed a theoretical model on the social level that incorporates two important elements (instead of one) for the explanation of violence and aggression: social stressors and social support systems. This model assumes that the probability of violence and aggression as a reaction to stress will increase when social support systems fail or malfunction. Stress has been related to aggressive behavior by Halleck (1967), who argued that aggression may be considered an adequate response to stress—which in turn may arise from a variety of sources (both external and internal to the individual).

Social support systems are an essential part of the model, for they are conceived as mediators between the social stressors and the reactions to which they are presumed to lead. Examples of social support systems include feelings of national solidarity (on the macrolevel) and family ties and stable networks of friends (on the microlevel). Several previous studies (analyzed by Dooley and

Catalano [1980] and Leavy [1983]) have reported that social support appears to decrease the production of health and behavioral problems that usually result from stressful life changes. The basic assumption here is that the greater the strength and stability of the social support systems, the greater the ability of individuals and the society to cope with stressful events and situations.

This stress model has received considerable empirical support from previous studies which were based on it (Landau, 1984; Landau and Beit-Hallahmi, 1983; Landau and Raveh, 1987). The findings of other studies, although not based on this model, are consistent with it (see, among others, Avison & Loring, 1986; Brenner & Swank, 1986; McDowall, 1986).

We consider this model to be appropriate for application to family violence as well. As a matter of fact, the findings of many previous studies are compatible with this model:

1. Unemployment as well as other stressful life events encountered by family members were found to be related to family violence (see, among others, Galdstone, 1965; Gelles & Straus, 1985; Gil, 1970; Young, 1964).
2. Social isolation (conceived in this context as lack of social support) is considered by a number of studies to be a major correlate of family violence (Helfer & Kempe, 1972; Moden & Wrench, 1977; Smith, 1973; and many others).

The advantages of applying this model to family violence are both theoretical and practical. The model provides conceptual tools for the prediction and identification of factors that might enhance or reduce the probability of family violence. As a result, it can serve as a basis for research in this field. At the same time it can also provide practical tools for treatment professionals in assisting family members to cope with and resolve the problem of violence within the family.

It should be made clear that the stress-support model is not being suggested as a deterministic "explanation" of family violence. Similarly, it is not intended to "psychologize" the problem or exonerate violent spouses (usually men in cases of severe violence) through the magic formula of stress support. As shown before, family violence is deeply rooted in the structure of society and is now recognized as a social problem rather than just a matter of personal pathology. The stress-support model is not intended to replace other perspectives on this topic (e.g., the feminist one), but hopefully it will add another useful dimension to the analysis of this social problem and help those affected to deal with it.

It should be noted that family violence is but one of the possible applications of the stress-support model. Only future research in this field will tell how successful this and other applications will be. So far, the chances of analyzing violence on both the individual and social level within the same theoretical model look very promising.

BIBLIOGRAPHY

Avison, W. R., & Loring, P. C. (1986). Population diversity and cross-national homicide: The effects of inequality and heterogeneity. *Criminology*, *24*, 733–749.

Brenner, M. H., & Swank, R. T. (1986). Homicide and economic change: Recent analysis of the Joint Economic Committee Report of 1984. *Journal of Quantitative Criminology*, *2*, 81–103.

Calvert, R. (1974). Criminal and civil liability in husband-wife assaults. In S. Steinmetz & M. Straus (Eds.), *Violence in the family* (pp. 88–92). New York: Harper & Row.
Curtis, L. (1974). *Criminal violence: National patterns and behavior*. Lexington, MA: D. C. Heath.
Davidson, T. (1978). *Conjugal crime: Understanding and changing the wifebeating pattern*. New York: Hawthorn Books.
Dobash, R. E., & Dobash, R. (1979). *Violence against wives*. New York: The Free Press.
Dollard, J., Doob, L. W., Miller, N. E., Mowrer, O. H., & Sears, R. R. (1939). *Frustration and aggression*. New Haven, CT: Yale University Press.
Dooley, D., & Catalano, R. (1980). Economic change as a cause of behavioral disorder. *Psychological Bulletin*, *87*, 450–468.
Feierabend, I. K., & Feierabend, R. L. (1966). Aggressive behaviors within politics, 1948–1962: A cross-national analysis. *Journal of Conflict Resolution*, *10*, 249–272.
Galdstone, R. (1965). Observations of children who have been physically abused by their parents. *American Journal of Psychiatry*, *122*, 440–443.
Gelles, R. J. (1982). Domestic criminal violence. In M. E. Wolfgang & N. A. Weiner (Eds.), *Criminal violence*. Beverly Hills, CA: Sage.
Gelles, R. J., & Straus, M. A. (1985). Violence in the American family. In A. J. Lincoln & M. A. Straus (Eds.), *Crime and the family*. Springfield, IL: Charles C Thomas.
Gil, D. G. (1970). *Violence against children: Physical child abuse in the United States*. Cambridge, MA: Harvard University Press.
Helleck, S. (1967). *Psychiatry and the dilemmas of crime*. New York: Harper & Row.
Helfer, R. E., & Kempe, C. H. (1972). *Helping the battered child and his family*. Philadelphia: Lippincott.
Henry, A. F., & Short, J. F. (1954). *Suicide and homicide*. New York: The Free Press.
Hovland, C. I., & Sears, R. R. (1940). Minor studies of aggression: Correlation of lynchings with economic indices. *Journal of Psychology*, *9*, 301–310.
Knutson, J. F., & Mehm, J. G. (in press). Transgenerational patterns of coercion in families and intimate relationships. In G. Russell (Ed.), *Violence in intimate relationship*. New York: Spectrum Press.
Landau, S. F. (1983). Haim hahevra haisraelit alima yoter meaherot? In A. Hareven (Ed.), *Haim kashe lihiot Israeli*. Jerusalem: Van Leer Foundation.
Landau, S. F. (1984). Trends in violence and aggression: A cross-cultural analysis. *International Journal of Comparative Sociology*, *25*, 133–158.
Landau, S. F., & Beit-Hallahmi, B. (1983). Aggression in Israel: A psychohistorical perspective. In A. P. Goldstein & M. Segall (Eds.), *Aggression in global perspective*. New York: Pergamon Press.
Landau, S. F., & Raveh, A. (1987). Stress factors, social support and violence in Israeli society: A quantitative analysis. *Aggressive Behavior*, *13*, 67–85.
Leavy, R. L. (1983). Social support and psychological disorder: A review. *Journal of Community Psychology*, *11*, 3–21.
Levinger, G. (1966). Sources of marital dissatisfaction among applicants for divorce. *American Journal of Orthopsychiatry*, *26*, 803–897.
Lieberson, S., & Silverman, A. R. (1965). The precipitants and underlying conditions of race riots. *American Sociological Review*, *30*, 887–898.
Maden, M. F., & Wrench, D. F. (1977). Significant findings in child abuse research. *Victimology*, *2*, 196–224.
McDowall, D. (1986). Poverty and Homicide in Detroit, 1926–1978. *Victims and Violence*, *1*, 23–34.
Minchin, L. (1982). Violence between couples. In P. Feldman (Ed.), *Developments in the study of criminal behavior: Vol. 2. Violence*. London: Wiley.
Moonman, J. (1987). Violence in the home. In E. Moonman (Ed.), *The violent society*. London: Frank Cass.
Newman, G. (1979). *Understanding violence*. New York: Lippincott.
Pasternak, R. (1987, June 6). Violent behavior of children at school and family relationships. *Haaretz*. (Daily newspaper in Hebrew).
Pelton, L. H. (1978). Child abuse and neglect: The myth of classlessness. *American Journal of Orthopsychiatry*, *48*, 608–617.
Ransford, H. E. (1968). Isolation, powerlessness, and violence: A study of attitudes and participation in the Watts riots. *American Journal of Sociology*, *73*, 581–591.
Smith, S. M. (1973). *The battered child syndrome*. London: Butterworths.

Star, B. (1980). Patterns of family violence. *Social Casework*, *61*, 339–346.
Stark, R., & McEvoy, J. (1970, November). Middle class violence. *Psychology Today*, *4*, 52–65.
Steele, B. F., & Pollock, C. B. (1974). A psychiatric study of parents who abuse infants and small children. In R. E. Helfer & C. H. Kempe (Eds.), *The battered child* (2nd ed.). Chicago: University of Chicago Press.
Straus, M. A. (1974). Foreword. In R. J. Gelles (Ed.), *The violent home: A study of physical aggression between husbands and wives*. Beverly Hills, CA: Sage.
Straus, M. A. (1978). Wife beating: How common and why? *Victimology*, *2*, 443–458.
Straus, M. A. (1979). Family patterns and child abuse in a national representative American sample. *Child Abuse and Neglect: The International Journal*, *3*, 213–225.
Straus, M. A., Gelles, R. J., & Steinmetz, S. K. (1980). *Behind closed doors: Violence in the American family*. New York: Doubleday.
Wolfgang, M. E. (1958). *Patterns in criminal homicide*. New York: Wiley.
Young, L. R. (1964). *Wednesday children: A study of child neglect and abuse*. New York: McGraw-Hill.

4

Victims in Disasters

Daniel E. Della-Giustina
Safety Studies, West Virginia University

INTRODUCTION

Disasters, both major and minor, occur frequently enough that one can evaluate each incident and comparatively analyze the problems. There are victims in all disasters. Most individuals and organizations responding to a disaster have not had prior experience, and since an *immediate* response to victims' needs is so vital, there is a tendency to see the situation and the response it requires as unique. Studies show that individuals and teams can be assembled in advance and trained in disaster control and remedial action in aiding victims. If such teams had been trained and in place during the disasters at Chernobyl, Bhopal, and Indianapolis, the resulting injury and loss of life could have been measurably reduced.

The primary emphasis here will be on the social disruption caused by the physical effects of disasters. This is a particularly useful way of examining disasters, since disaster agents create demands with which a community must cope. Such demands are created at the very time when the community's problem-solving ability may be severely damaged by the impact of the disaster.

Two types of demands are made. Demands of the first type, which are generated by the disaster agent as it strikes the community, are called *agent-generated demands*. In responding to these demands, the community will in turn be confronted with a new and more general set of demands, called *response-generated demands*. Both sets of demands must be given consideration in developing a comprehensive disaster-response plan.

Community consensus in the aftermath of such widely publicized disasters as Chernobyl, Bhopal, and Indianapolis indicates the need for advance planning through an organized community effort. In any given disaster situation, the characteristics and consequences of the disaster agent are all part of the "larger picture." Successfully coping with disaster agents requires thorough planning

Daniel E. Della-Giustina received a Ph.D. in Higher Education, with emphasis in safety and health, from Michigan State University. He has published over 60 articles on safety and has presented scholarly papers at numerous meetings and conferences. He is currently the editor of *The Safety Forum*, published by the American School and the Community Safety Association.

Dr. Della-Giustina has appeared as an expert witness in safety and health liability cases for the past 14 years in numerous cities throughout the United States. He has served as a consultant to various public, volunteer, and industrial fire brigades on the issues of disaster preparedness and emergency systems. He is currently the chairperson of the Safety Studies Department at West Virginia University, where he has been a faculty member for the past 12 years.

based on the anticipated impact of the disaster and the anticipated response to victims' needs. Such planning requires the combined efforts of legislative leaders, social agencies, and citizens' groups.

DISASTERS

On a national scale, major disasters are commonplace. During the last 25 years there has been an average of 19 disasters a year that necessitated a declaration of disaster by the President of the United States. In addition to these major disasters, each year there are many incidents that are more localized and that, for various reasons, do not lead to a presidential proclamation of disaster. Such incidents, while in one sense minor disasters, can be fairly destructive in terms of casualties.

Reports of Soviet evacuation measures describing a 12-mile-long row of 1,100 buses taking people away from the area around the Russian nuclear plant in Chernobyl made reality out of what had theretofore been conjecture. More than 90,000 persons were evacuated from the vicinity of the plant. In Bhopal, India, over 2,500 persons died from the methyl isocyanate leak—the worst industrial disaster ever recorded. The Indianapolis Coliseum explosion resulted in 81 deaths and approximately 400 injuries, even though the physical damage was confined to one part of the building.

Disasters can be divided into man-made (technological) disasters and so-called natural disasters (e.g., floods, hurricanes, volcanic eruptions, tornadoes, blizzards, earthquakes, etc.). Technological disasters include structural fires, radiological accidents, and explosions. Frequently there is little advance warning in disasters such as these.

Disasters have phases or periods: a warning period, a threat period, an impact period, an inventory period, a rescue period, a remedy period, and a restoration period. Obviously, the warning period is the most opportune time for providing community information and possible evacuation. Advance warning does not always occur, and in such cases it is important to do as much as possible to offset the lack of warning. Disaster planning is an attempt, prior to the actual occurrence of a crisis, to facilitate recognition of emergency demands and to make the community response more effective. It is an exercise in anticipating what might be required for any relevant group or organization.

Disaster agents vary along different dimensions. These dimensions and their variants can be combined in a multitude of ways. Thus, it is nearly impossible to develop a simple yet meaningful typology of disaster agents. Nevertheless, knowledge of how disaster agents may differ along one dimension is still useful for emergency planning. Such knowledge should alert the planner to possible variants that have to be taken into account. Furthermore, in certain localities some dimensions are more likely than others to be operative and to vary.

Disaster agents vary in terms of their predictability. An explosion or an earthquake is considerably less foreseeable than a flood which is brought about by a series of more precisely measurable factors. In fact, for some weather phenomena it is possible to obtain for specific localities the gross probabilities that a particular disaster agent will strike. For example, the chances there will be hurricane force winds in certain Florida cities in any given year have been calculated.

Disaster agents also vary in terms of their frequency. Although natural disasters may be relatively rare, there are certain locales which can be labeled as disaster prone. To illustrate, some regions in the Ohio Valley are susceptible to flooding, other areas (e.g., in the Midwest) are subject to tornadoes, and the Gulf coast is frequently confronted with the threat or occurrence of hurricanes. Thus, there are geographic, climatic, and other conditions which present the possibility of particular kinds of disaster and represent a sustained threat. Here again, gross figures for frequency can be obtained for some disaster agents. The National Weather Service has not only calculated tornado incidences by month (May has the highest rate), by state (Texas has the most), and by square mile (a square mile in Oklahoma has the most), but it has also calculated the threat when high tornado incidence and dense concentration of population are taken into account.

Another factor to consider is the controllability of the disaster agent. Some situations allow for intervention and control, which reduces the potential impact of the disaster agent. For example, flooding can often be anticipated and at least partially prevented, whereas other disasters, such as earthquakes and tsunamis (so-called tidal waves), allow no such luxury.

The following factors all concern time but should not be confused. Disaster agents differ in their speed of onset. For example, impact is sudden in tornadoes and flash floods, whereas other floods crest gradually. Also, some types of agents, such as earthquakes, may impact an area repeatedly in a matter of hours. The length of forewarning is the period between warning and impact. Tidal waves generated by an earthquake illustrate the distinction between the previous two factors. The length of forewarning of tidal waves may be several hours, but their actual speed of onset, once initiated, is very rapid. Disasters also differ in their duration of impact. A tornado impacts an area for only a few minutes, but a flood's impact may be sustained for several days. The worst time combination from the viewpoint of damage potential is a disaster agent that is rapid in onset, gives no warning, and lasts a long time. An earthquake with strong aftershocks is an example of such a combination.

The final differentiating characteristics of disaster agents are their scope of impact and intensity of impact. The scope of impact is essentially a geographic and social space dimension. A disaster can be concentrated in a small area, affecting few people, or dispersed over a wide area, affecting large numbers. Intensity of impact reflects a disaster's potential to inflict injuries, deaths, and property damage. These two factors should be clearly distinguished. For example, an explosion, though highly destructive, may affect only a limited geographic area, whereas a flood may be of low intensity but affect a broad geographic area and many people. This, of course, has important implications for the degree of disruption of local community affairs. A destructive but localized disaster, though tragic, may have only minimal consequences for the community at large. Conversely, a diffuse but less destructive disaster may be extremely disruptive to everyday community living.

There are several discernible phases in the history of any disaster. The predisaster phase is the everyday situation in the community. A preimpact phase begins with the earliest sign of possible danger; it is the period from the initial warning to the actual impact. The warning may be official, as in the case of a weather bulletin, or spontaneous, as when a passerby spots a gas leak. The impact phase is the period when the disaster actually strikes. As mentioned earlier, this period may be of short or long duration; it may last a few minutes (tornado) or several weeks or more (flooding). The emergency phase is the period of response to the immediate demands presented by the agent. Recovery is the final phase and includes attempts to mitigate any long-term effects of the disaster agent and return the community to normal conditions.

TWO TYPES OF DEMANDS

As mentioned above, there are two types of disaster demands. Agent-generated demands are caused by the disaster agent as it impacts the community. In responding to these demands, the community will then be confronted with a new and more general set of demands, namely, response-generated demands. Both sets of demands must be given consideration in developing a comprehensive disaster-response plan.

Agent-Generated Demands

Warning

Some disasters (e.g., explosions, earthquakes) allow for little if any warning. However, many disasters occur with some prior indication of danger. In these situations, warning can be the most important element of the organized disaster response and can help minimize human and material loss. Warning includes detecting and predicting the occurrence of a disaster agent, disseminating information about the agent and about protective action to the public and community organizations, and receiving such information from available sources. Total warning is possible only in certain kinds of disaster. Hurricanes provide significantly more warning time than do most explosions. Of course, an important problem in all warning systems is getting people to accept the threat as legitimate and serious.

Preimpact Preparations

This demand assumes that warning has occurred and there is time to make some preparations. Preparation tasks include the readying of human and material resources for response, the institution of measures to lessen the actual impact of the disaster agent, and the taking of steps to limit the consequences of impact. Preparation of resources might include activating equipment, calling up personnel, stocking goods, and so on. Measures to lessen impact might include sandbagging or diking, immunization, or placing residents in shelters. The best example of a measure to lessen the consequences of disaster would probably be the evacuation of individuals from a projected impact area.

Search and Rescue

The basic demand here is to locate, rescue, and transport entrapped persons to places of safety and assistance. A directly related demand is to have the necessary equipment and qualified personnel to undertake rescue efforts. For example, in some cases heavy earth-moving equipment may be required, along with trained people to operate that equipment safely and efficiently.

Care of the Injured and Removal of the Dead

For most of us, the term *disaster* usually signifies a catastrophe involving major loss of life, injury, and property damage. Measures must be taken to care for casualties. The injured must be moved rapidly from the impact area to locations where medical help (triage teams) and supplies are available. Assignment of priorities for treatment through the establishment of a triage system often becomes mandatory, since it may mean the difference between life and death. The dead also present a disaster demand. Fatalities must be removed from impact area to a permanent or temporary morgue facility. In addition, the dead must be identified, the causes of death determined and certified, and the bodies released to claimants for burial. This requires the mobilization of qualified personnel, including coroners, fingerprint experts, and funeral directors.

Welfare Demands

Measures must be instituted to provide for the basic needs of survivors. Among these are food, clothing, and shelter, although the specific requirements will vary considerably depending on a variety of circumstances. In addition, disaster workers require some of these same services if they are to operate effectively.

Restoration of Essential Community Services

In order to attain a high degree of recovery in the immediate postimpact period, the community must restore services necessary for its functioning. Restoring, at least temporarily, such services as gas, electricity, telephone, water, and transportation thus becomes very important. Casualty care depends on maintaining many of these services in hospitals and on transporting victims to medical centers. Telephones or two-way radios may be crucial for communication and assessment of disaster needs.

Protection Against Continuing Threats

Hazards may be created by damage to buildings, live power lines may be exposed, rockslides may be imminent, and aftershocks or tidal waves following earthquakes may cause additional damage. There may also be public health problems. Water and food supplies may be polluted, and animal carcasses must be removed before decomposition begins. Perhaps most important of all, there is the need to combat the fires that frequently break out even when the prime disaster agent is of a nonfire nature. All secondary threats create demands which must be addressed, since they could be as damaging as the initial disaster agent (in case of fire, often more damaging).

Community Order

Several specific demands are included here, such as guarding property, patrolling danger areas, and especially directing traffic near the scene of impact. There is also the more general demand of ensuring that community resources, both public and private, are used for community needs.

Response-Generated Demands

Communication

Rapid and accurate communication is the basis of effective emergency response. Without adequate communication, the other emergency-response demands cannot be met effectively. One of the major demands in a disaster is information, including information about victims, essential resources, crises, the location of services, and the confirmation of the warning. Thus, communication must be given careful consideration in planning. Without communication, coordination becomes impossible. Given the heavy informational demands, existing communication networks may be inadequate or may break down. There may be a scarcity of skilled personnel to operate facilities. Also, traditional channels may no longer be appropriate. In this case, new channels must be opened, misinformation kept at a minimum, and legitimate requests for information fulfilled.

Continuing Assessment

A virtually constant demand in disaster situations is an overall appraisal of what is happening. If no reliable data are available, assessment will be inadequate and confusion will result. Assessment is crucial because of its direct relationship to organized action. Appropriate actions are determined on the basis of perceived needs at any given time or location during disasters.

Mobilization and Utilization of Human and Material Resources

Disasters, just as everyday situations, require the utilization of human and material resources. Personnel must be recruited, trained, and mobilized. Necessary resources must be acquired, maintained, and allocated for appropriate activities. Disaster situations present acute problems in the allocation of crucial human and material resources. Equipment may not be located at points where it is most needed. Specially trained personnel may not be immediately available, and there is no time for training. The location of relevant resources in the community may not be known; hence valuable supplies may go untapped. Given these possible contingencies, the central demand is to effectively utilize all available resources. Human and material resources must be joined together in the most useful way to meet disaster demands.

Coordination

The need for coordination underlies much of what we have been discussing; it is the essence of good planning. In normal times, overall coordination of the community is generally not critical, as various community organizations can carry out their activities in large measure independent of one another. However, during disasters cooperative measures are necessary to allocate the resources of the community so that high-priority needs are met. Problems and situations must be assessed and decisions made. Information gaps have to be filled. Resources have to be allocated and distributed. Coordination is therefore a key to planning.

Control and Authority

Coordination is impossible without some system of overall control and distribution of authority. There must be people who have responsibilities, who are in charge, and whose authority is legitimate. A general tendency in disaster situations is for new authority patterns to emerge. An individual's authority may be legitimatized by his or her technical competence, preparation, or degree of information about the ongoing situation. The role of police departments in disaster coordination is a good example.

In any given disaster situation, the characteristics and consequences of the disaster agent are part of a global picture. However, in the planning process it is necessary to break the whole down into parts so that the situation becomes manageable. Attempting to react to the global picture is ineffective and inefficient.

Disaster research studies have identified organized planning as the primary means of successfully aiding disaster victims. Through international communication and cooperation, the existing response framework can be investigated and strengthened by means of a critical review of the state of the art in victim assistance.

BIBLIOGRAPHY

Center for Planning and Research. (1980). *Manual for developing EOC standard operating procedures.* Palo Alto, CA: CPR.

Dynes, R. R. (1975). *Organized behaviors in disaster.* Columbus, OH: Disaster Research Center.

Dynes, R. R., & Quarantelli, E. L. (1977). *Role of local civil defense in disaster planning.* Columbus, OH: Disaster Research Center.

Federal Emergency Management Agency. (1981, July). *Disaster operations: A handbook for local governments* (CPG 1-6). Washington, DC: Author.

Grant, H. D., Murray, R. H., & Berger, J. D. (1982). *Emergency care* (3rd ed.). Bowie, MD: Robert J. Brady Company.

Quarantelli, E. L. (1979). *Studies in disaster response and planning.* Columbus, OH: Disaster Research Center.

Quarantelli, E. L. (1982). *Delivery of emergency medical services in disasters: Assumptions and realities.* New York: Irvington.

Snell and Associates. (1980). *Overview assessment of the California Master Mutual Aid Program.* Playa Del Rey, CA: Author.

System, Inc. (1981). *Guide for emergency evacuation management and operations.* Los Altos, CA: Author.

5

Ethnic Interaction and Ethnic Violence in India: A Case Study in West Bengal

P. K. Bhowmick
Faculty of Science, University of Calcutta

INTRODUCTION

Interethnic tension is a serious problem in India today. One form of tension centers around the tribes in India. It may be of two types: (1) tribe–nontribe and (2) intertribal. In this chapter, attention has been focused on a tribe which shows signs of being a cause of both types of tension. The tribe has a peculiarity, in that it is gradually being forced into a separate identity by the others around it—those who are tribal as well as those who are nontribal.

The beginning of the process may be traced back to India's colonial past. The Lodhas have fallen victims to a process of labeling by their neighbors, including the administrative apparatus of the polity with which they had only a marginal connection. Because of a process which they had no control over or even awareness of, the Lodhas came to be stigmatized as a criminal tribe (in 1871). This process dislodged the Lodhas from their forest habitat and their forest-dependent way of life without providing them with a socially accepted means of livelihood.

After independence, thanks to the dissemination of knowledge (furnished by the anthropologists and enlightened administrations) about the factors precipitating the crisis, the Lodhas were denotified, with the ostensible purpose of erasing the stigma attached to them. But it nevertheless continued to haunt them, if not legally, at least socially. The Lodhas have been given this or that concession, but no comprehensive understanding or solution of their problem has yet been achieved. As a result, the Lodhas continue to be victimized by the surrounding social situation. While many of them are even today charged with recidivism, others suffer from the lack of opportunities for getting established in life. Consequently, the problem of the Lodhas continues to be simply a law and order problem, but nobody cares to look at the victims themselves, including

Prabodh Kumar Bhowmick is a professor of anthropology and the Dean of the Faculty of Science at Calcutta University, where he received all his academic degrees. Professor Bhowmick has published more than 200 papers and a dozen books on sociocultural and anthropological topics. He recently completed a manuscript on the Chenchus of the forests and plateaux, a hunting and gathering tribe in transition. He is editor-in-chief and coeditor of scholarly journals and has traveled widely to deliver lectures and speeches on developmental anthropology and related subjects at national and international conferences.

their perspective and *weltanschauung*. The result may be a more serious problem in the future. The Lodhas, because of their perpetual deprivation and constant forced isolation from the rest of the society, may go in search of a separate ethnic identity, either on their own or in concert with others who are similarly disinherited. This may well add to the ethnic problems now plaguing India.

Peace and harmony has not always prevailed among human societies, neither among primitive societies nor among modern urban societies. The individuals of a society generally try to maintain some kind of conformity among themselves, and in this way they try to constrict or avoid the disruptive forces that cause tension and disorder. Obviously, forms of social order, norms, and values are evolved for this purpose. To have all these in operation, sometimes a society forms political organizations whose social mechanisms are supposed to induce the members to abide by the rules through a central power and the imposition of law. Informal organizations have respect for religion, because religious beliefs are also considered to be a very important means of social control. These social mechanisms are in existence in various forms in many societies. During the long march of human societies from archaic to complex and sophisticated social orders, there have been many examples where interactions of groups pigmented the larger social canvas with shady patches of violence and victimization.

Different concepts regarding crime, tort, and sin have occurred in different societies. One may pick examples at random.

> *Crime is an offence against the community, a tort is a wrong against an individual. Primitive groups regard many of the crimes in our law as mere torts but they always consider certain actions intolerable and punish them collectively, which is the test of crime. (Lowie, 1947, p. 285)*

In the same way, as mentioned earlier, supernatural sanctions are also important in controlling human behavior.

> *Sins are kinds of deviant behaviour that are believed to call forth punishment by supernatural forces. In the Trobriand islands, incest is a sin: an individual who engages in this behaviour is punished by a devinely imposed skin affliction. Supernatural forces who punish social deviants are found in every culture, there are ghosts, spirits, giants . . . . (Nanda, 1980, p. 251)*

In many cases, a central power and formal, rigid systems of operating law make the social system function harmoniously. Conflicts are resolved through generally accepted norms and procedures or sometimes through legitimate coercion. Ultimately, the question of legitimacy arises (i.e., the question of who has the right to hold or use power). All power is embedded in the cultural matrix of the society, and thus it conforms to the customs and traditions of that society.

Attempts to gain control over power and resources and to sustain large population groups result in feuding or war:

> *The distinction between feuding and warfare is one of scale and organisation. Feuding usually involves relatively small numbers of people and contains an element of surprise. War involves more people and has an element of planning and organisation. (Nanda, 1980, p. 261).*

Feuding and war are among the situations which are studied by victimologists.

ETHNIC INTERACTION AND INDIAN HISTORY

India is peopled by varied ethnic groups, and we find there variegated cultural life. Besides, India has given birth to all types of civilization—from hoary Stone Age cultures to modern, complex societies. Many lithic tools have been unearthed from different parts of India. At the same time, we find certain special traits which clearly signify distinct cultures and different ethnic groups. A long history, processes of stress and strain from interactional involvements, and gradual adjustments to geophysical and ethnic situations have resulted in certain blendings which cannot be overlooked. All these factors have contributed to the molding of a distinctive life-style or cultural configuration. A definite negroid ethnic strain, possibly from thc West, came to the mainland; in the course of time, it was gradually pushed back by other racial strains. Another cultural strain, introduced by an austroasiatic group, penetrated the mainland, and ultimately this strain and culture fully engulfed the people who were of varied racial strains, thus leading to a process of blending. A Mongoloid racial strain is easily identifiable, but this strain did not easily interact with the people of the mainland. This strain is very clearly identifiable in the north and the northeast portion of the country. Naturally, long historical interactions and some other compelling factors molded the history of India, which is nothing but the story of conflict and composition.

It is believed that the so-called Indian tribal groups were slowly pushed back into the inhospitable regions of the country by other groups who possessed superior power, skill, and technology and who tried to gain control over the resources. Naturally, a long period of interaction and conflict is shrouded in the depths of history. The greater powerful groups fought each other to eke out an existence. There are approximately 450 tribal communities, all of which are identifiable groups. Their total population is 51,628,638, which is 7.76% of the total Indian population of 685,184,692 (1981 census). Members of these groups are hunters and gatherers, pastoral or swidden cultivators, or settled agriculturists. Some make a living from cottage industries. Of course, a majority work as day laborers or wage earners in agriculture and modern industry. For administrative purposes, 76 groups have been classified as "primitive tribal groups," and special assistance has been and is being given to them to lift their standard of living.

More than a century ago, in 1871, a few groups of people, both tribal and nontribal groups, were considered to be "criminal tribes." This classification was due to their supposed criminal activities. The stigma of criminality was inflicted on them by the British rulers in India. There were 153 such groups. Their treatment included many restrictions regarding movement, which made it casy for the police to keep surveillance over the *dagis*, or marked recidivists, of the criminal tribes. After independence, however, the Criminal Tribes Act was repealed (in 1952). This erased the stigma of criminality that was attached to criminal tribe members. The number of people affected was 27,102,180. From then on, the groups were treated as denotified communities. Naturally, special treatment for them was suggested in order to provide correction, economic growth, and rehabilitation. At present, a few of these groups have been included in the list of primitive tribal groups.

CRIMES IN TRIBAL INDIA

The pattern of crime, as we conceive it, may sometimes vary from group to group. Among the Toda, a pastoral people of southern India, female infanticide was customary. If the first-born baby was a girl, then she was killed by putting her in a desolate place within three days of the birth. Head-hunting occurred among the Nagas, and burial of captured individuals was considered creditable among members of the Ao Naga Society. Killing an unknown man during the month of *Jaistha* (May–June) on the night of the new moon (*Amabasya*) and sprinkling his blood on the paddy fields by the Oraon was intended to placate the spirit of Mahadania, who causes drought and famine. Human sacrifice (*meriah*) by the Khond group of Orissa had a different purpose. Frazer (1864), following Macpherson, describes this subject very clearly:

> *The sacrifices were offered to the earth goddess, and were believed to ensure good crops, and immunity from all diseases and accidents. In particular, they were considered necessary in the cultivation of turmeric, the Konds arguing that the turmeric could not have a deep red colour without the shedding of blood.*

The Santals have a very different attitude toward the *dain* (witch). She is believed to create epidemics in the form of infanticide, and the bewildered villagers rush to the sorcerer (witch doctor) to find out the reason for this. The witch doctor is known as the *jan guru*. He calculates using occult practices, sometimes shouts with a foaming mouth, utters indistinct doggerel, and creates an eerie atmosphere which stupifies the bewildered villagers. Then suddenly he arrives at a conclusion and points his finger at a widow who doesn't have a child, uttering that she is the root of all malaise in the village. The Santals, without any verification, rush out in a group to kill her by throwing stones or by beating her with a heavy stick as if she were Satan incarnate. Sometimes she is burnt alive. These are very common sights in Bengal even today. Every year, newspapers report witch hunting of this type. These violent crimes are happening among the Santals—a docile and honest tribal community in India.

Elwin, in his *Maria Murder and Suicide* (1950), described various cases of homicide and suicide. He gave glaring examples from various tribal groups in which suicide is very common. He also gave a rough analysis of the causes of murder in 100 cases (Elwin, 1950, p. 51). See Table 5-1 for a summary of Elwin's analysis. The Marias are a tribal group who live in central India and practice

Table 5-1 Causes of homicide in 100 cases

Cause of homicide	Number of cases
Robbery or accusation of robbery	8
Quarrels over property	15
Suspicion of magic or witchcraft	5
Insanity	5
Resentment at abuse or word magic	9
Revenge	6
Family quarrels	16
Sex motives	17
Alcohol	19

Source: V. Elwin, *Maria murder and suicide*.

Table 5-2 Causes of suicide in 245 cases in Bastar

Cause of suicide	Number of cases
Insanity	20
Disease	52
Leprosy	6
Grief on account of bereavement	17
Love affairs	11
Quarrels over property	3
Quarrels between wife & husband	55
Other domestic quarrels	43
Fear of scandal	11
Intoxication	1
Economic (starvation & financial ruin)	3
Fear of courts and officials	3
Bad treatment by employers	2
Failure in school examination	1
Not properly reported	17

Source: V. Elwin, *Maria murder and suicide.*

agriculture. Table 5-2 gives the causes of suicide among all the tribes of the area during a 10-year period.

Elwin gave a clear picture of suicide as practiced among the tribes of Bastar in central India. Similar examples from Malinowski are also available in his famous book *Crime and Custom in Savage Society* (1940). He described the suicide of a Trobriand islander. The suicide occurred after the victim was accused of incest by his fellow villagers.

> *For this there was only one remedy, only one means of escape remained to the unfortunate youth. Next morning he put on festive attire and ornamentation, climbed a coconut palm and addressed the community, speaking from among the palm leaves and bidding them farewell. He explained the reasons for his desperate deed and also launched forth a veiled accusation against the man who had driven him to his death, upon which it became the duty of his clansmen to avenge him. Then he wailed aloud, as is the custom, jumped from a palm some sixty feet high and was killed on the spot. (Malinowski, 1940, p. 78)*

Traditionally, the criminal tribes have forest or pastoral economies. Some members practice weaving, mat making, trading in beads and bangles, and scavanging. A few typical cases can be cited. The Minas of Punjab are skillful burglars and dacoits, like the Lodhas of West Bengal. The Sannyasis of Uttar Pradesh, Punjab, and Rajasthan are expert dacoits, and at the time of committing dacoity, they pelt stones. The Jadnas are swindlers who pretend to turn metals into gold. The Gopalas engage in stealing cattle and selling them elsewhere. The Manga Mudis are cattle poisoners as well as cattle thieves. They also steal goats and sheep. The Chapperbands are known for pilfering. Sometimes they counterfeit coins. The Kaladis and Konda-Doras indulge in crime after the growing season. The Bauris are experts at household burglary and nighttime cattle stealing. They have been known to steal jewelry off the bodies of sleeping women. The Bauris sometimes pose as gentlemen of high caste, cheat the members of other groups by marrying their daughters, and plunder them at their convenience. The Soonariahs are daytime pickpockets and also commit petty thefts. The women of the Bedar community of Maharastra are mostly prostitutes.

Some become mistresses to pave the way for burglary. The Hanri women marry well-to-do Muslims and disappear with their wealth at the first opportunity. The wives of Kaikadis become temporary wives of others. The Muggarudi women cleverly pilfer clothes from the washing line. They have been known to appear stark naked before policemen to bewilder them and make them forget their duty. The Waghari women are persistent beggers who often steal the ornaments worn by children.

The above are a few of the activities of some members of the ex-criminal tribes of India. By engaging in these activities, they subsist as social parasites. Though there are police actions and other people are well acquainted with the nature of their activities, these groups are able to eke out an existence.

THE LODHA: A WEST BENGAL CASE

The Lodhas are one of the primitive tribal groups in India, and they were treated in the past as a criminal tribe prior to the revocation of the Criminal Tribes Act in 1952. They live mainly in the rugged jungle terrain of West Midnapore (in West Bengal), but some are found in the contiguous regions of Orissa and Bihar. The total number in and around the Midnapore district is 30,000. They speak a corrupt Bengali dialect, with some admixture of the Mundari tongue. The Lodhas constitute one-third of the total number of active criminals in the district. The pattern of their criminal activities is shown in Table 5-3.

Many reports against the Lodhas have been registered, though at present few Lodhas have been sent up for trial. The criminal leanings of the Lodhas are due to economic depression and territorial displacement. They belong to a group of hunters and gatherers. They considered themselves a part of nature, and economic symbiosis for their expanding families was not at all difficult. But the permanent land settlement introduced by Lord Cornwallis attracted others to the forest, and therefore the Lodhas became strangers in their own home. They were surrounded by agrarian, land-grabbing communities, like the Santals, the Mundas, and the Mahatos. The naturalistic worldview of the Lodhas and their way of living (i.e., the material culture) was put under attack by changes in sociopolitical and ecological conditions. The impact of the surrounding communities severely affected their traditional patterns of economic life, which had justified their symbiotic philosophy. This impact ultimately tilted the balance of the whole society. In such circumstances, pilfering, petty thefts, and stealing

Table 5-3 Pattern of major crime in the Midnapore district (1961)

Type	Reported cases	True cases	Lodhas involved in cases
Murder	86	72	—
Dacoity	110	108	6
Robbery	123	107	—
Burglary	1516	1486	127
Theft	1715	1583	111

articles from the houses of the neighbors, as well as the clandestine sale of jungle products, were first resorted to by individuals. In the course of time, they developed into group activities. Amidst poverty, the unsympathetic attitude of neighbors, and the stoic apathy of the then ruling government, criminality cut a deep gorge into their society, a gorge which the people rolled down into helplessly. Lodha criminal activity is nothing but a survival strategy. Since the Lodhas could not refashion their life-style, they had no other alternative but to tread the path of criminality, which was their last resort for keeping body and soul together.

The Lodhas in general, especially the criminals, maintain relationships with certain people who are in the habit of receiving stolen property at rock-bottom prices. The Lodhas, knowing very well that they are being cheated, are not able to avoid the snares of these wily people, who pretend to have concern for them. When Lodhas are arrested or jailed, these people look after the families and sometimes even spend money to defray the cost of legal proceedings or for other purposes. Thus, the nexus between the Lodhas and these supposedly helpful neighbors binds the Lodhas hand and foot with ties which are very difficult to break. However, some welfare programs have been started by the government in different parts of the district in order to improve the Lodhas' economy and provide them with education and other benefits.

There is another aspect of the problem. After the introduction of the Panchayati Raj, a good number of the Lodhas gradually became associated with village administrations. A few of them affiliated themselves with local political parties. They entered the last election, which CPI and CPI-affiliated candidates won. Naturally, this gave them the opportunity to mix with other sections of the people, thus bridging the gap that had prevailed for such a long time among these communities. Such political involvements have created more tension and factionalism in a few villages—as a result of party ideologies. In many cases, village or tribal solidarity or communal integrity has been threatened.

SINCE DENOTIFICATION

The Lodhas were freed from restrictions on movement and other constraints, but the stigma of criminality has constantly haunted them. Prolonged criminal activity and the steps taken by the government to maintain law and order have caused them to have a certain bent. The reasons are analyzed below:

1. Economic and territorial displacement caused the Lodhas to lose their livelihood and eroded their self-confidence.
2. Because of their ignorance of any art or craft that might serve certain needs of the general economy, they have failed to find any room in the larger sociocultural order.
3. Since legitimate routes to earning a livelihood were totally denied, the Lodhas took routes that were considered devious by those in the wider socioeconomic order. The stigma of criminality that consequently came to be attached to the Lodhas brought in its train a thoroughly negative social assessment of them.
4. Police oppression, punishment, and torture disturbed the Lodhas' cohesion and solidarity. Repeated arrests and prolonged incarceration, sometimes on "got

up" charges, completely shattered familial bonds and bred in the Lodhas a sort of "atomized," selfish, and irresponsible mentality.

5. Extreme poverty exposed the Lodhas to various forms of exploitation by the village worthies, who in many cases were the brains behind the crimes committed by the Lodhas.

6. As a result of being compelled to sell the stolen articles to others at a very low price and thus being "cheated," the Lodhas came to regard non-Lodha people as dishonest and tyrannical.

7. The stark reality of a life of starvation killed any zeal or enthusiasm for a better life. Indeed, it killed the Lodhas' desire and capacity for fighting back. They slipped into indolence and incapacity, into utter despondency and total apathy regarding any kind of change or innovation.

8. The ever-present fear of police torture or intimidation by neighbors made the Lodhas almost birds of passage. Their homes hold no attraction for them. Signs of loss of the sense of belonging to an organized social life (anomie) are evident among the Lodhas.

9. The above facts have made the Lodhas withdraw from the wider socio-cultural milieu and have prevented them from making any attempt at altering the situation. Their age-old timidity and coyness have got a firmer grip on them because of the totally hostile environment—an environment which they have no control over and which they do not even desire to have control over.

In spite of the welfare programs for the Lodhas, they are subject to victimization, including mass killings (see Table 5-4). The image profile constructed during the operation of the Criminal Tribes Act cannot be wiped out within a short time.

An account of a mass killing of Lodhas appeared in *RAIN*:

> *It was 26 September 1979. The people of the whole of Bengal and its border regions were celebrating the Great Puja Festivals. In parties they were visiting the temples and Puja pandels and enjoying the festivities.*
>
> *Suddenly there came a crowd numbering several thousands, lethally armed and beating drums. They brought with them a few cartfuls of country liquor. They were a mixed group of tribals. They came to wreak vengeance on a group of "criminals" who were hiding in a vast stretch of sugar cane plantation along the basin of the river Subarnarekha. The beating of*

Table 5-4 Mutilations and killings of Lodhas

Place	Year	Number killed	Number mutilated
Dhanghari (Binpur PS)	1961	1	3
Jhargram	1968	5	12
Patina (Gopiballavpur)	1979	19	—
Ganua (Narayangarh)	1981	8	9
Numenigeria (Jhargram)	1982	2	—
Kesiari	1982	3	—
Baghapa/Chakua & Chandri (Jhargram)	1982	8	—

> *drums echoed in the jungle on the river banks. The noise and uproar almost rent the sky when the mob found and held forty-five men they were in pursuit of. They tied them with twisted straw ropes like animals and beheaded nineteen of them, one after another. The bodies were thrown into the river and taken into custody. The angry mob was retaliating against another tribal group for their having committed dacoity and rape in their villages. Then they went back shouting all the way like a victorious army.*
>
> *These victims were the Lodhas, who live in the rugged terrain of the Bengal-Bihar-Orissa border where there is an abundance of forests. In the few months before the incident, they had committed a series of dacoities and robberies and in a few cases had molested women belonging to the Santals and other tribal groups. The law and order situation greatly deteriorated at this place. The police failed to suppress or apprehend them and ultimately the people took the law into their own hands. The tribals declared "gira," a traditional form of Santal war against others, by making a knot from the bark of* Sal *tree, (Shorea Robusta) and by beating "kara," their traditional war drum. (Bhowmick, 1981, p. 6).*

AMELIORATIVE MEASURES

It should be mentioned that the ameliorative measures taken by the government and by voluntary organizations have not always produced good results. In most cases, the measures have been stopped. The difficulties were due to a wrong diagnosis of the problem. In pursuing development work among the Lodhas, three points should be kept in mind:

1. *The Lodhas are a problem-ridden people.* They have many psycho-emotional problems. Chronic social neglect by the greater society has dwarfed their minds and activities. Laziness, reluctance to do any hard labor, and parasitism have made them unfit for any manual work. Therefore, any sort of action such as "shock therapy" will not do them any good. Since they have developed parasitic tendencies, they do not hesitate to cheat the government.
2. *Many of the Lodhas' neighbors create trouble for them.* These neighbors directly or indirectly insist that the Lodhas engage in criminal activities in order to benefit them. They do not want further welfare to be provided to the Lodhas, for then they will no longer have the advantage of cheap labor. It has been observed that economic goods (e.g., goats, bullocks, and even building materials) given to the Lodhas are sold to the neighbors for just a song. In such circumstances, welfare measures become meaningless. The neighbors include various persons belonging to political parties, and these persons have easy access to local police officials. In some cases, a changeover to new receivers of goods aggrieves the old receivers, who try to take revenge against the Lodhas, even arranging to have them murdered.
3. *The government administration in some cases creates more problems than it solves.* In most of the cases, it does not understand the existing problems and its plans are misguided. The result is failure.

All attempts at amelioration should be looked into very carefully. The main goal should be the overall development of the Lodhas. Some welfare activities are being performed by voluntary organizations. The activities at Bidisa are especially praiseworthy. Recently, a "Lodha cell" has been organized by the government. Panchayat members have been involved in some welfare work, including tank excavation, goat and poultry rearing, and so on. It should be mentioned that the money is being provided entirely by the Indian government, since the Lodhas are categorized as a primitive tribal group.

THE DANGER OF DEMOCRACY

The Left Front Ministry has been in power in the state for over 10 years. This ministry has undertaken all development activities through the local Panchayats. In most cases, especially in tribal areas where tribesmen become Panchayat members, development work faces a serious obstacle. These groups of people, who have no understanding of planning and little experience in development work, want to play a vital role and often try to dominate efficient government officials. There are many instances where such officials not only were denied proper respect but were even insulted. As a result, they withdrew instead of involving themselves in development activities. Also, sometimes the Lodhas, just to evade arrest by the police, take refuge behind political leaders. They reap political advantages, and therefore crime and antisocial activities are on the ascendency in many places.

CONCLUSION

The above account may appear at first to be an analysis of a small and not very significant tribe in India. The connection with the issue of interethnic conflict may not be obvious. But a little reflection immediately suggests that the Lodhas have been subjected to much suffering because of their specific identity, which they are constantly made conscious of by others around them.

Mass killings of Lodhas have been considered to be among the consequences of ethnocultural interaction. The Lodhas as a group have developed their life-style in interaction with their environment and the neighboring ethnic groups. Their life-style has been molded by this interaction, and as a consequence the group has a distinct image profile. This image profile even today has changed very little, because there has been an almost total absence of educational opportunities and socially acceptable economic opportunities for the group. Therefore, the group is still not in a position to face the many difficulties that threaten its existence. Until systematic opportunities for the group are provided, the Lodhas will not be able to change their status. Naturally, all development work for them should be properly designed to give it shape and to withstand unnecessary political interference.

The political and administrative apparatus of the state sometimes loses stability. The people then cannot keep faith with the administration, and hence they take the law into their own hands. In such cases, the demoralization of the state administration should be checked, and the amount of political interference should be reduced to avoid danger to the development work. Such situations can lead to violent eruptions, which in turn can threaten social stability as well as security. Violence should be discouraged by all means possible, and victims of violence should be given restitution while being shown sympathy and affection by state leaders.

Anthropologists, like the rest of society, concur with the analysis of existing conditions—but with a difference. They search for the origins of a problem and try to discover clues about the future. What may be set aside by others as presently inconsequential appears to have a deeper significance in the creative imagination of anthropologists, who try to see the connection, if any, between a particular problem of an individual or a group and what may be called larger public and historical issues. Anthropologists therefore have to highlight issues which are obvious and hence do not engage the attention of others. These issues, because of the lack of consideration they receive from politicians, policy makers, and administrators, get more and more complicated and attain a form and proportion that proves unmanageable in the long run.

At least, this is the case for what are deemed critical ethnic problems in India today. The clamor for the recognition of an ethnic identity for the Nagas, the Khasis, the Mizos, and even the Gorkhas and the Akalis is not the result of chance events but the culmination of a long process. The Lodhas may today be dismissed as just a problem tribe which should be provided with material help. That they might ultimately grow into a powerful ethnic group and pose a threat to the prevailing political order may seem very unlikely. Yet, although their numerical strength is not impressive, it is not necessary that a separatist movement ostensibly demanding political recognition of ethnic identity be gigantically strong. Certain communities, each of which taken by itself would not have sufficient strength, can come together and organize to form a sociopolitical movement. That the Lodhas cannot be confirmed in their old criminal identity would be the conclusion of anybody who had faith in the various measures instituted for their amelioration. However small the number of the Lodhas getting education, the Lodhas no longer live in isolation. They are drawn more and more into the vortex of the political life of the nation. Of course, they are not yet allowed their legitimate share of power and resources or even of recognition. The resultant simmering discontent may arouse and confirm their consciousness of being separate. The negative stereotypes of other tribes, let it be said, may have an important role in confirming this view of themselves. In any case, their discontent will have several important consequences:

1. It will widen the gap between the Lodhas and certain other tribal groups.
2. It will perpetuate and even widen the gap between the Hindus and Muslims in the vicinity.
3. It will force the Lodhas to close up their ranks, forge a bond of unity with certain other tribal communities which share a similar fate, and become part of a separatist movement.

Hence, not neglect or condescension but an adequate understanding of the problems of different underprivileged communities, irrespective of their current strength and size, is needed if there is to be a long-term solution to interethnic violence in a country like India.

BIBLIOGRAPHY

Bhowmick, P. K. (1956). Physical affinities of the Lodhas of Midnapur. *Man in India*, *56*(2).
Bhowmick, P. K. (1963). *The Lodhas of West Bengal.* Calcutta: Punthi Pustak.
Bhowmick, P. K. (1968). Occupational changes in two villages in Bengal. *Man in India*, *48*(1).
Bhowmick, P. K. (1968). Development scheme as factors of social and economic changes: A case study of the Lodha rehabilitation centre at Daharpur in Midnapur District, West Bengal. *Journal of Social Research*, *11*(1).

Bhowmick, P. K. (1970). Welfare programmes and administration for development and integration: A case study of the Lodhas of West Bengal. *Tribe*, *7*(1).
Bhowmick, P. K. (1976). *Socio-cultural profile of frontier Bengal.* Calcutta: Punthi Pustak.
Bhowmick, P. K. (1976). Problems of denotified tribes: A case study of the interaction of government and diverse ethnic groups in fringe Bengal. *Man and Life*, *2*(1,2).
Bhowmick, P. K. (1978). Approach to tribal development. *Bulletin of the Department of Anthropology, Dibrugarh University*, *7,8*.
Bhowmick, P. K. (1981). Rehabilitation of a denotified community: The ex-criminal Lodhas of West Bengal. *Journal of the Royal Anthropological Institute, 44.*
Bhowmick, P. K. (1983). The Lodha: A denotified community of West Bengal. *Man in India*, *63*(3).
Bhowmick, P. K. (1984). Development anthropology. *The Eastern Anthropologist*, *37*(4).
Bhowmick, P. K. (1985). Tribal situation in West Bengal. *Indian Anthropologist*, *15*.
Bhowmick, S. (1987). *Tribal odyssey: A journey between two worlds.* Calcutta: ISRAA.
Bhattacharya, S. K. (1987). *Souvenir*. Calcutta.
Census of India (1981). Series 1, Parts 2 & 3. New Delhi.
Daily, F. C. (1916). *Manual of criminal tribes operating in Bengal.* Calcutta.
Elwin, V. (1950). *Maria murder and suicide*. Bombay.
Haikerwal, B. S. (1934). *Economic and social aspects of crime in India.* London.
Kapadia, K. M. (1952). The criminal tribes of India. *Sociological Bulletin*, *1*(2).
Lowie, R. H. (1947). *An introduction to cultural anthropology*. New York.
Malinowski, B. L. (1940). *Crime and custom in savage society*. London.
Nanda, S. (1980). *Cultural anthropology*. New York.

III

THE VICTIM AND THE JUSTICE SYSTEM

6

When the Battered Woman Becomes the Defendant

Lenore E. A. Walker
Walker & Associates, Denver, Colorado

INTRODUCTION

American statistics suggest that approximately 12% of all homicides in this country are committed by women, most of whom are battered women who kill their abusive partners in self-defense (Browne, 1987). In at least 50–80% of the cases (the numbers vary, along with the recordkeeping of the FBI), assault was reported one or more times to the police prior to the homicide. In most of these family violence cases, the lethality danger was ignored or not noted. Newer proarrest policies recommended by the Attorney General's Task Force on Family Violence (1984) ensure that more victims than ever are being offered services when assault is reported to the police. Still, the lethality potential is not sufficiently noted, and a small but significant percentage of assault victims may resort to violence or other criminal acts for their own protection. Some of these women will undoubtedly become defendants in a criminal proceeding.

Recent examination of women prisoners indicates that approximately 80% of them have been victims of incest, sexual abuse, and physical battery (Bauschard, 1986). Crimes involving money and property (e.g., embezzlement, forgery, and burglary) and drug-related crimes may well have been committed by women at the demand of their batterers. Both direct and indirect threats of further violence frequently motivate these criminal acts. Rarely has justification been used as a defense for these battered women, and although it is becoming a more popular defense, I believe that the battered woman who becomes a defendant today may be in greater legal jeopardy than in earlier days—as a result of the very programs created to help her when she is the victim. This danger can come from advocates or even untrained mental health professionals who unwittingly help the victim to release her angry rage without giving her the

Lenore E. A. Walker holds a doctoral degree from an accredited psychology department at Rutgers, The State University of New Jersey. She has focused her research and clinical work on battered women, abused children, and other victims or survivors of men's violence. Her independent practice, Walker & Associates, provides psychotherapy, psychological consultation, forensic evaluations, and expert witness testimony in this area. She is the author of numerous books and articles on victims of violence, including *The Battered Woman* and *Women and Mental Health Policy*. She has lectured around the world and has attended many international women's conferences. Dr. Walker is the 1987 recipient of the Distinguished Contribution to the Profession for Public Service award of the American Psychological Association Board of Professional Affairs and the 1988 recipient of the World Leadership Award of the World Congress of Victimology.

skills to manage it. It can also come from a failure to protect her right to remain silent by breaking confidentiality, such as when records and testimony are introduced without securing informed consent. Finally, it can come from setting up programs which she is told will keep her safe without ensuring that such programs are truly effective.

JUSTIFICATION STANDARDS

In many cases, the battered woman defendant's actions can be justified or excused on the basis of fear of further abuse or retaliation. Self-defense in homicide cases and duress in other criminal matters is predicated on proving the facts which demonstrate that the woman has a *reasonable perception of imminent danger*. The redefinition of both *an objective reasonable woman* and *subjective reasonable battered woman's perceptions*, as well as the understanding that for many battered women the danger of great bodily harm or death is always imminent, has caused the modification of these legal standards for justification defenses (Blackman, 1987). Several cases helped establish these new standards.

In *State v. Wanrow* (1977), the Washington Supreme Court decided that "in our society, women suffer from a conspicuous lack of access to training in and the means of developing those skills necessary to effectively repel a male assailant without resorting to the use of deadly weapons" (p. 548). The reasonable woman is more likely to perceive the need to arm herself with a weapon to defend against a man who has learned to use parts of his body to inflict injury. This decision has broadened the definition of a reasonable woman to explain the reasonable battered woman's use of a weapon when the man has none other than the deadly parts of his body. *Wanrow* also affirmed the use of jury instructions which changed the language to specifically refer to the female gender instead of using the more typical generic male language. This step is important in broadening the reasonable person standard to include women as well as men.

The lead case which argues for extending the imminency question was *State v. Garcia* (Bochnak, 1981). Here, the issue before the court was whether Inez Garcia, after being raped by two acquaintances who threatened to come back and repeat the sexual assault when they left, reasonably perceived that she was still in imminent danger when she shot one of the rapists several hours later. The court affirmed her contention that imminent does not necessarily mean immediate when they granted her a new trial. These men knew her habits and where she lived, so their threat was likely to be acted on. She was subsequently acquitted on grounds of self-defense at her new trial.

Garcia and similar cases have demonstrated that the period of imminent danger is broader than is traditionally conceived in regard to male-to-male fights. Some states, particularly in the West (e.g., Colorado), have passed new laws expressly permitting the use of deadly force in defense of a person's home or other personal property. These so-called "make my day" laws, named after a line in a Clint Eastwood movie, have not yet been widely applied to family violence, but they have been applied in cases of strangers who break into people's homes. In one Colorado case, this statute was used to justify not filing charges against a woman who shot and killed a man who had been harassing her as a Peeping Tom on and off for a long period of time.

Browne (1987) has found that several factors, mostly involving the batterer's behavior, differentiated her sample of battered women who killed in self-defense from those who did not strike back with such force. The women who killed demonstrated fear and terror, which produced a feeling of desperation. The frequency and severity of abuse, threats to kill, and danger to children or other loved ones and the presence of other correlates of violence (e.g., destruction of property and assaults on others) were all associated with those who commit homicide in self-defense. In the 110 cases that have been evaluated at Walker & Associates, factors such as sexual abuse of the children, marital rape, and alcohol or methamphetamine abuse and a combination of terror and rage producing desperation are associated with women who harm or kill the abuser (Walker, in press). Thus, the research supports defining the reasonable battered woman's perception that she is in imminent danger of serious bodily injury or death in a broad range of situations, some of which might not have been included prior to the new court decisions.

A reasonable perception, of course, does not have to be proven accurate in the legal standard, such as happened in one of our cases, where the woman saw the glint of metal in a poorly lit room—and mistook a cigarette lighter for a gun. Since her batterer had just beaten her and said he was going to get a gun and shoot her, the jury found it was reasonable for her to believe he was going to keep his threat, even though she misperceived the lighter for the gun.

There is a relatively new acceptance in the United States of the introduction of expert witness testimony on the *battered woman syndrome* as a way to meet the self-defense standards when battered women kill their abusers (Schneider, 1987; Walker, 1984b, 1987a). This testimony is also being allowed in duress and other defenses involving battered women. Such testimony is typically offered after a thorough psychological evaluation, including a review of the abuse history and an assessment of the woman's current state of mind, to determine if she acted in accordance with the expected effects of a *posttraumatic stress disorder* (PTSD), which is caused by the psychological trauma from the battering. The battered woman syndrome is a subcategory of the more formal psychiatric diagnosis of PTSD found in the *Diagnostic and Statistical Manual of Mental Disorders* Third Edition, Revised (American Psychiatric Association, 1987). Its presence or absence depends on meeting the diagnostic criteria—like any other diagnostic category—and not just on the defendant's self-report data, although her abuse history is of course important. This diagnostic category is usually used for a justification rather than a mental health defense in most cases (Sonkin, 1987; Browne, Thyfault, & Walker, 1987; Walker, 1987b).

BATTERED WOMEN WHO KILL IN SELF-DEFENSE

The admissibility of psychological testimony to support a justification defense has been slowly evolving out of case law decisions over the past 10 years. *Ibn-Tamas v. U.S.* (1979) was the first case to deal directly with the issue, and in ruling that the knowledge to be provided by an expert would be beyond the ken of the average juror and would be more probative than prejudicial if it were admitted, the court set the stage to encourage other state courts to admit such testimony. Decisions in other states, such as Georgia (*State v. Smith*, 1981), Maine (*State v. Anaya*, 1981), Illinois (*State v. Mennis*, 1983), Washington (*State v. Allery*, 1984), New Jersey (*State v. Kelley*, 1984), New York (*People v. Torres*,

1985) and Florida (*Hawthorne v. State*, 1985), ruled that a woman who presents evidence of having been repeatedly battered as justification for her otherwise criminal behavior is entitled to a psychological evaluation and the opportunity to put such evidence before the triers of fact. Although, the U.S. Supreme Court has not yet ruled on such a case, there was a written dissent issued by two dissenting justices (Powell and Marshall) when the majority refused to grant *certiorari* to hear *Moran v. Ohio* (1984), noting that "the battered woman's syndrome as a self-defense theory has gained increasing support over recent years" (286).

Other decisions have kept the testimony out, such as *State v. Thomas* (1981), an Ohio case where the ruling was that such evidence was more prejudicial than probative (the only such ruling to date), and have narrowed the definition of a *reasonable victim* to someone who does not appear to initiate the encounter or any aggression which results in a homicide (*Burhle v. State*, 1981) or hires someone else to do the killing (*State v. Martin*, 1984). In the *Kelley* decision, the New Jersey Supreme Court went further than most other courts by using the new domestic violence legislation to declare that battered women are intended to be treated as a special class (civil protection laws probably would not have passed if these women were not vulnerable to being harmed again).

Once the admissibility issues became somewhat resolved through an increasing number of favorable decisions, especially the *Kelley* and *Hawthorne* decisions, the major issues then became whether or not the defendant was battered as she claimed and what the relevance was of the battered woman syndrome for those victims or defendants who did not behave according to the expected reasonable person or battered woman stereotypes. Jones (1981) has described many of the false notions concerning women who kill, and I have described myths about battered women, many of which are still prevalent (Walker, 1979).

Although the data demonstrate that most battered women fight back at some time (Walker, 1984a), the stereotype is that the "good victim" is passive and never tries to defend herself. Most battered women learn that they are hurt worse when they attempt self-defense, but sometimes they take the risk to bolster their faltering self-esteem. Others may have been trained to fight back, having learned at an earlier period to cope with pain by turning it into angry and aggressive feelings. Our research demonstrated the typical progression of affect went from feeling shock and surprise after the first battering incident to anger and hostility after later incidents (Walker, 1984a, p. 175).

In the same study, 92% of the battered women interviewed thought that the batterer could kill them and 54% thought in some circumstances they could kill him. In addition, 74% admitted thinking about him dying, but only 11% admitted trying to bring about his death by their actions. Nine of the 400 in that sample were successful. When asked who they thought would be most likely to die during a battering incident, 87% of the women interviewed thought it would be them. In almost one-half of the cases (48%) the batterer threatened to commit suicide and in 36% of the cases so did the woman (Walker, 1984a, pp. 177–178). Obviously, the issue of dying is an important issue in these relationships. Most battered women do fantasize about the batterer's death during the course of a battering relationship, but very few actually take steps to bring it about. Yet, should evidence of this common occurrence be introduced in a homicide trial, it may preclude the admissibility or believability of self-defense as a justification.

These data have relevance for those who work as attorneys, advocates, service providers, and researchers in the field of victimology. Many interventions with battered women can later be used to demonstrate a lack of reasonableness, imminency, or even "good victim" type characteristics should these women become defendants. Several cases are presented here to illustrate the potential for problems despite the best intentions of the victimologists.

Fear and Anger

The healing process for battered women includes, among many goals, the validation of angry feelings at their oppression. If a therapeutic intervention proceeds along the expected lines, then the client's angry feelings will be expressed slowly and within the client's control (Walker, 1987b). Without helping her work through these angry feelings, the battered woman will be less likely to heal and become a survivor. However, if too much rage is touched off too quickly, it can result in homicidal or suicidal behavior on the part of the victim. These cases may or may not involve self-defense, depending on whether and for how long the batterer has ceased his abusive behavior. In several of our homicide cases, the physical battering had stopped, but the batterer continued to abuse the victim psychologically through direct or indirect means (e.g., financial or legal harassment). This danger is a real one both for advocates untrained in therapy skills and for therapists untrained in the psychology of battered women.

In the case of P.L., a 35-year-old battered woman who shot and killed her abusive husband, it became clear that the homicide occurred in direct relation to the marital therapy treatment the couple was undergoing at the time. The therapy notes indicated that as the therapist tried to shift the balance of power using appropriate and standard family therapy techniques based on family system theory, the other family members became more angry with P.L., since she did less to make their lives comfortable. The shift in power tipped the lethality potential here. The husband became more of a bully as he grabbed more of the power (at the therapist's urging), particularly in taking over the management of the family business, which had previously been P.L.'s function. He refused to let her enter the business without his permission. No longer able to feel needed through cooking, doing the laundry, and providing other housekeeping services to the family (given up with the therapist's encouragement) and isolated from her business (given up as a result of her husband's demands), P.L. felt displaced and without value to her family.

As P.L. began to become more depressed, she acted out in aggressive ways, including taking a loaded gun into a therapy session and threatening to kill herself with it. She later said she wanted both the therapist and her husband to see her die. When the therapist called the police, fearing P.L. was a danger to herself and the others, P.L. ran out of the office and successfully eluded them. The shift in power in that family came too soon, before the violence was under control. Achieving control can take a long time in family therapy, if it occurs at all.

P.L. became so scared by the escalation in her feelings of fear and anger that they combined in a lethal way. She voluntarily went to a mental health facility, but she left after 24 hours when they would not deal with the family violence issues. She then went to a local battered women's shelter, but they refused her admission because she now had a mental health hospitalization record. She went back home. Following the next battering incident, which included her husband's humiliating her by seriously beating her and threatening to kill her in front of others, P.L. did not commit suicide as she threatened but took the gun and shot and killed her husband instead.

P.L. probably would not have killed her husband even after that abusive incident had her perception of the violence not been altered by the family therapy. The therapist kept detailed notes of P.L.'s steady deterioration and her own frustration of not being able to effectively intervene. Battered women do not perceive therapeutic neutrality; they believe that one is either totally on their side or does not like them and will cause them harm. At the same time, advocates who are usually less well trained in therapeutic techniques sometimes unwittingly set up types of situations which push the family dynamics toward a homicide. Ironically, the victim-witness program which did not ever get involved in assisting P.L. did provide assistance to her husband's adult children, who testified against P.L. in the trial. She lost her long-standing victim status once she became a defendant.

Blaming the Victim

Sometimes a homicide is precipitated by inadequate therapy that is not well supervised and in which the victim is made to feel like the responsible party. Although many of the more overt ways of blaming the victim are no longer common, battered women are still being blamed by invalidating their perceptions of danger when there is no direct proof but the dynamics of abuse are evident.

In the case of S.B., her battering husband was referred to social services after her children and several of their friends disclosed he had been sexually abusing them. Although she believed that the sexual abuse had happened and considered divorcing her husband, the peer advocacy program they were referred to kept her hoping that he would change. He attended therapy sessions, as did she, with a therapist recommended by the program. The oldest daughter was assigned to a group, but no treatment was available for the younger ones. S.B. felt that she was being told she was as "sick" as he was, even though she had not known about his behavior. She became angry that he was not being held accountable for his misdeeds.

Meanwhile, the oldest daughter recanted her story about the sexual abuse by her father because, as she later told me, she overheard girls in the group discussing other group members in her school cafeteria. Behaving as a typical victim who is fearful of retribution from confrontation, she did not tell anyone and simply refused to discuss her own situation. She reasoned that since her father was not allowed to live in the house, she was safe at least. She did not realize that one of the repercussions would be that her original story would become invalidated as the father's therapist came to know him and believe that he was incapable of the kind of abuse he had been accused of. Without physical evidence of the sexual abuse, the younger children were not involved. The three other children's stories never changed, but they had not been required to attend these group sessions.

Feeling disbelieved, both the mother and the daughter became more resistant to treatment and more unwilling even to try to defend their positions. The father, who never missed a session, looked better and better, whereas the mother and daughter were labeled vindictive and emotionally disturbed. They became more and more frightened that the system would not be able to protect them from this violent man, and indeed, just as their fears predicted, he was declared no longer dangerous by his therapist and was allowed by social services to move back into the family home. Although they never ruled on the truthfulness of the original sexual abuse claim because a treatment plan was already in progress, the records cast suspicion on its veracity. It should be mentioned that they provided family treatment, a modality considered questionable by others in the domestic violence field (Walker, 1988).

S.B. was terrified when her husband moved back in but felt powerless to do anything about it. He did not physically abuse her or the children but went back to his psychologically intrusive and oppressive ways. The children and she were ordered to work for hours at a time doing chores he wanted done. She believed he was trying to tire them out so they would sleep through his molestation, one of the earlier accusations of how he had harmed them. S.B. decided her only way to keep the children safe was to let them all sleep together, in one room, while she sat up watching them through the night. This allowed her very little uninterrupted sleep and she quickly became exhausted.

The fights escalated between S.B.'s husband and her oldest daughter, who told her mother that she wanted her father dead. He had taken to carrying a loaded gun with him at all times, often threatening to kill himself as a way to get the family more engaged again. They all began wishing he would do it. The homicide occurred after the daughter told the mother that her father tried to molest her again. There is some question as to whether the molestation ever occurred. S.B. became terrified that she could no longer protect her children and that social services would not protect them. That night she shot and killed him while he lay in bed, probably asleep. When questioned, the child admitted telling the mother about the alleged sexual abuse incident and having no remorse that the father was dead. Neither did any of the other children have remorse; they stood and cheered after the mother shot him.

In this case, the fear and anger escalated when the program failed to deliver promised services to this family. Instead of giving the mother clear information about the low success rate in curing child sexual abusers, she was led to think that the authorities believed the family could be reconstituted. Both she and the eldest child were led to believe that their fears and suspicions were unfounded and that they were making too much of a big deal. This is merely a subtle way to blame the victims for their situation. Once the abuse recurred, neither one felt any confidence in the system, and S.B. reasonably perceived the need to defend her children from further harm.

CONFIDENTIALITY ISSUES

Many victim programs supported by the prosecutor's office keep records that may be wrongfully turned over to the state when the victim is charged with a crime. This could result in the breaking of confidentiality by disclosing a victim's statements without her permission. In the case of S.B. (reported above), the records from the volunteer group were turned over to the state attorney without discussion with her. Some volunteers and even some professionals have never been taught how to separate their impressions from observations when writing anecdotal entries in a client's record. Someone might include a statement such as "The client wanted to kill her husband" instead of the more accurate "The client stated she wished her husband dead when he was beating her" or "The client was so angry, I thought she might wish her husband dead." This could make a tremendous difference to the victim who becomes a defendant. It could also affect the program's legal liability in a variety of ways, including giving rise to a charge of negligence in not reporting a prediction of dangerousness. Sonkin (1986) describes the recent U.S. case law concerning a therapist's duty to warn a client who is in such danger of being harmed.

There is a new trend toward protecting information about a victim's psychotherapy, even when the issue of her consent or the impact from the violence is part of the defense. The case law is developing around rape victims who refuse permission for the defense to obtain their treatment records. In *Bond v. District Court* (1984), the Colorado Supreme Court ruled that the trial court judge must balance the defense's need to know with the victim's right to privacy to maintain the healing from psychotherapy before the records are given to the defense. Therapists should respond to a subpoena with a request to have it "quashed," and if this fails, they should then request that the attorney file a motion for what has become known in Colorado as a *bond hearing* in order to protect the records. In the last six cases where we have requested this, the records were ordered protected in five of them. In all the cases a report was required, and in some a deposition from the treating psychologist was ordered as well. But at least the motion kept the raw treatment progress notes from being circulated to all parties in the lawsuit. Only in one case were some of notes given to the defense.

Most state licensing laws include some version of the American Psychological Association (APA) Code of Ethics, which requires a psychologist not to disclose any raw data which includes therapy notes and raw test data to anyone not trained in its proper interpretation. Certainly, lawyers are not often trained in psychological interpretation. I usually refuse to comply with a *subpoena duces tecum* ordering me to turn over all my records and instead request a hearing before the court. Sometimes I must hire my own attorney to represent me; other times the attorney for the client and I have a mutual interest in protecting the records and he or she can represent me. I make the argument that two bodies of law conflict, the administrative code (which requires me to follow the APA Code of Ethics and the Standards for Providers of Psychologists in order to protect my license) and the criminal or civil rules of evidence. In more than half of my cases, the judge ruled to protect the records. In those cases where there was an unfavorable ruling, I handed the sealed envelope containing the records to the judge and stated in the record that I would not break the ethical code but would follow the judge's order and let the judge turn the records over if the judge so wished. In a few cases where I followed this procedure, the judge reconsidered and refused disclosure when faced with the responsibility.

In one particular case, C.R. was convicted of murder and sentenced to 12 years in prison largely because the battered women's shelter turned over their records and volunteer advocates testified against her. This shelter's funding came directly from the prosecutor's office and the director was a member of the victim-witness team. When the homicide occurred and C.R. told of having previously received victim services when her abusive husband was prosecuted, the shelter's records, including the anecdotal notes from C.R.'s shelter stay, were turned over, even without a subpoena accompanying the request. Statements which were attributed to her and used to support the claim she had a "violent nature" were admitted at the trial through this procedure. C.R. was not the "good victim" expected on the basis of stereotypes of battered women, and her self-defense plea was rebutted with the information disclosed. As a result of C.R.'s unhappy fate, the state shelter network conducted workshops on how to write records and how to protect them should such a situation occur again.

Another trial involved P.E., who had been a shelter resident and had received out-client services prior to killing her abuser. In P.E.'s case, her records and her advocates' testimony would have been quite useful in establishing the reasonableness of her perception of danger and the need to use deadly force. However, the prosecutor put pressure on the advocates not to testify. While not directly linked by funding, the program was dependent on the prosecutor's cooperation in protecting the battered women when their abusers were arrested for assault. Therefore, they decided not to testify, fearful that an upset in the basically positive relations with the prosecutor's office would place the entire program in jeopardy. Many other battered women programs are in a similar position, as are other victim support services.

LEGAL LIABILITY ISSUES

Many of the above mentioned cases involve the legal liability of the therapist, the program, and perhaps third parties such as motels, apartments, and shopping centers for failure to provide protection for a subsequent crime victim. Civil actions for personal injury account for a larger share of court time in most U.S. jurisdictions. Under our system of law, it is not uncommon for a battered woman to be a witness or party in a criminal action against her abusive spouse, a civil action against him for physical and psychological damage to her, a divorce action with a custody fight, a dependency and neglect action filed in juvenile court to prevent child abuse, and a juvenile action of delinquency for a teenage child who is demonstrating acting out behavior. It is also not unusual for additional litigation to be filed against professionals for malpractice. Charges can also be filed with the licensing boards controlled by the attorney general's office and with the ethics and grievance committees of the various professional associations. Each of these actions can occur in a different courtroom, with none of the judges involved required or in some cases permitted to talk to each other.

The cost of such liability has not yet outweighed the cost of providing services to violence victims, but I predict it soon will, especially as batterers become more sophisticated in manipulating the legal system. It can take years for a professional to be absolved of any wrongdoing given the backlog of cases. Liability insurance carriers often recommend settlement in lieu of the rising costs of litigation. This occurred in one case against a psychiatrist whom I was hired to be an expert witness for. This psychiatrist involuntarily hospitalized an alcoholic batterer and then was sued when the battered wife returned home. In cases where batterers are also accused of child sexual abuse, professionals hired by either side have been known to file ethics, malpractice, and even slander charges against one another. In many cases, the professionals involved are guilty of malpractice when the battered woman is hurt by the batterer. Sometimes the service provider does not pay sufficient attention to the clues of escalating dangerousness, such as in P.L.'s case (described above). Other times there is a direct denial of danger or even exploitation of the victim. The proliferation of available literature on intervention services for victims of violence can be argued to have set a new community standard against which the professional is judged.

Denial of Danger

K.C. is a formerly battered woman in her mid-30s. She appears to be pretty until someone looks closely at her face, now paralyzed on one side from the bullets that her abusive ex-husband fired into her at close range. Her internal injuries are numerous and she will never live a fully active life as an able-bodied person again. She warned everyone that her ex-husband was going to kill her, but most who heard her labeled her an hysterical woman.

K.C. and her ex-husband were ordered by the judge to exchange visits with their young child in the presence of a named therapist at the local mental health center. The therapist was busy, perhaps untrained in domestic violence, and did not understand the high lethality potential in such cases. He saw the ex-husband for two sessions, pronounced him nondangerous, and told K.C. she was crazy and exaggerating her fears. Apparently satisfied with his "successful" treatment, he allowed the visitation exchange to continue but did not protect the woman and child as ordered.

On the day she was shot, the ex-husband was late in returning the child and the therapist was too busy to find a safe place for K.C. to wait, despite her pleas. He left her standing in the hall, alone, a ready target when her ex-husband came into the building. Taking advantage of the opportunity to kill her, he took out the gun he typically carried on his person, threw her to the ground, and repeatedly shot her at close range. Much to his and her surprise, she survived, but with seriously disabling physical and psychological injuries. The children who witnessed this brutal attack also have psychological scars.

The ex-husband pleaded guilty and has been sentenced to prison. The therapist and the mental health center were sued for millions of dollars and resolved the case in an out-of-court settlement on the morning right before the trial was due to begin, probably for close to the insurance policy limit. Just the cost of defending such a lawsuit would bankrupt most victim service programs that do not carry liability insurance.

Denial of Abuse

In many states, there has been a movement toward legislating mandatory joint custody of children in a dissolution of marriage action. Obviously, involuntary joint custody of children in a situation where there has been spouse abuse will be dangerous due to the power differences between the abuser and the battered woman. Joint custody will keep the battered woman under the batterer's dangerous control. Research documenting the behavior of children who repeatedly witness battering demonstrates it is akin to war survivor behavior (Rosenberg & Goodman, 1987). In some states, such as Colorado, joint custody is not mandatory in cases where there is a history of domestic violence. The burden of proof, however, is on the battered woman. Therefore, it is in the self-interest of the batterer who wants custody to deny his abusive behavior. Custody evaluators who do not properly investigate for battering and recommend joint custody will probably be liable for malpractice should the mother or child be harmed (Chesler, 1986).

Misdiagnosis

Although the battered woman syndrome, like other PTSDs, is not always considered a mental disorder by itself (it can coexist with other more serious disorders), it is not unusual for battered women to be court ordered to undergo psychological evaluation. Differential diagnoses can be made to distinguish the psychological injury from battering, rape, and other traumas on the one hand and symptoms arising from more serious disorders on the other. However, not all mental health professionals have been trained to distinguish these. A misdiagnosis can result in legal or other jeopardy to the woman, can further damage her self-esteem, and can block access to proper treatment.

The American Psychiatric Association in developing the 1987 revision to the *Diagnostic and Statistical Manual of Mental Disorders*, approved new diagnostic categories which can be easily confused with PTSDs (American Psychiatric Association, 1987). In an attempt to placate dissenting groups—both groups in the American Psychiatric Association and groups representing the other mental health professions—the psychiatrists placed these categories in a special appendix. Psychologists have voted not to use these diagnoses because the inadequate data base renders their reliability and validity questionable. But they have been numbered and could thus be used to misdiagnose battered women and other violence victims. These categories are *self-defeating personality disorder* (formerly masochistic personality disorder), *sadistic personality disorder*, and *late luteal dysphoric mood disorder* (formerly premenstrual dysphoric mood disorder). As a concession, the psychiatrists added an exclusion for battered women and other violence victims, but the language is unclear enough to confuse even those well trained in the field (Walker, 1987c). Litigation is expected to be introduced in those cases where it can be demonstrated that one of these diagnoses caused a victim harm. The American Psychiatric Association representatives have argued to have these diagnoses included in the 1992 revisions of *International Classification of Diseases* (ICD-10), which might occur unless member countries protest to the World Health Organization, which is the publisher.

CONCLUSION

In conclusion, the rise of programs to meet victims' rights to services has not always considered changes in the legal rights due to what is now being called *feminist jurisprudence*. As victimologists, we must look at the unintended effects of our actions. In some cases, we cannot predict that the victim will become so frightened that she kills the abuser. In other cases, such as those described above, it is apparent that the danger of someone dying is quite high no matter what our intervention. Although we refer offenders and provide services to them, it is apparent that we will not always be successful in stopping their abusive behavior. We must anticipate failures and create structures to allow victims to voluntarily return for our assistance without fear of further harm. It is our responsibility to clarify the community standard by which we will be judged. Otherwise we must be prepared to allow those less knowledgeable to do it for us. I suggest we should anticipate that in a small number of cases the reempowered victim will have no choice but to kill or be killed and thus we should design our policies to protect her in case she becomes a defendant.

BIBLIOGRAPHY

Attorney General's Task Force on Family Violence. (1984). *Report*. Washington, DC: Department of Justice.

American Psychiatric Association. (1987). *Diagnostic and Statistical Manual of Mental Disorders* (3rd ed., DSM-III-R). Washington, DC: Author.

Bauschard, L. (1986). *Voices set free: Battered women speak from prison*. St. Louis: Women's Self Help Center. Available by direct order from Women's Self Help Center, 2838 Olive, St. Louis, MO 63103.

Blackman, J. (1986). Potential uses for expert testimony: Ideas toward the representation of battered women who kill. *Women's Rights Law Reporter*, *9* (3,4), 227–238.

Bochnak, E. (Ed.) (1981). *Women's self defense cases*. Charlottesville, VA: The Michie Company Law Publishers.

Bond v. District Court, in and for Denver County, 682 p. 2d 33 (Colo. 1984).

Browne, A. (1987). *When battered women kill*. New York: The Free Press and Macmillan.

Browne, A., Thyfault, R. K., & Walker, L. E. A. (1987). When battered women kill: Evaluation and expert witness testimony techniques. In D. J. Sonkin (Ed.), *Domestic violence on trial* (pp. 71–85). New York: Springer.

Burhle v. State, 627 p. 2d 1374 (1981).

Chesler, P. (1986). *Mothers on trial*. New York: Consortium Press.

Hawthorne v. State, 408 So. 2d 801, 805 (1982), remand rev'd, 470 So. 2d 770 (1985).

Ibn-Tamas v. U.S., 407 A 2d 626 (Washington, DC, 1979).

Jones, A. (1981). *Women who kill*. New York: Holt, Rinehart & Winston.

Moran v. Ohio, 469 U.S. 948, 83 L.Ed. 2d 285 (1984).

People v. Torres, 128 Misc. 2d 129, 132, 448 NYS 2d. 358, 361 (Sup. Ct. 1985).

Rosenberg, M., & Goodman, G. (1987). The child witness to family violence: Clinical and legal considerations. In D. J. Sonkin (Ed.), *Domestic violence on trial* (pp. 97–126). New York: Springer.

Schneider, E. (1986). Describing and changing: Women's self defense work and the problem of expert testimony on battering. *Women's Rights Law Reporter*, *9*(3,4), 195–222.

Sonkin, D. J. (1987). *Domestic violence on trial*. New York: Springer.

Sonkin, D. J. (1986). Clairvoyance vs. common sense: Therapist's duty to warn and protect. *Violence and Victims*, *1*(1), 7–22.

State v. Allery, 101 Wash. 2d 591, 682 P. 2d 312 (1984).

State v. Anaya, 438 A. 2d 892 (1981).

State v. Garcia, CR. No. 4259, Sup. Ct., Monterey County, California (1977).

State v. Kelley, 97 NJ 178, 478 A. 2d 364 (1984).

State v. Martin, 666 S.W. 2d. 895 (1984).

State v. Mennis, 118 Ill. App. 3d 345, 455 N.E. 2d 209 (1983).

State v. Smith, 247 GA. 612, 277 S.E. 2d 678 (1981).

State v. Thomas, 66 Ohio St 2d 518, 423 N.E. 2d 137 (1981).

State v. Wanrow, 88 Wash., 2d 221, 559 p.2d. 548 (1977).

Walker, L. E. A. (1979). *The battered woman*. New York: Harper & Row.

Walker, L. E. A. (1984a). *The battered woman syndrome*. New York: Springer.

Walker, L. E. A. (1984b). Battered women, psychology and public policy. *American Psychologist*, *29*(10), 1178.

Walker, L. E. A. (1986). A response to Elizabeth M. Schneider's Describing and changing: Women's self-defense work and the problem of expert testimony on battering. *Women's Rights Law Reporter*, *9*(3,4), 223–225.
Walker, L. E. A. (1987a). Intervention with victims. In I. Weiner & A. Hess (Eds.), *Handbook of forensic psychology*. New York: Wiley.
Walker, L. E. A. (1987b). Inadequacies of masochistic personality disorder diagnosis for women. *Journal of Personality Disorders*, *1*(2).
Walker, L. E. A. (Ed.), (1988). *Handbook on sexual abuse of children*. New York: Springer.
Walker, L. E. A. (in press). *Battered women's self defense* (Working Title). New York: Harper & Row.
Walker, L. E. A., & Edwall, G. E. (1987). Determination of child custody and visitation in battering relationships. In D. J. Sonkin (Ed.), *Domestic violence on trial* (pp. 127–152). New York: Springer.

7

The Impact of Police on Victims

Wesley G. Skogan
Center for Urban Affairs, Northwestern University, Evanston, Illinois

INTRODUCTION

Victims traditionally have been the "forgotten participants" in the criminal justice system, valued by the police only for their role in reporting crimes when they occur and appearing in court as witnesses. Studies of the police have highlighted the extent to which their function is to deal (often inadequately) with victims' problems rather than "fight crime." Police officers who respond to calls represent the sole contact that the majority of victims have with the criminal justice system, for most crimes are never solved and many do not even warrant a follow-up visit from a detective. As responding officers provide the primary link between victims and the state, any attempt to improve the lot of crime victims inevitably will depend on the active assistance of these officers.

There is little systematic information on how the police deal with victims and what the effect of that treatment is. Surveys indicate that most Americans have a favorable opinion of the police before an emergency contact, but many come away from the experience unhappy. Past research suggests that victims want information, recognition, advice, support, protection, and reassurance and that they often do not get these from the police.

Lack of information is one of the biggest complaints. Victims feel frustrated by a lack of feedback about progress in their case or its probable disposition (Kelly, 1982). They know very little about police or court procedures and may have unrealistic expectations about the capacity of the police to solve their case. Several studies indicate victims have little knowledge about programs available to them or where to turn for assistance with practical problems (Elias, 1983; Ziegenhagen, 1976).

Victims want recognition of their status as injured parties and they want their situation to be taken seriously. This highlights the importance of the rituals of police work—listening to the victim's story, questioning neighbors, searching for physical evidence and fingerprints, and filling out forms. Victims also need advice on what to do, assistance with pressing problems, and sympathy. Shapland (1984) found that "caring and supportive attitudes [on the part of police] were the main subject for victim praise." Ironically, many "professional" responses by the police to those with whom they come in contact are at odds with the

Wesley G. Skogan is a professor of political science and urban affairs at Northwestern University. His research focuses on victimization and citizen reactions to crime problems and on the police. He recently completed work on his new book, *Disorder and Community Decline*, to be published by The Free Press.

needs of victims. Police officers often appear impersonal, if polite. They can be preoccupied with technical efficiency and unwilling to venture an opinion outside of their traditional area of expertise. Victims, on the other hand, tend to rate police officers by the amount of time and trouble the officers take to help them (Maguire, 1982). Patrol officers can be under pressure to complete incident reports quickly and get back "in service"—surely not a victim-oriented criterion of police service.

Finally, victims need reassurance and protection, and the police are important symbols of the provision of protection. It appears that important general sources of fear are isolation and the feeling that nobody will come to one's aid. The rapid appearance of the police, considerate attention by them, and (perhaps) their continued visibility may help alleviate the fear of crime which follows victimization.

This paper examines the impact of variations in some of these aspects of police treatment of victims. It utilizes data from a two-wave panel survey which identified a sample of crime victims, inventoried their contacts with the police, and gathered their impressions of the quality of service they had received. The interviews also gathered data on two potential consequences of their treatment by the police: (1) their fear of crime and their perceptions of neighborhood crime problems, and (2) their general assessment of police service. The impact of the police on these victims seems to have been salutary. The findings support the contention that what the police say and do for victims makes a difference in how victims view their predicament and enhances their support for the police.

Because this was a panel study, it was possible to take into account both the personal characteristics of the victims and their fear and perceptions of the police *before* the crimes took place. This increases our confidence in the conclusions concerning the causal consequences of variations in the way in which they were treated by police.

THE DATA

Data to assess the impact of policing on victims were gathered in personal interviews with 1,738 residents of seven selected neighborhoods in Newark, New Jersey, and Houston, Texas. The neighborhoods had relatively high crime rates and featured a mixture of single family homes and rental apartments. Respondents in Newark were virtually all black; in Houston, blacks, whites, and Hispanics were represented in all of the areas. Households were randomly selected from lists of all residential addresses in each neighborhood. Individual respondents were then chosen at random from among household residents 19 years of age and older. The data are available from the Criminal Justice Data Archive at the University of Michigan.

Victimization was measured by yes-no responses to 17 "screener" questions. Each question asked about a specific recent experience, and together they covered both completed and attempted incidents in a variety of crime categories. This analysis is based on all 299 panel members who were victimized between the two waves of interviewing and who also had contact with the police during this period. These 299 victims constitute 38% of the 792 interwave victims identified in the survey; as in all victim surveys, the majority of incidents were not reported to the police. In this group, 82% were interwave victims of property crime and 18% were victims of personal crime. The most frequent form of property victimization was simple theft (57%), followed by burglary (36%). Among personal crimes, robbery and actual assault (as opposed to threats of assault) were most frequent (6% each).

Four indicators of fear of crime were employed in this analysis. Two concerned personal crimes. *Worry about personal victimization* was measured by combining responses to questions about the extent to which respondents were worried about being robbed and assaulted in their neighborhood. *Concern about area personal crime* was measured by responses to questions about "how big a problem" robbery, assault by strangers, and sexual assaults were in the area. Two other measures focused on property crime. *Worry about property crime* was measured by combining responses to questions about how worried respondents were about being burglarized and having their car stolen or damaged. *Concern about area property crime* was measured by responses to questions about "how big a problem" burglary, auto vandalism, and auto theft were in the neighborhood.

There were two measures of general attitudes toward police officers active in the study areas. Assessments of *police demeanor* were measured by combining responses to questions about how polite, helpful, and fair local police were; assessments of *police task performance* were measured by two questions concerning "how good a job" area police did in preventing crime and keeping order.

The critical explanatory variable in this study—the perceived quality of the treatment received by these 299 victims from the police—was measured in the following fashion. In the second wave of interviews, respondents were asked whether or not they had initiated any of six different types of contacts with the police. Those who had were asked a series of follow-up questions regarding the experience. If they reported more than one type of self-initiated contact during the period, they were asked about the most recent of them. Responses to four follow-up questions were combined to form the *quality of treatment* measure for this study:

1. Did the police clearly explain what action they would take in response to your contact?
2. Did you find the police . . . ("very helpful" to "not at all helpful")?
3. When you talked to the police were they . . . ("very polite" to "very impolite")?
4. How fairly were you treated by the police that time? Were they . . . ("very fair" to "very unfair")?

The only follow-up item excluded from this measure was a hypothetical reporting-in-the-future question, which was not related to the other responses.

All of these multi-item scales were single factored. Their reliabilities (Cronbach's alpha) ranged from .75 to .82 and were very similar for the two waves of the survey. The reliability of the quality of treatment measure was .79.

An important aspect of the study is that these data were collected in two interviews with each respondent, spaced 10–11 months apart. The "panel" feature of the data helped solve a key methodological problem, namely, that there are multiple, confounding determinants of victimization, people's willingness to call the police, and people's attitudes toward crime and the police. These include race, class, age, and gender. This makes it risky simply to correlate measures of police contacts with indicators of their apparent consequences, for any observed correlations could be due to the joint effects of other factors. As in past research, it would be possible to develop measures of some of those confounding factors and control for them statistically. However, since there are many of them, some factors may inadvertently be left out of the analysis, others may be poorly measured, and some are doubtless unknown. A useful (if inevitably only partial) solution to the "confounding" problem was to interview the respondents twice. The first interview established "baseline" information on fear and general perceptions of the police. Then, a second wave of interviews remeasured these things to assess *changes* in attitudes during the intervening period. Changes between Wave 1 and Wave 2 then could be related to the respondent's experiences with the police between the interviews. Panel data are not a perfect solution to the confounding problem. A special difficulty is that the consequences of other events which take place between the two waves of interviews can be confused with "victimization effects," especially if they co-occur to some extent with victimization. Further, because there is inevitably error in the measurement of variables, the Wave 1 data do not fully adjust the Wave 2 data for their "true" levels during the first period, and some variance in the Wave 2 measures really reflects their prior levels.

These panel data were collected as part of an evaluation of areawide policing projects in the two cities. To control for the possible confounding effects of the programs, the multivariate analyses presented below include measures of the treatment or control condition of each respondent.

FINDINGS

By and large, the impact of the police on these victims seems to have been somewhat beneficial. Between Wave 1 and Wave 2, their opinions of the police serving their area grew more favorable. This is documented in Table 7-1, which indicates that, on average, they were more likely to think the police were polite, helpful, fair, and doing a good job on second questioning. All but one of those shifts were statistically significant, and all were in a favorable direction. The same differences appear when victims residing in the evaluation treatment and control areas are examined separately. In both cases, victims as a whole were more favorable toward the police after being victimized.

Table 7-2 resembles Table 7-1, but it reports before-and-after levels of worry and concern about crime. Unlike Table 7-1, it does not point to any dramatic changes in levels of fear attendant upon victimization. Scores on measures of worry and concern about personal and property crime evidenced only one significant change, and that was in a more fearful direction. The same minimal differences appear when victims residing in the evaluation treatment and control areas are examined separately. However, it may be instructive that this apparent stability runs counter to the general pattern in these data. Victimization *was* related to increased worry and concern among all victims in the Houston and Newark panel survey, and it led them to adopt more personal and household precautions (cf. Skogan, 1987). However, this pattern did not hold among the minority of victims who came into contact with the police. Thus, the pattern of "nondifferences" reported in Table 7-2 hints that those contacts may have had positive consequences.

Table 7-1 Changes in victims' general attitudes toward the police

Measures of general attitudes	Mean scores		Two-tailed significance	*N*
	Before	After		
Demeanor				
In general, how polite are police in this area when dealing with people? (1–4)	2.97	3.22	.001	227
In general, how helpful are police in this area when dealing with people around here? (1–4)	2.74	2.92	.04	236
In general, how fair are the police in this area in dealing with people around here? (1–4)	2.98	3.09	.10	222
Task Performance				
Now, let's talk about the police in this area. How good a job do you think they are doing to prevent crime? (1–5)	2.71	3.10	.001	269
How good a job are the police in this area doing in keeping order on the streets and sidewalks? (1–5)	2.73	3.11	.001	267

Note that all items were scored in a "positive" direction, e.g., higher scores indicate the police were perceived to be polite, fair, doing a good job, etc.

To this point, we have seen that victims who came into contact with the police were more favorable toward them afterward, and, counter to the general pattern in the same surveys, they were not more fearful despite their recent experience with crime. The critical question remains, Can this stability or change over time in victims' opinions of the police and perceptions of vulnerability to crime be attributed to the character of the service these victims received?

Table 7-3 examines this problem by relating the quality of treatment scale described above to measures of fear and assessments of police performance. The partial correlations presented in Table 7-3 indicate how strongly variations

Table 7-2 Changes in victims' worry and concern about crime

Measures of worry and concern	Mean scores		Two-tailed significance	*N*
	Before	After		
Worry about personal crime victimization	2.13	2.06	.25	291
Concern about area personal crime problems	1.76	1.69	.09	290
Worry about property crime victimization	2.32	2.40	.05	251
Concern about area property crime problems	2.18	2.20	.54	298

Note that all items were scored in a "positive" direction, e.g., higher scores indicate the higher levels of concern and worry. All of the scale scores have a range of 1–3.

Table 7-3 Impact of the perceived quality of contacts with the police

	Correlation with quality of treatment scale[a]		
Measures of consequences	Partial correlation	Two-tailed significance	*N*
General police performance			
Police demeanor	+.45	.001	263
Task performance	+.36	.001	283
Personal vulnerability			
Worry about personal crime victimization	−.12	.04	291
Concern about area personal crime problems	−.11	.07	290
Vulnerability to property crime			
Worry about property crime victimization	−.05	.41	251
Concern about area property crime problems	−.04	.46	298

[a]Controlled for Wave 1 scores, age, race, housing tenure, household composition, gender, residence in a program or control area, and city.

in the manner in which victims perceived they were treated are related to those consequences. The partial correlations take into account the perceptions of respondents *before* the incident, as well as their age, race, gender, and other personal characteristics, their treatment or control condition in the project evaluation, and their city of residence.

Table 7-3 indicates that good treatment made somewhat of a difference. Victims who thought the officer(s) they talked to were helpful, fair, polite, and informative were more likely to think that the police in general were the same way and performed their job well. They also were less likely than those who thought they were treated badly to feel vulnerable to personal crime. However, only about one-half of the fear-of-crime measures were significantly related (or nearly so) to the quality of treatment measure; there was no apparent effect of police contacts on perceptions of area property crime. Perceptions of property crime were linked to the quality of treatment by the police in the hypothesized fashion, but the correlations were not significant. The most dramatic effects of contacts with the police were reserved for attitudes toward the police.

SOME CAVEATS

The data presented above constitute only an indirect test of the frequent contention that police actions at the scene of the crime affect victim perceptions of their fate and shape their assessments of how effectively the system can function in their behalf. The principle problem with the data is that we cannot directly link the victimizations recalled in this survey with a specific follow-up contact with the police. Rather, we only know that during the period between the two waves of interviewing these residents of Houston and Newark both were victimized and initiated a contact with police in their city. The two actions were not necessarily linked, although probably the bulk of the contacts examined here did involve calling the police in response to the crime. However, it is also possible that *other* supportive contacts with the police may also influence a victim's perceptions, not just contacts immediately following a crime. In any event, the findings here support the notion that what the police say and do for victims makes somewhat of a difference in how they view their predicament and enhances their support for the police.

BIBLIOGRAPHY

Elias, R. (1983). *Victims of the system*. New Brunswick, NJ: Transaction Books.

Kelly, D. (1982). *Victims' reactions to the criminal justice response*. Paper presented at the meeting of the Law and Society Association, Denver, CO.

Maguire, M. (1982). *Burglary in a dwelling*. London: Heinemann.

Shapland, J. (1984). Victims, the criminal justice system, and compensation. *British Journal of Criminology*, *24*, 131–149.

Skogan, W. G. (1987). The impact of victimization on fear. *Crime and Delinquency*, *33*, 135–154.

Ziegenhagen, E. (1976). Toward a theory of victim-criminal justice system interactions. In W. McDonald (Ed.), *Criminal justice and the victim*. Newbury Park, CA: Sage.

8

The Police and the Victims of Everyday Conflicts: First Results of a Study of Police Mobilization and Patrol Dispatches in the Federal Republic of Germany

Thomas Feltes
Institute of Criminology, University of Heidelberg,
Federal Republic of Germany

INTRODUCTION

The first part of this chapter presents an overview of police and victim research in West Germany. In the second part, a study of police alarms and emergency calls is presented, with data on the reasons for and the number of alarms and calls in 32 West German cities of more than 200,000 inhabitants. Criminal offenses account for less than 25% of all calls and patrol activities. Nearly the same percentage are for different kinds of help for very different kinds of victims. Conflict solutions—settling family conflicts and neighborhood disturbances—constitute another part of day-to-day police work; 30–50% involves traffic problems. Police alarms and emergency calls have been declining since 1981. Until 1981, the number of calls to the police had been constantly on the rise. In major cities, the police receive an emergency call every 1 or 2 minutes. Significantly, the socially deprived are both the objects and subjects of calls for police help.

The job of police officers has become more complex and broader over time. This is recognized by practitioners, scholars, and the general public. Equally, it is obvious that the police have more tasks than crime fighting. Functions like "peacekeeping," "order maintenance," and "service provision" represent a large part of police work (Flanagan, 1985, p. 10). Several developments have taken place to classify police tasks. Law enforcement, order maintenance, protection, and crime prevention are mentioned and discussed most often in West Germany and in the United States.

Thomas Feltes studied law, education, psychology, and sociology at the University of Bielefeld, where he earned a doctoral degree at the Faculty of Legal Science. He taught and conducted research at universities, police high schools, and academies in Bielefeld and Hamburg and is currently an assistant professor (Hochschulass.) at the Institute of Criminology of the University of Heidelberg.

The author is grateful to the North Atlantic Treaty Organization for funding the meeting where this paper was presented and to the University of Heidelberg, Faculty of Law, for the travel grant.

RESEARCH ON POLICE IN WEST GERMANY

Although theoretical and especially political discussions about police and police functions are common (Busch et al., 1985; Werkentin, 1984) and lots of studies are done in foreign countries (Reiner & Shapland, 1987), empirical police research is very rare in West Germany (Sack, 1987). None of the West German research institutes—except ours—is actually engaged in this kind of criminological research, and there were only two or three studies in the early 70s on police and their proactive work (Feest & Blankenburg, 1972; Feest & Lautmann, 1971). In particular, the patrol units have never been the object of criminological reflections by those outside the official system. The reason for this lack may be twofold. First, West German police forces, in contrast to police forces in the United States, for example, are secret, hidden organizations. For example, the exact number of police officers is kept secret,[1] and the "work" of the German police has never been controlled by public committees like the McDonald Commission in Canada. Some years ago, after some bitter conflicts between police officers and demonstrators had occurred, committees named "Police Watching the Police" were founded in some cities. However, there was neither official nor even informal support given by the political parties. Only the West German Green Party became involved. Second, nobody controls the effectiveness of the German police. Even in times of financial crises the government had and has enough money to provide for the police and their technical equipment. Official reasons for these expenses include "increasingly violent demonstrations," terrorism, and rising crime rates. But nobody asked for a proof of efficiency.

On the other side, criminological researchers in the 80s were not interested in the police, neither in their function as stigmatizing social control agents nor in their positive functions. Even at the beginning of the 80s, when "diversion" as a new strategy was discussed and victim-offender programs were implemented in some cities, nobody seemed to realize that it is essential to include police as partners in any such program. Only now, in the last 2 or 3 years, are police being recognized as important for handling juvenile delinquents and for optimizing the treatment of victims, especially victims of sexual abuse.

VICTIM–OFFENDER RESEARCH IN WEST GERMANY

The situation is nearly the same for research on victims. We did some studies on rape victims (Weis, 1982), but research on other victims is only starting to be done and questions like "What do victims really want?" or "What are the main problems victims have?" are only starting to be asked. Some surveys on victimization were done in the 70s (Plate et al., 1985; Schwind, 1984; Schwind et al., 1975; Stephan, 1976; Villmow & Stephan, 1983), but no consequences for the treatment of individual victims followed. We have not had a National

[1]There are about 170,000 police officers on duty in West Germany. I tried to find out how many police officers are on duty or on shift in different cities in Germany, but police offices and ministries denied to name the number. About 60% of the 170,000 police officers are patrol police officers. Due to a failure rate of about 40% (illness, school, overtime compensation, vacancies), less than 14,000 police officers are on shift on average. About 6,000 officers are on the street; the others are busy with paper work and station tasks. Therefore, there is a proportion of 10,000 citizens per patrol police officer doing his or her job outside the police station (see Feltes, 1984).

Crime Survey until now, but the Bundeskriminalamt is currently preparing some projects. The first pretest for one project has just been finished using telephone interviews in Heidelberg. All in all, our knowledge about the significance of crime reporting, determinants of reporting, and the consequences of nonreporting is very modest.[2] But due to some newer studies, we know a little more about the public opinion on offender restitution.

One study, by Klaus Sessar (Sessar et al., 1986; Sessar, 1984), on public attitudes toward offender restitution in West Germany showed that restitution is accepted by the public for a wide range of crime problems. Forty-seven and a half percent of all respondents ($N = 1365$) supported private settlement (restitution) in the case of property crimes and 20.5% in the case of violent crimes. For both types of crimes, victims had a higher percentage of support than nonvictims. Only 7.0% called for criminal sanctions in the case of property crimes and only 17.6% in the case of violent crimes. Thus victimization, unlike fear of crime, has no positive effect on the call for criminal sanctions (people with higher fear scores prefer more formal criminal sanctions). These results are criticized by some other researchers, who argue that Sessar's results were predetermined by his questions. Schädler and Baurmann found in their study that less than 15% of all victims agree there should be some kind of noncriminal settlement.[3]

Janssen and Kerner have just conducted research on police officers' perceptions of the problems of crime victims. In this study about 600 patrol officers and detectives of the Hamburg police filled out mailed questionnaires. Although the data are just being entered into a computer, preliminary reviews of the questionnaires indicate that victims very often call the police because no other immediate help is available. On the one hand, police officers reported little knowledge about the consequences of victimization. Only a few had victimology "classes" during their training. On the other hand, it was often mentioned that not only do victims of classical severe victimization (e.g., rape, robbery, and aggravated assault) need intensive help but so do burglary victims, for example.

In the course of a research project entitled "The Meaning of Formal and Informal Sanctions Within the Scope of Everyday Conflict Work-up," Hanak, Stehr, and Steinert interviewed 234 persons. In less than 8% of a total of 1,100 conflict situations reported by these persons, the law was mobilized. The readiness to mobilize the law is restricted to relatively few fields of conflict. People are the most prepared to consult a lawyer or to go to court in connection with tenancy agreements. Another important field is business life. Generally, the mobilization of the law serves mostly as a strategy to create a certain amount of pressure on one's opponent and attain one's goals. This is consistent with earlier studies that show that victims who bring criminal charges against somebody often have other than "penal" reasons for making the charges, for example, personal reasons like revenge, insurance, to put pressure on the "offender" for financial purposes (Kürzinger, 1978).

Criminal law played a subordinate role in the cases studied by Hanak, Stehr, and Steinert. In all, less than 15% of all conflict situations were settled by "sanctions," and informal sanctions predominated over formal ones. Only in

[2]For the status of world research, see Skogan (1984).

[3]The results of this study are not yet published. The information was given to the author by Schädler himself.

less than 1% of all cases was the opponent formally prosecuted. Generally, very few conflicts were settled by means of communication; they are instead absorbed (i.e., the victim accepts the conflict or the situation) or remain unsettled. Obviously, the readiness for direct settlements of conflict is quite low. Even in cases where an official demand is touched (e.g., when the victim has the right to claim for damages or to demand compensation), victims tend to absorb the conflict.

I should mention that since 1986 official West German police statistics contain data on the victim-offender relationship. Some of these data are given in Table 8-1.

POLICE: THEIR ROLE AND FUNCTION IN WEST GERMANY

In many cases, police have to function as coordinators for the administration of damages. This is usually required by the insurance company. Police also are supposed to deal with situations involving threats and nuisances and to settle neighborhood conflicts and domestic disputes. Further, police play an important role in the settlement of traffic conflicts and in the redress of various molestations (disturbances and brawls). In these areas, their work is relatively effective. But these services have only partly to do with their legal tasks. In the field of prosecution police work is rather ineffective. From other studies and research, we learn that police clear up less than 10% of all crimes committed by unknown offenders. This raises the clear-up rate from 42% to 47% (Steffen, 1976). In all other cases, the victim provides the police with the name of the suspect and sometimes even the suspect him- or herself (e.g., in the case of shoplifting).

Of the two functions of police, namely, to preserve the *law* and maintain *order*, in reality maintaining order function is dominant. But in public, media, and political discussions, preserving the law is always pushed in the foreground, especially in connection with violent demonstrations and terrorism.

This use of the police force led to great frustration among West German police officers and to discontentment with their profession. In fact, younger

Table 8-1 Victim-offender relationships in West Germany

Crime	Number of victims	Close relation	None
Murder	572	58.7%	13.5%
Murder, attempted	556	47.3	34.4
Manslaughter	361	77.3	10.0
Manslaughter, attempted	1,435	59.0	21.8
Rape	3,105	42.7	28.1
Rape, attempted	2,526	21.8	51.6
Robbery	24,155	8.3	59.1
Robbery, attempted	6,406	8.1	62.5
Dangerous and grievous bodily injury	66,493	32.6	39.6

Source: Polizeiliche Kriminalstatistik 1986, p. 35.

The percentage of close relations is higher for women in cases of murder (63.9%), attempted murder (59.8%), and dangerous and grievous bodily injury (57.9%).

police officers are essentially more discontented than older ones (Feltes & Hermann, 1987). One reason for this may be that in the daily routine of police work the aspect of "helping others" can be realized less and less nowadays, although for nearly all police officers this aspect was crucial for their choice of vocation (see below).

As service functions predominate in the everyday routine of police work, citizens are increasingly confronted with discontented police officers, who, moreover, often come from different neighborhoods and social classes than the citizens they deal with. In recent years, police officers who attended a high school have been chiefly employed. Structural changes in the police force system (e.g., centralization) have meant that police officers nowadays only rarely work in the area in which they live. Furthermore, police officers are often transferred to other cities after their training.

Our interviews with police officers have shown that especially members of the lower social classes call the police for their service and conflict-settlement functions. As far as criminal prosecution is concerned, the offender and the victim often come from the same social class, usually the working class or "lower middle class." In cases in which one of the opponents belongs to a considerably higher or lower social class than the other, police are called more often by the person who belongs to the higher class. But as Hanak has shown, in very few of the conflicts are the opponents members of different social classes (in about 15% of his cases).

As a first conclusion, we may say that police and victims and their mutual relationships are quite unexplored in West Germany, but things are getting better.[4]

WEST GERMAN POLICE AND DISCRETIONARY POWER

Police in West Germany, as in other countries, I suppose, are unspecified agents used by citizens for a range of purposes which exceeds by far the very specific duties set down in the West German criminal, procedure, and police codes. Unlike U.S. police, West German police don't have any discretionary power. Theoretically, every offense noticed by a police officer and mentioned in the criminal code or in other bylaws must be registered and prosecuted. Only the state attorney may dismiss cases and use discretionary power. Nevertheless, the reality is different. Our evaluation of patrol police diaries established that West German police officers make use of some kind of "informal discretionary power." Especially in neighborhood disputes, family conflicts, and minor offenses (e.g., damage of property), police officers on shift make discretionary decisions. They use techniques such as immediate conflict solution and take immediate actions to help people in everyday conflicts.

[4]Criminological research in West Germany was mainly engaged in the labeling discussion, with some empirical studies at the beginning of the 70s, and in treatment and offender therapy at the end of the 70s and beginning of the 80s. It is now looking for new tasks, since the evaluation of treatment and therapy didn't give sufficient results.

RESULTS OF TWO EMPIRICAL STUDIES ON THE WEST GERMAN POLICE

The aim of our research was twofold. First, we wanted to determine how many people call the police, how many patrol dispatches are run and what the different kinds of emergencies are. Second, we wanted to discover whether there is any difference between the reality of everyday police work and the professional self-assessment of police officers.

Police Mobilization in West Germany

Our just finished study on Police Mobilization and Patrol Dispatches included all of the 31 German cities with more than 200,000 inhabitants. We received the data from the Police Offices.[5]

Number of Telephone Calls on the Police Emergency Line

Figure 8-1 shows that the rate of telephone calls in 10 West German cities where data were available is similar. There were about 30,000 to 40,000 calls per 100,000 inhabitants (or between .3 and .4 calls per person). For example, in Hamburg there were .3 calls per person and in Berlin, .36 calls per person. Compare this with data collected by Clifford Shearing (1984, p. 14) for certain North American cities. In Toronto, there were .39 calls per person (in 1971); in Montreal, .44 calls per person (in 1969); and in New York, .65 calls per person (in 1969).

The number of calls received by the operator from other police divisions varies between 10% and 40% of all calls for assistance received by the police in the West German cities. Therefore, we included only "switchboard" calls (911 calls) in our study. Our findings indicate that about 90% of the calls came from citizens; the others came from alarm companies, post- and taxi-lines, and so on.

Concerning trends in the number of calls during the last few years, one very interesting phenomenon should be mentioned: There was a steady increase in the rate of calls per 100,000 inhabitants until the beginning of the 80s. Figure 8-2 shows this for Hamburg. Data for other cities show the same trend. But since 1980–1981, the rate was stable or even decreased in some cities. This at least occurred in bigger cities. As we will show later on, the rate of patrol dispatches did not decrease. This rate is still going up in all of the cities included in our study.

It is furthermore noteworthy that there seems to be no causal connection between the rate of criminal offenses registered by the police and the number of emergency calls. In Hamburg, for example, the rate of calls remained almost the same between 1978 and 1986, whereas the rate of registered offenses increased during the same period from 10,630 to 16,230 (see Fig. 8-3). In absolute

[5]The data were partly incomplete and only partly usable for comparison. The reason for this is that we do not have an equalized switchboard documentation system yet. A computerized system will be implemented in some cities in the next years.

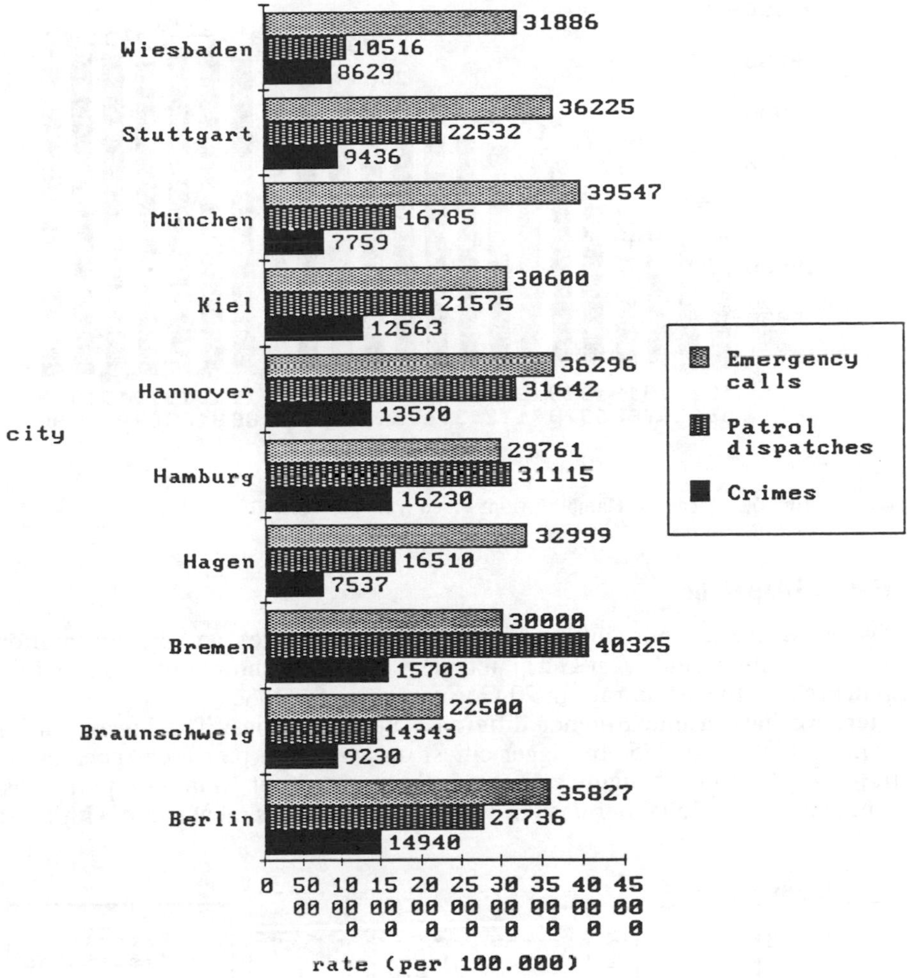

Figure 8-1 Emergency calls, patrol dispatches, and crimes in 10 German cities, 1986 (rates per 100,000)

figures, there were 515,000 calls in 1982 but only 468,000 in 1986. In Frankfurt, calls went down since 1981 by 19%, whereas the rate of criminal offenses rose by 32% (see Fig. 8-4). The same is true for some other cities (see Table 8-2).

There is another reason for supposing that the number of registered offenses is not an indicator of the number of calls: In 1986 there were approximately the same rate of calls in Munich, where 7,755 offenses per 100,000 inhabitants were registered, and in Frankfurt, where 21,385 offenses were registered. We don't know the efficiency of those calls and we also don't know how police officers handle different kinds of calls.

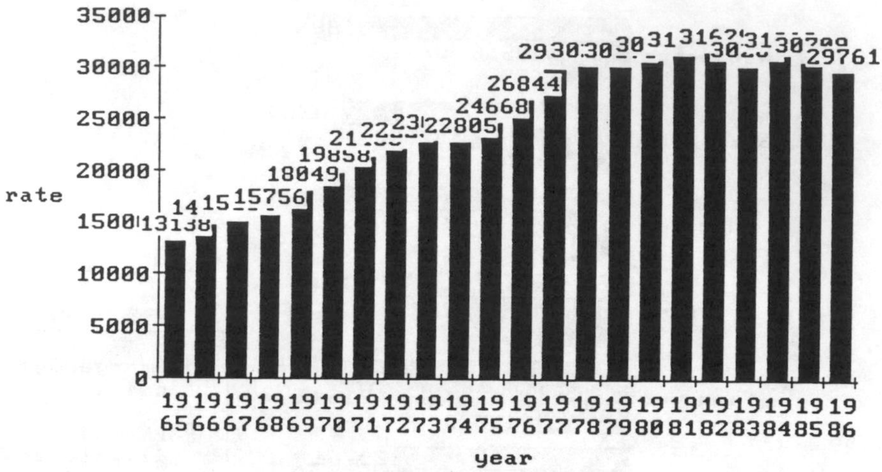

Figure 8-2 Emergency calls in Hamburg, 1965–1986 (rate per 100,000)

Patrol Dispatches

We have obtained more information on patrol dispatches, and the information is better for comparing West German cities. Figure 8-5 shows the rate of patrol dispatches and the crime rate in 20 German cities for 1986.

Here we have a much higher difference between cities: The lowest rate is 6,725, the highest 40,325. In bigger cities, on average a patrol car goes on an action every minute. Roughly estimated, there are about 10 million patrol dispatches per year (27,000 per day) in West Germany. This means that with three

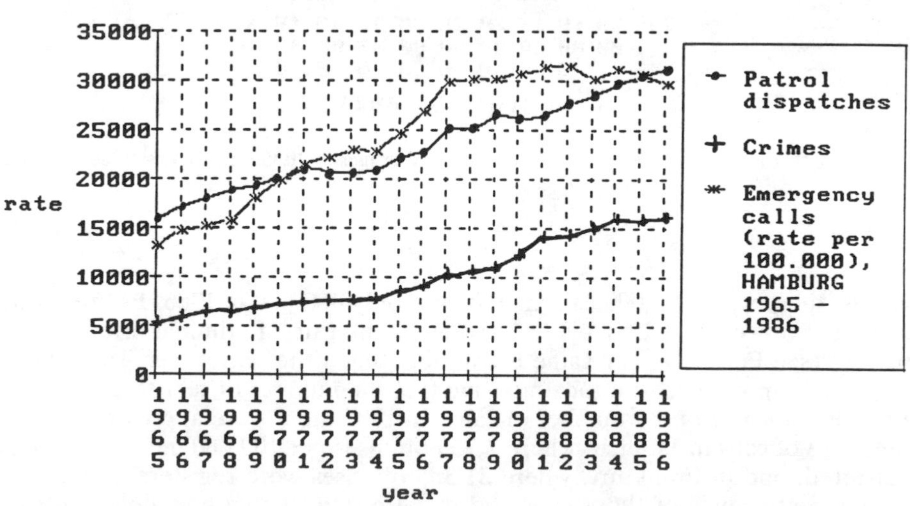

Figure 8-3 Emergency calls, patrol dispatches, and crimes in Hamburg, 1965–1986 (rates per 100,000)

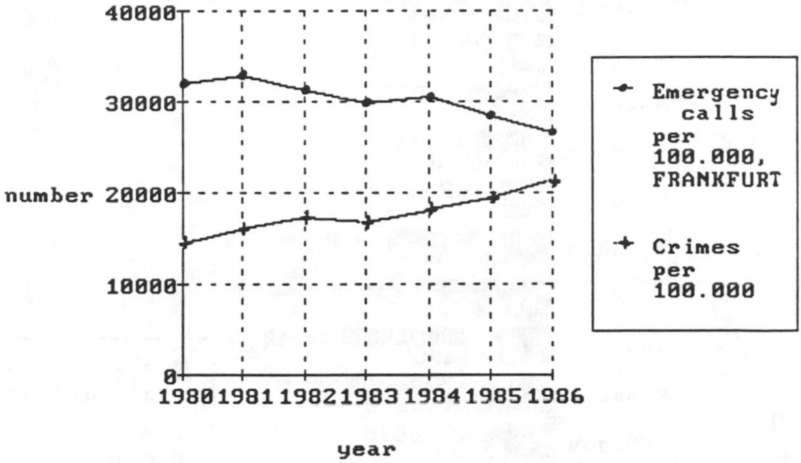

Figure 8-4 Emergency calls in Frankfurt (rate per 100,000)

shifts per day, each police officer has to run one to two dispatches per shift (or, for each car, some three actions per shift).

Rates of patrol dispatches are quite different, even in cities with about the same population. For cities with roughly 200,000 inhabitants, patrol dispatch rates are between 6,725 per 100,000 (Augsburg, 245,500 inhabitants) and 21,575 (Kiel, 244,600 inhabitants). For cities with roughly 500,000 inhabitants, the rates are between 20,420 (Duisburg, 516,500 inhabitants) and 40,325 (Bremen, 524,700 inhabitants). For cities with more than one million inhabitants, the rates are

Table 8-2 Calls and crimes in 1981 and 1986 (per 100,000)

City	1981	1986	Difference
Frankfurt			
Calls	32,928	26,633	– 19%
Crimes	16,202	21,385	+ 32
Hamburg			
Calls	31,307	29,761	– 5
Crimes	14,125	16,230	– 15
Hannover			
Calls	37,394	36,296	– 3
Crimes	10,537	13,570	+ 29
Berlin			
Calls	40, 475	35,827	– 12
Crimes	13,277	14,941	+ 13
München			
Calls	41,731	39,547	– 5
Crimes	6,956	7,759	+ 12

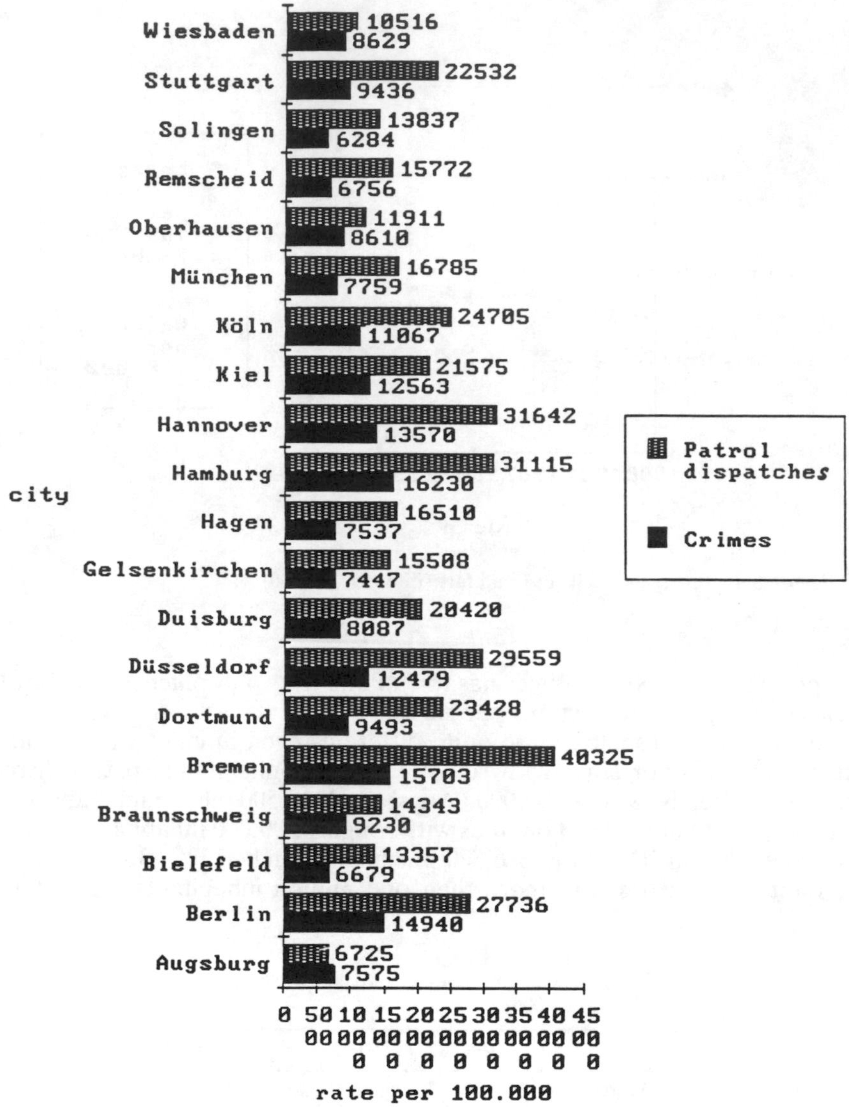

Figure 8-5 Crimes and patrol dispatches in 20 West German cities with more than 200,000 inhabitants (rates per 100,000)

between 16,785 (München, 1,269,300 inhabitants) and 31,115 (Hamburg, 1,575,700 inhabitants). There seems to be no significant correlation between the number of inhabitants and the rate of patrol dispatches.

It was already mentioned that the number of patrol dispatches is still increasing. In contrast to the number of calls, the increase in patrol dispatches did not stop at the beginning of the 80s. Figure 8-3 indicates this for one city (Hamburg).

The total number of patrol dispatches in Hamburg (and in Munich too) has nearly doubled in the last 20 years. In Hamburg, the number increased from 16,000 (per 100,000) in 1965 to more than 31,000 in 1986; in Munich the increase was from less than 10,000 to about 17,000.

The major part of the everyday routine work of West German police consists of different types of traffic accidents, events, and offenses. The rate ranges from 25% to almost 60% in different cities. "Real crimes" (i.e., patrol dispatches on the grounds of a supposed or actual offense) are rather exceptional (from 16% to 28%). Brawls and quarrels are the cause for action to a similar extent (up to 25%), as are different kinds of help and assistance (e.g., aiding drunken and helpless persons). The rates for types of patrol dispatches in two cities are shown in Fig. 8-6.

The Self-Assessment of Police Officers and Their Assessment of Public Opinion

In 1981, we interviewed a sample of 431 police officers to get their self-assessment and their opinions on different questions concerning police functions. Some of the questions are listed below and the results are shown (see Table 8-3). One major finding was that police officers rate public opinion of police work and of the functions of the police worse than it actually is. The police officers significantly underestimated public opinion. As shown in another study some years ago, the public has a better opinion of police officers and their work than police officers themselves have (Kerner, 1980). This conflict between police officers' estimates of how they are perceived by the public and how the public actually looks at the police is reported in other research as well.

Furthermore, the police officers want more discretion in settling everyday conflicts, especially when juvenile offenders are involved. As for cooperation with social workers in everyday conflicts, this is not possible for most of police officers in typical criminal cases, but it is very possible with social problems like drug abuse, alcoholism, suicide, and family conflict. Police officers would also cooperate with social workers when victims need special help.

Cooperation between the police and other social institutions is rated by the police officers as very poor.

In a second part of our study, social work students were interviewed. The results show that the attitudes and self-assessments are quite different between the two groups. Some results are shown below. Social workers rate themselves as a kind of "helper elite" with very critical political attitudes. For example, they rate themselves more "left wing" than they are. Nobody else but social workers are qualified to help others, and their own work stays rather uncriticized. Any possibility of stigmatizing people (especially juveniles) through social work is denied.

CONCLUSIONS

All in all, two different tendencies can be observed. On the one hand, the demand for help or intervention by the police constantly rose until the beginning of the 80s. As shown earlier, the rise of criminal offenses (as registered by the police) was only partly responsible for this. Rather the readiness or ability of

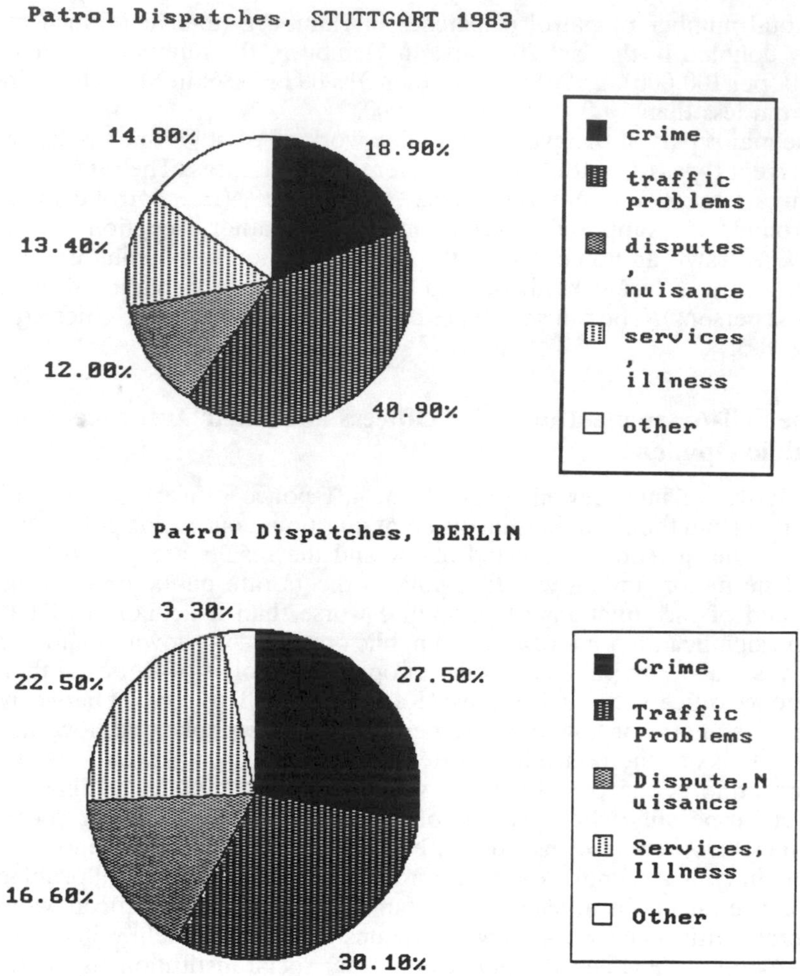

Figure 8-6 Composition of patrol dispatches in Stuttgart and Berlin

people to settle conflicts by means of communication decreased. Victims are less ready and able to help themselves. Official authorities are increasingly called in to settle conflicts. Even the rise in registered offenses can be explained by this phenomenon, at least partly. On the other hand, the police are less and less capable of accomplishing the task of keeping order and settling conflicts adequately and for the benefit of the victims concerned. This might be one reason for the stability or, in some cases, the decrease in the rate of emergency calls in many cities since the beginning of the 80s.

Police officers themselves are eager to help other people. But changes in the structure of police work and the police system, as well as political decisions (e.g., the decision to declare the defeat of "violent demonstrations," terrorism,

Table 8-3 Police officers' self-assessment and assessment of public opinion

Question:
There are people, especially scholars, who tell us that delinquents are "people like you and me."
A. What do you think about this statement?
B. How do you feel about other people and this statement?

	A (police)	B (other people)
It's correct	54.2%	29.6%
It's not easy to decide	21.7	25.7
It's wrong	24.1	44.7

Question:
There are projects called "diversions" (informal disposal of criminal prosecutions against juveniles).
A. How do you feel about such projects?
B. How do you feel about other people and their opinion?

	A (police)	B (other people)
Agree	48.1%	17.4%

Question:
How do you feel about the following statement: "The police are quite often engaged in conflicts (i.e., demonstrations) which the government and social policy should have to cope rather than police officers"?
A. Your opinion?
B. How do you feel about other people's opinion?

	A (police)	B (other people)
Agree	86.2%	64.0%

Question:
A. How do you feel about the following statements?
B. How do you feel about other people's opinion?

POLICE OFFICERS . . .	A YES (police)	B YES (other people)
Want to help others	82.6%	42.0%
May break a law to help other people	22.6	13.6
Are critical toward society	60.0	31.6
Are critical toward police	33.3	17.2
Are satisfied with their job	37.0	36.4
Work hard on their job	41.6	22.2
Are red-taped (bureaucratic)	49.3	76.4
Are well trained for their job	46.4	25.7
Are not interested in political questions	11.3	26.8
Vote against nuclear power	5.6	11.8
Vote for the social democrats	12.3	13.2

and violent crime as the main tasks of the West German police), complicate the police officers' job unnecessarily. Now as never before citizens call the police to solve a wide range of problems. Victims call the police in order to find an institution and people in this institution who are able to help them physically and psychologically. Therefore, the role and the functions of the West German police have to be discussed again taking into account some new considerations.

BIBLIOGRAPHY

Busch, H., Funk, A., Kauß, U., Narr, W.-D., & Werkentin, F. (1985). *Die Polizei in der Bundesrepublik*. Frankfurt, New York: Campus.

Feest, J., & Blankenburg, E. (1972). *Die Definitionsmacht der Polizei*. Düsseldorf: Bertelshann.

Feest, J., & Lautmann, R. (Eds.). (1971). *Die Polizei*. Opladen: Westdeutscher Verloc.

Feltes, T. (1984). Polizeiliches Alltagshandeln: Eine Analyse von Funkstreifeneinsätzen und Alarmierungen der Polizei. *CILIP, Bürgerrechte und Polizei*, *19*(3), 11–24.

Feltes, T., & Hermann, D. (1987). Zufriedene Polizisten? Die Einschätzung der Berufssituation und der Ausbildung durch Polizisten. *Die Polizei*, *3*, 73–77.

Flanagan, T. J. (1985). Consumers' perspectives on police operational strategy. *Journal of Police Science and Administration*, 10–21.

Kerner, H.-J. (1980). *Kriminalitätseinschätzung und innere Sicherheit*. Wiesbaden: BKA-Forschungsreihe.

Kürzinger, J. (1978). *Private Strafanzeige und polizeiliche Reaktion*. Berlin: Duncker and Humblot.

Plate, M., Schwinges, U., & Weiss, R. (1985). *Strukturen der Kriminalität in Solingen*. Wiesbaden: Bundeskriminalamt.

Reiner, R., & Shapland, J. (Eds.) (1987) Why police? Special issue on policing in Britain. *The British Journal of Criminology*, *27*(1).

Sack, F. (1987). Wege und Umwege der deutschen Kriminologie in und aus dem Strafrecht. In H. Janssen, R. Kaulitzki, & R. Michalowski (Eds.), *Radikale Kriminologie*. Bielefeld: AJZ.

Schwind, H.-D. (1984). Investigations of non-reported offenses. In R. Block (Ed.), *Victimization and fear of crime around the world*. Washington, DC: U.S. Department of Justice, Bureau of Justice Statistics.

Schwind, H.-D., et al. (1975). *Dunkelfeldforschung in Göttingen*. Wiesbaden: Bundeskriminalamt.

Sessar, K. (1984). *Public attitudes towards offender restitution in Germany*. Paper presented at the annual meeting of the American Society of Criminology, Cincinnati, OH.

Sessar, K., Beurskens, A., & Boers, K. (1986). Wiedergutmachung als Konfliktregelungsparadigma? *Kriminologisches Journal*, *18*(2), 86–104.

Shearing, C. D. (1984). *Dial-a-cop: A study of police mobilization*. Toronto: University of Toronto, Centre of Criminology.

Skogan, W. (1984). Reporting crimes to the police: The status of world research. *Journal of Research in Crime and Delinquency*. *21*(2), 113–137.

Stephan, E. (1976). *Die Stuttgarter Opferbefragung*. Wiesbaden: Bundeskriminalamt.

Steffen, W. (1976). *Analyse polizeilicher Ermittlungstätigkeit aus der Sicht des späteren Strafverfahrens*. Wiesbaden: BKA.

Villmow, B., & Stephan, E. (1983). *Jugendkriminalität in einer Gemeinde*. Freiburg: Max-Planck-Institut.

Weis, K. (1982). *Die vergewaltigung und ihre Opfer*. Stuttgart: Enke.

Werkentin, F. (1984). *Die Restauration der deutschen Polizei*. Frankfurt, New York: Campus.

9

Interviewing Victims of Crime

Malcolm D. MacLeod
University of St. Andrews, Scotland

INTRODUCTION

Creating and maintaining good working relationships with the public are everyday problems faced by investigating police officers. Nowhere in the legal system is their success more important than in their relationships with victims of crime. The attitudes formed by victims during and after police investigations can significantly affect the level of cooperation and support which the police can ultimately expect to enjoy (see Block, 1971; Koenig, 1980; Homant, Kennedy, & Fleming, 1984).

Negative attitudes held by victims can often be attributed to the dissatisfaction felt with regard to particular police actions. Percy (1980) and Poister and McDavid (1978), for example, have argued that victim satisfaction is dependent on how close actual police response times match expected response times. On a broader base, others have simply identified the quality of the interaction between the victim and the investigating police officer as the principal determining factor (e.g., Carlson & Sutton, 1981; Scaglion & Condon, 1980).

One important facet of the quality of this relationship was revealed in a study conducted by Shapland, Willmore, and Duff (1985). They found that the willingness of victims to give continued cooperation was dependent on the amount of feedback received by victims regarding the progression of police investigations. It would appear that it is only when a person's rewards are increased that he or she is likely to show the police willing cooperation. Wiley and Hudik (1974), for example, found greater cooperation for the investigation of crimes against persons than for "victimless" crimes.

A central component of any police-victim interaction is the interview. It is probable, therefore, that the quality of these interactions is to a large extent dependent on how interviews are constructed and conducted. The fact that some victims form negative attitudes toward the police and can show an unwillingness to cooperate with investigations is indicative of some basic problems in police training (see MacLeod, 1987). A number of gaps have to be negotiated during

Malcolm MacLeod was awarded his doctorate in 1987 from the University of Aberdeen, having submitted a thesis on police interviewing techniques. He has worked for several years as a Research Fellow on the Person Identification Project funded by the Home Office and has recently been appointed as a lecturer in the Department of Psychology at the University of St. Andrews. His research interests lie in the field of psycholegal research, with particular interest in victim memory for complex events; the development of investigative interviewing techniques; and the examination of factors which can affect credibility assessment.

police training. One of these is the acquisition of interviewing skills, despite the fact that interviewing is considered "bottom-line" for such a close contact profession as policing (Shepherd, 1986). The study of witness protocols may provide valuable information as to where training could prove most beneficial. One such study, in which 135 incidents of assault were examined, is reported here. The implications of this kind of research for the future development of interviewing skills are discussed.

THE POLICE INTERVIEW

The principal reason for the lack of interviewing skills among police lies in the commonly held belief that interviewing techniques cannot be taught (Kettle, 1981). Indeed, the current standing orders to the Scottish police forces (Grampian Police, 1984, sect. 6) state clearly that "the ability to question a witness skilfully is innate." The consequence of such a view is that the development of interviewing skills, almost without exception, is dependent on the "sitting by Nellie" approach (Shepherd, 1986), that is, learning via the study of an experienced officer in the course of his or her duties. This approach has the disadvantage that bad as well as good techniques can be passed on from one police officer to the next.

Also, much of the relevant information currently available to the police takes the form of interrogation manuals (e.g., Inbau & Reid, 1967; O'Hara, 1973; Aubry & Coputo, 1980). Little attention, in contrast, has actually been given to the study of interview techniques. Instead, the impression gained is that interrogation and interviewing practices are synonymous. This is not necessarily the case, even though both are essentially methods of collecting information. Indeed, the progress of some criminal investigations may even be hampered by such a view, since the difficulties of interviewing victims can be quite different from the difficulties encountered during the interrogation of suspects.

It is clear, therefore, that if police interviews are to be efficient and effective, changes need to be made in the ways in which police officers are trained to interview. Cannell and Kahn (1954) argue convincingly that the validity of the information obtained via interviewing is dependent on the skill with which interview techniques are applied. This, in turn, is dependent on how well the interviewer is trained. That an interviewer requires training and practice in the use of his or her skills in order to achieve an acceptable level of proficiency must be axiomatic (MacLeod, 1987).

What precise forms police interview techniques should take remains unclear, however. Currently, there is a dearth of empirical work concerning the actual kinds and quantities of information typically elicited from police interviews. Yet until such material is gathered, there can be little justification for advancing the use of any particular technique or procedure.

The findings from some archival studies, however, have recently shed some light on this problem, especially those which have used protocols from witnesses to real-life events as the source of raw data (e.g., MacLeod, 1985; MacLeod & Shepherd, 1986; Yuille, 1986). This approach has a number of advantages. Not only does its use permit the examination of factors such as violence (often at levels beyond those normally considered desirable or permissible in the laboratory), but it also permits the identification of aspects of the police interview where the development of new techniques could potentially increase recall for particular kinds of information.

AN EXAMPLE

One such study involved the examination of 135 incidents of assault which occurred in the city of Aberdeen during 1982. Each statement was coded into its constituents, that is, action and description details. Each action detail was then categorized according to the person who had performed the action, whereas description details were categorized according to whom or what the description concerned. There were four referents:

1. the witness him- or herself
2. the victim
3. the accused
4. the periphery (i.e., any other people present at the incident and where the incident took place)

Two frequency scores were obtained for each referent (one for action detail and one for description detail). Consequently, eight frequency scores were calculated to give a numerical index of the content of each statement. (Retest reliability averaged around 80%.)

ANALYSIS

The data were analyzed using an unequal cells analysis of variance (ANOVA). Scores had first been transformed ($\log(x + 1)$) to obtain a better approximation to the normal distribution of homogeneity of variance generally preferred for parametric analyses. The following text and figures refer to these transformed data. (Despite the difference in cell sizes, cell variances were homogeneous.)

A 4 (Type of Witness) × 2 (Type of Incident) ANOVA was employed. The dependent variables were the frequency of action and description details reported.

RESULTS

An ANOVA indicated a significant main effect for Type of Witness, $F(3, 371) = 47.37$, $p < .001$. The length of statements given by victims differed significantly from all other witness types. Victims reported the most information, whereas bystanders reported the least ($p < .05$). The reasons for these differences may lie in the fact that the information available to passive observers can differ greatly from the information available to those who are actively involved—simply because of differences in physical proximity. For bystanders, however, the victim can also be an additional competing stimulus which can limit the processing of information about other persons and objects (see Fig. 9-1).

Differences in the kinds and amounts of information reported can also be due to the way in which the available information is processed. Type of Witness, for example, was found to influence significantly the particular kind of information reported, as indicated by interactions between Type of Witness and Type

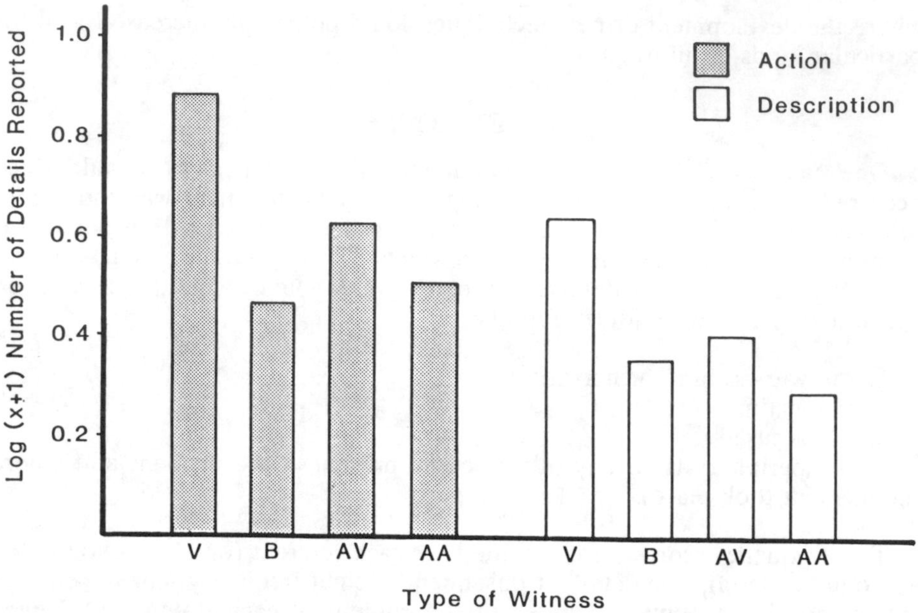

Figure 9-1 Action and description details reported about victim by witnesses to assaults. V = victims, B = bystanders, AV = associates of victims, AA = associates of accused.

of Referent ($F(9, 1113) = 15.96, p < .001$) and also between Type of Witness, Type of Referent, and Type of Detail ($F(9, 1113) = 4.04, p < .001$). Indeed, significant effects for Type of Witness were present for all four referents. The largest effects concerned the report of information about the witness him- or herself and the victim ($F(3, 371) = 64.26, p < .001$, and $F(3, 371) = 60.64, p < .001$, respectively). (Level of self-referent information reported by victims is synonymous with level of victim referent information reported by victims.) A series of Newman-Keuls tests indicated that for each of these referents victims differed from all other witness types ($p < .01$).

The report of information concerning the accused showed a smaller yet highly significant effect, $F(3, 371) = 10.24, p < .001$. Newman-Keuls tests indicated that the source of this effect could be attributed once again to the comparatively large number of details reported by victim witnesses (see Fig. 9-2). The accused is likely to have been perceived as the most important stimulus in the victim's environment, whereas bystanders may have attached little importance to the accused because of factors such as the delay in labeling the event as an emergency (see Piliavin, Piliavin, & Rodin, 1975).

The analysis also revealed that more information was reported about both the witness him- or herself and the victim in "injury" cases than in "no injury" cases ($F(1, 371) = 6.45, p = .012$, and $F(1, 371) = 7.64, p = .006$, respectively). In contrast, witnesses to "no injury" assaults reported more information concerning the accused than did witnesses to "injury" assaults, $F(1, 371) = 9.19, p = .003$ (see Fig. 9-3).

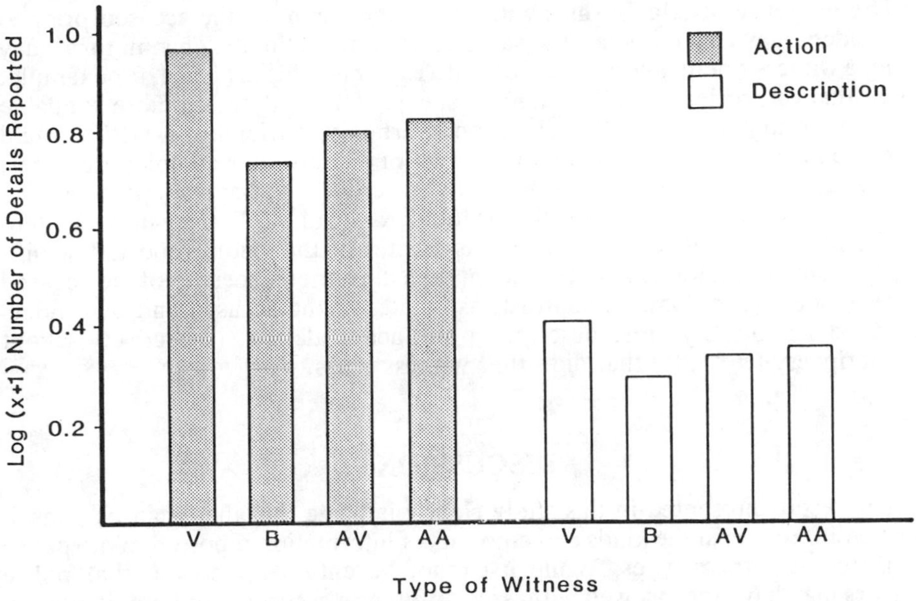

Figure 9-2 Action and description details reported about accused by witnesses to assaults. V = victims, B = bystanders, AV = associates of victims, AA = associates of accused.

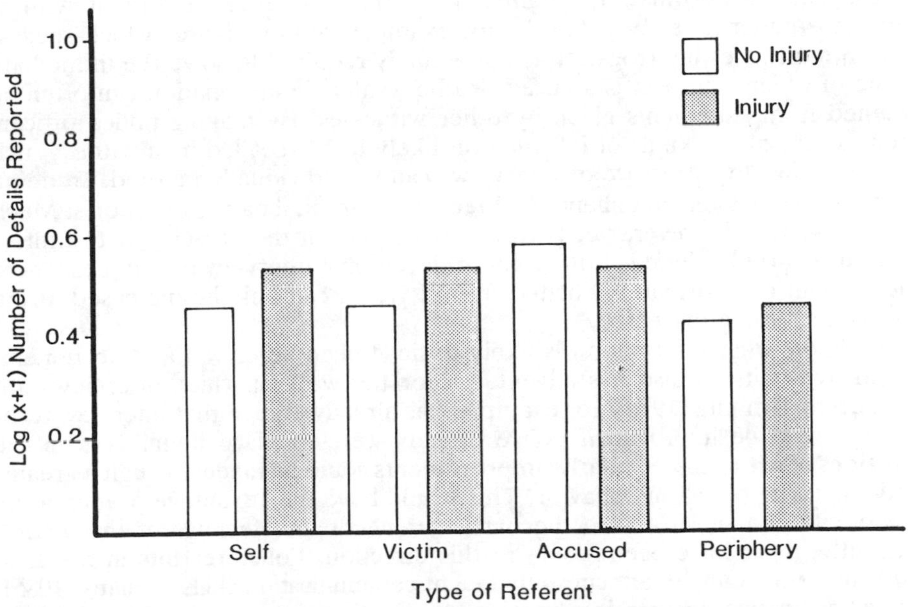

Figure 9-3 Referents reported by witnesses to "no injury" and "injury" assaults.

The existence of relationships with either the victim or the accused prior to an incident may also influence the salience of certain stimuli. This, in turn, may affect a witness's perception of an incident. Taylor and Fiske (1975), for example, argue that categories related to salient aspects of a situation are more available as a way of understanding that situation. Certainly, a friend of a victim would be more likely to show sympathy to that victim than would a complete stranger. Consequently, empathizing observers are more likely to have adopted the victim's phenomenological perspective (Gould & Sigall, 1977; Regan & Totten, 1975). Indeed, the data indicate that associates of the victim reported significantly more information about the victim than did either associates of the accused or bystanders ($p < .05$). In contrast, associates of the accused and bystanders reported significantly more description and action details, respectively, about the periphery ($p < .05$) that did other witness types.

DISCUSSION

The results presented in this study clearly indicate that there can be considerable differences in the kinds and amounts of information reported to the police by different witness types. While it cannot be entirely ruled out that police officers may have interviewed witnesses differently according to type, it is more likely that the observed differences are due to witness factors such as the particular roles played in the incident.

In a recent report by the Metropolitan Police (1985), it was noted that too often victims of crime are interviewed in exactly the same way as other witness types. Yet the information obtained from the differential nature of witness reports is undeniable. Witt (1973), for example, reports figures which suggest that in most cases interrogation is not actually required to solve the immediate crime of which a suspect is accused. Rather, valuable information can often be gleaned from statements given by other witnesses. By making police officers more aware of the kinds of information likely to be recalled by a witness such as the victim, the structure of interviews can be individually tailored. In doing so, it may be possible to enhance further the differential nature of reports. Much more research, however, needs to be conducted on the veracity of the information reported. There is little point in developing interview techniques where the amount of information elicited from a victim can only be increased at the cost of increasing inaccuracy.

To know what information is likely to have been perceived and be remembered by a witness also has advantages for the ways in which interviews are conducted. Schmitz (1978), for example, has already argued that interview techniques could be improved if police officers were to place themselves in the positions of witnesses. Similarly, improvements could be made through a greater understanding of victim behavior. This would have the advantage of increasing receptivity and sensitivity to the particular needs and feelings of the victim. Recently, there have been moves in this direction. Police recruits in the East Midlands, for example, are currently taught communication skills (Adams, 1985), and a human-awareness training program presently being run in the Metropolitan Police is primarily concerned with the development of interpersonal skills (see Bull, 1986; Bull & Horncastle, 1986).

Attention has also been drawn to the need for specialized training of police officers to deal with victims of crime. Yuille (1986), for example, in commenting on the training adopted by the Royal Canadian Mounted Police, suggests that the major problem in training is the lack of specification of when certain interviewing techniques should be employed and when others should be avoided. While there is merit in such a point of view, specialized training should not take place at the expense of developing basic interviewing skills. It should always be remembered that police officers have to deal with a variety of situations (some extremely emotionally charged) which do not always permit the use of preorganized question sets. Rules and specifics can fail to add up to a general integrated system or conceptualization of interviewing (Shepherd, 1986). It is important, therefore, that an investigating police officer has at his or her disposal the general principles of interviewing in addition to any specialized skills necessary to deal with victims.

The value of this can most readily be seen where juvenile or sexually abused victims (who may be very distressed and confused) have to be interviewed. In such instances, it is important that all the necessary information is gathered during as few interviews as possible in order to lessen any trauma to the victim resulting from having to recall the incident repeatedly over an extended period of time. The effectiveness and efficiency of such police interviews depend heavily on the police officer's skills in conversation and listening. No amount of special sets of questions could be expected to compensate for poor performance on any of these basic skills.

The solution, therefore, has to lie in the development of training programs that would enable police officers to obtain a firm grasp of the basic skills of interviewing. This could be accomplished with a mixture of formal and informal teaching and with adequate feedback regarding an individual interviewer's strengths and weaknesses. An important part of any such training program should also be the dissemination of knowledge regarding the mediating factors that can affect eyewitness behavior of the type discussed here. Ultimately, police officers who have a wider knowledge of such factors would be more sensitive in their interviewing of victims of crime.

BIBLIOGRAPHY

Adams, J. (1985). *Communication skills training with new recruits.* Paper presented at NATO Conference on Police Selection and Training: The Role of Psychology, Skiathos, Greece.

Aubry, A. S., & Coputo, R. R. (1980). *Criminal interrogation.* Springfield, IL: Charles C Thomas.

Block, R. (1971). Fear of crime and fear of the police. *Social Problems*, *19*, 91–101.

Bull, R. (1986). An evaluation of police recruit training in human awareness. In J. C. Yuille (Ed.), *Police selection and training: The role of psychology.* Dordrecht, The Netherlands: Martinus Nijhoff.

Bull, R., & Horncastle, P. (1986). *Metropolitan police recruit training: An independent evaluation.* London: The Police Foundation.

Cannell, C. F., & Kahn, R. L. (1954). The collection of data by interviewing. In L. Festinger & D. Katz (Eds.), *Research methods in the behavioral sciences.* London: Staples Press.

Carlson, H., & Sutton, M. (1981). A multi-method approach to community evaluation of police performance. *Journal of Criminal Justice*, *9*, 227–234.

Gould, R., & Sigall, H. (1977). The effects of empathy and outcome on attribution: An examination of the divergent perspectives hypothesis. *Journal of Experimental Social Psychology*, *13*, 480–491.

Grampian Police. (1984). *Scottish criminal law, police duties and procedure* (Vols. 1, 2). Aberdeen, Scotland: Aberdeen University Press.

Homant, R. J., Kennedy, D. B., & Fleming, R. M. (1984). The effects of victimization and the police response on citizens' attitudes toward police. *Journal of Police Science and Administration*, *12*, 323–332.

Inbau, F. E., & Reid, J. (1967). *Criminal interrogations and confessions* (2nd ed.). Baltimore, MD: Williams & Wilkins.

Kettle, M. (1981). More light on policing. *New Society*, *56*, 265.

Kirk, R. E. (1968). *Experimental design: Procedures for the behavioral sciences.* Monterey, CA: Brooks-Cole.

Koenig, D. (1980). The effects of criminal victimization and judicial or police contacts on public attitudes toward local police. *Journal of Criminal Justice*, *8*, 243–249.

MacLeod, M. D. (1985). *Perspectives on an assault: Varying accounts by different witnesses.* Paper presented at NATO Conference on Police Selection and Training: The Role of Psychology, Skiathos, Greece.

MacLeod, M. D. (1987). Psychological dynamics of the police interview. Unpublished Ph.D. thesis, University of Aberdeen, Scotland.

MacLeod, M. D., & Shepherd, J. W. (1986). Sex differences in eyewitness reports of criminal assaults. *Medicine, Science and the Law*, *26*, 311–318.

Metropolitan Police (1985). *Child sexual abuse investigation and detection techniques.* Interim working party report, Metropolitan Police.

O'Hara, C. (1973). *Fundamentals of criminal investigation* (3rd ed.). Springfield, IL: Charles C Thomas.

Percy, S. (1980). Response time and citizen evaluation of police. *Journal of Police Science and Administration*, *8*, 75–86.

Piliavin, I. M., Piliavin, J. A., & Rodin, J. (1975). Costs, diffusion, and the stigmatized victim. *Journal of Personality and Social Psychology*, *32*, 429–438.

Poister, T., & McDavid, J. (1978). Victims' evaluations of police performance. *Journal of Criminal Justice*, *6*, 133–149.

Regan, D. T., & Totten, J. (1975). Empathy and attribution: Turning observers into actors. *Journal of Personality and Social Psychology*, *32*, 850–856.

Scaglion, R., & Condon, R. (1980). Determinants of attitudes toward city police. *Criminology*, *17*, 485–494.

Schmitz, H. M. (1978). *Course of events in a crime: The reconstruction and description of criminal offences in police-witness interrogation.* Washington, DC: National Institute of Justice.

Shapland, J., Willmore, J., & Duff, P. (1985). *Victims in the criminal justice system.* Aldershot, England: Gower.

Shepherd, E. (1986). Interviewing development: Facing up to reality. In J. C. Yuille (Ed.), *Police selection and training: The role of psychology.* Dordrecht, The Netherlands: Martinus Nijhoff.

Taylor, S. E., & Fiske, S. T. (1978). Salience, attention and attribution: Top of the head phenomena. In L. Berkowitz (Ed.), *Advances in experimental social psychology* (Vol. 11). New York: Academic Press.

Wiley, M. G., & Hudik, T. (1974). Police-citizen encounters: A field test of exchange theory. *Social Problems*, *22*, 119–127.

Witt, J. W. (1973). Non-coercive interrogation and the administration of criminal justice: The impact of Miranda on police effectuality. *Journal of Criminal Law and Criminology*, *64*, 320–332.

Yuille, J. C. (1986). Meaningful research in the police context. In J. C. Yuille (Ed.), *Police selection and training: The role of psychology.* Dordrecht, The Netherlands: Martinus Nijhoff.

10

Victim-Offender Mediation as the Preferred Response to Property Offenses

Burt Galaway
School of Social Work, University of Minnesota, Minneapolis

INTRODUCTION

Two years experience with a victim-offender reconciliation program (VORP) in Minneapolis–St. Paul, Minnesota, confirms previous experiences regarding the feasibility of implementing a VORP. The program primarily serves victims of juvenile burglary and their offenders. In the first two years, 165 offenders participated; these offenders had a total of 162 victims, of whom 54% (87) decided to meet their offenders. One hundred and twenty-eight agreements were negotiated, involving 99 offenders and 84 victims. Forty-four percent of the agreements called for monetary restitution, 17% for personal service restitution, 6% for both monetary and personal service restitution, 10% for community service restitution, 2% for both community service and monetary restitution, and 20% for apologies only. Two percent had other requirements. For victims who experienced monetary loss, the mean loss was $745 (including amounts reimbursed by insurance companies); offenders who negotiated monetary restitution obligations had a mean obligation of $247. Seventy-nine percent (101) of the agreements were successfully closed. Implementing a VORP is feasible. Programs of this nature provide victims opportunities to participate in the criminal and juvenile justice process, serve penal objectives, have an impact on recidivism equal to or greater than other penal measures, provide a reasonable response to the serious overcrowding of prisons and jails, and will enjoy con-

Burt Galaway is a professor at the School of Social Work, University of Minnesota. He received the Ph.D. degree (social work, sociology) from the University of Minnesota and the M.S. degree (social work) from Columbia University. His social work practice experience has been in child welfare, corrections, and victim service agencies. He has done research in the areas of restitution, criminal justice, spouse battering, victim-offender mediation, and child welfare. In 1982, Dr. Galaway was the recipient of a research fellowship from the New Zealand National Research Advisory Council and spent 12 months as a senior research fellow with the New Zealand Department of Justice. Dr. Galaway is author or coauthor of several books and articles.

The Institute where this chapter was originally presented was partially funded by *Victimology: An International Journal* and by the North Atlantic Treaty Organization. Additional support for preparation of the chapter provided by the Minnesota Citizens Council on Crime and Justice, sponsor of the Hennepin and Ramsey Counties victim-offender mediation programs. The points of view expressed in this chapter, however, are those of the author and do not necessarily represent the policy or points of view of *Victimology, An International Journal*, NATO, or the Minnesota Citizens Council.

siderable support from both victims and the general public. Victim-offender mediation should be systematically implemented as the preferred response to property victimizations by offenders.

At the Third International Institute on Victimology, held in Lisbon, I proposed a model for a penal-corrective process to provide crime victims with an active role in the justice system (Galaway, 1985). The model was derived from Leslie Sebba's (1982) concept of an adversarial-retributive model for victim involvement in the justice system, which he contrasts with a social welfare–social defense model. Essentially the model requires property offenders to develop and carry out restorative plans. In other words, their penalties consist of activities designed to bring about an improvement in the condition of their victims and their communities. The term *penal-corrective* is used to refer to sanctions which are formally imposed on an offender after guilt has been established and which can be enforced through use of the power of the state. The term *corrective* means that the purpose of the sanctions is to bring about a correction of the harm done rather than a correction of the offender.

The model also has features similar to, but not necessarily with the same philosophical underpinnings as, victim-offender reconciliation (or mediation) programs (Umbreit, 1986; Chupp, 1988; Peachey, Snyder, & Teichsoob, 1983; PACT Institute of Justice, 1984). In February 1985, we implemented a VORP in the metropolitan area of Minneapolis and St. Paul, Minnesota (Hennepin and Ramsey Counties). The first year's experience of the Hennepin County (Minneapolis) project was reported at the Second World Congress of Victimology, held in Florida in 1986. I report the first two years' experience of the combined Twin Cities programs. This experience indicates that it is feasible to implement VORPs. Over half of the victims will participate, practically all meetings result in the development of an agreement, and nearly 80% of the agreements are completed. This experience confirms previous, although less well documented, experiences with similar programs.

The feasibility of implementing a VORP is clear, although establishing feasibility is, of course, quite different than establishing that such programs are desirable. Several arguments can be mustered to support the proposition that victim-offender reconciliation should become the preferred response for property offenders. These programs provide victims with opportunities for meaningful participation in the juvenile and adult justice systems. Mediation and the contracts negotiated as a result of mediation may fulfill penal objectives and may be as effective as other measures in accomplishing utilitarian objectives related to a reduction in recidivism. Such programs may result in a reduction in the use of prison and jail space for property offenders in jurisdictions that are experiencing overcrowding and are confronting the need to commit massive sums of money to prison and jail construction and operation. Finally, a growing number of surveys from around the world indicate that these programs will enjoy considerable public and victim support even when presented as an alternative to the more severe sanctions of prison and jail.

VICTIM–OFFENDER MEDIATION IN MINNEAPOLIS–ST. PAUL

The Minneapolis–St. Paul project is sponsored by the Minnesota Citizens Council on Crime and Justice, a nonprofit, nongovernment agency which engages in criminal justice and victim policy development as well as the provision of direct services, including crisis intervention for crime victims. The program was designed primarily to serve juvenile burglars and their victims. Burglaries were selected to deal with relatively serious property offenses and to rationally limit the number of referrals to guard against the danger of being overwhelmed with referrals. The project has received a few adult referrals and has also received some juvenile referrals for offenses other than burglary, including an armed robbery and a sexual assault case. The first referrals were made in February 1985; 183 offenders, including 8 adults, had been referred to the project by the end of 1986. The project accepts all referrals, although 18 of the offenders did not participate in the program.

Referrals are made by probation staff involved in completing pre-sentence investigations. After the referral, a VORP case manager begins contact with the victim, first by letter, second by telephone, and third by personal visit. The VORP case manager also arranges to meet with the offender and his or her parents before telephoning or visiting the victim. During the visit with the offender and the parents, the case manager secures perceptions of losses, discusses VORP procedures, and prepares the young person for participation in the victim-offender meeting. Parents are not encouraged to participate in the victim-offender meeting, although they are not prohibited from doing so. The meeting with the offender and the parents usually occurs between mailing the introductory letter and telephoning the victim.

The case manager telephones the victim to schedule a visit at the victim's home or business to discuss the VORP program. The preference is to explain the program and invite victim participation during a visit, although sometimes the case manager must provide information about the program during the telephone conversation. During the visit, the case manager will ask the victim to review the victimization, including perceptions of losses, and will provide the victim with an opportunity to discuss reactions to both the victimization and experiences with the criminal justice system. The VORP program will be explained and the victim will be invited to participate.

Meeting the offender prior to meeting the victim can create inconvenience if a victim declines to participate, as this decision must then be discussed with the offender. Becoming acquainted with the offender, however, is helpful in responding to victim questions and in providing information to use for a decision about participating. The case manager, having first met the offender, is better prepared to meet with the victim. If the victim agrees to participate, the VORP case manager arranges a meeting and serves as a neutral facilitator. The location for the meeting is discussed during the preliminary visit with the victim. The location should be convenient for the victim. One hundred and twenty-eight victim-offender agreements have been negotiated. Meetings for 23% (29) were held in victims' homes, 40% (51) at victim's places of business or work, 11% (14) at institutions where offenders were incarcerated, 15% (19) at neutral locations in victims' communities, 6% (8) at the VORP office, and 5% (7) at other locations.

The meeting between victim and offender has two distinct phases. First, victim and offender are given an opportunity to share reactions regarding both the victimization and their experiences with the criminal justice system and to ask questions of each other. The second phase of the meeting focuses on the damage that was done and the development of an agreement by which the offender can make amends to the victim. Apologies are extended by the offender and accepted by the victim in the course of most meetings. Upon completion of the negotiations, an agreement is put in writing, signed by all participants, and presented to the probation officer for approval.

The 165 youths who participated had a total of 162 victims; some youths had more than one victim and in some cases more than one youth had the same victim. Fifty-four percent (87) of the victims agreed to participate. Victims who have declined to participate usually indicated that they did not want to go to the trouble of attending a meeting with the offender, most often because the losses were small or they didn't think that it was worth the bother or that a meeting would serve any useful purpose. Table 10-1 shows the type of victim for both participating and nonparticipating victims. Sixty-seven percent (109) of the victims were individuals or households and 13% (21) were owner-operated businesses. Only 20% (32) of the victims were large organizations. Organizational victims were more likely to participate in VORP than individual victims; 43% of the individual victims participated compared to 76% of the owner-operated businesses and 75% of the other organizations.

Ninety-five percent (128) of the 135 victim-offender meetings have resulted in negotiation of an agreement acceptable to both victim and offender. None of the agreements have been altered or rejected by either probation officers or judges. The agreements have provided for monetary restitution (where the offender makes a money payment to the victim), community service restitution (where the offender and the victim agree that the offender will make repayment through contribution of labor to a community organization), or personal service restitution (where the offender makes payment by providing services or labor directly to the victim). Sometimes only an apology is requested, and occasionally there are miscellaneous requirements.

Table 10-2 shows the distribution of agreement by the type of restitution to which the victim and offender agreed. The two agreements in the "other" category provided for behavioral commitments. In one case, the victim was the father of the offender, who had run away from home and returned to burglarize his home. Another victim, an owner of a small business, suggested to the offender the choice of 30 hours community service or 30 hours doing school work at home; the offender agreed to the homework.

Table 10-1 Victim participation by victim type

Victim type	Victim participation					
	Yes		No		Total	
Individuals/households	(45)	43%	(62)	57%	(109)	100%
Owner-operated business	(16)	76	(5)	24	(21)	100
Managed business	(10)	77	(3)	23	(13)	100
School	(4)	67	(2)	33	(6)	100
Other government organization	(4)	67	(2)	33	(6)	100
Charitable, religious, or social agency	(6)	86	(1)	14	(7)	100
Total	(87)	54	(75)	46	(162)	100

Table 10-2 Agreements by type of restitution

Type	Number and percentage	
Monetary restitution	(56)	44%
Personal service restitution	(22)	17
Both personal service and monetary restitution	(8)	6
Community service restitution	(13)	10
Both community service and monetary restitution	(2)	2
Apology only	(25)	20
Other	(2)	2
Total	(128)	100

Table 10-3 summarizes victim losses and the terms of the restitution agreements. Seventy-one of the 84 victims experienced, after insurance settlement, financial losses averaging $349; in addition, insurance companies for 15 victims experienced losses averaging $1,964. From the offender perspective, 87% (86) of the offenders were involved in acts resulting in losses directly to victims or to insurance companies averaging $631 per offender; 85% (84) of the offenders caused victim damages not covered by insurance averaging $295 per offender. Although 80% of the victims experienced loss, only 56% negotiated monetary restitution with the offenders. Victims negotiating monetary restitution negotiated for a mean of $313, compared with a mean loss of $743. Fifty-nine percent (58) of the offenders agreed to monetary restitution averaging $252 per offender. Twenty-seven percent (27) of the offenders agreed to personal service restitution averaging 36 hours, and 15% (15) agreed to do community service averaging 39 hours.

Responsibility for monitoring compliance with the agreements is shared by VORP case managers and probation officers. VORP case managers maintain contact with victims and probation officers maintain contact with offenders. VORP follow-up with victims is done by telephone. When a failure to comply with the terms of an agreement occurs, the VORP case manager contacts the probation officer and a joint decision is made as to what action might be required. If necessary, an attempt will be made to get the parties back together to renegotiate the terms of the agreement. All agreements include a date by which the restitution obligation is to be completed.

All of the agreements (cases) included a target completion data and have been closed. Fifty-two percent (66) have been closed as fully completed by the target date, 19% (24) as fully completed after the target date, 9% (11) as renegotiated and completed, and 21% (27) as not completed. The first three types of closures are considered successful closures; thus the overall successful closure rate is 79%. The completed agreements have resulted in monetary restitution to direct victims of $8,280, monetary restitution to insurance companies of $3,096, community service restitution of 489 hours, personal service restitution of 127 hours, and $90 contributed to charity. Twenty-eight offenders completed other requirements (usually apologies).

Table 10-3 Victim losses and the terms of restitution agreements

		Agreement (n = 128)			Offenders (n = 99)			Victims (n = 84)		
	Total	No.	%	Mean	No.	%	Mean	No.	%	Mean
Losses										
To direct victim	$24,801	(105)	82%	$236	(84)	85%	$295	(71)	80%	$349
To insurance company	$29,457	(19)	15%	$1550	(19)	17%	$1550	(15)	15%	$1964
Total	$54,258	(110)	86%	$493	(86)	87%	$631	(73)	82%	$743
Restitution plans										
Monetary										
To direct victim	$11,505	(64)	50%	$180	(58)	59%	$198	(47)	56%	$266
To insurance company	$ 3,096	(6)	3%	$516	(6)	6%	$516	(3)	4%	$810
Total	$14,601	(66)	52%	$221	(58)	59%	$252	(48)	57%	$313
Personal service restitution	969 hr.	(30)	23%	32 hr.	(27)	27%	36 hr.	(18)	21%	54 hr.
Community service restitution	585 hr.	(15)	12%	39 hr.	(15)	15%	39 hr.	(10)	12%	59 hr.

FEASIBILITY OF VICTIM–OFFENDER MEDIATION

Determining the feasibility of victim-offender mediation involves answering questions such as these: Are victims willing to participate? Are victims and offenders able to reach mutually acceptable agreements? Are offenders able to comply with the terms of the agreements? The 2-year experience of the Minneapolis–St. Paul program suggests that the concept is feasible; 54% of the victims chose to participate in the program, 95% of the meetings resulted in agreements, and 79% of the agreements were satisfactorily completed. Monetary restitution was negotiated in 50% of the agreements; offenders responsible for monetary restitution had a mean obligation of $252. Other agreements called for community service, personal service restitution, or apologies only. This experience suggests that victims are reasonable in their requests, take into consideration the youth and resources of offenders, and negotiate agreements which offenders are able to, and actually do, complete.

The Minneapolis–St. Paul experience mirrors information available from the National VORP management information system maintained by the PACT Institute of Justice (Gehm, 1986). During the first year of operation (July 1, 1985, through June 30, 1986) data on 311 cases were reported by nine different American VORP programs (the Minneapolis and St. Paul programs were two of the nine). Sixty percent (183) of the cases resulted in a victim-offender meeting, 27% (81) did not result in a meeting because of victim unwillingness, 6% (17) did not result in a meeting because of offender unwillingness, in 2% (5) of the cases the victim could not be found, in 2% (7) the offender could not be found, and in 4% (13) the matter was resolved without a meeting (data were missing for 5 cases). Ninety-four percent of the meetings resulted in a signed agreement. Sixty-one percent (105) of the agreements called for monetary restitution; the mean amount of monetary restitution negotiated was $175 (the highest amount was $3,100).

These experiences are further confirmed by a growing body of research. In the first year, the Minnesota Restitution Center found that 31 of 44 victims were willing to travel to the state prison to meet their offenders and negotiate restitution agreements (Galaway & Hudson, 1975, p. 359). A study of victims from 19 American restitution programs found that 46% would want to meet with their offenders to develop restitution contracts in future cases of victimization, 36% would not want to meet, and 18% did not respond (Novack, Galaway, & Hudson, 1980). A study in the Tulsa juvenile court found 71% of the victims willing to meet their offenders (Galaway, Henzel, Ramsey, & Wanyama, 1980, pp. 42–48). Cannady (1980) found that 17 of 19 victims of juvenile offenders placed on probation in Charleston, South Carolina, reported a willingness to meet their offenders, and Kigin and Novack (1980) reported that 74% of 176 victims of juvenile offenders in St. Cloud, Minnesota, thought that they should be involved with their offenders in determining restitution obligations. Shapland, Willmore, and Duff (1985), in a study of victims of violent crime (assault, sexual assault, and robbery) in Great Britain, found that 17% of the Coventry victims and 19% of the Northampton victims would have liked to have met with the offenders and judges to work out sentences. Thirty-two percent of the victims in the Florida plea bargaining research attended plea bargaining conferences (Heinz & Kerstetter, 1979). A survey of a random sample of the public of

Columbia, South Carolina, found that half of the respondents show a willingness to be involved in personal service restitution if they were victimized through malicious damage to their homes (Gandy & Galaway, 1980).

There is also a growing body of research evidence to support what was discovered by the Minneapolis–St. Paul program and other VORPS, namely, that victims will not be vindictive in their negotiations with offenders. The Florida plea bargaining research found that "contrary to the expectations of some observers the victims did not demand the maximum authorized punishment" (Heinz & Kerstetter, 1979). Victims in the Minnesota Restitution Center program agreed to participate in negotiating restitution contracts with the full understanding that the outcome of the process would be a much shorter period of prison time for the offenders (Hudson & Galaway, 1974). Directors of five juvenile restitution programs argued that victim involvement is an essential ingredient of juvenile restitution programs, and they note that "the stereotype of the outraged, vindictive victim has been used as an excuse to exclude victim involvement for the sake of protecting the child from retaliation. The stereotype has not been born out by experience" (Maloney, Gilbeau, Hofford, Remington, & Steensen, 1982, p. 5). Henderson and Gitchoff (1981) found from their clinical work with crime victims that victims were willing to accept noncustodial sentences and restitution. Shapland's study of victims of violent crime in England found that "both in their wishes at the beginning of the case as to what sentence should be passed and in their reactions to the actual sentence, victims were not punitive" (1981, p. 6). Mcguire's study of burglary victims in England found victims were not the punitive "hang em, fog em, lock em up forever" people that popular myth suggests (1979). The 1982 British crime survey inquired of respondents identified as victims about the treatment they thought their perpetrators deserved to receive. Only half thought their offenders should be brought before the courts and only 10% said they should be imprisoned for their offenses (Hough & Mayhew, 1983, p. 28). Hagan, on the basis of his Canadian findings, states that "full exposure of the victims to the criminal justice process involves fewer risks than agents of the system may have previously assumed" (Hagan, 1983, p. 217). Forty-eight percent of the victims in a St. Cloud, Minnesota, study of juvenile offenders and their victims reported that no punishment other than restitution should be imposed (Kigin & Novak, 1980).

Finally, there is clear emerging evidence that restitution obligations will be completed. A juvenile restitution initiative funded by the Office of Juvenile Justice and Delinquency Prevention discharged 14,012 youths during the first two years, and 86% of the closures were considered successful (success means that the youth completes restitution obligations and does not re-offend while in the program) (Schneider, Griffith, & Wilson, 1982). The National Assessment of Adult Restitution Programs examined adult programs in the United States and found completion rates ranging from 52% to 91% (Hudson, Galaway, & Novak, 1980). McEwen and Maiman's study in Maine found that terms of small claims orders which had been negotiated between victim and offender were more likely to be completed than those that had been judicially ordered (1981).

The experience of the Minneapolis–St. Paul program, the collective experience of other VORP projects, and the available research indicates that mediation between crime victims and offenders is feasible. Concerns that victims do not want to participate, that mediation sessions might become explosive, or that victims will make unreasonable demands given the limited means of offenders are exaggerated and are not supported by experience or research. Most of the documented victim-offender mediations to date have involved juvenile property offenders and their victims. A few reports, however, of the use of the victim-offender mediation with adult offenders and with offenders who have committed violent crimes are beginning to emerge. Forty-five percent of the cases reported to the national VORP management information system involved adult offenders and 5% involved personal offenses. Case studies of the use of victim-offender mediation with offenders who committed crimes of violence are being reported (Umbreit, 1986, 1988). Victim-offender mediation is a feasible approach with juvenile property offenders and victims, may be feasible with adult property offenders and victims, and a more extensive experience base is required to access the feasibility of the practice with juvenile and adult offenders who have committed crimes of violence. But concluding that a concept can be implemented is not the same as concluding that the concept is sound social policy.

VICTIM-OFFENDER MEDIATION AS SOCIAL POLICY

Should social policy encourage the development of victim-offender mediation programs? There are several reasons to support such programs as a matter of public policy. The extent of support might range from cautious experimenting with a few pilot programs to wholesale reallocation of criminal justice resources to victim-offender mediation.

To begin with, we have been committing huge sums to jail and prison construction. The U.S. federal and state prison population increased by 76% between 1980 and 1987, with 546,659 persons in state and federal prisons at the end of 1987 (U.S. Bureau of Justice Statistics, 1987). As of December 31, 1987, the federal and state prison population was at 173% of design capacity (U.S. Bureau of Justice Statistics, 1988, p. 5). Americans have sharply escalated corrections and penal expenditures over the last decade; between 1977 and 1985 corrections expenditures nearly doubled (U.S. Bureau of Justice Statistics, 1987). Most of the increase has been for prison and jail construction and operations. Between 1977 and 1985, the proportion of state and local corrections budgets used for institutions increased from 74.4% to 83.5% while the proportion used for probation and parole decreased from 17.6% to 12.4% (U.S. Bureau of Justice Statistics, 1987). We have been experiencing a cancerous growth of the prison and jail industry, a growth which threatens to sap resources which are vitally necessary for health, education, and social welfare needs. But are we any safer?

Continuing reports from crime victimization surveys suggest increasing probabilities of being victimized by crime. A recently released projection (Koppel, 1987) suggesting that 83% of 12-year-olds will be victims of violent crimes sometime during their lives attests to the general ineffectiveness, perhaps bankruptcy, of our current system of responding to crime and crime offenders. These troubling projections have occurred during a time of increased harshness and increased spending for prisons and jails. If the present programs are ineffective, as the evidence suggests, an appropriate public policy position is to abandon what is ineffective in the response to crime and offenders and transfer resources to programs based on new principles.

Restitution, including victim-offender mediation, may be as effective as more expensive penalties. A study of adult parolees found that a group released from prison early to a restitution center had fewer new convictions than a matched group released to parole after serving a normal period of incarceration (Heinz, Galaway, & Hudson, 1976). Similar results were found in a 2-year follow-up of randomly selected adult offenders released to the Minnesota Restitution Center compared with a control group of offenders who completed prison (Minnesota Department of Corrections, 1976). A study of 250 offenders in the Tulsa, Oklahoma, juvenile restitution program found those who had contact with victims were less likely to recidivate than those who did not (Guedalia, 1979). Cannon and Stanford (1981) reported 19% of offenders were rearrested among juvenile restitution cases in a 6-month time period, compared with 24% for a nonrestitution group. Hofford (1981) reported a recidivism rate of 18% for youth in a juvenile restitution program, compared with a 30 percent rate for those on regular probation. Rowley's 6-year post hoc study of juvenile offenders referred to a restitution diversion program and a matched group processed through the juvenile court found substantially less recidivism among the restitution diversion group (Rowley, 1988). Recent field experiments (Schneider, 1986) on the use of restitution for juvenile offenders, including one project in which restitution took the form of victim-offender mediation, offer impressive evidence that restitution may be more effective in reducing recidivism than short-term detention, probation supervision, or mental health counseling.

The emerging crime victims movement suggests that crime victims are isolated from criminal and juvenile justice processes despite a desire on the part of many victims to participate in criminal and juvenile justice matters. Victim-offender mediation provides this possibility to victims. Further, mediation programs facilitate communication between victims and offenders, encourage offenders to assume responsibility to victims and communities for their conduct, and provide better opportunities for informal social control over the behavior of offenders than programs which isolate and separate offenders from their communities and the persons they have harmed.

Finally, there is a growing body of research evidence to indicate that the general public will accept sanctions of restitution, community service, and victim-offender mediation as an alternative to imprisonment for property offenders. The work of Hough and Mayhew (1985), Shapland (1982), and Shaw (1982) in England, Van Dijk (1984) in Holland, Galaway (1983) in New Zealand, Doob and Roberts (1983) in Canada, Gandy in Colorado (1975) and in South Carolina (1978; Gandy & Galaway, 1980), Thomson and Ragona (1987) in Illinois, the North Carolina Center on Crime and Punishment (Hickman-Maslin, 1986), and Sessar (1989) in Germany indicate strong public support for using restitution instead of imprisonment for property offenders. The consistency of these findings, which run counter to the ideology and perceptions of many criminal justice officials, challenges the accuracy of perceptions that the public is demanding imprisonment. Martin Wright (1987), after reviewing the research, arrives at this conclusion:

> *What these surveys show, however, is that many members of the public, including victims, are ready to shift the whole basis of the debate. Instead of debating as judges and magistrates do, whether to use harsh or lenient punishment, a substantial number of people are beginning to say "use reparation sanctions instead of punishment."*

The most reasonable conclusions are that victim-offender mediation programs are feasible to implement and are sensible as public policy. The public may be more likely than criminal justice professionals to support development of victim-offender mediation programs as the preferred penalty for property offenders.

BIBLIOGRAPHY

Cannady, L. (1980). *Evaluation of the Charleston Juvenile Restitution Project Final Report*. Washington, DC: Metametrics.

Cannon, A., & Stanford, R. (1980). *Evaluation of the Juvenile Alternative Services Project*. Tallahassee: Florida Department of Health and Rehabilitative Services.

Chupp, M. (1988). Reconciliation procedures and rationale. In M. Wright & B. Galaway (Eds.), *Mediation and criminal justice: Victims, offenders, and community* (pp. 56–68). London: Sage.

Doob, A., & Roberts, J. (1983). *An analysis of the public's view of sentencing*. Toronto: University of Toronto Centre of Criminology.

Galaway, B. (1984). *Public acceptance of restitution as an alternative to imprisonment for property offenders: A survey*. Wellington, New Zealand: Department of Justice.

Galaway, B. (1985). Victim participation in the penal-corrective process. *Victimology: An International Journal, 10*(1–4), 617–630.

Galaway, B., Henzel, M., Ramsey, G., & Wanyana, B. (1980). Victims and delinquents in the Tulsa Juvenile Court. *Federal Probation, 44*(2), 42–48.

Galaway, B., & Hudson, J. (1975). Issues in the correctional implementation of restitution to victims of crime. In B. Galaway & J. Hudson (Eds.), *Considering the victim: Readings in restitution and victim compensation* (pp. 351–360). Springfield, IL: Charles C Thomas.

Gandy, J. (1975). Attitudes toward the use of restitution. In B. Galaway & J. Hudson (Eds.), *Offender restitution in theory and action* (pp. 119–129). Lexington, MA: D.C. Heath.

Gandy, J., & Galaway, B. (1980). Restitution as a sanction for offenders: A public's view. In J. Hudson & B. Galaway (Eds.), *Victims, offenders and alternative sanctions* (pp. 89–100). Lexington, MA: D.C. Heath.

Gehm, J. (1986). *Reports from the National VORP Management Information System*. Valparaiso, IN: PACT Institute of Justice.

Guedalia, L. (1979). *Predicting recidivism of juvenile delinquents on restitutionary probation from selected background, subject, and program variables*. Unpublished doctoral dissertation, The American University, Washington, DC.

Hagan, J. (1983). *Victims before the law: The organizational domination of criminal law*. Toronto: Butterworths.

Heinz, A., & Kerstetter, W. (1979). Pretrial settlement conference: Evaluation of a reform in plea bargaining. *Law and Society Review, 13*, 349–366.

Heinz, J., Galaway, B., & Hudson, J. (1976). Restitution or parole: A follow-up study of adult offenders. *Social Service Review, 50*(1), 148–156.

Henderson, J. H., & Gitchoff, C. T. (1981, November). Victim perceptions of alternatives to incarceration: An exploratory study. Paper presented at First World Congress on Victimology, Miami, FL.

Hickman-Maslin Research. (1986). *Report prepared for North Carolina Center on Crime and Punishment based on a survey of registered voters in the state of North Carolina*. Raleigh, NC: North Carolina Center on Crime and Punishment.

Hofford, M. (1981). *Juvenile Restitution Program final report*. Charleston, SC: Trident United Way.

Hough, M., & Mayhew, P. (1963). *The British Crime Survey.* (Home Office Research Study No. 76). London: Her Majesty's Stationery Office.

Hough, M., & Mayhew, P. (1985). *Taking account of crime: Key findings from the 1984 British Crime Survey* (Home Office Research Study No. 85). London: Her Majesty's Stationery Office.

Hudson, J., & Galaway, B. (1974). Undoing the wrong: The Minnesota Restitution Center. *Social Work, 19*(3), 313–318.

Hudson, J., Galaway, B., & Novack, S. (1980). *National Assessment of Adult Restitution Programs final report*. Duluth, MN: University of Minnesota School of Social Development.

Kigin, R., & Novack, S. (1980). A rural restitution program for juvenile offenders and victims. In J. Hudson & B. Galaway (Eds.), *Victims, offenders, and alternative sanctions* (pp. 131–136). Lexington, MA: D.C. Heath.

Koppel, H. (1987, March). *Lifetime likelihood of victimization*. Washington, DC: U.S. Department of Justice, Bureau of Justice Statistics.

Maloney, D., Glibeau, D., Hoffard, M., Remington, C., & Steenson, D. (1982, May-June, July-August). Juvenile restitution: Combining common sense and solid research to build an effective program. *New Designs for Youth Development*, pp. 3–8, 1–6.

McEwen, C., & Maiman, R. (1981). Small claims mediations in Maine: An empirical assessment. *Maine Law Review*, *33*, 237–268.

Mcguire, M. (1982). *Burglary in a dwelling*. London: Heineman.

McKnight, D. (1981). The victim-offender reconciliation project. In B. Galaway and J. Hudson (Eds.), *Perspectives on crime victims* (pp. 292–298). St. Louis: C.V. Mosby.

Minnesota Department of Corrections. (1976). *Interim evaluation results: Minnesota Restitution Center*. St. Paul, MN: Author.

Novack, S., Galaway, B., & Hudson, J. (1980). Victim offender perceptions of the fairness of restitution and community service sanctions. In J. Hudson & B. Galaway (Eds.), *Victims, offenders and alternative sanctions* (pp. 63–69). Lexington, MA: D.C. Heath.

PACT Institute of Justice. (1984). *The VORP book*. Valparaiso, IN: Author.

Peachey, D., Snyder, B., & Teichroeb, A. (1983). *Mediation primer: A training guide for mediators in the criminal justice system*. Kitchner, Ontario: Community Justice Initiatives of Waterloo Region.

Rowley, M. S. (1988, June). Vermont juvenile court diversion: Concurrent use of victim and community restitution. Paper presented at International Symposium on Restitution and Community Service Sentencing, Minneapolis, MN.

Schneider, A. (1986). Restitution and recidivism rates of juvenile offenders: Four experimental studies. *Criminology*, *24*(3), 533–552.

Schneider, P., Schneider, A., Griffith, W., & Wilson, M. (1982). *Two year report on the National Evaluation of the Juvenile Restitution Initiative: An overview of program performance*. Eugene, OR: Institute of Policy Analysis.

Sebba, L. (1982). Victims role in the penal process: A theoretical orientation. *American Journal of Comparative Law*, *30*, 217–240.

Shapland, J., Willmore, J., & Duff, P. (1985). *Victims in the criminal justice system*. London: Gowen.

Shaw, S. (1982). *The people's justice: A major poll of public attitudes on crime and punishment*. London: Prison Reform Trust.

Thomson, D., & Regona, A. (1987). Popular moderation versus governmental authoritarianism: An interactionist view of public sentiments toward criminal sanctions. *Crime and Delinquency*, *33*(2), 337–357.

Umbreit, M. (1986). Victim/offender mediation: A national survey. *Federal Probation*, *50*(4), 53–56.

Umbreit, M. (1988). Violent offenders and their victims. In M. Wright & B. Galaway (Eds.), *Mediation in criminal justice: Victims, offenders and community* (pp. 99–112). London: Sage.

U.S. Bureau of Justice Statistics (1987, March). *Justice expenditure and employment, 1985*. Washington, DC: U.S. Department of Justice.

U.S. Bureau of Justice Statistics (1988, April). *Prisoners in 1987*. Washington, DC: U.S. Department of Justice.

Van Dijk, J. J. (1985). Public perceptions and concerns: On the pragmatic and ideological aspects of public attitudes towards crime control. *Justitiele*, Verkenningen 1.

Wright, M. (1987, June 2). What the public wants: Surveys of the general public including victims. *Justice of the Peace* (London), *151*(23).

11

Victim Support Programs: Between Doing Good and Doing Justice

Jacquelien Soetenhorst
Social Faculty, University of Amsterdam, The Netherlands

INTRODUCTION

The victim movement is an international phenomenon. Though the activities of people participating in this movement have many things in common, there are also differences due to structural and cultural national characteristics. In Holland, one of the most noticeable aspects is the growing number of victim support programs at the local level. This chapter presents a brief account of recent policy measures taken by the Dutch government regarding these programs. The main purpose is to clarify the question that victim support programs face at the moment: *What should the content and reach of the aid offered to the target group be?* This autumn we hope to begin an action research project in order to collect the necessary data to arrive at an adequate answer to this question.

Before this can be done a more theoretical analysis is necessary, one that offers insight into the different forces which confront victim support programs. One interesting fact about these programs is that they are situated both in the field dominated by the helping professions (doing good) and in the criminal justice field (doing justice). The demand made on the helping professions is to expand psychotherapeutic aid, whereas the criminal justice system has its own demands. The competing demands tend to "neutralize" the innovative potential of these programs as expressions of a grass roots movement. At the end of the chapter is a formulation of conditions that seem to be necessary to protect the project against complete absorption by either the helping professions or the judicial system and to strengthen its innovative potential.

During the past twenty years I have been confronted with the practical questions that arise in the field of criminal justice. These questions have varied depending on the historical situation, which in turn was defined by the dominant socioeconomic and cultural climate. After World War II, there was a general understanding in The Netherlands that it was necessary to rebuild society. The

Jacquelien Soetenhorst studied law at the University of Leiden, The Netherlands. For many years she practiced as a lawyer, returning to teach at Leiden University in 1972. After the 1975 publication of her thesis, *Tradition and Innovation in the Criminal Justice System*, she became a member of the research team of the Social and Cultural Planning Office in The Hague. Since 1982, she has been a professor at the University of Amsterdam. Dr. Soetenhorst is the author of three books and many articles in the field of deviance and control.

value orientation was based on prewar conditions (*prewarish* meant quality in those days). On the issue of crime and delinquency, initiative was left to the religious-oriented democratization, which was backed by the government. But by the second half of the 60s, this consensus on issues like crime and delinquency had broken down. The rise in the level of welfare for the majority of the population, combined with the process of democratization and secularization, resulted in a cultural climate that was highly critical of established and routinized practices, especially in the field of law and order. The positions of the power elite in politics, law, and administration came under critical attack. On one occasion, the mayor of Amsterdam wept during a television interview when attacked on his policy against demonstrators. In the field of criminal justice, the dominating topic was how to depenalize and decriminalize behavior that was then defined as criminal by the law (Packer, 1968). Prescriptions regarding moral behavior were seen as outdated. In the pluriform liberal society that was envisaged for the near future, political rights such as freedom of expression were emphasized. Humanization and tolerance were considered important values. In the field of criminal law, this meant that the rehabilitative value of prison sentences was questioned. They were to be avoided. If sentencing was inevitable, programs were to be developed in such a way that damage to offenders having to endure a prison sentence would be reduced to a minimum level. Conditional release and the development of "open prison" facilities were stimulated. For prevention of juvenile delinquency and other undesirable activities, emphasis was laid on community programs. An analysis of the debates in Parliament at that time indicates that the ability of social workers to handle this type of problem was highly rated (Social and Cultural Report, 1982).

Integration rather than exclusion was the aim of the societal reaction regarding crime. Both cost-benefit calculations and humanistic values provided the necessary arguments for an antirepressive criminal justice policy. The sentencing practice of the judges should be geared toward monetary fines and conditional sentences. As crime statistics showed a slight but not alarming increase in crime rates, there was hardly any protest against this approach (Allen, 1981). The Netherlands became well known for its humanistic antirepressive attitudes. The proportion of people in prison in The Netherlands was remarkably low. Experts from all over the world went there in order to study this phenomenon (Downes, 1982).

But by the second half of the 70s, there was some disruption in the atmosphere of satisfaction: Policy makers began to show signs of nervousness as it became clear that the data on crime were not up to date. Crime levels were much higher than the data suggested, and more serious crimes, like burglary, were increasing relatively quickly. This in turn produced a situation in which prison space was insufficient, which became the prime issue for policy makers in the coming years. The probability that citizens—especially in the bigger cities—would become victims of crime was on the increase. Car theft by drug addicts became a special nuisance, apart from more disturbing forms of crime, like mugging. These developments were reported regularly in victim surveys. Victims began to express their discontent through the media, thus strengthening the ever-present latent urge among the public for more effective "weapons in the fight against crime." Inefficiency of the apparatus, combined with an increasing demand on police services, public prosecutors, and the courts, created serious problems by the middle of the 80s, including the problem of how to satisfy the needs of victims of crime. The present mayor of Amsterdam, Van Tijn, who was one of the critical socialists a decade ago, publicly expressed regret about his former lenient attitude. An impressive policy effort was started by the Dutch government on the crime problem. Victim programs are part of this effort. In my previous paper for the victimology group, I reported on these developments (Soetenhorst, 1985).

This chapter briefly discusses the developments since then regarding the victims of crime. However, its main focus is on the different ideological (normative) orientations of both professionals and volunteers working within the framework of the "crime movement." The position will be defended that it is absolutely necessary to clarify the relationship between *doing good* (interventions of the helping professions) and *doing justice* (judicial interventions) in order to make our efforts to cope with the crime problem less incidental and less dependent on fluctuations in the sociocultural and socioeconomic climate, which, as we have seen, lead to unprincipled movements back and forth of public opinion. We do not need another regretful mayor.

RECENT POLICY DEVELOPMENTS REGARDING ASSISTANCE FOR THE VICTIMS OF CRIME

In Holland, public attention began to be focused on the position of the victims of crime at a relatively late date. Political attention had long been focused on war victims. However, in 1974 a fund was created for the victims of crimes of violence. The financial means were modest and the selection of victims to benefit from this fund was rigid. Only when serious physical or psychological damage could be proved was the victim able to meet the requirements of the fund. Also, the amount of money a victim could claim from the offender for damages during the criminal procedure was increased (at this moment the maximum is $750).

It was the feminist movement which initially focused public attention on the weak position of victims of violent crime. The introduction of shelter homes for battered women made visible the lack of adequate aid. In 1982, Parliament requested the Minister of Justice to appoint a committee to work out proposals for the better treatment of victims by the police and judicial authorities. This committee published its report in 1984. In 1986, concern for the victims of crime was expressed in the government's Declaration of Policy as a field of main concern. A national plan entitled Society and Criminality (1985), was worked out by the Ministry of Justice and accredited by Parliament; it includes policies concerning the victims of crime. These policies follow three lines:

1. Two government instructions (one for the police and one for the public prosecutor's office) on how to deal with the victim of a crime were published. Since April 1987, the victim must be informed of his or her rights and the state of affairs concerning his or her case.
2. A committee was appointed in order to work out proposals aimed at strengthening the position of the victim in court. Extension of the procedural or participatory rights of the victim seems to be necessary, as up till now the victim could only try to bring in a modest damage claim during the criminal procedure.

3. There was stimulation to develop services to help crime victims. (The Minister of Justice allocated $1,500,000 for these activities.) This third policy will be analyzed further in the following paragraphs.

WHAT KIND OF ASSISTANCE DO CRIME VICTIMS NEED?

Typification of Organizations

The last two years has shown a rapid increase in projects for crime victims at the local level. The 54 projects are meant to support all crime victims (not a specific type of victim). The type of support consists of initial aid in the form of information and advice about the legal aspects; practical assistance like changing locks, going to the police, and referrals to specialized agencies for therapeutic or legal aid; and last but not least mediation between the victim and the offender or other agencies, such as probation services or insurance companies. The organizational structure of these projects varies. Some of them are closely connected to police offices, whereas others function as independent agencies subsidized by the local authorities. Yet others are connected with family care or mental health agencies. The participation of volunteers also varies. The majority of the programs use volunteers, but the proportion of volunteers versus professionals varies, just as do the tasks performed by volunteers on a day-to-day basis. Since 1986, the projects, with a single exception, are connected by the National Association of Victim Support Programs. This national organization is subsidized by the Ministry of Justice. The basic questions faced by those involved in these programs are, *How do we reach the victims of crime? What kind of support do we offer?* In other words, what should be the content and extent of the aid given to victims?

The Social Construction of the Victim by the Helping Professions

Need becomes a tricky issue when related to a quota of help or support to be offered. The type of assistance offered often defines the need (Lipsky, 1982).

Research among victims indicates that they are primarily interested in being able to talk to a sympathetic listener, and for this a low grade of professionalization would be sufficient. However, professionals—functioning in these projects as coordinators—indicate there is a development toward "psychotherapeutization" of the aid offered. A possible explanation might be the high level of unemployment, especially among women with a degree in psychology or social work, who thus tend to participate as volunteers. For them the work is attractive because they gain experience and are able to continue to hope to move to a paid position eventually. This situation stimulates the tendency to define the need of victims in terms of mental health care. This might be reinforced by the standing practice of giving war victims psychiatric care. Psychiatrists and researchers working in this field have authority and thus defining power. They redefine the problems of victims of violence in psychiatric terms. In a recent study, for instance, the concept of "violent crime" is redefined in such a way that it includes property crimes such as pickpocketing and burglary (Van der

Ploeg et al., 1985). The client-image fitting these constructions is the dependent female whose needs are largely immaterial and who is thus willing to receive the help offered in existing therapeutic programs.

In conclusion, unless victim support programs take strong measures to resist this development, they will tend to disappear or to be transformed and eventually integrated into the mental health field.

The Needs of Victims from the Perspective of the Criminal Justice System

The second external influence on these projects comes from another quarter. Because victims who want to take advantage of the criminal justice system have to report their complaint to the police, it is considered the responsibility of the Minister of Justice to develop an adequate policy on their behalf. The minister has to deal with a judicial system that is completely geared toward the rights and duties of the offender. In this context, the victim is perceived primarily as someone that might be of help in gathering testimony or proof for the case. The police, hardened by experience, tend to perceive the victim as a possible liar. "We can type out an official report on 'stolen goods' knowing that this registration is meant to cheat the insurance company," a police officer remarked in testimony given to the Small Crime Committee in 1986. The victim movement, especially groups like Women Against Sexual Violence, exposed these practices and demanded rights for the victim. The right to be informed on the case at all stages, legal assistance in court procedures, influence on whether to prosecute, limitations on the interrogation procedure, and even a say in the demanded sentence—these are some of the most provocative claims. The social construc-

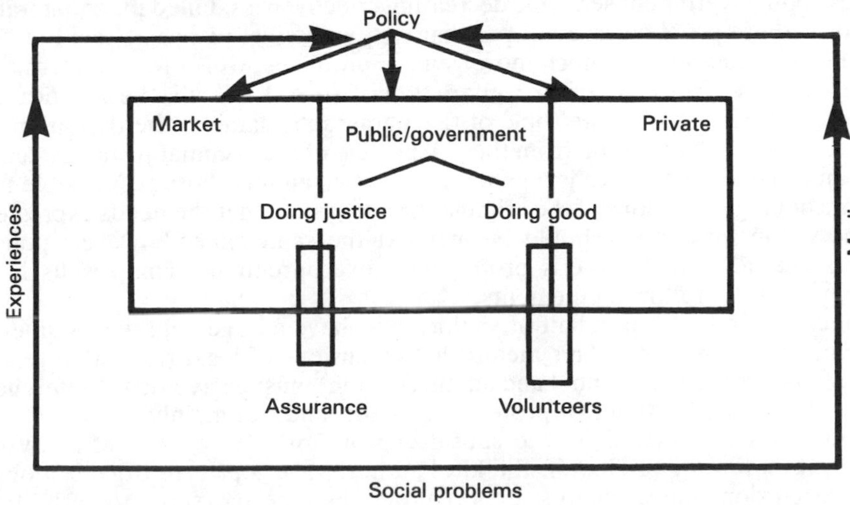

Figure 11-1

tion of the client in this perspective consists of the accountable adult who has a good deal of civil competence and who wants to realize his or her rights.

The Need for Legitimation of the Criminal Justice System

Though one might conclude from this perspective that the reconstruction of victims' needs would lead to an extension of victims' rights, this has not been the case up till now. There may be some rhetoric and some symbolic changes in procedural law, but on the whole the Minister of Justice has refrained from developing an active policy. The public prosecutor's office in Holland historically has had an independent and very strong position in relation to the Minister of Justice. One might expect resistance from the public prosecutor's office on any substantial extension of victims' rights, because this would automatically result in a reduction of the discretionary power of the public prosecutor. The stand that the representative of the Dutch government took in the debate on the U.N. declaration on the rights of victims illustrates this. Van Dijk, director of the research office of the Ministry of Justice, discussed this point during the international meeting organized for the centenary of the Dutch Criminal Code. Van Dijk (1986) stated, "The opposition of the Dutch delegation to the original paragraph in the U.N. Declaration relating to 'the right to be present and be heard at all stages of the proceedings' is a reflection of the reservations about the idea of the victim as a party which is rooted deeply in the structures and traditions of the Dutch criminal justice system." Thus the involvement of the judicial system is not so much rooted in the desire to extend the rights of the victim. The system needs to be sure of the trust and support of the citizens—citizens who hear every day more news about the lack of grip the police and the authorities have on the crime problem. At this same occasion, Professor 't Hart (1986) placed the crisis of the criminal justice system in a broader framework. According to his vision, "Capacity problems, overburdening, excess demands upon government services, decreasing effectiveness, failed planning, raising costs: these problems are not peculiar to the criminal justice system but are specific manifestations of much more general problems, which form the crux of the discussion on 'the crisis of the welfare state' " (p. 81). What is the significance of these observations for the topic of this paragraph, namely, the definition of the needs of victims of crime from the perspective of the criminal justice system? We can conclude that there is a general consensus among those responsible for the functioning of sections of the criminal justice system that the needs expressed by the victim movement should be met. At the same time, however, policy makers are faced with serious problems of overburdening. This results in a strategy with the following elements.

Policy investments on behalf of victims must have a large degree of visibility combined with low costs. This means that extensions of legal rights that result in increased costs (in personnel and administration) must be avoided. Preference is given to services with a low professional status and run mainly by volunteers on conditions formulated by the subsidizing authority (e.g., the Ministry of Justice, the Ministry of Health, the local authority, or a private organization).

In conclusion, unless victim support programs take measures to resist this development, they will stay marginal (in extent and content) and the extension of legal rights will be symbolic in character.

VICTIM SUPPORT PROGRAMS AS A SOURCE OF SOCIAL INNOVATION

In the previous sections, I sketched the sometimes contradictory forces these projects experience, with one foot in the field of the helping professions and the other in the criminal justice field (see Table 11-1). Up till now very little attention has been given to the fact that these projects are rooted in the victim movement. The term *social movement* refers to scattered, often invisible activities of loosely organized citizens who share (often temporarily) a certain commitment to a social issue. Social movements become manifest in different countries, like the women's movement or the peace movement. The victim movement is also an international phenomenon.

Systematic comparative research is not yet available, but research performed on a national level indicates strong differences between the Western nations on such issues as the level of organization, expressed aims, professionalization, and participation of volunteers. A social movement consists of grass roots initiatives surrounding a social issue. Scattered, often weakly organized citizens are attracted by an issue defined as a metaphor (Schön, 1979). The ability of the generative metaphor is to attract and bind people with completely different motivations, backgrounds, and political views.

The word *victim* has this binding capacity, but it generates different actions. Although this point can only be mentioned in passing here, we should be aware of the fact that the practice of defining undesired life events in terms of victims and offenders has a strong emotional and societal impact. The impact, namely, the necessity to maintain order (Durkheim, 1906; Girard, 1978), is reflected in the emotions involved. The societal order is disturbed or experienced as threatening. These strong emotions are clarified by the work of Lerner (1980). According to Lerner, we all use certain schemata (schematic notions about reality) in order to accept the world as basically "normal and just." Becoming a victim is one of those events that shatters this outlook on socicty. "The belief in a just world" is affected. In order to cope with this tension, people tend to blame the victim for the occurrence of the unwanted situation. On the basis of these insights, one might expect that some of the people attracted by the mctaphor "victim support" are highly emotionally involved. For instance, in contrast to volunteer projects generating aid for the elderly, the subject matter of volunteer programs for victims is much more explosive. Neighborhood watch projects

Table 11-1 A comparison of doing good and doing justice

	Doing good	Doing justice
Ideological orientation	Altruistic/solidarity	Fairness/exchange
Frame of reference	Responsibility/contextual connections	Individuation/separation/ categorization
Definition of the problem	Suffering/inability	Lack of knowledge
Type of action	Support/influence behavior/ influence environment	Information/procedural assistance
Organizational context	Mental health care	
Limits	No need/no money/ selection of clients	No need/overburdened/ selection of clients

illustrates this. Some of the watchers picture themselves as gunslingers, whereas others merely seek preventive or self-help measures. Some victims are mainly interested in stiffer prison sentences, whereas others seek fair reparation for damage done.

Before we can define the innovative ability of the Dutch victim movement, research is necessary. In the first place, more information is needed about the projects started for victims of crime (e.g., the formal goals, the offered assistance, the method and styles of handling clients, the proportion of volunteers, the normative orientations on issues that need to be solved, etc.). We hope to commence such research this fall. In the second place, it is necessary to have an analysis of the "voice of the victim in the media." There are indications that representatives from victim projects who appear on television programs express on the whole a moderate view on crime issues. The professionals involved in these projects perform a key role. As they are now meeting each other within the framework of the national organization on victim aid programs (mentioned in the introduction) it is possible for them to exchange attitudes and opinions on actual themes and thus define a shared standpoint.

My impression, based on personal contacts, is that on this level there is a serious effort to develop a policy that moderates the repressive elements of the movement and explores the possibilities of mediation techniques, preventive measures, and political action of a more structural nature. In my view, the impact of the victim movement occurs on two levels: (1) It improves the individual aid offered to the victims of crime, and (2) it improves the societal response to those situations that involve both victims and offenders.

The introduction mentioned the specific Dutch climate regarding the approach to offenders. Some analysts of this climate, such as David Downes (1982), ascribe the comparatively mild punitive climate to the Dutch political structure. Different religious parties (pillars) worked out a system that stresses "decorum, negotiation, accommodation and pragmatic tolerance (by no means the same as sympathy) for the interests and values of other groups" (Downes, 1982, p. 340). As this is not the place to elaborate on the "special nature" of the Dutch political climate concerning crime issues, I merely state that this special nature reappears in the Dutch version of the victim movement. The innovative potential lies in the discretion left to the projects to organize their activities according to their own goals.

However, studies on social movements make clear that the critical force of a movement, and thus its innovative potential, at the same time presents a threat to the status quo, which serves as a countervailing power. Ralph Nader, leader of the U.S. consumers movement, defines consumers as *victims of the system*, thus making use of the victim metaphor. He pleads for legal advocacy, stating that "a primary goal of our work is to build countervailing forces on behalf of citizens. . . . Must a just legal system not accord victims the power to help themselves, and deter those forces that victimize them?" (cited in Handler, 1978).

Handler (1978), who analyzed 34 grass roots initiatives, reached the conclusion that most of the projects ended up in a deal with the authorities. This is especially true when such projects are organized on a national level, for then a central point is created, which in turn gives rise to the need to control their activities. Handler observed,

> *Instead of competition organ groups vying for government benefits, there is consensus politics. Government deals with the most powerful, best organized interests in society and tends to sanction and support bargains already struck, which further strengthens the entrenched groups. The partnership system fails to take into account unarticulated interests of weak and poorly organized groups. The present system, instead of fostering change, increases benefits and advantages for elites and perpetuates the status quo.* (p. 4)

Handler formulated a couple of conditions the projects must fulfill in order to prevent the process of absorption. The most outstanding conditions are these:

- Projects must develop widespread and constant political support.
- Projects must get financing from different sources.
- Projects must generate new activities that are consistent with their goals.

In conclusion, the innovative potential of victim programs is apparent, both on the microlevel of individual aid and on the macrolevel of dealing with social problems involving crime victims. However, forces directed toward "consensus politics" tend to redefine the activities in such a way (self-help, neighborhood watch, informal social control) as to result in a loss of innovative capacity.

CLUES FOR THE DEVELOPMENT OF AN ORGANIZATIONAL DESIGN FOR VICTIM SUPPORT PROGRAMS

What concrete suggestions can be derived from the conclusions reached up till now with regard to the central question: *What is the ideal content of the aid given to the victims of crime?* After the above exploration of the societal forces these projects face, we can formulate the following statements (to be tested by further research).

1A. People have different ideas about what victim support programs should offer.

1B. Each vision "generates" a specific program of activities (recipe of action).

Explanation. Victim support programs can be seen as providing a form of care that needs special skills, such as skills in psychotherapy. Either specialized facilities are necessary or these skills must be integrated into existing mental care services. These programs can also be seen as providing a service (from the side of the police and judiciary). In this framework, the content of the aid consists of information on victims' rights and reference to existing facilities. Finally, they can be seen as presenting a countervailing societal force on behalf of marginal, weakly organized citizens. As such, they need discretionary power in organizing their activities.

2A. It is necessary to be aware of the limits of these projects in the face of the dominant political climate regarding government responses to social problems. Present characteristics of this climate are as follows:

—a preference for volunteers working with trained professionals (social work level)

—a low level of institutionalization
—strong instruments of control by conditional subsidies and centralization of negotiating power
—an extension of information rights of victims instead of a substantial extension of services

2B. Within these limits, those in charge of victim support programs should clearly formulate their goals and the means by which they intend to achieve these goals. Projects, of course, can have different aims.

2C. Training programs combining skills from the helping professions and judicial skills should be developed both for volunteers and for professionals working with volunteers.

Explanation. The combination of different goals might disappoint those involved in a project. Extension in the form of professionalization is not favorable. Thus training programs should be developed to teach laypersons some basic skills.

3. In order to protect the innovative potential of these projects (their grass roots origin), decentralization or adjudication of discretionary power to the lower levels of the organizations is desirable.

Explanation. If this does not happen, the projects might end up consolidating the status quo. By separating the realm of the "victim" from the realm of the "offender," they strengthen the existing definitions, thus missing the chance to transcend these definitions by exploring alternative approaches in dealing with undesired life events.

BIBLIOGRAPHY

Allen, F. A. (1981). *Penal policy and social purpose*. New Haven, CT: Yale University Press.
Downes, D. (1982). The origins and consequences of Dutch penal policy. *British Journal of Criminology*, *4*, 325–362.
Durkheim, E. (1906). Determination du fait moral. *Bulletin de la Societé Francaise de philosophie*, *4*.
Girard, R. (1978). *Des choses cachées depuis la fondation du monde*. Paris: Grasset.
Handler, J. (1978). *Social movements and the legal system*. New York: Academic Press.
Lerner, M. E. (1980). *The belief in a just world: A fundamental delusion*. New York: Plenum Press.
Lipsky, M. (1982). *Street-level bureaucracy: Dilemmas of the individual in public services*. New York: Russell Sage Foundation.
Packer, H. (1968). *The limits of criminal sanctions*. Stanford, CA: Stanford University Press.
Schön, D. (1979). Generative metaphor: A perspective on problem setting in social policy. In A. Ortony (Ed.), *Metaphor and thought*. London: Cambridge University Press.
Social and cultural report. (1982). The Hague, The Netherlands: Government Printing Office.
Soetenhorst, J. (1985). Victim support programs: Lever for change? *Victimology: An International Journal*, *10*, 687–698.
't Hart, A. C. (1986). Criminal policy in the Netherlands. In J. J. M. Van Dijk et al. (Eds.), *Criminal law in action: An overview of current issues in Western societies*. Arnhem, The Netherlands: Joudaquint.

Van der Ploeg, H. M. (1985). Psychologic research on the (lack of) demand for aid among the victims of violence. Lisse, The Netherlands: Swets & Zeitlinger.

Van Dijk, J. J. M. (1986). Victim rights: A right to better services or a right to active participation. In J. J. M. Van Dijk et al. (Eds.), *Criminal law in action: An overview of current issues in Western societies.* Arnhem, The Netherlands: Joudaquint.

IV

THE CHILD VICTIM AND RELATED ISSUES

12

The Legal and Diplomatic Response to the International Abduction of American Children

Michael W. Agopian
Criminal Justice Department, California State University, Long Beach

INTRODUCTION

A worldwide problem is the abduction of children by noncustodial parents following divorce. Frequently, such child abductions occur in cases where parents are from different national or cultural backgrounds. Typically, after a divorce, one of the parents desires to take the child to his or her country of origin. Although no data are available to gauge the extent of child abductions by a noncustodial parent worldwide, this chapter presents findings regarding American children abducted from the United States to a foreign country. It also examines the policy of Office of Consular Affairs (OCA), Department of State, regarding child abduction and analyzes a proposed legal remedy, the Hague Convention on the Civil Aspects of International Child Abduction.

International child abduction by a noncustodial parent poses complex challenges to all national systems of justice. Diplomatic relations are affected, jurisdictional conflicts arise, investigations may become complicated and costly, and cultural traditions are threatened. Such complexity may send a subtle signal to divorcing parents that international child abduction is a form of self-help following divorce.

The attractiveness of divorcing parents to engage in international child abduction may be fostered by family law courts. This problem is rooted in a fundamental question: If one court has given custody or guardianship of a child to parent A, why would another court in another country award custody to parent B? There appear to be at least three possible reasons for this predicament: (1) The second judge (who is outside of the country) may disagree with or mistrust the prior custody order. (2) The second court may disregard the initial

Michael W. Agopian is associate professor of criminal justice at California State University, Long Beach. He is the author of the pioneering book *Parental Child Stealing* (D.C. Heath, 1981) and has conducted extensive research regarding missing children and child custody. His research publications cover both social science and the law and include the areas of forcible rape, drug treatment, dispute resolution programs, and innovations in court processing of offenders. His Ph.D. was completed at the University of Southern California in 1980.

This research was supported, in part, by a grant from the Scholarly and Creative Activities Program at California State University, Long Beach, CA.

custody judgment in favor of a local resident. Sensitive to possible inequities of language, finances, or customs, the second court may be more sympathetic to a parent returning to his or her homeland and professing to love and take responsibility for a child. (3) Forsaking joint custody, parents may view international child abduction as a method of insuring full-time parenting privileges.

A good deal of activity has recently been directed toward the problem of missing children in the United States (Agopian, 1981). For the first time, federal laws have been implemented, including the Parental Kidnapping Prevention Act (18 USC 1037), the Missing Children's Act (28 USC 534), the Missing Children's Assistance Act (PL 98-473, sec. 401-73). The National Center for Missing and Exploited Children has also been created. In 1984, President Reagan proclaimed May 25 as Missing Children's Day.

Individual states have also vigorously responded to the plight of missing children (Agopian, 1982). Every state has created or updated laws. Eighteen have implemented felony offenses, and 23 others provide an optional felony or misdemeanor statute.[1] Statewide information clearinghouses, reward funds, and search programs have been developed. The plight of missing children has become a national concern. All of these efforts, however, have been directed at missing children who are sequestered within the United States (Hoff, 1982).

A new and serious type of child abduction concerns the transportation of victims across international boundaries. Such abductions may occur after a custody decree has been issued or prior to a custody determination. This type of child abduction involves a blatant determination to circumvent legal action or to deprive a parent of judicial recourse to obtain guardianship within the United States.

THE FREQUENCY OF AMERICAN CHILDREN ABDUCTED TO FOREIGN COUNTRIES

The data below concern parental child abduction cases in which the victims were removed from the United States and reports were filed with the OCA. From 1973 to the close of 1986, a total of 2,292 cases of international parental child abduction were reported. The most dramatic increase was between 1982 and 1986, during which there were 1,674 cases—73% of the total cases since OCA instituted reporting. During the 1973–1986 period, 1,020 victims were transported to Europe. This was followed by the inter-American region (Mexico, Central America, South America, and the Caribbean), with 542 cases. East Asia and Pacific countries reported 236 cases, and 126 children were spirited to African locations. Table 12-1 presents international child abductions from the United States to world regions from 1973 to 1986.

[1]As of January 1987, states which prescribe a mandatory felony offense for parental child abduction are Alabama, Colorado, Idaho, Illinois, Indiana, Kentucky, Maine, Minnesota, Mississippi, Montana, New Jersey, New Mexico, North Carolina, North Dakota, Oregon, Rhode Island, Vermont, West Virginia, Wisconsin, and Wyoming. As of January 1987, states which prescribe an optional felony or misdemeanor charge for parental child abduction are Alaska, Arizona, Arkansas, California, Delaware, District of Columbia, Georgia, Hawaii, Kansas, Maryland, Massachusetts, Michigan, Missouri, Nevada, Nebraska, New Hampshire, New York, Ohio, Oklahoma, South Carolina, South Dakota, Utah, and Washington.

Table 12-1 Parental child abduction cases reported to Citizens Consular Services by year and region

	Year														
Region[a]	73	74	75	76	77	78	79	80	81	82	83	84	85	86[b]	Total
AF	0	0	0	0	2	0	14	12	12	26	24	11	9	16	126
ARA	0	0	1	7	7	15	29	14	53	102	112	88	66	48	542
EAP	0	0	0	0	2	0	3	39	12	5	51	30	58	36	236
EUR	1	0	2	5	53	50	64	75	87	164	139	134	158	88	1020
NEA	0	0	2	1	4	3	2	15	32	43	62	69	78	57	368
Total	1	0	5	13	68	68	112	155	196	340	388	332	369	245	2292

[a]AF = African Services Division, ARA = Inter-American Services Division, EAP = East Asia/Pacific Services Division, EUR = Europe and Canada Services Division, NEA = Near East/South Asia Services Division.

[b]As of October 17, 1986.

Perhaps the most significant question concerning the problem of international child abduction is, What destination is sought by offending parents who abduct children? Because the present cases involved an enormous range of locations—58 different countries or jurisdictions—only the 15 most desired destinations for offenders are presented in Table 12-2.

Most parents involved in child abduction seek refuge in the Federal Republic of Germany (13%, or 163). Mexico was the second destination of choice (11%, or 137), followed by the United Kingdom (6%, or 73) and Italy (5%, or 66). The above four countries accounted for 35% (439) of the parental child abductions reported to the OCA.

THE U.S. CONSULATE RESPONSE TO CHILD ABDUCTION

The OCA operates as an information exchange in cases of international child abduction. Working with American embassies, the OCA provides indirect assistance and support to locate children wrongfully detained or transported outside the United States. The OCA can only assist in determining the welfare and whereabouts of American children abducted by a parent and transported to a foreign country. The OCA cannot intervene in child custody disputes, which are deemed private legal matters.

The principal tool of the OCA in missing children cases is the Consular Welfare and Whereabouts Search. In this procedure, a foreign service post attempts to locate a missing child and ascertain the child's state of health. This process may be implemented directly by U.S. consular staff or with the assistance of local foreign authorities. If a child is located and contact and evaluation are

Table 12-2 Destination countries for child abduction victims (only top 15 countries listed)

Destination	Number	Percentage
Federal Republic of Germany	163	13%
Mexico	137	11
United Kingdom[a]	73	6
Italy	66	5
Canada[a]	37	3
France[a]	32	3
Brazil	29	2
Greece[a]	29	2
Ecuador	29	2
The Netherlands	27	2
Trinidad	23	2
Spain[a]	21	2
Australia[a]	20	2
Philippines	17	1
Yugoslavia	17	1
Total	720	57[b]

[a]Countries that have ratified the Hague Convention on the Civil Aspects of International Child Abduction.

[b]Base for percentage is 1,255 cases. This is the total cases for which specific destination information is available. Change due to new information system implemented in 1982.

completed, then a report of the child's condition will be provided to the searching parent. If the welfare and whereabouts investigation indicates that the child is or was abused, the U.S. official will request local authorities to remove the child to protective custody (Agopian, 1984, 1985). Consular officials cannot take custody or force a child to return to the United States.

Basically, the OCA, through U.S. representatives, can assist in parental child abduction cases by

1. assisting parents to locate missing children abroad
2. monitoring and reporting on the welfare of American children upon the request of a parent
3. furnishing general information, short of legal advice, concerning foreign and domestic laws and procedures which might be of assistance in obtaining or locating a child
4. providing lists of foreign attorneys who have expressed a willingness to represent American citizens
5. alerting local authorities or social service agencies if it appears that a child is being abused or neglected
6. imposing passport controls in appropriate cases

Should a dispute over custody of a minor (a person below 18 years of age) be involved, revocation or denial of a passport to the minor is possible. Denial of a passport to a minor requires the following conditions: (1) an application to the Department of State with evidence and documents that an arrest warrant and felony criminal charges are pending on a parent, (2) a court order from the country from which the passport is sought that specifies custody of the child has been given to the person who has requested the passport denial or hold, or (3) the custody order issued in the country where the child is held forbids the child's departure from that country without the court's permission.

The passage of the Parental Kidnapping Prevention Act in 1980 provided for assistance by the Federal Bureau of Investigation in certain parental child abduction cases, namely, cases involving interstate or international flight to avoid prosecution. Utilization of the Fugitive Felon Act allows for federal investigations and requests of extradition to prosecute the original state felony charge. It should be noted that extradition of an offending parent does not return a child to the legal guardian. Also, the U.S. Department of Justice has been extremely restrictive in issuing Unlawful Flight to Avoid Prosecution warrants in parental child abduction cases. Since the passage of the Parental Kidnapping Prevention Act, Department of Justice guidelines for unlawful flight warrants have necessitated "independent credible information that the child is in physical danger or is then in a condition of abuse or neglect." In addition, the basic requirements for international extradition include the following:

- The charge must be a crime under the legal systems of *both* countries.
- Punishment for the offense charged must exceed one year.
- The offense charged must be specified in mutual treaties.
- The cost of the extradition process must be absorbed by the requesting country.

THE HAGUE CONVENTION ON INTERNATIONAL CHILD ABDUCTION

Because parental child abduction is not specifically included in prior international treaties of which the United States is a party, legal cooperation and reciprocity were unavailable. A historic step was taken on October 30, 1985, when President Reagan signed the Hague Convention on the Civil Aspects of International Child Abduction. In his letter of transmittal to the Senate, President Reagan said of the Hague Convention,

> *The convention would represent an important addition to the State and Federal laws currently in effect in the United States that are designed to combat parental kidnapping—specifically, the Uniform Child Custody Jurisdiction Act now in effect in every state in the country, the Parental Kidnapping Prevention Act of 1980, the 1982 Missing Children's Act and the Missing Children's Assistance Act. It would significantly improve the chances a parent in the United States has of recovering a child from a foreign Contracting State. It also provides a clear-cut method for parents abroad to apply for the return of children who have been wrongfully taken to or retained in this country. In short, by establishing a legal right and streamlining procedures for the prompt return of internationally abducted children, the Convention should remove many of the uncertainties and the legal difficulties that now confront parents in international child abduction cases. (Reagan, 1985)*

The Convention was ratified by the U.S. Senate on October 9, 1986. Senate advice was given to deposit the instrument for international ratification after Congress provides implementing legislation. On April 29, 1988, President Reagan signed PL 100-300, the International Child Abduction Remedies Act (see 42 USC 11601-10). This implemented the Hague Convention in the United States effective July 1, 1988.

The design of the Hague Convention is simple and direct. It seeks to promptly return a child who has been abducted from his or her country of residence and to facilitate visitation rights across international borders. It does not attempt to determine custody. The Convention seeks to restore the factual situation prior to the child's removal. The international offender would be denied any advantage due to the removal of a child. After return of a child to his or her country of habitual residence before the abduction, disputes about custody rights can be settled.

The Convention reflects a worldwide concern about the effects on children of parental abduction and a desire to deter such action. The Convention will apply to children under 16 years of age and will require a child's return to his or her original country regardless of a custody order previously issued or of predecree removals. Visitation rights are also partially addressed in the Convention. To promote reciprocal obligations, the Convention will apply only when a child has been taken from one ratifying country to another ratifying country. Adherence to the Convention articles is voluntary. To date, eight countries have ratified the Hague Convention: France, Portugal, Switzerland, Hungary, Canada, the United Kingdom, Australia, Luxembourg, and Spain.

The Hague Convention will provide an important addition to U.S. state and federal laws designed to combat parental child abduction. It would augment the

Uniform Child Custody Jurisdiction Act in effect in every state and the Missing Children's Act of 1980. The Convention will significantly improve the chance a parent in the United States has of recovering a child from a foreign country.

DISCUSSION

International child abduction by a parent is usually a manifestation of an unusual and complex family tragedy. In addition to the victim's injury, such an offense may be illustrative of a deeper human drama. What motivates a parent to resort to the international abduction of a child? Although preliminary, the following considerations should help in understanding more fully what may be the final effort of a desperate and determined parent to retain possession of a child.

First, with the ease of international travel and the expansion of multinational corporations, U.S. citizens may be marrying foreign spouses in greater numbers. After returning to the United States and establishing a family, a foreign parent may become disappointed in the new country, develop homesickness, or face marital strains. Seeking family support or the comfort of being in the homeland, the parent leaves the United States with the child (or children) against the desire or without the knowledge of the other parent. Simply, the foreign-born spouse may have a change of heart and desire to reside in his or her country of origin. This scenario could easily be repeated, for example, in European countries where U.S. military forces are present. In fact, Germany, Italy, and the United Kingdom are the preferred destinations to hide a child.

Second, for some offenders, international flight might appear as an opportunity for self-help, in particular, an opportunity to gain a legal advantage in a foreign court. Fearful of inferior representation in U.S. courts (possibly due to financial limitations, language, or nationality), the abducting parent desires a custody award from his or her homeland. Aware of the complexity of international law, increased expenses for investigations, or logistic impediments, an offending parent might seek refuge in a country adhering to different legal and cultural principles from those prevalent in the United States. This may account for international child abductions to countries in the Middle East, Mexico, or South America.

Third, some parents, especially foreign-born fathers, may become aware of the judicial bias within the United States of awarding child custody to mothers. Determined to retain possession of a child, an offending parent might see no value in obtaining an affirmative court order from any country. For such a parent, international flight provides the most effective course to evade or frustrate U.S. justice.

A significant concern in cases of international child abduction perpetrated by parents is the welfare of the victims (i.e., the abducted children). It may be that victims are accorded unusually lavish and compassionate treatment because the offenders seek to persuade them of the benefits of the "new home." Often the thrill of air travel, gifts, interaction with grandparents, and the adventure of being abroad are utilized to assuage fears arising from the abduction. For other children, however, travel to a new country brings with it painful and unpleasant experiences. They have to adopt a new language and they lose contact with family and friends. The general comfort of the U.S. home may never be replaced. For these victims, international child abduction by a parent is viewed as an enduring tragedy.

The motivations of offenders and the degree of injury victims experience are only two of the many complex dynamics within this complex family crime. Yet it appears that these two areas more than any others propel the search for a remedy to the international abduction of children by parents. This study offers preliminary data that signal the extent and seriousness of abductions of children to foreign countries. Further investigation is needed to determine specific motivations of offenders, patterns and characteristics of the offense, injuries to victims, and outcomes of cases.

BIBLIOGRAPHY

Agopian, M. W. (1981). *Parental child stealing*. Lexington, MA: D.C. Heath.

Agopian, M. W. (1982). Legislative reforms to reduce parental child abduction. *Journal of Juvenile Law*, *6*, 1–26.

Agopian, M. W. (1984). The impact on children of abduction by parents. *Child Welfare*, *6*, 511–519.

Agopian, M. W. (1985). Impact on victims of parental abduction. *Crown Counsel's Review* (Canada), *4*, 7–10.

Hoff, P., et al. (1982). *Interstate child custody disputes and parental kidnapping: Policy, practice and the law*. Washington, DC: American Bar Association.

International Child Abduction Remedies Act, 42 USC Sec. 11601–11610.

Reagan, R. (1985). Letter of transmittal on October 30, 1985, and letter of submittal from Secretary of State George Shultz to the President (October 4, 1985). *Federal Register*, *51*, 10495–10497.

13

Child Victims of Abuse and Neglect: A Portuguese Research Project

Eliana Gersão
Center for Judiciary Studies, Ministry of Justice, Lisbon, Portugal

INTRODUCTION

The purpose of this chapter is to report on the findings of a research project carried out in 1985 and 1986 by the research unit of the Centro de Estudos Judiciários (Training School for Judges and Public Attorneys). The research concerned maltreated and neglected children.

The research was based on a questionnaire addressed by mail to priests and local authorities in a sample composed of 500 communities.

The research focused mainly on children who were maltreated or neglected *by their own families.* It tried to determine the most current kinds of maltreatment and neglect as well as some of the more evident characteristics both of the families where such problems exist and of the children who are victimized.

The research also dealt with children who beg in the streets in order to determine their numbers and to find out the reactions of people witnessing these situations.

Last, the questionnaire included some questions addressing what people felt about physical punishment of children.

CHILD PROTECTION IN PORTUGAL AND RELATED RESEARCH

The problem of child victims of abuse or serious neglect is a cause for worry among the different services and agencies dealing with children. Concern for the situation of such children is particularly felt by juvenile courts, as it is their legal responsibility to protect them (Act No. 314, October 27, 1978).

Juvenile courts have a long tradition in Portugal. They were set up in 1911 by the Children's Welfare Act. The fact that Portuguese legislation helped pioneer the institution of juvenile courts is a matter of great pride to us.

Eliana Gersão is the director of the research unit of the Center for Judiciary Studies in Lisbon. Previously, she was the director of the observation center for juvenile offenders in Coimbra. She studied law at the University of Coimbra, has earned several fellowships for study abroad, and has taken part in several important international conferences. She has published extensively, particularly in the area of juvenile delinquency.

The Children's Welfare Act entrusted to juvenile courts intervention in cases of children and juveniles up to the age of 18 who are abused, abandoned, or in need of care, as well as cases of children up to the age of 16 who are maladjusted or delinquent.[1]

Juvenile courts have exercised this dual function up to the present. Traditionally these courts have intervened mostly in cases of juvenile delinquents or of children who might be living on the fringe of society.[2] However, their actions in defense of abused or seriously neglected children have intensified in recent years. This development does not necessarily mean that such cases are becoming more frequent. Rather, there is greater awareness of the problem on the part of the courts and of the services dealing with children and the public in general. Thus, many situations that some years ago were ignored or looked on with indifference are now presented to juvenile courts.

The training school for judges and public prosecutors has been especially dynamic in the field of protection of maltreated or neglected children. The work of its research unit (Gabinete de Estudos Jurídico-Sociais) has been particularly relevant in this area.

Among several other activities, a research project carried out in 1985 and 1986 to provide the first global image of the country's reality stands out.[3] This research is not only the most comprehensive study undertaken in Portugal on this matter so far but also one of the first empirical investigations in the field of victimology in the country. It was based on a questionnaire sent by mail to priests and authorities responsible for *freguesias* (the smallest administrative units), in a sample of 500 parishes.[4] It mostly covered child victims of abuse or serious neglect inside the family. Child begging and serious accidents suffered by children were also taken into account.

First, the research attempted to uncover the most common types of abuse and neglect. Then it tried to find out the characteristics most often associated with families where such problems occur and the characteristics most often associated with the children involved.

RESEARCH RESULTS

A quarter of the parishes which answered the questionnaire stated that there were abused children in their area. A third of those parishes confirmed the existence of seriously neglected children. Abused or neglected children were reported to exist in 580 families. If we extrapolate this number for the country as a whole, we obtain a total of 18,141 child-abusing families, or 62 such families

[1]Regarding juvenile delinquents under 16, the Children's Welfare Act provides for the exclusive application of welfare measures, forbidding the imposition of penalties. This principle, which has been in force in Portugal ever since 1911, has never been subject to any restriction. Nor, since 1911, have children under 16 been able to be remanded in prison.

[2]Such cases mainly involve vagrancy, begging, prostitution, and alcohol abuse. Today, according to the Penal Code (in force since 1983), such cases are not in principle considered crimes where adults are concerned.

[3]This research was done by Fausto Amaro and is published. See Fausto Amaro, Crianças maltratadas, negligenciadas ou praticando a mendicidade [Children abused and neglected or reduced to begging], *Cadernos do CEJ*, Lisboa, 1986.

[4]Other research techniques would involve more expensive means than those available.

per 10,000. In 3,862 families (13.2 per 10,000), physical maltreatment occurred; in the remaining ones, psychological abuse or failure to provide adequate care took place.

The most frequent types of abuse were beatings (16.3%)[5] and want of the most basic care: The child was dirty, in rags, or inadequately clothed (52.8%); was not properly fed (33.1%); was not looked after when ill (20.7%); or was not given sufficient attention (19.7%). A significant number of cases of psychological abuse, such as constant scolding (39.3%), lack of love (38.2%), and interdiction of playing (11.2%), were mentioned. The respondents also noted cases of children not sent to school (15.2%) or compelled to do excessive or dangerous work for their age (respectively 10.1% and 7.9%). Cases were also pointed out of children locked up and confined (5.1%) and even tied up (1.1%).

A relationship seems to exist between child abuse and the predominance of cultural patterns which accept physical punishment as a legitimate educational tool. The questionnaire also included some questions on attitudes in order to find out the feeling of the population toward corporal punishment of children. The opinion that "parents have the right to inflict corporal punishment on their children as long as they don't overdo it" was prevalent in the districts where higher rates of abuse were reported. Lower rates of abuse were found in the districts where more critical attitudes were expressed toward corporal punishment, the predominant opinion being that "parents overdo it when they beat their children, as there are other ways of educating them."

As to the characteristics of families that abused or neglected their children, the emerging "portrait" points to low cultural and financial status as typical. In more than 50% of the cases, the parents were illiterate or had not finished primary school. Their jobs were almost invariably included in the less qualified groups.[6] The households were large (with three or more children) and the parents were quite old (the father was over 50 in 27.8% of the cases). It was also common to find alcoholism (84.5%),[7] violence or aggression (55.7%), and mental retardation or illness of at least one of the parents (30.9%). It was also frequently the case that these families were marginalized or isolated ("those who get on with nobody") (25.7%).

The picture of family disorganization presented by the respondents fits with their opinions about why parents mistreat or neglect their children. They mentioned primarily lack of education, culture, or ability to educate on the parents' side (22.4%). Financial difficulties were considered a determining factor of such behavior only by 9.5% of those interviewed.

With regard to the personal characteristics of the children, it was found that abuse and neglect fell mostly on children 6 to 14 years of age (75%). In this age group, the victims were mostly boys (57.8%), contrary to the case of younger children (up to 6 years of age), where girls predominated (67.7%).[7]

[5]Percentages are based on the total number of children reported as being subject to abuse or neglect.

[6]These results can be explained by the types of abuse to which the respondents were more sensitive (situations of lack of basic care). But there are other explanations for this, which will be mentioned later.

[7]The percentage are calculated in relation to the total number of families reported to abuse or neglect the children under their care.

The research also covered child begging. It aimed quite simply at obtaining some information on the size of the problem and on public attitudes about it. Although child begging was not considered to exist in the majority of the parishes which answered the questionnaire, some of them (5%) acknowledged its existence. Cases of begging usually seem to involve gypsy children, many of them nomads.

Tolerance was the prevailing attitude in the face of such situations. The respondents stated that in their area people gave alms to children whenever they could. This attitude is in agreement with the explanation they gave for the cases of child begging they knew about. Basically they think children beg for economic reasons.

Finally, the research covered the question of serious accidents involving children. This seems to be a problem of quite worrying dimensions. Indeed, almost all the parishes which answered the questionnaire confirmed the existence of serious accidents in which children were victims. These accidents often involved children being run over (34.8%) and poisoned or intoxicated (9.6%). The remaining 55.8% were falls, burns, and drownings. Ten percent of the accidents were fatal.

LIMITATIONS OF THE RESEARCH

First of all, we are aware that concepts such as abuse and neglect are fluid (except in extreme cases, where abuse or neglect is quite blatant and unequivocal). There is a great deal of subjectivity in the assessment of cases of this nature, which depends on, among other factors, opinions about the position and rights of children in today's world and about how they should be reared. Thus, the data collected have to be interpreted not so much as reflecting reality but as corresponding to the situation as felt by those questioned.

We know as well that the cases reported to us do not constitute more than a small part of the reality, the tip of the iceberg, one might say. The majority of the incidents take place in the privacy of family life and are not known outside. This is especially true of abuse, particularly when there are no visible marks on the body or when the victim, due to his or her age or other special reasons (e.g., mental retardation), does not leave the family circle or is unable to complain.

We must not be deceived by the fact that the cases reported came invariably from destitute families of the lowest social and economic strata. We know that there are also abused or neglected children in more privileged families. Nevertheless, abuse and neglect occur, as a rule, in more subtle ways and are therefore more difficult to discover. Besides, privileged families, due to their social position, are not in principle the objects of suspicion and consequently of attention on the part of the respondents.

CONTRIBUTIONS AND IMPACT OF THE RESEARCH

In spite of its limitations, the research project had a great impact in the country. Representatives of the several services and agencies dealing with children were present at a meeting in which the results of the research were disclosed. In turn, the data collected were widely publicized by the media. Lately the Centro de Estudos Judiciários has been asked to participate in meetings on this subject in different parts of the country. These meetings have mainly brought together judges, public prosecutors, pediatricians, and social workers who have tried to utilize their various skills in order to achieve quick, efficient, and adequate means of protection for victimized children.

Thus, in a significant way, this research contributed to ending the silence and indifference that until then surrounded the situation of these children. Even if there is no other benefit, this simple fact more than justifies the work put into it.

14

Participants in the United States Child Care Industry as Victims of the Fear of Crime

Vergil L. Williams
Department of Criminal Justice, University of Alabama, Tuscaloosa

Velma A. Williams
Child Development Associate Training Program, University of Alabama, Tuscaloosa

This paper deals with the fear of crime. More precisely, it deals with public reaction to the fear of crime. Given the technology of modern media, crimes that are abhorrent or just unusual become widely known to the general public. Ordinarily, nothing much comes of such wholesale reporting of crimes that interest the public. But, on occasion, one finds an unexpected public reaction to the news of a crime or series of crimes.

The crime or crimes at issue here involve reports of sexual abuse of young children attending preschool or day-care programs. Staff members of the centers were arrested and charged. Publicity was enormous, as is documented below. The 1984 McMartin case in California became a focal point, but other reports of child abuse by day-care providers surfaced. In retrospect, it does not appear

Vergil Williams presented his first paper on victimology at the First International Symposium on Victimology in Jerusalem, Israel, in 1973. He has followed developments in the field since that time. He served as chairman of the Department of Criminal Justice at the University of Alabama from 1977 to 1987, where he currently holds the rank of professor. His contributions to the criminal justice literature include three books: *Introduction to Criminal Justice* (1982), *Dictionary of American Penology* (1979), and *Convicts, Codes and Contraband* (1974). He has published articles in *Crime and Delinquency, Journal of Criminal Justice, Corrections Today, Journal of Police Science and Administration*, and other journals in the field.

Velma Williams has been involved professionally in early childhood education programs since she received an MS in human development from the University of Alabama in 1981. Currently, she is a consultant in the Child Development Associate Training Program at the University of Alabama in Tuscaloosa. In that capacity, she trains Head Start teachers and other caregivers in preschool programs for a Child Development Associate credential. Additionally, she is the director of an afterschool program for elementary school children. She has presented papers on child development issues at international conferences in London, Munich, Paris, and Rome.

that there was a crime wave or any more child molestation than normally goes on in so large a nation as the United States.

The large-scale publicity concerning the McMartin case and related incidents probably resulted from a combination of factors. People are concerned about the welfare of young children in general. In particular, people are protective of young children in matters of a sexual nature. A cultural value is to preserve the sexual innocence of children in our society for as long as possible. Further, there is nearly always great public indignation when those entrusted with the care of our children violate that trust. These factors make stories about possible criminal conduct of child care workers eminently newsworthy.

The publicity about the McMartin case yielded an unexpected crisis in the child care industry. Insurance companies decided that child care was a high-risk enterprise. Consequently, child care providers suddenly found that (1) their liability insurance was cancelled, (2) they could not renew their policy when it expired, or (3) renewal was possible only at vastly more expensive rates. Yet subsequent investigations and Congressional hearings did not turn up any evidence that would justify such a monumental reaction from insurers. Liability insurance claims filed by child care providers are few and tend to involve only small sums paid out for routine mishaps such as playground accidents. No one could document that any liability insurance claim has ever been filed due to a child care worker physically or sexually abusing a child entrusted to his or her care. In short, the insurance industry's sudden decision to classify child care as high risk appeared to be an irrational response to fear of a particular type of crime. Media publicity evidently played a key role in these events but is not the only factor in the insurer's reaction, as will be demonstrated.

The result of the insurance industry's reaction to the McMartin case was clearly to make child care both harder to obtain and more expensive for users. Some child care providers could pass these higher costs on to their customers (depending on the elasticity of demand in their local markets). Others could not and were forced out of business.

This paper is not about the victimization of children. Many other studies address that issue. It is argued here that a relatively small amount of crime has triggered a societal response that raised the cost of an essential service for thousands of families. It is argued that these cost increases are unjustified by reality. They were not caused by the existence of crime but by the irrational fear of crime. This paper explores the mechanisms by which these events occurred and the concept of mass victimization that can be attributed to the fear of crime. It attempts to explain the exact mode by which a large segment of the public became victimized by the fear of crime.

BACKGROUND: THE EVENTS TRIGGERING THE FEAR OF CRIME

In November 1985, the National Association for the Education of Young Children (NAEYC) reported that its headquarters in Washington, DC, was receiving some 200 calls per week from child care centers throughout the country. Examples of the telephone comments from child care givers are as follows (Liability Insurance Update, 1985, p. 53):

"I've never had an insurance claim, but my policy was cancelled."
"I'm calling everywhere for insurance, but in the meantime I need proof of a policy to renew my lease."
"I've been setting aside funds for the Center Accreditation Project, but now I need to use them to cover my increased insurance premiums."
"I can't believe I have to choose between closing my program or operating without insurance."
"This is a nightmare!"

The informal comments quoted above capture the sense of crisis that was underway in the child care industry throughout the United States. The NAEYC was prompted to do an empirical study on the magnitude of the crisis. Their formal findings are summarized in the following section. Before reviewing that material, it is necessary to review some of the events that triggered the liability insurance crisis.

The McMartin Preschool case in Los Angeles began early in 1984, when the founder of the preschool program and several teachers were charged with sexual molestation of young children in their care. As this is being written, California has embarked on a trial of Peggy McMartin Buckey, age 60, and her son Raymond, age 28, for 99 counts of sexual molestation of children. Charges against the school's founder and four former teachers have been dropped due to lack of evidence. The five have filed a $50 million defamation and negligence suit (Lacayo, 1987).

Publicity about the McMartin case was comprehensive and on a national scale, and it seemed to stimulate reporting on other accusations of child abuse. The *Los Angeles Times* reported the first events of an accusation of child abuse by a former employee in the McMartin case on February 3, 1984. An inspection of a newspaper index is revealing. In 1983, before the McMartin case, the *Los Angeles Times* had a total of 54 entries on child abuse. In 1984, that category of entries jumped to 220 (many front page stories), and it was 209 in 1985. The publicity was not limited to California. Index examination reveals that the *Washington Post* had only 15 entries on child molesting in 1983 but had 105 entries in 1984 and 103 in 1985. The *Christian Science Monitor* had 3 entries on the topic in 1983. There were 23 entries in 1984 and 18 entires in 1985. The *New Orleans Times-Picayune* had 25 child abuse entries in 1983. In 1984, there were 88 entries, followed by 74 entries in 1985.

Several rational explanations suggest themselves for the increase in the reports of child abuse or molesting. Possibilities include the following: (1) There was a sudden and dramatic increase in child abuse; (2) the amount of child abuse had been underreported, but the publicity surrounding the McMartin case opened the floodgates for more honest reporting; (3) the media perceived a lurid interest in the phenomenon and began to report it more prominently and consistently than before; (4) there was an increased determination on the part of authorities to unearth child abuse; and (5) events have resulted in a spate of false charges against innocent people. It is beyond the scope of this study to render judgment as to which of the above, if indeed any, explanations are accurate. It is sufficient for our purposes to note that publicity on child abuse increased noticeably following the McMartin case. For example, by 1985, the more perceptive began to comment publicly about the unusual amount of publicity surrounding the social problem of child abuse. A professor of political science on the editorial advisory board of *The Progressive* published an article entitled "Invasion of the Child Savers: How We Succumb to Hype and Hysteria," in which she raises serious questions about the accuracy of media reports on child abuse (Elshtain, 1985).

An attentive audience for the hype and hysteria noted by Professor Elshtain (1985) appears to be the insurance industry. As demonstrated in the following section, that industry seems to have set rates based on the publicity about child abuse rather than by use of traditional actuarial techniques.

REACTION OF INSURANCE INDUSTRY TO CHILD ABUSE PUBLICITY

There are two key types of evidence to document that there is a liability insurance crisis for the child care industry in the latter part of the 1980s. The NAEYC undertook a national survey to gather data and to confirm whether there actually was a crisis. The other confirmation of the crisis situation comes from hearings held by the U.S. Congress. The latter confirms basic information gathered by the former. Some of the findings of the NAEYC Child Care Liability Insurance Survey (1986) are discussed in this section.

It was in November 1985 that NAEYC surveyed a random national sample of 1,000 child care providers. The purpose of the survey instrument was to assess recent changes in the availability, affordability, and coverage that these child care providers had experienced with their liability insurance (NAEYC, 1986). The 269 returns—out of 1,000 survey instruments—constituted a 27% return rate. Out of the 50 states, returns were received from 43 states. A goodly portion of day-care for young children is provided by commercial child care centers. There were 219 of these centers that responded to the survey. Other respondents included 24 family day-care homes and a small number of Head Start programs (NAEYC, 1986).

The survey returns did verify that a liability insurance crisis among child care providers did develop following the McMartin case and the increase in publicity. In the year preceding the NAEYC survey, about two-thirds of family day-care homes and more than one-third of child care centers experienced either cancellation or nonrenewal of their liability insurance. The rate for Head Start programs was 27%. Some 60% of the programs had experienced a rate increase the previous year (NAEYC, 1986).

The magnitude of the rate increases is interesting. Of the businesses reporting increases, half had their rates doubled. Thirty-eight percent of family day-care homes experienced at least a tripling of their rates. A small number reported rate increases exceeding 500%. Additionally, the more expensive liability insurance that is available is more narrow in coverage. It is now common for liability policies to specifically exclude court costs arising from child abuse allegations (NAEYC, 1986). This exclusion provides an important piece of evidence in our attempt to link the insurance industry behavior to the fear of crime.

Insurance companies normally have an actuary whose job it is to calculate rates and risks and to establish premiums based on claim history and other tangible evidence. One must ask whether the circumstances justified the insurance industry behavior that created the child care liability insurance crisis. The available evidence does not support the claim that there was a sudden discovery of unprofitability and high risks, despite statements by insurance industry officials in Congressional hearings. U.S. Representatives George Miller and James Florio held hearings on the liability insurance crisis. Insurance officials testifying could not produce evidence of major losses due to insuring child care providers (NAEYC, 1986).

The NAEYC survey (1986) did not uncover anything in the claims history of care providers to justify the insurance crisis. Nine out of 10 child care programs have never filed any kind of claim against their liability insurance. Of those that have filed claims, 81% reported that total claims from the inception of their business were less than $500. The largest claim reported was one for $15,000. These claims were under general liability coverage for such things as minor accidents or broken equipment. Allegations of child abuse and subsequent claims would be covered under professional liability insurance. No such claims were made or paid out in the year covered by the survey. One of the most interesting facts unearthed by the survey was a comparison of total claims paid by the insurance companies with total liability insurance premiums paid by the child care providers. Amounts totaling less than 3% of the premiums were paid out by insurance companies (NAEYC, 1986).

This section has outlined the basic nature of the liability insurance crisis that developed following significant media activity on the McMartin Preschool case and similar allegations of child abuse or molestation. It is argued that the child care industry and the users of child day-care have become victims of crime in a special way. The following section explores the relationship between anticipation of crime and public reaction.

THE MEDIA AND THE FEAR OF CRIME

There are studies of the fear of crime and its relationship to news reporting. As early as 1951, sociologists were studying media reports of crime and their impact on people's perception of crime (Davis, 1951). Black and Long (1973) used econometrics to establish that there is a link between reported crime levels and subjective evaluations of potential victimization— that people do develop more fear of crime when they hear (or read) about crimes being committed. Heath (1984) argues convincingly that stories about crime reported locally cause more fear of crime and anticipation of victimization than crimes reported in the national press that occurred in some distant place. That is, a resident of Little Rock, Arkansas, may not be unduly disturbed to read about the McMartin Preschool case in *The Christian Science Monitor*. However, that same reader would react differently to a report in the local paper concerning a similar crime in Little Rock.

The work of another researcher confirms and extends Heath's work. In doing a comparison between the state of Texas and the state of Tennessee, Thomas Dull (1983) sought to investigate whether there is a positive relationship between the official incidence of crime as reported in the media and people's perceived likelihood of victimization. The idea was to compare perception of crime in a high-crime state (Texas) to that in a low-crime state (Tennessee). Dull used the concept of anticipatory victimization wherein a person feels likely to become a victim of a specific crime within a year. He concluded that reports of high-crime rates in the community did increase fear of crime. Looking at the work of Heath and Dull, it appears that the perception of local crime can be statewide.

Other researchers have detected social reaction related to media publicity on crime. Jones (1976) did a study on the amount of crime presented in newspapers compared with the amount reported in the Uniform Crime Reports. A number of people have examined the impact of newspaper crime reporting on perceptions and fear of crime (Baker, Nienstedt, Everett, & McCleary, 1983; Davis, 1951; Gordon & Heath, 1981).

Reviewing the literature on reporting of crime makes it clear that there is widespread agreement among researchers that comprehensive reporting of crime can increase the fear of crime and trigger societal reactions unsuited to the immediate danger. The small sample of such literature offered in the preceding paragraphs leads the authors to believe that the insurance industry officials reacted inappropriately to the publicity about the McMartin Preschool case. Their fear of crime in this area meant possible loss of profits, and they moved to avoid that without a rational assessment of actual risk. That move created a crisis in the child day-care industry and made thousands victims of an irrational fear of crime.

The next section further explores the concept of child care users and providers as victims. Before proceeding, the authors wish to point out that we do not blame the media for the victimization under discussion. In our view, the media are doing their job in reporting that which is newsworthy. We agree with Heath's view: "Fear is not attributable to sensationalistic reporting style on the part of the newspaper, but rather to the sensationalism intrinsic to the crime itself" (1984, p. 275). Although it is not our objective to affix blame, the frequent references to the publicity may give the reader the impression that we are blaming the press. This is not our intention.

A CONCEPT OF MASS VICTIMIZATION THROUGH FEAR OF CRIME

Has anyone suffered because of the day-care liability insurance crisis? If so, who are the victims? If there are victims, in what sense are they victimized? This section addresses those questions. Earlier sections have argued that there is a positive relationship between events (primarily the McMartin Preschool case) that triggered large-scale media publicity and, in turn, created a fear of crime among insurance industry officials to the point of causing them to make an irrational response.

If liability insurance premiums increase drastically for child care providers, what are the consequences? The answer to that question depends on the market structure of the child care industry or, more specifically, on the elasticity of demand for the service in a particular geographic area. If a child care provider is providing services in a community without much competition, it may be possible to shift most or all of the increased costs to the users of the service in order for the providers to maintain a reasonable profit margin (inelastic demand). If there are a number of child care providers in a community and the situation is highly competitive, it may not be possible for the provider to pass along the costs (elastic demand). In the latter circumstances, the provider must absorb the costs. This might then destroy the profit margin and force the provider to close up business in order to avoid losses. To further complicate the analysis, some child care providers serve poor working mothers under Head Start and Title XX programs that provide government subsidies. These programs prohibit increasing fees for the users. A final complicating factor is that child care providers have the option of daring to operate without liability insurance. The influence of this latter factor is lessened due to a circumstance noted by the NAEYC (1986), namely that child care licensing offices in 24 states require licensed centers to maintain liability insurance. We can only speculate that child care providers who are not required by state law to have liability insurance would at least feel some sense of deprivation or anxiety if they tried to operate without liability insurance.

To assess elasticity of demand for any product or service is a lengthy and complex task. One can, however, gain some clues from the NAEYC survey (1986). In response to the crisis, most child care programs (95%) plan to remain in business. This indicates that the child care providers estimate that they can pass on all or part of the increased costs to users and that the part of the increased costs that cannot be passed on in higher fees can be made up by cutting costs to produce a lower quality service. Head Start programs, subject to governmental regulations, have less choice, since they cannot increase their rates. Some 11% cite closing as a likely response. The others must cut back on the quality of service to survive. Almost 50% of the larger child care centers (providing services for the majority of users) and 21% of the smaller ones planned to raise parent fees. Few programs involved in the survey indicated a willingness to remain in business without liability insurance (5% of child care centers, no Head Start programs, and 25% of family day-care programs).

In summary, it safely can be said that child care providers in the United States perceive at least a fair degree of inelasticity of demand for their services. They believe that they can continue in business by passing along a part of the cost of increased liability insurance premiums to customers and that they can further protect their profit margin by reducing costs and quality of service. As a practical matter, one might surmise that most of the cost of increased liability insurance premiums will be passed on to users of child day-care. If one accepts that premise, the social injustice question then evolves about the users of child day-care services. Who are they?

Since a considerable portion of the increased liability insurance premium for child day-care apparently can be passed along to users, it is apparent that it is the users who are bearing the burden of the increased costs. In essence, more income is being transferred from the users of child care services to the profit margins of insurance companies. Does this involuntary transfer of wealth constitute social injustice? The answer to this question depends on who uses the child care services—whether the users are essentially the same social class as the stockholders of the insurance companies. One is aware that investors or stockholders are among the most economically privileged of our society, and the most financially secure often are older Americans whose children are grown or nearly so. One would suppose, at least at first blush, that an involuntary transfer of income from younger (less affluent) Americans to older (more financially secure) Americans is the result of the child day-care liability insurance crisis. If so, there is a dimension of social injustice occurring.

Reasonably good answers are available concerning the demography of day-care users. Ruopp, Travers, Glantz, and Coelen (1979) published a report of a national study of day-care. The U.S. Department of Health and Human Services (Calhoun, Grotberg, & Rackley, 1980) also made available the results of a comprehensive study at about the same time. These formal studies are a bit out of date, but informal reports are available to update these academic pieces (e.g., Wallis, 1987).

By 1978, it was reported that 52% of America's families with children under 13 had a work-related need for some type of child day-care. In other words, more than half of all mothers of young children were in the work force. This figure is up from 20% in 1950 (Rouopp et al., 1979). Currently, it is close to 60% (Wallis, 1987). As for determining the socioeconomic class of working mothers of young children, researchers report that labor force participation is highest among single-parent families. Among two-parent families, the labor force participation of mothers is greater in situations where the father's income is low (Rouopp et al., 1979). Currently, 70% of working mothers claim to be in the work force because of economic necessity (Wallis, 1987).

Another way of looking at family expenditures on day-care for young children is as a proportion of total family budget. In 1975, if a family had to purchase day-care services for even one child, that expenditure would be the fourth largest item in the family budget after food, housing, and taxes (Rouopp et al., 1979).

Without belaboring the point, authors would like to point out that demographic data indicate that in the majority of cases an American family that purchases child day-care does so because it is essential to the family budget that the mother of the family's young children be in the labor force. Thus, the majority of those in need of child care services are among those who are struggling for survival or at least struggling for a solid footing in the American middle class. Few of these aspirants have succeeded to the point of becoming investors in American corporations such as insurance companies. Of course, a few have some dollars in retirement funds that invest in a multitude of corporations, but it is not reasonable to believe that most child care users share in the rewards of insurance industry profits. From our research, we conclude that an involuntary transfer of income from the relatively poor to the relatively prosperous is occurring because of the child care industry liability insurance crisis. In short, the crisis resulting from the fear of crime has been costly to American society in that it has created a new class of victims. The victimization manifests itself in terms of increased costs of child day-care for Americans struggling to achieve or maintain middle-class status. There is victimization that results from irrational public responses to media reports of a particular type of crime.

We briefly survey a media-driven societal response to fear of a particular type of crime that resulted in a new form of social injustice. The subsequent liability insurance crisis following extensive but inaccurate reporting on massive amounts of child abuse by child care providers has adversely impacted the lives of millions of Americans, both economically and psychologically. All nations with a free press are vulnerable to the same type of unexpected development. The parameters of this problem are deserving of additional study.

BIBLIOGRAPHY

Baker, M. H., Nienstedt, B. C., Everett, R. S., & McCleary, R. (1983). The impact of a crime wave: Perceptions, fear and confidence in the police. *Law and Society Review*, *17*, 319–335.

Block, M. K., & Long, G. L. (1973). Subjective probability of victimization and crime levels: An econometric approach. *Criminology*, *11*, 87–93.

Calhoun, J. A., Grotberg, E. H., & Rackley, W. R. (1980). *The status of children, youth, and families—1979.* Washington, D.C.: U.S. Department of Health and Human Services.

Davis, T. R. (1951). Crime news in Colorado newspapers. *American Journal of Sociology*, *57*, 325–330.

Dull, T. R. (1983). A two Southern state comparison between UCR crime rates and the anticipation of victimization. *Southern Journal of Criminal Justice*, *8*, 16–32.

Elshtain, J. B. (1985). Invasion of the child savers: How we succumb to hype and hysteria. *The Progressive*, *49*, 23–26.

Gordon, M. T., & Heath, L. (1981). The news business, crime, and fear. In D. Lewis (Ed.), *Reactions to crime* (pp. 227–250). Beverly Hills, CA: Sage.

Heath, L. (1984). Impact of newspaper crime reports on fear of crime: Multimethodological investigation. *Journal of Personality and Social Psychology*, *47*, 263–276.

Jones, E. T. (1976). The press as metropolitan monitor. *Public Opinion Quarterly*, *40*, 239–244.

Lacayo, R. (1987, May 11). Sexual abuse or abuse of justice? *Time*, p. 49.

National Association for the Education of Young Children. (1985). Public policy report: Liability insurance update. *Young Children*, *41*, 53–55.

National Association for the Education of Young Children. (1986). *Final report of the child care liability insurance survey*. Mimeographed.

Rouopp, R., Travers, J., Glantz, F., & Coelen, C. (1979). *Children at the center: Summary findings and their implications*. Cambridge, MA: Abt Books.

Wallis, C. (1987, June 22). The child-care dilemma. *Time*, pp. 54–60.

V

SEXUAL VICTIMIZATION AND OFFENSES

15

Rape Law Reform in Canada: Evaluating Impact

Patricia Begin
Research Branch, Library of Parliament, Ottawa, Ontario, Canada

INTRODUCTION

On August 4, 1982, Bill C-127, An Act to Amend the Criminal Code in Relation to Sexual Offences and Other Offences Against the Person, was passed by the House of Commons in Canada. On January 4, 1983, it became Canadian law. The sexual assault provisions of Bill C-127 made fundamental amendments to the *Criminal Code* with respect to the substantive, procedural, and evidentiary aspects of Canada's rape and indecent assault laws.

Bill C-127 followed more than a decade of criticism and lobbying by women's groups and other interest groups advocating reform in policy and in law with respect to rape in Canada. Critics in a number of common law jurisdictions, including Canada, were advancing two interdependent analytical frameworks for the reexamination and reform of rape laws. One viewed rape as a crime of violence—an abuse of power—and not as a crime of uncontrollable sexual passion perpetrated by a "sick" stranger (Clark and Lewis, 1977a, pp. 133–146; Smart & Smart, 1978, pp. 91–93; Box, 1983, p. 137). The other viewed the rules of law related to evidence and procedure in rape trials as practices which harassed and degraded victims and denied to women the right to individual and sexual autonomy and equal rights under the law (Edwards, 1981).

It was argued by many critics that the rape law and societal perceptions of rape complainants influenced the behavior of victims and criminal justice system practitioners. That is, empirical evidence suggested that the law itself was a factor in victims' reluctance to report, in the police tendency to treat complaints as fabrications, and in the failure to prosecute and to convict.

Respecting victim reluctance to officially report sexual attacks, the "dark figure" of sexual assault—that is, the relatively large difference between the number of sexual assaults experienced by victims and the number reported to

Patricia Begin was employed as Research Criminologist in the Criminal Law Unit, Policy, Programs and Research Branch, Department of Justice Canada. She holds a master's degree in sociology from Carleton University, Ottawa, Ontario. Ms. Begin's main areas of research responsibility with the Department of Justice included sexual assault, child sexual abuse, and family violence. Sociolegal research has been planned, designed, and carried out in these substantive areas to facilitate the development of criminal law policy and to evaluate its impact.

The views expressed herein are those of the author and do not necessarily represent the views or policies of the Department of Justice of Canada.

police—has been examined in victimization surveys conducted in both Canada and the United States (Solicitor General of Canada, 1985; Committee Sexual Offences Against Children and Youth, 1984; Bureau of Justice Statistics, 1985). In 1982, in Canada, the Ministry of the Solicitor General conducted a victimization survey in seven major urban centers that involved more than 61,000 telephone interviews. Respondents were asked to report on incidents which had occurred between January 1 and December 31, 1981. The survey estimated approximately 17,300 sexual assault incidents, of which about 90% involved female victims (sexual assault included rape, attempted rape, molesting, or attempted molestation). Fewer than 40% of the female sexual assault victims reported their victimization to the police (Solicitor General of Canada, 1985, pp. 2–3). Of those victims who failed to report their victimization, 44% articulated a concern about the reaction and attitudes of the police and courts toward this type of incident (Solicitor General of Canada, 1985, p. 4).

In addition to the relatively low rate of victim reporting, research also showed that the processing of rape complaints through the criminal justice system involved a progressive process of elimination. Official discretion was operative at each successive stage. For the year 1982, of the number of rapes "reported or known" to the police, approximately 31% were recorded by police as "unfounded." By way of comparison, in that same year, 4% of all assault complaints were recorded as unfounded (Statistics Canada, 1983). The "unfounding" of a complaint of rape did not necessarily mean that a rape had not occurred. Stanley (1984) summarizes complainant attributes identified in research on rape in Toronto and Vancouver that had influenced the filtering of rape complaints and the classification of cases as founded or unfounded.

> *The major factor in the judgement made to proceed with a case or to terminate investigation was . . . the character of the reporting victim. If the victim was drunk when she was first interviewed by the police, if she was a runaway teenager who did not live at home and was unemployed, if she was between the ages of thirty and forty years of age and separated, divorced, or living "idle," unemployed or on welfare, or receiving psychiatric care, generally the police would not pursue the case. Further, if the woman was not hysterical when she reported the crime, or if she waited too long to report the crime, or if she knew the offender, or if she voluntarily accompanied the offender to his residence, or accepted a ride in his car, it was likely that the police would not designate the case as "founded."* (pp. 38–39)

Further, if a complaint of rape was determined to be founded by police, the likelihood of an alleged offender being charged, sent to trial, and convicted was minimal.

Unfortunately, there is a dearth of contemporary information in Canada on convictions and sentencing patterns. The limited and dated information to draw upon indicates that in 1971 there were 2,107 reported rapes in Canada. Of these reported rapes, 1,230 were classified as founded by the police. Yet only 119 persons were charged and only 65 of the accused were convicted of rape or a lesser charge. Thus, 54.7% of those charged with rape were convicted of some offense, whereas in the same year the overall conviction rate for criminal charges was 86% (Kinnon, 1981, p. 34).

Legally, a convicted rapist could be sentenced to life imprisonment. Canadian sentencing data derived from six correctional jurisdictions reveal that in 1982, of those convicted of rape and attempted rape who were admitted to penitentiaries with sentences of 2 years or more, 69% were sentenced to between 2 and 5 years (Hahn, 1983, p. 40). This is one of the empirical "facts" that motivated the call for reform. What were regarded as in need of reform included the definition of rape, the groups protected by the law, the sentence structure, and the evidentiary and procedural rules that governed rape trials. These features of the rape law were seen as influencing the rate of reporting rape victimizations, the police founding rate, the outcomes of prosecutions, and sentences.

The remainder of this paper will discuss these matters in the following way. The next section discusses each feature of the rape law that critics had struggled to reform. Following this discussion is an overview of the law reform process and a description of the features of the new law. The final sections of the paper lay out the program of research to evaluate the rape law reform in Canada. Included is a discussion on considerations associated with an impact study of criminal law reform.

HISTORICAL CONTEXT AND THE LEGAL ISSUES

Definition, Groups Protected, and Sentences

Until January 1983, four criteria set by statute determined whether an act of rape had occurred: (1) The act had to involve sexual intercourse, that is, penetration; (2) the act had to be committed by a man with a woman; (3) the act had to occur without her consent unless the consent was extorted by threats or fear of bodily harm, was obtained by impersonating her husband, or was obtained by false and fraudulent representations as to the nature and quality of the act; and (4) the act had to occur outside the bounds of marriage (*Criminal Code*, R.S.C. 1970, c.C-34, s.143). Each of the features of the rape law was criticized for the narrow focus on what rape is, who can be raped, and who is culpable.

First, given the gender-specific character of rape, a sexual attack by a man against a man, a woman against a woman, or a woman against a man were not offenses encompassed by the rape provisions of the *Criminal Code*. It was acknowledged that rape and other sexual offenses are typically committed by men against women and reflective of historically specific, socially structured, unequal power relationships between the sexes. Critics nonetheless assailed the focus of the law on nonconsensual heterosexual sex to the exclusion of other forms of nonconsensual sexual acts and advocated that all persons should receive "equal protection of and responsibility under the law, regardless of sex" (National Association of Women and the Law, 1981, pp. 2–3).

Second, and related to the above, the rape law offered protection only from nonconsensual sexual intercourse. Other forms of sexual violation involving varying degrees of violence and coercion were outside of the scope of protection potentially afforded to victims by the rape law. This critique generated the position that forcible sexual acts were in essence assaultive and could have equally serious consequences for victims. "Non-consensual sexual contacts are first and foremost assaults and should be defined by the nature and degree of violence used rather than the kind of sexual contact" (Kinnon, 1981, p. 39).

Third, the rape law granted a man an absolute right to sexual access to his wife. That is, the codified law stated that husbands could not be charged with raping their wives. Or, to state the obverse, the law did not protect wives from sexual intercourse with their husbands against their will. This feature of the rape law, which fundamentally sanctioned coercive sex between spouses, was condemned by critics as "one of the most serious deficiencies in the . . . offence of rape" (National Association of Women and the Law, 1981, p. 9). Further, it informed the feminist argument that rape laws had historically developed to protect the property interests of men (Clark and Lewis, 1977a, pp. 110–123).

Backhouse and Schoenroth (1983, p. 49) have argued that the spousal exemption in rape law derives from a statement made by Sir Matthew Hale circa 1678:

> *The husband cannot be guilty of rape committed by himself upon his lawful wife, for their mutual matrimonial consent and contract* the wife hath given up her self *in this kind unto her husband which she cannot retract. (Hale, 1800, p. 628; emphasis added)*

Fourth, a man convicted of having sexual intercourse with a woman who was not his wife and without her consent was legally liable to be sentenced to *life imprisonment*. This maximum suggested that, in law, rape was indeed regarded as a very serious offense. The limited statistics reveal that in the main a life sentence was imposed only for rapes categorized as "heinous" or "sadistic," those in which the victim suffered serious physical injury. Research that has been conducted on rape and associated violence has concluded that a small proportion of rapes have had such extreme consequences (Box, 1983, p. 137).

The problem for reform advocates was that the statute law was completely silent on the aggravating circumstances associated with the commission of a rape in determining a sentence. The rape law provided no guidelines or parameters for sentencing, generally resulting in seemingly arbitrary and light sentences. A chasm existed between the legally possible and legal practice. In point of fact, in 1971 in Canada the average sentence for a conviction of rape was estimated to be 4 or 5 years (Clark and Lewis, 1977a, p. 57). Further, it was noted that juries were reluctant to convict accused rapists where the potential sentence did not reflect the severity of the alleged offense (Justice and Legal Affairs, 1982a, p. 7).

Some critics expressed the belief that the rape law and the associated maximum penalty derived from the conception that rape was an infringement of the sexual property of men—a raped woman was damaged goods. Ipso facto, the extreme sanction was not an expression of the idea that rape was a coercive infringement of the right of women to be autonomous and self-determining in their sexual relationships. In her submission to the Justice Committee on Justice and Legal Affairs, Clark articulated this view: "The rape law . . . had nothing whatsoever to do with giving women a right to sexual autonomy" (Justice and Legal Affairs, 1982c, p. 13). This position was buttressed by the defense of consent in rape trials. The defense of mistake about the existence of consent (e.g., the ambiguity of the complainant's behavior resulted in an error by the accused regarding consent) and the debate over its availability in rape trials was subjected to strong public criticism as a result of two high court decisions. In 1980, the Supreme Court of Canada, in *R v. Pappajohn*, ruled that a mistake of fact about consent could be an effective reply to a charge of rape and that the accused's mistaken belief need not be reasonable, only honestly held (Boyle, 1984, pp. 76–77; Watt, 1984, p. 224). The decision did not render reasonableness of mistake irrelevant to the process of determining honesty of belief, but it made clear that it is not required as a matter of law (McDonald, 1982a, p. 4). This Supreme Court of Canada precedent and a British predecessor (a 1975 judgment of the House of Lords in *Morgan* [Smart & Smart, 1978, p. 90]) were condemned by critics as constituting a "rapist's charter." They stirred demands that the belief in consent be based on reasonable grounds and that objective tests apply if the accused claimed to have entertained an honest belief that the victim had consented (Justice and Legal Affairs, 1982e, p. 16). In summary, the law of rape narrowly circumscribed what behavior or acts constituted the offense and to whom protection was extended and responsibility was applied. Also, the sentences imposed were variable and deviated significantly from the legally possible.

Evidentiary and Procedural Rules of Evidence—Rape Pre-1983

The common-law rules of evidence and procedure, when applied in a rape trial, often resulted in the harassment of complainants, rendering the trial process an ordeal for victims and negatively prejudicing their testimony. The rules that informed the conduct of rape trials were the doctrine of recent complaint, the corroboration rule, and the admissibility of evidence related to the reputation and sexual history of the complainant. These rules of law were assailed as indignities that "twice victimized" victims of rape (Kasinsky, 1978, p. 158).

Doctrine of Recent Complaint

At common law, although statements of a person made out of court may be used against that person when he or she is a witness in a judicial proceeding (either as an admission or for the purposes of cross-examination), one is not generally entitled to introduce evidence of statements made by the witness on other occasions for the purpose of confirming the witness's testimony. However, in rape cases a witness's out-of-court statements were admissible as an exception to the rule against self-serving statements. This exception, known as the doctrine of recent complaint, derived from the early common-law requirement that a victim of sexual assault was obliged to raise the "hue and cry" and "was based on a particular fear of false accusations in rape cases and the notion that the 'truly virtuous' woman who was raped would complain at the first reasonable opportunity" (Ruebsaat, 1985, p. 50).

The doctrine of recent complaint denied legitimacy to the quality of rape victims' experiences as victims and their reluctance to complain due to humiliation, confusion, embarrassment, or fear. This led one commentator to argue that "the doctrine of recent complaint was an aberration in the criminal law, for in most criminal cases the silence of the victim was an irrelevant issue" (Stanley, 1985, p. 47).

Corroboration Rule

Generally, at common law, the testimony of a witness to an incident was sufficient, if considered believable by a trier of fact, to establish the fact alleged. The requirement that the witness's testimony be corroborated by independent evidence where the witness was an accomplice in the crime, a child, or a complainant of rape or other sexual offenses constituted an exception to this common-law rule (Watt, 1984, p. 165). The statutory rule that corroboration was mandatorily required in prosecutions for certain offenses was enacted in 1892 and at that time did not relate to the common-law crime of rape. With respect to rape, an associated rule developed through case law which required that the judge caution the jury against accepting the complainant witness's testimony in the absence of independent corroboration (Stanley, 1985, p. 52).

This requirement for corroboration of the testimony of a complaint of rape reflected a dual concern: that an accused should not be convicted on the evidence of a single witness and that women were untrustworthy when it came to making complaints of sexual offenses (Stanley, 1985, p. 49). This statutory rule was repealed in 1976. However, the judicial practice of cautioning the jury continued. While no longer a rule of law, a "rule of practice" developed by which the judge in a rape case was to exercise judicial discretion in order to assist the jury in determining the weight they might give to the uncorroborated evidence of a complainant (Watt, 1984, p. 168; Boyle, 1984, p. 158; McTeer, 1978, p. 141). According to McTeer (1978), the unofficial rule was problematic because the practice of cautioning was "subject only to judicial discretion, but without any substantive guidelines for its exercise and without an explicit technical explanation of the law of corroboration" (p. 142).

Previous Sexual History of the Complainant

Until 1976, common-law rules governed the admissibility in rape trial proceedings of evidence of the complainant's sexual activity with persons other than the accused. The evidence was admissible if relevant to the existence or lack of consent of the complainant to sexual intercourse, the accused's belief in the existence of consent, or the credibility of the complainant (Stanley, 1985, p. 75).

In cases where the complainant's *consent* to intercourse with the accused was at issue, the defense was permitted to cross-examine the complainant about her prior sexual activity with the accused and her general reputation for chastity. This line of questioning was premised on the assumption that if the complainant had consented to sexual activity with the accused in the past, then it was likely that she had consented to this particular act of sexual intercourse as claimed by the accused (McTeer, 1978, p. 143). And where the line of questioning by the defense dealt with the complainant's reputation for chastity, the rationale for it was that a sexually active woman would be more likely to consent to intercourse than a chaste woman. The complainant was compelled to answer questions related to the above issues concerning consent, and her denial or refusal could be challenged or contradicted by evidence introduced by the defense (Watt, 1984, p. 188).

In cases where the complainant's *credibility* was at issue, the defense was permitted to cross-examine the complainant about her prior sexual history with persons other than the accused in an attempt to impeach her credibility. It was believed that if the moral character of the complainant was suspect, then her veracity or reliability was also suspect. In other words, a dubious link was established between the complainant's credibility and her penchant to be chaste—sexual autonomy implied dishonesty (Stanley, 1985, pp. 77–82). Because the credibility of the complainant in a rape case was a collateral issue, she could, however, refuse to answer—or the judge could exercise a discretion to exempt the victim from answering questions relating to her chastity. Further, the denial or refusal of the complainant to answer could not be contradicted (Watt, 1984, p. 188).

This rule of evidence, when applied to rape trials, was considered to prejudice the jury against the complainant[1] and to have the effect of turning the trial into a degrading and devastating ordeal for the complainant.

In an attempt to address the inequities suffered by victims and to encourage them to report rapes, Parliament introduced an amendment to the *Criminal Code*. It stated that no question could be asked as to the sexual conduct of the complainant with persons other than the accused unless reasonable notice had been given (with particulars of the evidence sought to be adduced) and the judge had decided, after holding an *in camera* hearing, that to exclude the evidence would prevent the making of a just determination of an issue of fact in the proceedings, including the credibility of the complainant. However, judicial interpretation of the amendment ultimately granted to the accused powers to cross-examine the complainant about her previous sexual conduct to an extent that went beyond what had previously been allowed. Watt (1984) notes two results reached by the courts that had the effect of undermining the potential positive effect of Section 142.

> *The phrase . . . "a just determination of an issue of fact in the proceedings, including the credibility of the complainant" elevated credibility, a collateral issue at common law, to the status of a material issue under the legislative provision. In consequence, [the complainant] could not refuse to answer questions as to her sexual history as her common law "privilege" was grounded upon the collateral nature of the issue and her denials in answer to the questions put, could be the subject of contradictory proof. Secondly, [the victim] was held to be a competent witness at the* in camera *hearing. (p. 190)*

In commenting on the judiciary's interpretation of Section 142, Boyle (1984) concludes, "It seemed that an amendment touted as an improvement in the position of the complainant had the opposite effect" (p. 135).

The 1976 amendment fell far short of the extensive changes to the rape law and trial process sought by most advocates of reform. They proposed a recon-

[1]LaFree, Reskin, and Visher analyzed trials and conducted interviews with 331 jurors who had heard cases of forcible sexual assault in Marion Country, Indiana, between July 1978 and September 1980. In those cases where the defense was either that the complainant had consented or that no sex had taken place, jurors were influenced by the character of the victim. The research found that eyewitness and other evidence, witnesses for the prosecution, the use of a weapon, and injury to the complainant were *not* determinants of the jurors' beliefs about the guilt or innocence of the accused prior to jury deliberation. Rather, "jurors in the consent–no sex cases were influenced by testimony about a victim's lifestyle. Any evidence of drinking, drug use, or sexual activity outside marriage led jurors to doubt the defendant's guilt, as did any prior acquaintance between the victim and the defendant" (LaFree, Reskin, & Visher, 1985, p. 400). Further, Hans and Vidmar reviewed research that has examined the impact of questioning victims rgarding their sexual life on the prosecution's case. The conclusions drawn from the research confirm the view that evidence of this nature prejudices the jury against the complainant. They write, "The results of these studies on jury decisions in rape cases, taken together, are troubling in some respects. One ubiquitous finding with implications for reform is the prejudicial effect of sexual behaviour of the victim on jury decisions. We have seen that it biases the case regardless of whether it is in any way pertinent to the legal issues" (Hans & Vidmar, 1986, p. 214).

ceptualization of sexual offenses. It was believed that if sexual offenses were defined, processed, and sanctioned as crimes of assault, that is, as interferences with others' physical persons without consent, the sexual life of the victims would no longer be an issue in rape trials and, by logical extension, the focus of liability for the offense would (appropriately) shift to the behavior of the accused. In turn, it was believed, behaviors would be modified. That is, victims would be less reluctant to report sexual attacks and the criminal justice system personnel would be more responsive to victims when victimizations occurred.

> *The adoption by the law, and the implementation in the law, of the view that rape is a form of assault would do much to ensure greater reporting, less impact on the victim and those around her, more successful outcomes, and a more rational basis for sentencing the offender. (Clark, 1977, p. 14)*

On the basis of this conception, it was advocated that a new legal framework of sexual offenses be developed. To achieve this objective, and in light of the substantial limitations that had been associated with the law, legal changes were sought in the definitions of what constitutes a sexual assault, the groups to whom legal protection extends, the sentencing structure, and the evidentiary and procedural rules which govern the legal processing of sexual assaults.

RAPE LAW REFORM IN CANADA

Rape law amendments or new statutes on rape have been enacted over the last decade in almost all states in the United States (Bienen, 1981) and in Australia (Sallman & Chappell, 1982), New Zealand (Barrington, 1984), and Canada.[2] In the early 70s, in Canada, the rape law, the rape trial process, and rape victims began to receive serious attention by feminist and other groups. Three groups—formal and grass roots women's organizations, academics, and government—have been identified as providing the impetus for the reform of rape legislation. These groups are also credited with having provided the intellectual, political, and legal inspiration that shaped the framework of the new sexual assault laws adopted by Parliament in 1982 (Clark, 1977; Andrew et al., 1982; Ellis, 1984).

[2]At the national level in Canada and internationally, the problem of rape has achieved a significant profile, since it has come to be seen by policy makers as part of the problem of violence against women. In 1981, the Canadian Federal-Provincial Task Force on Justice for Victims of Crime was established. In the 1983 report of the task force, *Justice for Victims of Crime*, seven recommendations were made that deal specifically with how the various systems (i.e., justice, medical, and social) should deal with victims of sexual assault (1983, pp. 162–163). At the Seventh United Nations Congress on the Prevention of Crime and the Treatment of Offenders, held in Milan, Italy, in 1985, a special report of the Secretary General, entitled *The Situation of Women as Victims of Crime* was presented. Included in this extremely informative paper, which draws its information from various international sources, is a section that addresses the sexual abuse of women (United Nations, 1985). Finally, at a 1986 meeting of Commonwealth law ministers held in Zimbabwe, a discussion paper was presented by the Commonwealth Secretariat entitled *Violence Against Women*. The paper, which concentrates on domestic violence and rape, was recommended by the Expert Meeting. Many of the issues the paper raises for the consideration of the ministers of the Commonwealth regarding the crime of rape and related sexual assault involve definitions, the groups protected, the sentencing structure, and the rules of evidence that govern rape trial proceedings. It is noteworthy that the recommended changes to rape legislation in many respects mirror those that were made to the *Criminal Code* of Canada in January 1983 (Commonwealth Secretariat, 1986).

The year 1972 marked the opening in Vancouver, British Columbia, of the first rape crisis center to provide victims of rape with counseling, public legal education, and support in the aftermath of a sexual attack (Andrew et al., 1982). Rape crisis centers have developed for two not necessarily mutually exclusive purposes. One was to fill the gap created by a dearth of community services to assist victims of a rape attack in coping with the particular problems they encountered as victims and as women. The second was to address the "secondary victimization" that rape victims experienced with criminal justice personnel and the criminal justice process (Clark, 1977, pp. 14–15). The strategic position of crisis centers as grass roots organizations that have direct experience with victims of rape provided fertile ground for workers to become organized and politicized regarding legal changes in the rape laws and the criminal procedure in rape cases. In point of fact, by 1978 a National Association of Sexual Assault Centres had been formed in Canada. When the association met in that year, a consensus was reached that Canada's rape laws needed radical reform and that the violent nature of the act must be stressed (Andrew et al., 1982, p. 10).

Coincident with the development and expansion of rape crisis centers in Canada was the rise of feminist and other research in North America on rape (Brownmiller, 1975; Clark & Lewis, 1977a, 1977b; Chappell, Geis, & Geis, 1977). Although feminists south of the border were the first to tackle the question, by 1973 Canadian research and interest in the area of rape had emerged. Feminist research generated sociohistorical accounts that documented the incidence of rape and rape laws, the processing of rape cases, and the treatment accorded to rape victims by the legal system. A significant theoretical contribution by feminists to an understanding of the formulation and history of rape laws is cogently articulated by Clark (1977):

> *The prevalent position among feminists is that rape is historically an offence not against persons but against property. In essence, it is an offence of theft and trespass, and as such, justifies punishment of the offender in accordance with the degree of damage caused in the trespass and the value of the goods stolen. On this theory, the only credible rape victims are those who are either virgins or those who are firmly ensconced within the bonds of monogamous marriage. This reflects the fact that women are socially and legally the property of particular men, their husbands or fathers, and that it is their sexual and reproductive functions which determine their property value. . . . Also, women who show a wanton disregard for those properties in terms of which their property value is assessed, who have histories of reputations for "promiscuity", or "lewd" and "unchaste" behaviour, forsake their right to be protected from attacks on their sexual organs. . . . rape laws are designed to protect only some women. (p. 11)*

This thesis was the outcome of research which showed that the law was prepared to protect women who were "true victims," that is, women who were in exclusive relationships with men. By extension, it exposed the law and trial procedures as a means of controlling women by disgracing those who lived independently and exercised sexual autonomy and by refusing to protect them from sexual attacks against their will (Edwards, 1981, p. 70; Kasinsky, 1978).

Accompanying the position that rape historically meant in law a crime against a man's sexual and reproductive property was the widespread consensus that the essence of rape in contemporary society was violence against women. It was held that if there was to be a correspondence between the essence of the offense and the law proscribing it, then the law must shift the emphasis away from women's reproductive capacity toward acknowledgment of the assaultive nature of a sexual attack, which involved a violation of the integrity of the person and was not limited to sexual intercourse (Ellis, 1984, p. 4). In light of this new conceptualization of rape, a reclassification of rape laws was called for that would recognize rape as an injury to the integrity of the victim's body. Two well-respected Canadian researchers in the area of rape advocated this reconceptualization of rape in the following manner:

> *So far as women are concerned, their sexual organs are no less, and no different a part of their person than their heads, eyes and limbs. . . . since sexual organs are just part of the body, an attack on the sexual organs is as threatening to life and health as an unprovoked attack on any of the other bodily parts. . . . [Therefore] the same standards which apply to assaults against other parts of the body should also apply to attacks against the sexual organs. (Clark & Lewis, 1977a, pp. 167–168)*

This position, in a somewhat modified form, was advanced by national women's organizations in Canada. As early as 1975, the Canadian Advisory Council on the Status of Women (CACSW) incorporated the rape issue and the need for law reform in relation to sexual offenses into its policy agenda. Two years later CACSW stated that one of its priority concerns would be "sexual offences in the *Criminal Code* and particularly rape and the plight of victims" (Canadian Advisory Council on the Status of Women, 1976, p. 1). In the same policy statement, the CACSW recommended that the *Criminal Code* be amended and that rape be replaced by four degrees of sexual assault (1976, p. 5). In the late 70s and early 80s, the National Association of Women and the Law (NAWL) and the National Action Committee on the Status of Women (NACSW) were identified as "the two groups . . . most visible . . . in lobbying for changes in rape laws" in Canada (Andrew et al., 1982, p. 10). In 1979, the NAWL recommended placing sexual assault offenses under the heading "Offences Against the Person and Reputation" in the *Criminal Code* and replacing rape with a four-tiered structure of sexual assaults (National Association of Women and the Law, 1979).

In 1978 the Canadian Law Reform Commission's *Working Paper on Sexual Offences* was released. The Commission recommended that a new offense of sexual assault be created to replace rape that would not distinguish between "unwanted sexual contact and unwanted sexual penetration for the purposes of the substantive law" and would consider "aggravating circumstances of the assault" at sentencing (Law Reform Commission, 1978a). The commission's rationale behind their proposed changes to the criminal law, which would delete rape from the *Criminal Code*, was that

> *to expunge from the Code all mention of that crime called rape, and to relegate it to a form of assault for all purposes would certainly effect a change in the characterization of the offence. . . . [That] however . . . in the view of the Commission, does not affect the reprehensible nature of the act. Whether the change would be more effective in terms of* increased protection for the dignity and inviolability of the person, *or whether its greatest value would lie in* alleviating the distress, humiliation and stigmatization that is associated with the present law *is not clear. Hopefully both results would follow. (Law Reform Commission, 1978a, p. 18; emphasis added)*

In November 1978, the Law Reform Commission's final recommendations on sexual offenses were released. The commission proposed that the offense of rape be replaced with two new offenses—sexual interference and sexual aggression—and that spousal immunity be abolished (Law Reform Commission, 1978b, p. 15).

In January 1981, the Minister of Justice introduced Bill C-53. The bill recommended replacing the terms *rape* and *indecent assault* with the terms *sexual assault* and *aggravated sexual assault*, thereby focusing on the violent nature of sexual offenses. In addition, substantial revisions to the laws of evidence applicable in rape trials were put forward, as well as proposals to reform the law in relation to the sexual exploitation of children and prostitution. When the Parliamentary Committee on Bill C-53 met in 1982, briefs were submitted from the following women's groups in Canada: the NAWL, the CACSW, the NACSW, the National Council of Women, the Quebec Federation of Women, and the Saskatoon Rape Crisis Centre. All submissions insisted that the assaultive, violent aspect be given predominance in the definition of assault (Justice and Legal Affairs, 1982a, pp. 5–6; 1982b, p. 48; 1982c, pp. 12–13; 1982d, pp. 4–5).[3] The Justice and Legal Affairs Committee, in considering Bill C-53, finalized its views concerning the law of rape and sexual assault but was unable to reach a consensus on those aspects of the bill concerning prostitution and children. The outcome was Bill C-127, considered by one commentator to be "the most sweeping reform of the *Criminal Code* in recent time" (Price, 1984, p. 10).

SEXUAL ASSAULT PROVISIONS OF BILL C-127

With the coming into force of Bill C-127 in January 1983, the law relating to the offense of rape was expunged from the *Criminal Code* and replaced by a trilogy of sexual assault offenses: sexual assault; sexual assault with a weapon, threats to a third party, or causing bodily harm; and aggravated sexual assault.

[3]Throughout the 1970s, when the recommendation that sexual assault be substituted for rape was being developed and advanced in Canada, opposition was silent or absent. In 1980, an article which has become the most referenced opposition to the proposed "desexualizing" of rape was published in Canada by Leah Cohen and Connie Backhouse. Their position is that rape is qualitatively different from other forms of physical assault, that the cultural underpinnings of rape cannot be eliminated simply by changing the name, and that the defense of consent is not altered by the amendments. They point out that what women experience as victims of a rape is not equivalent to what is experienced in other types of physical assaults. The act of rape transforms what for many women is a consensual act with a freely chosen partner into a "completely impersonal one used for the expression of hate, conquest or contempt" (Cohen & Backhouse, 1980, p. 101). The level of personal humiliation associated with rape renders the experience essentially different from other form of attacks against the body. Cohen and Backhouse also maintain that rape is an act which is produced by our culture and which entails "a peculiar overlap of violence and sex" that will not be eliminated by changing the name and emphasizing the violent component of the act (p. 101). Stated another way, they regard rape as a reflection of the lack of egalitarian principles and practices structuring gender relations in our culture.

In the same year in Britain, at the National Women's Liberation Conference in Leeds, a paper was presented in favor of keeping rape as a sex crime. It was argued that legislation which emphasizes violence would legitimate the current practice of doubting the veracity of rape victims unless they are injured. This practice has resulted in the "selective" investigation and processing of rape cases. Further, in those cases where a rape occurs and is believed to have occurred by the investigating authorities, without visible evidence of violence rape would be harder to prove than it is under the current law. The success of convictions under existing law is associated with a high degree of violence accompanying the rape. Therefore, defining rape as a crime of violence would serve to reinforce and "formalize the status quo" (McNeill, 1985, p. 115). The author concludes, "To separate rape off as a crime of violence would not lead to more successful prosecutions for rape. We would still need to prove by the marks that we had fought for our lives" (p. 118).

What constitutes a sexual assault is not defined and was left by the legislation for the courts to resolve. Each of these offenses carries maximum penalties ranging from 6 months to life imprisonment, depending on the aggravating factors associated with the sexual assault. Accompanying the nominal change from rape to sexual assault and the deletion from the *Criminal Code* of some crimes of coercive sexuality (rape, attempted rape, and indecent assault) are statutorily defined factors which vitiate the defense of consent to any form of assault, including sexual assault. These include the application of force to the complainant or third party, fraud, threats of force, and the exercise of authority. A further change to the substantive law is the legal recognition of sexual assault in marriage whether or not the spouses are living together at the time the offense is committed. Also, the law is gender neutral, thereby according men and women alike the same legal protection respecting sexual assaults.

In an attempt to redress the injustices of the legal processes in rape trials, the bill contains the following provisions. Corroboration is not required for a conviction, and a judge shall not instruct the jury that it is unsafe to find the accused guilty in the absence of corroboration. Further, the rules regarding recent complaint in sexual assault cases are repealed. With the exception of three specific circumstances, no evidence concerning the previous sexual history of the complainant with any person other than the accused is permitted.[4] Determination of the admissibility of such evidence in one of the three specific circumstances detailed in the *Criminal Code* takes place at an *in camera* hearing at which the complainant is not a compellable witness. Also, evidence of sexual reputation is not admissible for the purposes of challenging or supporting the credibility of the complainant. Finally, while an honest though unreasonable belief that there was consent is still theoretically a defense, the judge in a sexual assault trial is bound to instruct the jury to consider the presence or absence of reasonable grounds for that belief in determining whether or not it is honestly held.

In recognition of the significance of the fundamental changes to the law, the Department of Justice has undertaken an evaluation of the impact of the sexual assault provisions of Bill C-127.

Goals of Reform of Rape Law

Impact studies of law require (and assume) that legal goals are knowable. In point of fact, the goals of a law form "the basis for comparison—the *standard* against which reality is measured" in an impact study (Feeley, 1976, p. 499).

The goals of the sexual assault legislation articulated by proponents of the law reform in the period leading to the passage of Bill C-127 included these: (1) to make the law a more efficient instrument to repress sexual offenses by making

[4]Evidence concerning the sexual activity of the complainant with any person other than the accused is not admissable in sexual assault trials unless (a) it is evidence that rebuts evidence of the complainant's sexual activity or absence thereof that was previously adduced by the prosecution; (b) it is evidence of specific instances of the complainant's sexual activity tending to establish the identity of the person who had sexual contact with the complainant on the occasion set out in the charge; or (c) it is evidence of sexual activity that took place on the same occasion as the sexual activity that forms the subject matter of the charge, where that evidence relates to the consent that the accused alleges he believed was given by the complainant.

the criminal justice system more responsive (e.g., by assisting police, juries, and judges, teaching assailants a lesson, and bringing penalties in line), and (2) to improve the experiences of victims with the criminal justice system in general and the trial process in particular (e.g., by altering attitudes and alleviating distress, humiliation, and stigmatization) (Law Reform Commission, 1978a, p. 18; Kinnon, 1981, p. 79; Justice and Legal Affairs, 1982c, pp. 12–13; McDonald 1982b, p. 14). The third goal ascribed to the new law, elimination of sexual discrimination, is symbolic in essence and not necessarily amenable to the types of measures employed in impact assessments. (This goal was mentioned in the Minister of Justice's speech notes on Bill C-53.) In fact, Bienen (1980) notes in her impressive review of rape reform legislation in the United States that it is not possible to measure whether a rape law reform initiative is a reflection of a change in social attitudes toward women or whether the legislative change has produced a change in social attitudes. However, what is of importance is not the ability to determine causation but rather the role a legal reform in the rape area plays in educating professionals and thereby changing behavior and practices. The latter can be assessed in evaluation research.

Thus, the sexual assault legislation was intended to have an impact on a host of unique behaviors. These include victims' reporting behavior and experiences with the criminal justice process, criminal justice system practitioners' handling and processing of sexual assault complaints and cases, and the behavior of potential assailants.

LEGISLATION EVALUATION RESEARCH PROGRAM

The objectives of the evaluation of the 1983 sexual assault legislation are to describe and understand how the legislation was implemented, what procedures and methods were adopted, and how they are working. Also, the evaluation will attempt to determine whether the legislation has caused a change in, for example, the volume and types of cases going into the criminal justice system; the attributes of victims and offenders and the nature of their relationship; the police founding rate of sexual assault complaints; the lines of defense and the nature of evidence received by the triers of fact; the outcome of cases; and the experiences of victims, justice system practitioners, and sexual assault crisis center workers as well as their practices and attitudes. The evaluation will also attempt to determine any unintended consequences of the legislation on victims and on the criminal justice system.

The evaluation studies described below are process oriented (implementation) as well as outcome oriented (impact). Both qualitative and quantitative methods are employed in the research. Quantitative data will provide a foundation for causal attribution of both the intended and unintended effects of the law reform. The quantitative data are directed and supplemented by qualitative data to ensure a thorough understanding of the findings. The views and policies of sexual assault center staff and criminal justice system agents involved in implementing the law reform and the views of victims are regarded as crucial sources of information about the impact of the law. Using qualitative and quantitative methods and drawing information from a number of sources will enhance the comprehensiveness and confidence in the conclusions drawn about the impact of the law.

In planning for the evaluation research, it was determined that, at the minimum, a 3-year hiatus from the proclamation of the law to the start of the evaluation was necessary. Essentially, it takes time for legal reform to become public knowledge, begin to affect behavior, and become fully implemented. Two commentators have noted that "attempts to assess the impact of policy innovations require the passage of sufficient time to allow one to make sense of the complex interaction of motives and behaviour that implementation encompasses" (Casper & Brereton, 1984, p. 143). Further, it was necessary for a sufficient number of cases to have been decided and interpreted by the courts. Case law is an important indicator of the impact of legislative changes. The evaluation research program will be completed in the summer of 1988. Each of the field reports will be released, in English and in French, as a separate study. A synthesis report will be produced that draws together and interprets the findings from the various data sources, including statistical data, jurisprudence and legal issues, and the research findings from the six field studies. All reports were to be published and released in the fall of 1988. The following is a description of the research program.

Background Studies

In preparation for the full-scale evaluation, two background studies were carried out. These studies highlighted research issues that informed the framework of the evaluation. One study documents rape victims' sociolegal experiences with the Canadian criminal justice system prior to the amendment of the rape laws. The second study documents reported court decisions since the passage of the new sexual assault legislation (January 1983 to April 1985).

Field Research Studies

The field research component of the evaluation is the most comprehensive and in-depth aspect of the study. It is a key source of data for the evaluation and is taking place in six jurisdictions in Canada: Vancouver, British Columbia; Lethbridge, Alberta; Winnipeg, Manitoba; Hamilton, Ontario; Montreal, Quebec; and Fredericton, New Brunswick. These sites were selected to reflect the regional character of Canada. Data sources for the field studies include reviews of the police, Crown and sexual assault center files; interviews with or questionnaires filled out by key informants in the criminal justice system, sexual assault center workers, and victims; and monitoring of trials involving allegations of sexual assault. The file review will cover the pre–law reform period (1981–1982) and the post–law reform period (1984–1985). The field studies will permit the collection of detailed information on criminal justice system practices, on victims' experiences, and on key actors' opinions.

To ensure that definitions and measures are as valid as possible between research sites, the parameters for the field research studies are extremely detailed. The issues have been clearly articulated and an exhaustive list of data elements are listed for each of the research components. Also, the research does take account of variations in local priorities, concerns, and procedures in the administration of justice. Finally, all studies are coordinated from within the Department of Justice.

Other Studies

In addition to the field studies, there will be an analysis of case law that has emerged from the amendments to the *Criminal Code*. The sociolegal research study will review and analyze jurisprudence related to substantive, evidentiary, procedural, and constitutional legal issues that will have emerged in sexual assault case law. Statistical studies will also be conducted. One study will identify trends in the incidence, reporting, founding, and charging patterns associated with rape and sexual assault in Canada over a 10-year period. Another will examine the incidence of homicides that have occurred during the commission of rapes and sexual assaults. The intent of this study is to develop a statistical profile of the victims of rape and sexual assault homicides, and offenders, the offense (including situational contingencies), and the legal processing and outcomes of cases.

It is noteworthy that all "before and after" measures will be of different groups of victims and, in many instances, different practitioners in the criminal justice and other agencies. Also, categories of offenses are different between the two time periods, as are the groups to whom the law applies, the aggravating factors, and the rules of evidence, thereby precluding direct comparisons. These factors introduce shortcomings in measuring legal impact.

Methodological Considerations

From a review of prior research that has attempted to assess legal impact, two methodological considerations have emerged. One concerns the limit of *measuring* the impact of law on behavior and attitudes.

First, impact implies, inter alia, "effect" or "influence." Therefore, to refer to the impact of legal policy making is to take an instrumental view of law, that is, one which takes law to be an instrument to influence or order individual or group behavior to achieve particular ends or goals. Law is an independent variable. The pivotal question in legal impact studies is what has been the impact of the law on the behaviors, practices, experiences, attitudes, and so on, that the law was designed to affect.

An ideal impact research design would involve a control group design in which two jurisdictions, identical in every respect, would be randomly chosen. In one location, the law reform would be introduced; in the other, it would be withheld. The strategic issue in the impact assessment would be how to obtain estimates of the differences between legal behavior and practices in the two jurisdictions. From this determination, practices and behavior motivated by the law reform could be distinguished from other behavior or practices that would occur independent of, or in spite of, law reform. In Canada, the authority to enact criminal legislation is vested in the federal government and the authority to administer justice is vested in each of its provinces. Therefore, criminal legislation is legally extended to all Canadian jurisdictions, precluding a control population for the purposes of establishing a comparison group.

The second methodological consideration concerns the limit of legal prescription or proscription on motivating or modifying behaviors or attitudes. The notion that a law, once enacted and made public, becomes part of the stock of knowledge of society and affects behavior accordingly is not borne out by research. Kutchinsky's (1973) review of studies related to "knowledge and opinion about law" found no empirical evidence to support this covariance thesis regarding law and legal attitudes or behavior. This fact led him to conclude that "knowledge about law is neither a necessary nor a sufficient condition for conformity to the law" (Kutchinsky, 1973, p. 104). Historical factors and self-selection make it possible that behavior consistent with the goals of the sexual assault legislation may have occurred in any event, irrespective of the law reform. In fact, the law itself may be the result rather than the cause of these changes. Lempert (1966) regards selection as "the most severe threat which operates in a manner specific to socio-legal research" (p. 121). He goes on to state,

> *Any research design purporting to deal with the impact of a particular law on the behavior of a populace will have to make certain that the law is indeed more than an expression of the popular will of the people and that the people would be acting differently without the law. (p. 121)*

In Canada, historical factors that would potentially affect the behavior of victims, criminal justice system personnel, and offenders include the following:

- The changing status of and advances made by women in the social, economic, and political domains and the potential and the empowering effect of these developments.
- The visibly heightened awareness and focus on victims of crime in general and female victims in particular.
- The establishment of sexual offense investigation divisions in police forces where continuity and expertise have developed regarding the investigation of complaints and the gathering of evidence.
- The expansion of sexual assault support centers providing counseling and, in some centers, encouraging victims to report their victimization to police.

As noted above, the administration of justice in Canada is a provincial responsibility. Implementation of legislative initiatives by agents in the institutions of the criminal justice system are influenced by a number of extralegal factors, including attitudes, available resources, and formal and informal pressures emanating from inside and outside of the justice institutions in the 10 provinces. These can affect how evenly criminal legislation is implemented across the country.

In light of the limits of conducting legal impact research, inferences that are drawn in the research will be tentative rather than conclusive and explanations of relationships which are observed will go beyond the conceptually weak notion that the new law reform is the only factor to consider.

CONCLUSION

Elizabeth Sheehy (1985), in her concise and thoughtful review of *Sexual Assault* by Christine Boyle (1984), comments, "A major piece of research that Boyle has declined to tackle, given the timing of her book, is whether the new sexual assault amendments have in fact changed anything other than the name of the offense of rape" (p. 676). It is the intent of the evaluation research to determine what has changed since the 1983 amendments.

In this chapter I have attempted to highlight (1) some of the historical forces and issues which gave rise to the call for reform of Canada's rape law and (2) the goals and expectations associated with the law reform. The chapter also briefly describes the research program developed to assess the impact of this major legislative initiative, including some of the methodological challenges associated with the project. While the limits imposed on impact evaluations by the "real world" should not be minimized, one does not cease conducting research because the social world does not imitate an ideal research design. It is anticipated that the information and insights generated from this research will advance our knowledge and understanding of the impact of law reform; the experiences and needs of victims of sexual assault; the factors that influence discretion, processing, and outcomes of sexual assault complaints and cases; and the limits and possibilities of criminal law reforms to prevent or mitigate personal offenses that are overwhelmingly perpetrated by men against women.

BIBLIOGRAPHY

Andrew, K., Barnsley, J., Ellis, M., Lewis, D., McMurray, H., Ranson, J., & Riddington, J. (1982, October). Bill C-127: How did we get there? Where do we go from here?. *Kinesis*.

Backhouse, C., & Schoenroth, L. (1987). A comparative survey of Canadian and American rape law. *Canada–United States Law Journal*, *6*, 48.

Barrington, R. (1984). The rape law reform process in New Zealand. *Criminal Law Journal*, *8*, 307–325.

Bienen, L. (1980). Rape 111: National developments in rape reform legislation. *Women's Rights Law Reporter*, *6*(3).

Boyle, C. (1984). *Sexual assault*. Toronto: Carswell.

Box, S. (1983). *Power, crime and mystification*. London: Tavistock.

Brownmiller, S. (1975). Against our will: Men, women and rape. New York: Simon & Schuster.

Bureau of Justice Statistics. (1985, March). *The crime of rape*. U.S. Department of Justice.

Canadian Advisory Council on the Status of Women. (1976, September). *Rationalization of sexual offences in the Criminal Code*. Ottawa: Author.

Canadian Advisory Council on the Status of Women. (1982, March). *Justice regained: Brief of the Canadian Advisory Council on the Status of Women in respect of Bill C-53*. Ottawa: Author.

Canadian Federal-Provincial Task Force on Justice for Victims of Crime. (1983). *Justice for victims of crime*. Ottawa: Department of Supply and Services.

Casper, J., & Brereton, D. (1984). Evaluating Criminal Justice Reforms. *Law & Society Review*, *18*(1), 121–144.

Chappell, D., Geis, R., & Geis, G. (1977). *Forcible rape: The crime, the victim, and the offender*. New York: Columbia University Press.

Clark, L. (1977, November). Rape: A position paper. *Status of Women News*, *4*(2), 11–15.

Clark, L., & Lewis, D. (1977a). *Rape: The price of coercive sexuality*. Toronto: The Women's Press.

Clark, L., & Lewis, D. (1977b). *A study of rape in Canada: Phases "C" and "D" report of the Donner Foundation of Canada*. Toronto: Centre of Criminology.

Cohen, L., & Backhouse, C. (1980). Desexualizing rape: A dissenting view on the proposed rape amendments. *Canadian Women's Studies*, *2*(4), 99–103.

Committee on Sexual Offenses Against Children and Youth. (1984). *Sexual offences against children*. Ottawa: Department of Supply and Services.

Commonwealth Secretariat. (1986). *Violence against women*. Meeting of Commonwealth Law Ministers, Zimbabwe.

Edwards, S. (1981). *Female sexuality and the law*. Oxford: Martin Robertson.

Ellis, M. (1984, March). The sexual provisions of the Criminal Code. *Legal Services Society Schools Program Newsletter*, *8*(4), 3–6.

Feeley, M. (1976). The concept of laws in social science: A critique and notes on an expanded view. *Law & Society*, *10*, 497–523.

Hale, M. (1880). *History of pleas of the Crown*. Little-Britton: E. Rider.

Hahn, R. (1983). *Sentencing practices and trends in Canada*. Ottawa: Department of Justice.

Hans, V., & Vidmar, N. (1986). *Judging the jury*. New York: Plenum Press.
Justice and Legal Affairs, House of Commons. (1982a, April 27). Issue No. 78. Ottawa.
Justice and Legal Affairs, House of Commons. (1982b, May 6). Issue No. 82. Ottawa.
Justice and Legal Affairs, House of Commons. (1982c, June 1). Issue No. 91. Ottawa.
Justice and Legal Affairs, House of Commons. (1982d, June 9). Issue No. 95. Ottawa.
Justice and Legal Affairs, House of Commons. (1982e, June 17). Issue No. 98. Ottawa.
Kasinsky, R. G. (1978). The anti-rape movement in Canada. In M. A. B. Gammon (Ed.), *Violence in Canada* (pp. 151–167). Toronto: Methuen.
Kinnon, D. (1981). *Report on sexual assault in Canada*. Ottawa: Canadian Advisory Council on the Status of Women.
Kutchinsky, B. (1973). "The legal consciousness": A survey of research on knowledge and opinion about law. In C. M. Campbell, W. G. Carson, and P. N. P. Wiles (Eds.), *Knowledge and opinion about law* (pp. 101–138). Bristol, Great Britain: Barleyman Press.
LaFree, G., Reskin, B., & Visher, C. (1985). Jurors' responses to victims' behavior and legal issues in sexual assault trials. *Social Problems*, *32*(4), 389–407.
Law Reform Commission of Canada. (1978a). *Sexual offences*. (Working Paper No. 22). Ottawa: Author.
Law Reform Commission of Canada. (1978b). *Report on sexual offences 10*. Ottawa: Author.
Lempert, R. (1966). Strategies of research design in the legal impact study: The control of plausible hypotheses. *Law & Society Review*, *1*(1), 111–132.
McDonald, D. (1982a). *Rape and consent: The defence of mistake of fact* [Prepared for the Standing Committee on Legal and Constitutional Affairs]. Ottawa: Library of Parliament.
McDonald, D., (1982b). *The Evolution of Bill C-127* [Prepared for the Standing Committee on Legal and Constitutional Affairs]. Ottawa: Library of Parliament.
McNeill, S. (1985). Rape, sexuality and crimes of violence. In D. Rhodes and S. McNeill (Eds.), *Women against violence against women*. London: Onlywomen Press.
McTeer, M. (1978). Rape and the Canadian legal process. In M. A. B. Gammon (Ed.), *Violence in Canada* (pp. 135–150). Toronto: Methuen.
National Association of Women and the Law. (1979). *Recommendations on sexual assault offences*. Ottawa: Author.
National Association of Women and the Law. (1981). *A new image for sexual offences in the Criminal Code: A brief in response to Bill C-53*. Ottawa: Author.
Price, M. (1984). *A monitoring project of the new sexual assault legislation*. Report presented to the Alberta Law Foundation in conjunction with the Calgary Sexual Assault Centre.
Ruebsaat, G. (1985). *The new sexual assault offences: Emerging legal issues*. Ottawa: Department of Justice Canada.
Sallmann, P. A., & Chappell, D. (1982). *Rape law reform in South Australia: A study of the background to the reforms of 1975 and 1976 and of their subsequent impact* (Research Paper No. 3). Adelaide: Adelaide Law Review Association.
Sheehy, E. (1985). Sexual assault [Book Review]. *Ottawa Law Review 17*.
Smart, C., & Smart, B. (1978). *Women, sexuality and the law*. London: Routledge & Kegan Paul.
Solicitor General of Canada. (1985). *Female victims of crime*. (Canadian Urban Victimization Survey No. 4). Ottawa: Department of Supply and Services.
Stanley, M. (1985). *The experiences of the rape victim with the criminal justice system prior to Bill C-127*. Ottawa: Department of Justice Canada.
Statistics Canada. (1983). *Canadian crime statistics* (Catalogue 85-205). Ottawa: Department of Supply and Services.
United Nations. (1985). *Victims of crime: The situation of women as victims of crime*. Report of the Secretary General, Seventh United Nations Congress on the Prevention of Crime and the Treatment of Offenders.
Watt, D. (1984). *The new offences against the person*. Toronto: Butterworths.

16

Prostitution and Allied Offenses: The Overenforcement and Underenforcement of Unjust Law: The United Kingdom Experience

Susan S. M. Edwards
Ealing College and the Polytechnic of Central London

INTRODUCTION

Street soliciting by adult women continues to be an offense in some states in the United States and in the United Kingdom, Australia, and parts of Europe. For the most part, penal sanctions are draconian and retributive and street prostitutes are penalized, fined, and imprisoned. By contrast, the men who procure, pimp for, and ponce off (live off) these women are seldom prosecuted. In addition, a recently introduced law in the United Kingdom which provides for the prosecution of curb crawlers (the men who solicit women) is underenforced to the point of impotence. During the last few years in the United Kingdom, the United States, Canada, and Europe, the prostitution debate has been reopened by both right-wing legal reformers and left-wing feminists and socialists. Right-wing reformers demand tougher penal sanctions all around, and left-wing feminists remain divided. Some argue that prostitution should be decriminalized, claiming women have a right to sell their bodies if they choose. Others want penal sanctions to protect prostitute women from the excesses of sexual exploitation. In the U.K., the law penalizes the streetwalker, the most vulnerable of all. Prostitute women inhabit the threshold of victim-offender analysis. They are victims of male exploitation and a patriarchal and hypocritical bourgeois legal form. Reliance on reform of penal law to render prostitute women pro-

Susan S. M. Edwards is currently employed as a family law researcher by Ealing College, London, and as a lecturer by the Polytechnic of Central London. She is presently conducting research into prostitution, policing, employment, and the welfare of young women sponsored by the Nuffield Foundation, United Kingdom. She is also researching the impact of the new police policy on the policing of domestic assaults in London, research sponsored by the Police Foundation, United Kingdom.

Ms. Edwards would like to acknowledge the Nuffield Foundation for its financial support, Ealing College of Higher Education, London, for administering the grant, Gary Armstrong, her co-project worker, the Home Office Statistical Department, London, and the Metropolitan Police in London for their generous assistance.

tection or introduce equality in the penalization of men who consort with women is inevitably a contradiction in terms.

Streetwalking prostitute women are officially defined as "criminal offenders," offending against the laws governing street soliciting. The police respond to their street visibility by deploying a considerable amount of resources in cautioning, arresting, and prosecuting these women. Prostitute women are fined in the thousands, and some are sent to prison because of fine default. Research has shown that the childhood and adolescent backgrounds of prostitute women are very often characterized by sexual and physical assault, broken homes, and domestic violence (James, 1978a, 1978b; Bracey, 1983). Research has also shown that prostitute women often are single parents, are poor, and live in inadequate housing (Mukherjee and Scutt, 1981).

In 1985, 9,406 women were prosecuted summarily for streetwalking. By contrast, male punters (men who solicit women) and male ponces are rarely prosecuted, and the recent law regulating curb crawling is moribund. New crime prevention schemes that involve the local community and that are designed to combat the street problem (e.g., street lighting and blocking off roads and thoroughfares) simply move the prostitutes to another locality or, more insidiously, into clubs and parlors, where prostitute women are frequently controlled by male ponces and managers. In the United States, the Meese Report (1986) recognized that prostitute women are very often controlled by and involved in organized crime, but in the United Kingdom, government officials refuse to acknowledge the extent of their victimization. In these several ways, family background, economic impoverishment, and selective application of law ensure that prostitutes inhabit the crossroads of offender-victim analysis.

COMPARATIVE PROSECUTIONS

An analysis of women's engagement in prostitution and their victimization must begin with a comparison of prosecutions for streetwalking and allied offenses (Edwards, 1984). In 1979, prosecutions for prostitution in England and Wales totaled 3,167; in 1983, prosecutions had risen to 10,674; and by 1985, 9,406 women were prosecuted for streetwalking. These increases have been due, in part, to changes in legislation, changes in policing practice, to repressive public attitudes, and to a gradual erosion in women's economic opportunities. Figures for 1983, for example, clearly reflected the impact of the introduction by the Metropolitan Police of a "new" policing strategy on prosecution rates. In addition, in 1982, the Criminal Justice Act (s. 70) abolished immediate imprisonment for soliciting offenses. These legislative "reforms" may have contributed to an increasing number of women on the streets in 1983 and the years that followed. In addition, women's entry into prostitution has been affected by their worsening employment situation and by welfare reforms which have further impoverished women and single parents.

Although prosecutions of men for procuration have been steadily rising since 1979, when 225 men were formally dealt with, by 1985 only 542 men were prosecuted. Prosecutions for brothel keeping since 1979 have been roughly constant. In that year 115 women were prosecuted, and in 1985 there were 89 prosecutions. In 1986, 191 men were prosecuted for curb crawling. Looking to the disproportionate number of women prosecuted for prostitution compared with the relatively few men prosecuted for allied offenses, it is clear that prostitutes are victims not only of sexually repressive and unjust legislation and double victimization but also of male exploitation through control by pimps who are often beyond the reach of the law (see Edwards, 1986; Matthews, 1985, 1986; McLeod, 1982; Ohse, 1984; Russell, Frey, & Reichert, 1981; Russell & Owen, 1984). Turning to the question of convictions, there are wide differences in the conviction rate for men proceeded against for procuration and curb crawling, compared with women proceeded against for streetwalking (see Tables 16-1 and 16-2).

In this chapter, I shall argue that (1) the legislation and its enforcement unfairly penalizes the streetwalker; (2) the behavior of clients, punters, and business entrepreneur ponces is largely exonerated; and (3) even though there are laws to regulate and penalize such behavior, these laws have been underenforced, with the result that women prostitutes are left vulnerable and unprotected. Given the increasing control of prostitution by male managers, increasing threat of violence from pimps and punters, and the increasing threat of disease and AIDS, prostitute women today, as in the 19th century, are clearly victims of law, policing, and male punters and managers operating within the framework of bourgeois hypocrisy.

Prosecuting Women: Legal Overenforcement

In U.K. law, only women are defined as prostitutes and prosecuted for the offenses of loitering and soliciting in pursuit of prostitution. Despite the many forms that prostitution can take, legislation has been primarily concerned with the tightening up of the control of the street prostitute. Nowhere is this more evident than in the Street Offences Act of 1959 whose Section 1(1) makes it an offense for a woman to loiter or solicit for the purpose of prostitution. The aftermath of this act was characterized by the almost triumphant proclamation that the diminished visibility of street activity and the decline in prosecutions for soliciting were evidence of its overnight success. As Edwards (1984) writes

> *whilst the numbers of prosecutions and convictions for offences relating to prostitution declined drastically from the 19,663 before the introduction of the Act to 2,726 in 1960, this by no means reflected a real diminution in police activity or in prostitution.* (p. 30)

What was reflected was simply a change in police prosecution procedures brought about by the introduction of a system that provided for the cautioning of women on two occasions prior to arrest and charge. The apparently more lenient approach after 1959 was countervailed by the restoration of other police powers to their former 19th-century glory. These permitted a constable to "arrest without warrant anyone he finds in a street or public place and suspects with reasonable cause, to be committing an offence under this section" (Section 1(3)). Any women deterred from using the streets merely used other means of contacting clients, thereby avoiding police detection and ultimate imprisonment.

By December 1982, the Criminal Law Revision Committee, assisted by the Police Advisory Committee, published the working paper *Offences Relating to Prostitution and Allied Offences*. It was fourth such review in 50 years, its predecessors being the *Street Offences Report* of 1928, the *Wolfenden Report* of 1957,

Table 16-1 Prosecutions for loitering for the purpose of prostitution (1979–1984)

		1980			1981		
	1979	Total	17–21	21+	Total	17–21	21+
Total prosecutions	3167	3482	1324	2125	4324	1582	2706
Withdrawn/dismissed	142	140	44	93	182	55	124
Otherwise dealt with	14	8	2	6	7	1	5
Total found guilty	3014	3336	1278	2030	4127	1523	2571
Absolute discharge	14	25	9	15	39	17	22
Conditional discharge	578	513	185	320	686	267	409
Probation	279	324	144	180	379	155	224
Fine	1609	1880	758	1108	2389	889	1490
Community service order	42	116	39	77	115	32	83
Suspended sentence	245	254	75	179	288	90	198
Up to 1 month	78	108			144		
1 month up to 2 months	19	32			26		
2 months up to 3 months		85			31		
Over 3 months		2			3		
Other disposals	38	19			7		
Conviction rate[a]	95%	96%			95%		

[a]As a percentage of those prosecuted only. Source: *Criminal Statistics Supplementary Tables.*

and the working papers on vagrancy and street offences of 1974 and 1976. From January 31, 1983, in accordance with Home Office Circular 2/1983, following Section 71 of the Criminal Justice Act (1982), imprisonment for loitering and soliciting was abolished. Many claimed that this was a humanitarian move, but it was more likely to have been a politically expedient measure calculated to deal with the general problem of prison overcrowding. With the abolition of imprisonment, magistrates could no longer make community service orders or the suspended and partially suspended sentences that had hitherto been alternatives to custody. Since 1982, the probation order and the fine were the only remaining viable sentencing options. The result has been that, although the use of probation orders has declined, the number and quantum of fines has actually increased. In Sheffield, in November 1983, a 24-year-old woman was fined £650 after admitting only four offenses! Previously, an average fine for four offenses would have been about £100. Lord Justice Stephen Brown is one of a number of U.K. judges who have backed this "get tough" policy: "The magistrates in Sheffield deserve to be congratulated upon a careful and realistic approach to what undoubtedly appears to have been a major problem in their area" (*Sheffield Star*, March 8, 1985).

Despite the abolition of immediate imprisonment, the use of more and heavier fines has led to a rise in the number of women being sent to prison for fine default. In 1981, a total of 2,087 women were received into prison; 825 were fine defaulters, of whom 44 were prostitutes (constituting 2.1% of the total population). By 1983, receptions of women totaled 2,178. The number of prostitutes imprisoned for fine default was 1,041.

In 1987, the Metropolitan Police in London argued that the low level of fines imposed upon conviction was not proving a meaningful deterrent. However, court returns on sentencing and amount of fines ordered does not indicate that the level is especially low. Of 289 fines ordered in 289 convictions at Marylebone Magistrates Court from April 1, 1987, to July 10, 1987, 11% of the offenders

Table 16-1 (Continued)

1982			1983			1984		
Total	17–21	21+	Total	17–21	21+	Total	17–21	21+
6062	2151	3886	10674	3450	7210	8836	2379	6425
247	54	192	211	53	161	211	61	149
11	6	5	5	1	4	—	1	5
5804	1192	3688	10442	3390	7039	8605	2312	6263
30	9	21	62	13	48	114	26	88
746	257	480	800	270	528	706	97	501
448	176	272	251	109	142	184	74	110
3983	1488	2482	9294	2989	6298	7588	2014	5558
96	19	77	5	—	5	—	—	1
298	87	211	13	4	9	—	—	—
131			4			1		
12			1					
43			1					
1			—					
	11		5					
96%			98%			97%		

were fined under £25, 61% were fined between £30 and £50, 20% were fined between £60 and £75, and 8% were fined between £80 and £120. Fining by region continues to discriminate even further against the prostitute, who after all is poor and vulnerable. Magistrates courts vary considerably in the quantum of fine ordered per conviction. At Wolverhampton Magistrates Court in the West Midlands, for example, the rate is £250 per conviction.

But it is not just that women prostitutes face high fines and subsequent custody for nonpayment, they are also routinely detained in police cells overnight, pending court appearance. This is in evidence in London, where certain police stations adopt this policy as routine practice on the grounds that prostitute women who have addresses outside London (indeed, about 80% of women operating in London [Edwards & Armstrong, 1988]) are likely to jump bail and fail to appear in court the following morning. As a result, one London police station sometimes houses over 20 prostitute women nightly. This is ratified and in accordance with The Police and Criminal Evidence Act (1984), Part IV, Section 38(1)(a)(i) and (iii):

> *Where a person arrested for an offence otherwise than under a warrant endorsed for bail is charged with an offence, the custody officer shall order his release from police detention, either on bail or without bail, unless (i) his name or address cannot be ascertained or the custody officer has reasonable grounds for doubting whether a name or address furnished by him as his name or address is his real name or address; . . . (iii) the custody officer has reasonable grounds for believing that the person arrested will fail to appear in court to answer bail"*

The custody officer is also required by this section to make a written record of the grounds for detention. There is another side of the coin to this problem, which is that many prostitute women prefer not to give an address, as many keep their prostitution hidden from their families.

Table 16-1 Prosecutions for loitering for the purpose of prostitution (1979–1984)—(*Cont'd.*)

	1985			
	Total	14–17	17–21	21+
Total prosecutions	9406	44	2396	6966
Withdrawn/dismissed	197	6	50	141
Otherwise dealt with	4		3	1
Total found guilty	9161	36	2336	6789
Absolute discharge	134	—	37	97
Conditional discharge	694	12	197	485
Probation	174	6	68	106
Fine	8149	18	2031	6100
Community service order				
Suspended sentence				
Up to 1 month				
1 month up to 2 months				
2 months up to 3 months				
Over 3 months				
Other disposals				
Conviction rate[a]	97%			

[a]As a percentage of those prosecuted only.
Source: *Criminal Statistics Supplementary Tables*.

Underenforcement of The Law: Punters

Legislation, policing practice, and public pressure and concern have reflected a preoccupation with the streetwalker, whereas the activities of male punters have been outside the law. Nevertheless, although the law has not outwardly condemned the activities of male punters, it has not always condoned their behavior either. For example, consider the Vagrancy Act of 1898. Section 1(1) deemed a man who solicited prostitutes persistently as "a rogue and a vagabond," and according to Section 5 of the Summary Jurisdiction Act of 1848, a man found having sexual intercourse with a prostitute in a public thoroughfare should be charged with aiding and abetting her in the commission of the said offense.

But it took from 1898 to 1985 until any specific regulation of the male curb crawler was found in statute. This criminalization was resisted by prostitute organizations, including the English Collective of Prostitutes (ECP), who regarded such legislation as regressive. Nonetheless, there were abortive efforts to prosecute such men throughout the century, including the case of *Crook v Edmondson* (2QB:81), where the defendant was curb crawling in Preston (near Manchester) and was observed on two occasions to approach known prostitutes. Prosecuted under Section 32 of the 1956 act usually reserved for homosexual soliciting (the act states that "it is an offence for a man persistently to solicit or importune in a public place for immoral purposes"), the magistrates found there was no case to answer. The women were over 16!

In a later case, *R v. Dodd* (1977, Lexis), the court had to consider whether soliciting a 14-year-old girl from a car in a public street was an offense under the Sexual Offences Act of 1956. In the case of *Dodd*, however, since the girl was under the age of 16, it was a criminal offense to propose sexual intercourse

Table 16-2 Prosecutions and convictions for procuration, brothel keeping, and curb crawling

	1980		1981		1982		1983		1984		1985		1986	
	Pros.	Con.	Pros.	Con.	Pros.	Con.	Pros.	Con.	Pros.	Con.	Pros.	Con.	Pros.	Con.
Procuration	379	323	341	318	393	329	360	302	381	334	561	487		
S.T. ST Males	362	202	322	186	375	220	337	148	360	219	542	359		
CC	126	108	146	115	131	94	174	137	132	104	149	114		
SS Females	17	1	19	6	18	5	23	4	21	1	19	2		
CCT. CC	15	12	16	11	14	10	16	13	13	10	15	12		
Conviction rate for both[a]		85%		93%		83%		83%		87%		86%		
Brothel keeping														
Males	30	25	47	38	33	27	50	39	28	23	35	26		
Females	95	71	113	79	67	54	109	78	68	53	85	67		
Conviction rate for both[a]		77%		73%		81%		60%		79%		78%		84
Curb crawling														
Males													191	160
Conviction rate[a]														84%

[a]As a percentage of those prosecuted only.
Source: *Criminal Statistics Supplementary Tables*, Vols. 1, 2 (1980–1986 inclusive).

under Section 6 of the 1956 act and therefore could be deemed "immoral" under Section 32.

During the years immediately preceding the introduction of the Sexual Offences Act of 1985, which allowed for the prosecution of the curb crawler, police forces in England and Wales were already cautioning and in some cases arresting curb crawlers. As Matthews (1986) points out, in one area of London, Finsbury Park, a police subcommittee was set up toward the end of 1983 primarily to deal with this specific problem relating to prostitution. A special vice unit was organized by the police and operated from Stoke Newington Police Station to cover the whole area. "Intervention resulted in 460 women being cautioned, 659 women arrested, 453 kerb crawlers cautioned and a further 18 arrested, also 6 pimps and 6 ponces were arrested, together with 5 brothel keepers" (p. 9). Similar moves have taken place in other police forces outside London, where the Justice of the Peace Act (1361) was used to gain convictions. The London Police used the Metropolitan Police Act (1839) to charge curb crawlers with insulting behavior.

On September 16, 1985, the Sexual Offences Act provided for the prosecution of the curb crawler or punter for the first time. There have been, however, few arrests and prosecutions and fewer convictions. Criminal statistics for 1986 released following a question to the House in July 1987 indicated a provisional figure for 1986 of 190 prosecutions and 160 convictions. This compares with an estimated nine and a half thousand women convicted for prostitution. Regional differences in the number of men prosecuted for this offense are great. Figures for 1986 indicate that the Greater Manchester Police have had 56 successful convictions; the West Midlands Police, 71 convictions; and the Metropolitan Police, 3 convictions. Within the Metropolitan Police District itself, some areas have been more successful in getting prosecutions than others. The Street Offences Squad operating in Area 8, Westminster, for 1986 reported 2 curb crawlers and warned 49 others (Commissioner of Police of the Metropolis, 1986, p. 46). There are also wide regional variations in the application of the legislation. For example, the case against Colin Hart Leverton (QC), who was initially convicted of curb crawling at Wells Street Magistrates Court in London but later, on appeal, managed to get that conviction quashed, has had the effect of deterring prosecutions.

Interviews conducted by Sue Edwards and Gary Armstrong with the Street Offences Squad Police Station in London during June and July of 1987 indicate that the reluctance to arrest curb crawlers does not stem from a favorable application of police discretion regarding curb crawlers but instead is a response to legislation that is cumbersome and impossible to operate. As one officer explained, "The problem is the law. The law requires two overt acts. You can have a ten page statement saying you have followed him for one and a half hours and he still can get off." Another officer complained, "I mean the legislation is so unworkable, it has made our job very difficult. The main difficulty is this question of persistence; the man has to stop and solicit more than one girl." For the offense of curb crawling to be proven, the law requires the conduct to be "persistent" or likely to cause annoyance. Home Office Circular No. 52/1985, which was issued to chief officers of police lays down certain guidelines regarding the interpretation of the act. The test of persistent soliciting, it is made clear, "will of course be for the courts to decide," but the Home Office guidelines suggest that "soliciting of at least two women on the same occasion" is required, and the courts and the Crown prosecution service have clearly decided that a higher standard of proof is necessary.

It seems clear from its ratification in the Home Office guidelines that a moral perspective has intervened in "down criming" curb crawling offenses at the outset by cautioning rather than prosecuting offenders. As stated in the circular, "During the passage of the Bill through Parliament, attention was drawn to the particular need for care in deciding whether to charge individuals with offences under this Act, because of the possible implications for the reputation and family circumstances of a man accused of seeking the services of a prostitute." Home Office Circular No. 14/1985 drew attention to the use of cautioning of offenders as an alternative to prosecution.

Crime Prevention: The Police, Public, and Council Partnership

In an effort to get rid of the street prostitution problem, residents groups, police, and local councils have implemented ways of "designing out crime" as part of a situational crime prevention approach. In the Metropolitan Police area, particularly in Streatham, where the traditional method of the police arresting prostitutes for soliciting had not succeeded, local residents groups have produced leaflets and street lighting has been improved (Commissioner of Police of the Metropolis, 1986, p. 4). In Westminster and Camden, traffic schemes have been devised to combat curb crawling and prostitution. Paddington Division, in liaison with local community groups and Westminster's City Council, deployed a traffic scheme in Cleveland Square and Leicester Gardens which is thought to have discouraged curb crawlers, and street lighting there is being improved (Commissioner of Police of the Metropolis, 1986, p. 46).

But it is also well known that the 1983 "designing" out of prostitution in Kings Cross through saturation policing merely forced women out of the area into another. Prostitution then became a problem in nearby Finsbury Park. The impact of such schemes is to displace prostitution, and prostitute women and clients either move to other areas or else move off the streets into clubs and hotels, saunas and massage parlors. Some of these fronts for prostitution are organized for the benefit of prostitutes, punters, and entrepreneurs. Many are exploitive, and many are beyond the reach of the law or else benefit from the fact that the law is rarely enforced.

Underenforcement of The Law: Ponces

It was in the other arenas of prostitution that women were to experience the grossest victimization, control, and male violence. Increasing numbers of women prostituted themselves in clubs, saunas, and massage parlors. They lost their autonomy and were rapidly subjugated under the control of male managers, ponces, and pimps. Police claims that evidence of lawbreaking was difficult to establish meant that these enterprises were then, as now, largely outside police control. Women's vulnerability to male control and male violence had thus been increased.

This increasing control of female prostitution by entrepreneurs has been facilitated by the legislation itself. Since the Street Offences Act of 1959, women have become the victims of prostitution as an organized crime, controlled largely by male ponces and managers, though the extent of this actual control is hidden and often denied by the prostitutes themselves. In 1986, the Criminal Law Revision Committee, in its 17th report, *Prostitution: Off-Street Activities*, boldly addressed the question of exploitation and control of female prostitution through organized crime. In the opening remarks, the committee states, "All too often those who practice prostitution are likely to become victims of exploitation or contract venereal disease." The committee went on to recognize that the real mischief is the large-scale facilitation of prostitution and the insidious means used to control it. But even given the bold statements and suggestions for legal revision, nothing has been done to address these questions, and the insidious control continues. Meanwhile women prostitutes and drug addicts are increasingly at risk for AIDS.

The legislation relating to ponces is ambiguous and confusing. Most of the regulatory measures are contained in the Sexual Offences Act of 1956, where some offenses are sex specific (e.g., a man's living off of prostitution knowingly [Section 30] and a woman's directing or exercising control of prostitutes [Section 31]). Case law since 1956 demonstrates just how widely Section 30 (which concerns immoral earnings) has been interpreted and how difficult it has been to get a conviction. Lord Simonds recognized that the law was far too wide, too weak, and too ineffective with regard to "the tout, the bully or the protector" whom it was designed to catch (cf. *Shaw v DPP*, 1961, 125 JP 437). Police forces and policy advisors are quite clear that the concern is not with the simple ponce (e.g., an unemployed cohabitee or adult son) or with a situation where a man is a passive recipient. The concern is instead with the man who takes most of the earnings and organizes, controls, or assaults prostitute women. In accordance with Section 30, the prosecutor is required to prove that the defendant was living off the earnings of the prostitution, that he knew of the prostitution, and that he was receiving money. This section has resulted in prosecution of club owners, escort agency managers, taxi drivers, men living with prostitute women and exercising control over them, and men living with prostitute women and having no control whatsoever.

Under Section 30(1), it is for the prosecutor to prove that the defendant was living on the earnings of a prostitute. Under Subsection (2), it is for the defendant to prove he was not living on the earnings of the prostitute. In both cases, control need not be an element. The Criminal Law Revision Committee, in its 17th report, suggests that a new offense be framed, focusing on organizational control and direction of prostitution. The committee was in no doubt at all as to the heinous extent of control.

Activities of this kind take many forms and vary in gravity. Probably the most heinous form is when a man decides to take control of the practice of prostitution in an area: "He designates certain streets and premises such as clubs, as his territory and by threats or violence or bribery, ensures that all who practice prostitution in that area pay a part of their earnings to him" (Criminal Law Revision Committee, 17th Report, Para 2:11).

A whole series of cases has guided convictions and sentencing in such cases (cf. *Wilson*, 1984, CLR:173; *Grant*, 1985, CLR:387; *Farrugia*, 1979, 69 CAR:108). Sentencing practice, with the exception of *El Gazzar*, has clearly reflected the court's intention to distinguish between the passive and coercive ponce (cf.

Robinson Russell Bannerjee, 1986, 8 CF, CAR(S):102; *El Gazzar*, 1986, CLR:698; *Ross Visgkok*, 1987, 9 CAR(S):249). In cases where managers of saunas, clubs, and so on, or men living with prostitutes have exercised no control whatever, sentences have been minimal. Where there is control, sentences are more severe. *Parker* (1985, 6 CAR(S):444; Lexis; Enggen 19 July 1985) reveals the extent of control and coercion characteristic of some of these cases. In this particular case, the defendant Parker pleaded guilty at the Crown court on one count of living off immoral earnings (Section 30(1)) and one of aiding and abetting buggery in the form of bestiality. It was alleged that the appellant had introduced the woman with whom he was living "to prostitution and therefore had coerced her into continuing to act as a prostitute." It was said that the appellant was violent toward her and threatened to report her prostitution to the social services so that she would lose the custody of her child. On three occasions the woman ran away, but the appellant located her and brought her back. This scenario characterizes the coercion, the violence, and the fear that many women encounter. The threat of losing a child, the threat of exposure to the social services, or the threat of exposure to the police keeps many women under the control of ponces through fear. It was also alleged that Parker had advertised the woman's services in contact magazines and had received between £500 and £700 each week. The count of aiding and abetting buggery referred to an incident in which he took the woman to a club and forced her to have intercourse with a dog with a view to giving demonstrations in the future and making money out of the photographs that were made. Parker was sentenced to 4 years imprisonment for living on the earnings of prostitution and 3 years consecutive for aiding and abetting buggery. Parker had burnt the woman on one occasion, had slapped her, and had threatened to inform the social services so that she would lose custody of her child; as a result, she became ill and had to be hospitalized for a period of time. The appeal was dismissed and the sentence of 7 years upheld.

The law regarding procuration is equally problematic. Under Section 22 of the Sexual Offences Act of 1956, it is an offense to procure a women to become a prostitute. Again this section revolves around the belief and knowledge of the offense. For example, in the case of *R v. Brown* (1984 1, WLR:1211–1215), the appellant raised the defense that he had not procured her, because he believed that she was already a prostitute. The judge ruled that his belief, in this offense, was irrelevant. He changed his plea and was convicted. The appeal court responded by overruling this decision, declaring that his belief was indeed relevant and that if a man genuinely believed on reasonable grounds that the woman was a prostitute, he could not be said to be trying to procure her. Obviously, the classic defense in cases of procuration is that the defendant believed that the woman was a prostitute, a defense which most men charged with procuration will offer to the court for consideration. It is not only the belief aspect that makes conviction difficult but also the use of the wording "common prostitute." The case of *R v Morris-Lowe* (Court of Appeal Criminal Division October 26, 1984, CLR 1985:50) reflects the difficulty. In this case, the appellant advertised in the local newspaper for young women to train as masseuses. He stated that they would, if required by male customers, perform relief massage masturbation. He pleaded not guilty to the indictment, which contained three counts under Section 1(1) of the Criminal Act, of attempting to procure a woman for the purposes of common prostitution. He appealed on the ground that the offense under Section 22(1) of the Sexual Offences Act of 1956 specifies a "common prostitute." He said he had attempted to procure each woman to offer herself for prostitution, and the court had to decide whether the performance by a woman of a single act of lewdness with a man on one occasion for reward made her a prostitute or whether this was quite different from someone who was prepared for reward to engage in acts of lewdness with anybody who might hire her. It was decided that it was not an offense to procure a woman to become a common prostitute, and the convictions were quashed.

Sections 31 and 33 of the Sexual Offences Act have usually been applied in the prosecution of women, and Section 31 applies exclusively to women. The prosecutors have to prove more than is required for men prosecuted under Section 30(2) where living on immoral earnings is enough, cases brought under Section 31 require proof that the woman was exercising control. Section 33 applies to running a brothel. Many women organize together to combat social exploitation by men but, this is beyond the law. On April 21, 1978, Cynthia Payne (Madam Cyn) pleaded guilty to three counts of exercising control over a prostitute and to one count of keeping a disorderly house. She was convicted, fined, and sentenced to a term of imprisonment. She appealed. Her appeal revealed the hypocrisy of prostitution and the sex-specificness of a law which obviously prosecutes women for brothel keeping. Mr. Robertson, counsel for the appellant Cynthia Payne, had the following exchange with the investigating officer:

Q. As far as the clients were concerned, the 53 men, I think who were found and men who were observed going into the house on Decembe 6th, they were broadly speaking, middle-aged and elderly men?
A. There was a general cross-section, but principally middle aged and elderly.
Q. Of that cross section you had businessmen, managing directors and accountants?
A. Yes.
Q. You had barristers?
A. Yes, Sir.
Q. And solicitors?
A. Yes.
Q. Among those 53 men you had a Member of Parliament from Ireland?
A. Yes.
Q. You had a Member of the House of Lords?
A. That is correct.
Q. You had several Vicars?
*A. Yes. (*R v Payne, *Lexis [Enggen 15 May 1980]; cf.* R v O, *1983, CLR 401;* Kelly v Purvis, *QBD 1983:663;* Stevens and Stevens and Christy, *QBD 1987 July CLR)*

CONCLUSION

America, Canada, and Europe during the last few years have seen the publication of government inquiries on prostitution and pornography. On February 11, 1981, the European Economic Community placed a resolution on the position of women in the EEC. Article 55 asks the commission to conduct a systematic inquiry into the practices of procuring and trafficking in human beings for the purpose of prostitution and to carry out a study of the ways of harnessing the suppression of such activities within and between the 10 member states, of which Britain is one (Women of Europe, p. 89). Article 1 has still not been ratified.

In 1986, Hedy D'Ancona, the Dutch socialist member of the EEC, prepared a report on violence against women, documenting among others things the gross exploitation and victimization of women in prostitution. Hers has been another voice in the wilderness.

In the United Kingdom, there have so far been few who have seen prostitute women as vulnerable. However, many have been eager to focus on their potential for spreading the AIDS virus. The chief constable of the Greater Manchester Police in December 1986 made his views clear: "Why do prostitutes, whether infected with AIDS or not, continue to ply their trade regardless of the consequences?"

The AIDS health problem is already adding to the outlawing not only of gay men and drug addicts but of prostitute women. Stiffer laws in the United Kingdom will be aimed at those who infect others. Proposals are already being mooted for compulsory testing of prostitute women among others, following in the steps of 19th-century contagious diseases legislation. We are now moving into an era of greater regulation and overenforcement of laws regarding prostitute men. Any legislative measures in the future will be intended to increase control and will create further victimization.

BIBLIOGRAPHY

Barry, K., Bunch, C., & Castley, S. (1984). *International feminism: networking against female sexual slavery*. New York: International Tribune Womens Center.

Bracey, D. H. (1983). The juvenile prostitute victim and offender. *Victimology 8*(3–4).

Commissioner of Police of the Metropolis. (1986). *Report of the Commissioner of Police of the Metropolis*. London.

Criminal Law Revision Committee. (1974). *Working paper on vagrancy on street offences*.

Criminal Law Revision Committee. (1976). *Working paper on vagrancy on street offences*.

Criminal Law Revision Committee. (1982). *Working paper on offences relating to prostitution and allied offences*.

Edwards, S. (1984). *Women on trial*. Manchester, England: Manchester University Press.

Edwards, S. (1986, April 5). Fighting organized prostitution. *Justice of the peace*, *150*(14), 216–218.

Edwards, S. (1987). Prostitutes: victims of law, social policy and organized crime. In P. Carlen and A. Worrall (Eds.), *Gender crime and justice*. England: Open University Press.

Edwards, S., & Armstrong, G. A. (1988). Policing street prostitution: A profile of the SOS. *Police Journal*, July–Sept.

James, J. (1978a). Motivations for entrance into prostitution. In L. Crites (Ed.), *The female offender*. Lexington, MA.

James, J. (1978b). The prostitute as victim. In J. R. Chapman and M. Gates (Eds.), *The victimization of women*. London: Sage.

Matthews, R. (1985). Beyond Wolfenden: Prostitution politics and the law. In R. Matthews and J. Young (Eds.), *Confronting crime*. London: Sage.

Matthews, R. (1986). *Policing prostitution: A multi-agency approach*. Enfield: Middlesex Polytechnic.

McLeod, E. (1982). *Women working prostitution now*. London: Croom Helm.

Meese, E. (1986). The attorney general's report on pornography. Washington, DC: U.S. Department of Justice.

Mukherjee, S. K., & Scutt, J. A. (1981). *Women and crime*. Sydney, Australia: George Allen and Unwin.

Ohse, L. (1984). *Forced prostitution and traffic in women in West Germany*. Edinburgh: Edinburgh Human Rights Group.

Russell, K. V., Frey, V. H., & Reichert, L. (1981, July). Prostitution business and police: The maintenance of an illegal economy. *Police Journal*, pp. 239–249.

Russell, K. V., & Owen, C. (1984, January). Prostitution, women clients and the law. *Police Journal*, pp. 68–97.

Women of Europe. (1981). *Official Journal of the European Economic Community*, No. C50.

17

Sexual Victimization: Man's Struggle With Power

Joseph Giovannoni
Pacific Center for Sexual Health, Honolulu, Hawaii

INTRODUCTION

This chapter theorizes that sexual offenders have in common problems with power and control (issues) that they attempt to resolve through victimization. Sexual victimization frequently is carried out by males with feelings of inadequacy and powerlessness, a "macho man mentality," an obsession with sexual performance and experiences of rejection.

Sociocultural conditioning is shown to contribute to sexual victimization. Historically, through phallus worship, the penis has been viewed as a major symbol of power. One of the results for this conditioning is that men who feel powerless and inadequate use this symbol of power in an attempt to experience or regain a feeling of control and power in their lives. This same historical conditioning has given rise to the macho man mentality, which is reinforced by pornography. Pornography further contributes to sexual victimization by portraying women as submissive sexual objects. Pornography can fuel the sex offender's tendencies to victimize women and children.

The author believes that an understanding of the historical and sociocultural influences which contribute to sexual victimization, combined with an awareness of current attitudes and practices that reinforce such activity, is a necessary first step in the long road to reducing and preventing sexual victimization.

THE PENIS: A SYMBOL OF POWER

Historically, men have been socialized to use their male genitalia as a symbol of power. What happens, then, when men experience powerlessness with their sexuality? Is there a relationship between men's feelings of powerlessness and the sexual victimization of women and children?

Since the beginning of recorded time, erotic art has reflected a fascination with male genitalia as a source of power and gratification. In Pompeii, a pre-

Joseph Giovannoni, a certified sex therapist and educator, specializes in the assessment and treatment of sexual deviance and sexual dysfunction and has experience in treating sex offenders. He is the founder of the Pacific Center for Sexual Health and also acts as a consultant to Family Resource Centers in Hawaii. He maintains a private practice in Honolulu and has over 20 years experience in the field.

served house has a drawing of a man weighing his large penis on a scale as it is being measured. An 18th-century Japanese painter, Jichosai, depicted an entrant in a phallic contest: a man with a gigantic phallus on a wooden block being hauled by a crew of attendants. Twentieth-century men's bathroom graffiti reflect the same kind of preoccupation with the aggressive power of the penis—the bigger the better. To this day, the Japanese worship the penis through the phallic god Go-Shintai, a symbol of fertility in festivals. Historically and cross-culturally, men have equated the penis with power.

This focus on the penis as a symbol of power can lead men to feel vulnerable in sexual relationships. This is especially true with men who have suffered severe physical and emotional abuse in childhood. These men experienced powerlessness, confusion, and fear when they were abused. Trying to avoid repetition of these feelings and to regain and maintain power when they reach manhood becomes a critical psychological issue.

Unfortunately, the abused child often becomes the adult abuser. An abused child sees his abuser as someone with great power. He learns to associate power with abuse. If, as an adult, he feels powerless, it is natural for him to try and overcome these feelings by abusing someone else. In a society where male sexuality is focused on penis performance, a man can easily turn to his penis and his sexuality to express power.

Such men may use sexuality as a "means of compensating for underlying feelings of inadequacy" and "to express issues of mastery, strength, control, authority, identity and capability" (Groth & Birnbaum, 1979). Groth says that some men rape for power and that such men frequently masturbate to fantasies of sexual conquest and rape. A man who rapes because he is angry with women uses his penis like a sword to regain control and to hurt his victim.

MACHO MAN MENTALITY AND PENIS POWER

Traditionally, men and boys have been encouraged to build big muscles and to avoid expressing their feelings. Men are taught to be tough; therefore, their penises must also be tough. I have worked with 24 men who have been incarcerated for the rape of women and children. Initially, when seen as a group, they presented themselves as "tough guys." When they talked about their sexual exploits with women, they often exaggerated and competed with each other, bragging about their sexual prowess. The emphasis on good sex always was associated with what they could do with their penises—how well they "performed."

When I saw these men individually, however, their insecurity about sex began to exhibit itself. All of these men had had rigid, "macho-type" male role models who taught them that sexually they are as good as their phallus and that men are valued by how well they use it and how often. Several of the men had raped women while on dates. They could not understand why the women went with them to their apartments and then said no when they made their moves. They are baffled when I try to explain to them that their dates may have liked their company but not their phallus. Men who have been brought up to believe that their intrinsic worth is tied to the size of their penis find it very difficult to value themselves or believe that others may value them independent of that part of their anatomy.

PENIS PERFORMANCE AND SEXUAL FUNCTIONING

In my 15 years of experience as a sex therapist working with thousands of men who have sexual problems, I have found my clients to be very performance oriented. Many men who have suffered from impotence brought on by physical problems feel an overwhelming loss of control of their sexuality. The degree of loss experienced is much greater than the impairment caused by physical changes alone, however. This loss of function becomes much greater than it needs to be, because of a preoccupation with performance. These men overreact when they notice subtle changes in their sexual functioning. They are dismayed that their erections are not as they once were. Their penises are not as firm, and they notice a decrease in morning erections and difficulties with penetration. They view this diminished capacity as a lessening of their manhood and a theft of their power. Total dysfunction is not caused by the physical changes from illness but from the emotional changes brought on by the fear of failure. Men have been conditioned to equate failure of the penis with failure as a man and as a sexual human being.

Many men suffering from impotence seek an instant cure. They do not want to hear that what really caused their total dysfunction was performance jitters and fear of failure, not organic factors alone. Instead of learning to adjust to and enjoy the remaining function they possess, these men may turn to modern medicine for the "bionic" penis—the penile implant. For men who have organic impotence which cannot be treated successfully by medical and psychological intervention, these prostheses can be helpful. This includes men with spinal cord injuries, radical surgery, advanced diabetes, and advanced arterial sclerotic disease. Often, urologists are confronted by impotent clients who insist on having these prostheses. They want the ultimate erection—the perfect performance—without fail. These are men who could still regain adequate functioning with sex therapy and conservative medical interventions such as vasoactive medication to improve penile circulation (Zorgniotti & Lefleur, 1985). The popularity of penile implants reflects continued obsession with penis performance and phallus worship.

The focus of male sexuality on the penis denies men their innate ability to experience sensuality and tenderness with the rest of their body. This is commonly reflected by couples who come to therapy. The wife's complaint is that she does not get enough foreplay and that her husband's sexual focus is on intercourse (Masters & Johnson, 1970; Kaplan, 1974).

Over 500 sex offenders I have worked with report that they have a good sex life. However, their partners claim just the opposite. They say that the offender lacked sensitivity with regard to their needs and exhibited premature ejaculation. The offenders who molest children usually blame the children for seducing them. They minimize personal responsibility by claiming that their behavior is a result of uncontrollable urges. They talk as though their penis has a mind of its own. What I have observed is that they feel insecure about their sexual performance. Therefore, the offender seduces the child in order to regain mastery and power with his penis.

POWER-ORIENTED PORNOGRAPHY

Unfortunately, very early in life men are taught to believe that good sex is directly related to the size and strength of their penis, that organ between their legs, instead of the organ between their ears, their brain. Adult magazines, with their promises of manliness and sexual fulfillment, perpetuate this belief. One particular advertisement entitled "Men Who Measure Up" claims that it is natural to think that something bigger is better. This ad for the book *The Penis*, by Dr. Brian Richards, further seduces men into presuming that "the majority of women do think that a bigger penis is better."

Most men learn about sex through pornography, which perpetuates the image of women as submissive, passive sexual objects. The women in pornography are photographed "spread eagle" and are frequently portrayed as impatiently waiting for penetration by a large-sized phallus. One never sees a small phallus in pornography. Why? Pornographic material universally depicts large penises in order to maintain the myth that to be well-endowed is symbolic of manhood and power.

One popular pornographic magazine overtly expresses hatred of women in their jokes and cartoon drawings. For example, in one issue the three little bears are depicted in stereotypically sadomasochistic gear—leather clothes, chains in hand—standing at the door of their house grinning as a girlish-looking woman runs bruised and beaten away from them. Men who need to feel omnipotent identify with these magazines which sanction through publication the victimization of women.

Pornography often eroticizes the young woman. She has a perfect body, youthful smooth skin, and an innocent, naive pose. Many men fantasize having a virgin at least once in their life. Numerous incestuous fathers have explained to me that they turn to their daughters because of their own lack of sexual experience in adolescence. They regress to that age level as they reach for both the innocence of their daughters and a sense of sexual control which they do not have as adults. Despite the father's awareness that incest is socially and morally unacceptable, he turns to his daughter for sexual gratification. She is nonthreatening, and his feelings of powerlessness over his own life are so great that he allows his impulses to take charge. The mentality that allows for this kind of behavior is in part shaped by the type of pornography he reads. One of my clients was a navy father. He started reading pornography when he was out at sea. He came across a section of anecdotes about women who had sexually served their fathers. He found this sexually stimulating and fantasized about it. He kept the stories and masturbated while reading them. Seven years later he sexually molested his 9- and 10-year-old daughters.

MACHO MAN MENTALITY CONTRIBUTES TO SEXUAL VICTIMIZATION

Since men often are taught to be tough and unfeeling individuals, it is not surprising to find them insensitive to the pain they cause others. Also, men have not been culturally conditioned or primed to be caregivers to children. Consequently, they have difficulty identifying with the vulnerability of a child. This could be one explanation why more men than women are child abusers. Throughout history, men were the ones who fought the battles, raped, pillaged, and plundered. They dominated through aggression in order to get what they wanted. Characteristics like compassion and understanding are seen by many as being feminine—men are not supposed to be like that. Child molesters and rapists have a difficult time crying about their sadness. They feel very rigid and defensive. They often cannot understand the emotional damage they have caused their victims. They will minimize the harmful effects of the molestation and will blame society for making such a big issue of it.

This socialization of men to be tough also causes them to suffer a loss of humaneness and often to have difficulty accepting rejection. I have treated 300 incestuous fathers and have found that it is not uncommon for these men to blame their wives or girlfriends for depriving them of sexual gratification. The incestuous father feels he has an excuse to molest his daughter because his partner rejected his sexual advances. I call this an excuse, because on closer examination it is apparent that these men turn to children because they feel safer and more comfortable with a child. Also, these men use their incestuous sexual behavior to express anger at their partners, who they believe are rejecting them. Frequently, they explain their deviate conduct by saying their partners were "not being sexual enough." Resulting feelings of rejection, deprivation, and powerlessness lead them to try and regain a sense of control and power by being with a child who cannot say "No!"

These men come from all walks of life, and many are married and have children. I have seen teachers, grandfathers, teenagers, and even ministers in my practice, and the majority of these child molesters present an appearance of being very macho, muscular, and attractive. Often they struggle to be a pillar of strength. They try to meet the social image of the macho man—one who is always willing and able to have sex. Such an unrealistic image of how men are supposed to be has been ingrained in men's thinking since earliest times. A child is an easy conquest.

CHILD MOLESTING: A DISTORTED WAY OF REGAINING POWER

Such unrealistic expectations naturally give rise to feelings of powerlessness. In my work with men who have molested children, I have observed a strong relationship between these feelings of powerlessness and child sex abuse. Child molestation is their distorted way of expressing power. It is especially important to note that 60% of these men (in a sample of 500 offenders) were themselves victims of child molestation. Most of them experienced some form of physical, emotional, or sexual abuse as children. Powerless to fight back when *they* were physically abused and their masculinity violated, these men now molest those who are unable to resist *them*. Their victims now are the powerless ones. It is as if the abuser feels he was robbed of his sexuality and power as a child. He seeks to regain that power by reenacting the same script and reversing the roles.

Dr. David Finkelhor, from the University of New Hampshire, has developed a multifactorial analysis to explain the causes of sexual abuse. He notes that the child molester turns to children because of his need for power, omnipotence, and control. He has strong feelings of inadequacy and has experienced humiliation and powerlessness in his youth. As a child he often had a rigid role model who socialized him to view males as always being dominant. Finkelhor suggests that these are nonsexual motivations which influence a man to turn to children for sexual gratification (Finkelhor, 1984). It seems reasonable, however, to conclude that the motivational factors leading to sexual abuse identified by Finkelhor do indeed have sexual bases as well. My argument is supported by the previously stated hypotheses that there is a connection between the penis as a symbol of power and of manhood and sexual assault. In fact, sex could be considered a secondary motivational factor. Men who feel vulnerable and powerless still have sexual needs which they believe must be met. These needs are then satisfied by sexual abuse of a child or a woman. The abuser seeks to regain a feeling of power and control in his own life by controlling and physically overpowering others. In doing the forbidden, he experiences a charge of high energy caused by an increase in adrenaline in his system. This physiological response reinforces his deviant behavior.

The tough guy conditioning has created a thick armor which prevents the abuser from feeling the trauma of and consequences to the child who is abused. What remains uppermost in his mind is that someone or something else is responsible for his behaviors: His spouse is to be blamed because of her failure to provide sufficient sexual gratification; the child wanted it; or he was overpowered by drugs, stress, or whatever. The bottom line is that he has to protect his tough guy image—he must get what he wants or needs even if it means resorting to abusing a child. The excuses and rationalizations used by sex offenders show that they will not accept responsibility for their own criminal behavior. They will lie to maintain their deviance at all costs. This also provides them with excitement and power.

Let's summarize some factors which lead men to commit sexual assault: (1) Historically, men have been conditioned to believe their penis is a symbol of power. They have been taught to use sexuality as an expression of aggression and control. (2) Pornography creates an unrealistic macho man mentality, which eventually can lead to feelings of inadequacy. (3) Sexual assault is an expression of the feeling of being powerless. By imposing themselves on their victims, men who feel powerless display dominance and experience power over others.

HELPING MEN CHANGE

I have painted a pretty dismal picture of men's vulnerability to becoming a sexual perpetrator. However, all is not lost for today's potential sex abusers. The trend to socialize men to use their penises as power tools and sexual weapons to victimize women and children can be altered. Several areas need to be addressed simultaneously in order to stem this destructive tide.

The current standard of ultimate beauty and sexiness is the young, svelte, girlish-looking woman. We see this in all advertisements and commercials. Most of the world's highest-paid models are teenagers. Society needs to redefine the criteria for the ideal woman to include *all* age groups. Women in their 40s and 50s should be considered "sexy" as well.

Concurrently, mass media needs to deemphasize men as pinnacles of perfection and strength. Men can be portrayed as tender and vulnerable without being devalued. This is already beginning to happen through stories and movies about single fathers raising children or unemployed fathers put in a role reversal situation. Men are finding themselves in positions where they need to develop nurturing skills. As they do so, they are discovering new abilities and strengths. They are learning how to empower—not overpower—others.

Traditionally depicted as the "movers" and "shakers" of the world, men have been judged on their performance, in bed as well as in business. Men have to learn that the size of the penis does not determine good sex. It is what men do with their entire bodies, spiritual and emotional parts as well, that creates healthy sexual living. Men need to recognize that their most important organ is not the penis but the skin. Through the epidermis—the largest sensory organ—men can learn about their innate ability for tenderness, caring, gentleness, and comforting others. Historically, holy men have used touch (the laying on of hands) in their rituals. This demonstrates a different type of power, the power to heal and not to destroy.

Pornography, which has unfortunately gotten much bad press recently, needs to undergo a facelift as well. Current sentiment is to abolish pornography entirely. This movement traditionally has been fueled by proponents of the Moral Majority. I agree with them to some extent that contemporary pornography does much to undermine healthy sexual practices; however, we must be objective. Pornographic material has been the expression of the ultimate male sexual experience for centuries, and it is unrealistic to think that it can be eradicated. Pornography could, however, redirect its focus away from (1) sex acts which include violence; (2) partners who are childlike, passive, and submissive; and (3) penises which are (truly!) unnaturally large. Pornographic literature, then, could promote characteristics that are noninjurious and wholesome for society. Tenderness and human caring can and should be depicted in sexually explicit material.

These issues could also be addressed in the arena of sex education. This type of learning needs to take place both in schools and in the home. Teachers and parents need to demonstrate appropriate role modeling to allow children to assume both masculine and feminine traits. Young people need accurate information regarding sex. By the discussion of birth control methods, anatomy, pregnancy, and sexually transmitted diseases, sex becomes demystified to children and therefore less alluring.

Attention to parental responsibility can ensure that children are not sexualized too early. Through example, mothers and fathers can teach their children that affection can be expressed in caring nonsexual touch. Frequent hugs and other forms of positive human contact can do much to enhance the love, tranquility, and joy experienced in the home. (Sexual touch can be displayed in a playful nonviolent manner.) Assertive roles in the household can be assumed by both parents; children need to know that it is "okay" for women to be in a position of control.

Finally, all those who have contact with children need to be alerted to the signs of potential sex offenders—adolescents who may be turning to sex as a coping mechanism to deal with feelings of inadequacy and powerlessness. Clues such as talk that is demeaning of women, sex games which express regressed sexual aggression ("goosing," "grabbing ass," etc.), and extreme preoccupation with pornography need to be recognized. Moreover, professionals and parents should educate themselves on the symptomatology of victims of child sex abuse and know the resources available in the community to turn to for help.

When a sex offender is identified, he needs specialized treatment. His criminal thinking, which leads him to justify and rationalize his deviance, needs to be treated aggressively. A soft approach cannot be used. Traditional therapy which focuses on insight only assists such criminals in finding more excuses. These men have thinking errors that must be altered through persistent, vigilant confrontation with a therapist who can see through the excuses and rationalizations (Yochelson & Samenow, 1982). Sex offenders are very resistant to letting go of the thought and behavior patterns that give them a sense of power.

Sex offenders are in critical need of the kind of therapy that can enable them to change their thinking and help them find more gratifying and acceptable ways of expressing their sexuality. Deviance has become sexually gratifying; they need to be conditioned to find it unsatisfying. These men are the product of a society that gives them mixed messages: It is okay to *think* in deviant ways but there are laws against deviant *behavior*.

Strong support is needed from our legal system in order to reduce sexual victimization. The consequences of deviant behavior must be clear and severe if sex crimes are to stop. There should be mandatory therapy for all offenders. For those men who genuinely want to change, mandatory therapy can be a substitute for incarceration. For offenders who are not willing to try to restructure their belief system and who, therefore, continue to be a danger to society, there must be mandatory imprisonment as well.

Men have victimized themselves throughout the evolution of civilization. In trying to gain power over women, they have forfeited their ability to experience the harmony which results from a relationship based on support, mutual respect, cooperation, and sexual equality. As men and women try to achieve equality in relationships, the need for performance decreases. Sexual expression for a man then does not have to focus on how well he can perform with his penis. If he stops thinking he has to call on his penis to prove himself, he will never need to use his penis as the ultimate symbol of his sexuality, masculinity, and power in sexual assaults on women and children.

BIBLIOGRAPHY

Finkelhor, D. (1984). *Child sexual abuse: New theory and research*. New York: The Free Press.

Groth, A., & Birbaum, H. (1979). *Men who rape: The psychology of the offender*. New York: Plenum Press.

Kaplan, H. (1974). *The new sex therapy*. New York: Brunner, Mazel.

Kronhausen, P., & Kronhausen, E. (1968). *Erotic art: A survey of erotic facts and fancy in the fine arts*. New York: Grove Press.

Masters, W., & Johnson, V. (1970). *Human sexual inadequacy*. Boston: Little, Brown.

Yochelson, S., & Samenow, S. (1982). The criminal personality. In J. Aronson (Ed.), *A profile for change* (Vol. 1). New York.

Zorgniotti, A., & Lefleur, R. (1985). Auto-injection of the corpus cavernosum with a vasoactive drug combination for vascular impotence. *The Journal of Urology, 133*, 39–42.

18

The Sexual Victimization of Males: Victim to Victimizer: Clinical Observations and Case Studies

Robert E. Freeman-Longo
Correctional Sex Offender Treatment Program, Salem, Oregon

INTRODUCTION

The sexual abuse of males, including its long-term impact, has gained more attention in recent years. A review of the literature reveals that little has been written pertaining to this issue and that much of what has been written is conflicting. Clinical experience in working with convicted adult sex offenders suggests that there may be a significant relationship between childhood sexual abuse and subsequent sexually abusing behavior among males. In some cases it appears as though the sexual abuse of males impacts in ways which make it more difficult to treat male victims who become offenders than to treat offenders who have not been sexually abused.

Historically, sexual abuse has been viewed as a crime committed on a female by a male. This premise, which prevails even today, is based on myths and attitudes as well as statistics on reported crimes (i.e., the crimes reported to agencies such as victim advocate programs, children's protective services, and law enforcement agencies). Reporting statistics continue to indicate that women and female children are the primary targets of sexual abuse and sexual aggression. Estimates for the risk of becoming the victim of a sex crime range from 1 in 5 to 1 in 10 for rape perpetrated on women and 1 in 4 or 5 (for girls) and 1 in 9 or 10 (for boys) for sexual abuse prior to the age of 18, with the greatest risk being in the age period 8–13 (Department of Health and Human Services [HHS], 1985, p. 2). Since the majority of sex crimes are believed to go unreported, determining the actual number of victims of sex crimes becomes an impossible task regardless of whether or not the victim is male or female. In addition, cultural norms may play a significant role in determining which types of sexual behavior are considered to be abuse and which are not.

There are cultures and societies which advocate different attitudes and practices concerning children and sexuality. In 1985, the Dutch government proposed lowering the age of sexual consent from 16 to 12 years of age (*Age 12 Consent*,

Robert E. Freeman-Longo, M. R. C., is the director of the Correctional Sex Offender Treatment Program, Division of Mental Health and Department of Corrections, State of Oregon. Mr. Freeman-Longo is also a consultant in the area of assessing and treating sexual aggression.

1985). This legislation, had it passed, would have allowed adults to have legal consenting sex with children as young as 12 years old provided the minor was not coerced or seduced with gifts, promises, and the like.

In the eastern highlands of New Guinea there exists a tribe whose customary practice is to engage young boys in homosexual activity in order to prepare them for adulthood. The boys continue to practice homosexuality until marriage to a woman, at which time they become heterosexual, with an apparent lack of negative impact as a result of this life experience (*From Homosexuality*, 1985, p. 13). Such practices are cultural and not considered abusive by law or any other standard.

Little attention has been focused on the issue of sexually abused males (Cotton & Groth, 1982; Summit, 1983; Freeman-Longo, 1986; Porter, 1986; Reinhart, 1987). This is especially true regarding sexual abusers or offenders who themselves have been sexually abused and traumatized. Porter (1986) writes:

> *The overwhelming majority of perpetrators of sexual abuse are male, and a significant factor in the behavior of many perpetrators is a personal history of having been sexually victimized themselves. By no means, however, do all male victims of sexual abuse become perpetrators of sex crimes. In fact, of all such victims, probably only a small percentage may offend sexually. Sexually abusive behavior is related to a number of factors, of which a history of molestation is only one. Nonetheless, studies of incarcerated perpetrators of the most severe sexual abuses provide estimates that (1) up to 100 percent were sexually victimized as children and (2) more than half began their offending behavior as adolescents. (pp. 27–28)*

The majority of child molesters being reported to or apprehended by law enforcement agencies are males. Reinhart (1987) found in a study of 189 male sexual abuse victims that 96% were victimized by male perpetrators, 19% of whom were male adolescents. A study of sexual abuse in day-care centers reveals that "pedophiles can be attracted to day care programs, can abuse hundreds of children without being caught, are often not convicted after being arrested, and may have no criminal records even if they plead guilty to sexually abusing children" (HHS, 1985, p. 5). On the other hand, if one were to survey the average prison in the United States, one might find that as many as 20% to 25% of incarcerated felons have a history of sexually abusing behavior (Groth, personal communication, 1987). Clearly, there is a significant number of individuals in our society who are sexually abusing children. Most are males who are abusing male children to a significant degree.

There is little doubt that the sexual victimization of males is, at least in part, an unrecognized problem and that victimized males are neglected clients. This claim has credibility, at least in part, because male victims have a tendency to hide their victimization and are more likely to grow up and become sexual abusers and therefore remain neglected. If one looks at the agencies which work with the victims of sexual abuse, the above statement evokes more credence. The majority of these agencies employ women and tend to cater to female victims. This is especially true in the case of rape. Few males feel comfortable reporting a crime whose victims are usually female.

In recent years, some clinicians working with sexual aggressives, child molesters, and other paraphiliacs have reported that in fact many more male victims of sexual abuse may exist than are reported or even suspected. Abel (personal communication, March 1985) found that among 571 sexual offenders he evaluated and treated, 68.3% were pedophiles assaulting male children, 8.7% were pedophiles assaulting female children, 3.8% were incest offenders on male children, and 19.2% were incest offenders on female children. In addition, Abel reported that the average number of victims for offenders molesting female children was 23 and the average number of victims for offenders molesting male children was 281. Freeman-Longo (1985) found that among 53 sex offenders surveyed, 60% of child molestation victims were male and 40% were female (see Table 18-1). Abel (1986) found in a study of 371 sex offenders who exhibited touching behaviors in child molestation that the victims were 37.1% female and 62.9% male. These findings suggest that the number of sexual crimes committed against male children may be greater than those committed against female children.

Jones, Gruber, and Timbers (1981) conducted a study to examine their hypothesis that adolescent offenders, as a group, are at a higher risk for sexual victimization than nonoffending adolescents. Their original sample of 91 delinquent youths resulted in interviews of 42 females and 24 males. Half of the females reported being sexually abused, whereas none of the males did. Groth and Freeman-Longo (1987), however, report in an ongoing study of convicted sexual offenders that as many as 80% of their sample from four states say they were victims of sexual abuse and trauma. In addition, they find that among convicted sex offenders, both rapists and child molesters, the average age at the time of the first offense is 16. Given the above, it is apparent that there is a potential for a cycle of sexual abuse to occur.

A review of the literature reveals that little has been written that addresses what, if any, correlation exists between sexual abuse and sexually abusive or aggressive behavior. In addition, it is evident that research is needed to address what variables result in differences between individuals (i.e., why does one individual who is sexually abused become sexually abusive and another individual who is sexually abused not exhibit such behaviors). What has been written seldom addresses this phenomenon, and the data, when summarized, are conflicting. Petrovich and Templer (1984) studied a sample of 83 adult rapists and found 59% had been heterosexually molested. Most of their sample reporting sexual abuse (77%) had been abused on more than one occasion, and the abuse sometimes involved intercourse. The authors conclude that it is not certain that heterosexual molestation predisposes someone to become a rapist.

Pomeroy, Behar, and Stewart (1981) studied a small sample of referrals to the University of Iowa Child Psychiatric Department. Six boys and 10 girls had histories of sexual misbehavior and acting out. Of the sample, 1 boy and 5 girls

Table 18-1 Child molestation victim data (by age group)

	Female victims[a]				Male victims[b]			
	0–5	6–12	13–17	Total	0–5	6–12	13–17	Total
Child molestation	61	221	48	330	26	443	48	517
Rape	2	8	7	17	0	6	0	6

[a]Female child victim total = 347 (40%).
[b]Male child victim total = 523 (60%).

reported sexual abuse. Their findings indicated that "the sexual acting-out in the boys showed no consistent etiological factors," whereas the sample of girls "suggested that they were predisposed to sexual experimentation" by a combination of factors. Groth and Freeman-Longo (1987) find that sexual abuse is common in the histories of child molesters and rapists. Rapists report that 25% of the time their victimizers were women who engaged in fondling, oral sex, or intercourse with them. The study also indicates that the abuse occurred over long periods of time, and in most cases there were several different perpetrators for both the rapists and child molesters. Conte and Schuerman (1987) note that the impact of sexual abuse for boys may be greater when the abuse was of a longer duration, it occurred frequently, the sex was more intrusive (e.g., intercourse), and there was a closer relationship between the offender and victim.

Among researchers and clinicians working with child victims of physical abuse and neglect, there is general acceptance of the proposition that there is a cycle of abuse (Haynes, personal communication, May 1985). Simply stated, children who are victims of abuse or neglect are more likely to become abusers as adults. Presently there is a growing body of knowledge to support the notion of a sexual abuse cycle. In one recent survey, a major finding was that "there is a clear cycle of abuse begetting abuse: abusers who were abused as children, and mothers allowing their children to be sexually abused because their own fathers did it to them" (HHS, 1985, p. 6). Paperny and Deisher (1983) state, "In spite of conflicting data and a need for further research, there appears to be an association between maltreatment, abuse, and exploitation of adolescents, and violence or other offending behavior." Freeman-Longo (1986) notes, "If, in fact, the majority of sex offenders have been sexually abused themselves, then this observation may lend credence that there exists a cycle in sexual abuse."

Pithers, Buell, Kashima, Cumming, and Beal (1988) found a set of early precursors to sexual aggression among rapists and pedophiles. For rapists, physical abuse as a child, paternal absence or neglect, and maternal absence or neglect were significant factors in a list of 20 criteria. For pedophiles, paternal absence or neglect, precocious sexuality (less than 12 years of age at the time of first act of penetration not considered abuse), and sexual victimization (prior to the age of 12) were 3 of 20 high-frequency factors identified as early precursors to sexual aggression.

THE ETIOLOGY OF SEXUALLY ABUSIVE BEHAVIOR

There are several theories which address the etiology of sexual aggression. Some of the more popular are the biological-medical model, the psychodynamic model, the cognitive model, and the social learning model. These theories are all valid and have numerous case histories which support them. This author favors the social learning theory, which suggests that sexual aggression results from learned behaviors and environmental factors rather than from inborn causes. Paperny and Deisher (1983) state that "The adolescent sex offender and the emotionally and psychologically abusive adolescent may also learn their behaviors from modeling." Calderone (1983) states that "the peak period for sexual learning appears to coincide with that for learning language, that is, between 2–5 years of age. . . . as a result [of failing to teach children about sex before they reach adolescence] children reach adolescence with their natural eroticism maimed." Sexual abuse during childhood and the informative years may then result in inappropriate learning about sexuality or in experiences that provide a distorted view or understanding about human sexuality and human sexual response.

In working with sex offenders who molest children and who themselves have been sexually abused, we find that (1) the offender's offense(s) may be an anger reaction to his sexual victimization and feeling of powerlessness; (2) the offender's offense(s) may be a replication of what happened in his sexual victimization; or (3) the offender's offense(s) may be a modeling of his sexual victimization (his personal or misinterpreted view of his own sexual victimization may be that it wasn't that harmful to him and had pleasurable aspects to it, and in some cases it may be remembered as having been sexually arousing). Conte and Schuerman (1987) note that the professional literature "indicates that some children are profoundly traumatized by sexual abuse, some exhibit milder or transient problems, and some appear not to have been affected by the abuse."

The majority of the men we see are individuals whose motivational intent is in part fueled by anger. Often this anger is related, in varying degrees, to their own sexual abuse. Summit (1983) states,

> *For many victims of sexual abuse, the rage incubates over years of facade, coping, frustration, and counterfeit attempts of intimacy only to erupt as a pattern of abuse against offspring in the next generation. . . . The male victim of sexual abuse is more likely to turn his rage outward in aggressive and antisocial behavior. He is even more intolerant of his helplessness than the female victim and more likely to rationalize that he is exploiting the relationship for his own benefit . . . . child molestation and rape seem to be part of the legacy of rage endowed in the sexually abused boy. (p. 185)*

Our clinical experience with sex offenders who have been sexually abused reveals that it is often difficult for the offender to discuss his own victimization. The offender finds it easier to describe the pain and trauma he has inflicted on others than to disclose the fear and shame he experienced from his abuse. Many have never told anyone else about their exploits until they entered treatment and found it would be safe to disclose them. Concerns about being vulnerable and losing control are common blocks to admission.

Summit (1983) states,

> *Because of the extreme reluctance of males to admit to sexual victimization experiences and because of greater possibility that a boy will be molested by someone outside the nuclear family, less is known about the possible variations in accommodation mechanisms of sexually abused males. . . . While there is some public capacity to believe that girls may be helpless victims of sexual abuse, there is also universal repudiation of the boy victim. (p. 180)*

Some of the men we treat have replicated the abuse they experienced on their own victims. This often results from their internalization of the abuse and identification with the aggressor. In their own distorted thinking and subsequent behavior, they attempt to undo by redoing or resolve the trauma they experienced and make themselves feel better by recreating the abusive encounters. In such instances, the offender, in attempting to identify with his abuser, minimizes, in his thinking, the trauma he experienced. Although the offender may not necessarily have enjoyed the abuse he experienced as a child, he is able to minimize it by protecting the abuser through justifying the abuser's behavior or through identifying with him. This identification is accomplished through the reenactment of the victimization the offender experienced, as the following case history illustrates. (This case was related to the author by Barbara Mallas, Medford, OR, 1985.)

T.M. is a 30-year-old single white male charged with the sexual abuse of an 11-year-old white male over a 1-year period. T.M. stated, "The boy became an obsession with me." While in treatment, T.M. admitted to sexual molestation of 24 male children ranging in age from 3 to 17. He prefers ages 11 and 12. He began to molest younger males when he was 13 years old. T.M. revealed that while in jail he had been masturbating to the fantasy of his own molestation at the age of 7, but now, in his fantasy, he is the 30-year-old T.M. molesting himself at the age of 7.

In other cases, the offender who selectively abuses male children may report that he identifies with the male child victim. In such cases, the child may represent innocence and become symbolic of the offender's childhood. This is often the case when the offender reports feeling that he has missed out on his childhood and through the molestation seeks to recreate the childhood experience. Often such men see themselves in the child or children they ultimately abuse.

B.K. is a 48-year-old divorced white male who has molested over 100 children since he was 14. As a child he was molested by his father numerous times over several years. In an interview, when asked why he molested young boys, B.K. is quoted as having said, "I'm not exactly sure, I think I did identify with them. Very often I felt like I was also a child, and, I think in some ways I was trying to recapture that childhood that I felt I never had. I know there was other elements involved, because usually when I would start molesting [boys] my feelings about myself would be so low at that point that I would begin feeling the only person I could relate to was a child."

In some cases, our treatment program finds that there is an interesting potential link between childhood sexual abuse and later abusing behaviors. Sometimes an offender, when assessed on the penile plethysmograph, has shown sexual arousal while describing his own sexual victimization or listening to customized stimulus material which describes the abuse which occurred in the offender's life. In other cases, the offender clearly states that he finds his own victimization sexually arousing, as the following case histories illustrate.

D.P. is a 31-year-old divorced white male convicted of the sexual molestation of his 3-year-old daughter. He states he witnessed his father molest his sister. D.P. never told anyone about his own rape until entering treatment. He claims to suffer from delayed ejaculation of at least 1 hour during intercourse but of a shorter delay with masturbation. D.P. wrote in his thoughts-and-urges log, "While I was masturbating I had thoughts of how it felt when I was raped [age 16, by a black male stranger] and how I liked how it felt to have the penis in my ass. Those thoughts made me harder and easy for me to come."

M.D. is a 37-year-old single white male who was charged with the sexual abuse of numerous male children he coached in Little League baseball. As a child he was sexually abused by his father for a period of years, until his father was killed in an automobile accident. While in treatment, M.D. revealed in the laboratory that he was sexually aroused by thoughts of being sexually molested by his father.

CLINICAL OBSERVATIONS AND TREATMENT CONCERNS

In order to work with the offender's abuse and victimization issues, there are several areas that need to be considered. Obviously, in this situation, the clinician is treating both a victim and an offender simultaneously. It is important to keep that perspective during the therapy. It is our belief that in order to work with the abuse issues most effectively, certain criteria should be met by the offender. First, the offender should accept complete responsibility for his criminal or sexually offensive behavior. This helps in assuring that the offender doesn't fall into a victim stance and blame his crimes on his abuse or on others. Second, we find it helpful if the offender has worked with his anger for a while and appears to have some understanding of and control over his anger response. Finally, we feel it is important that he be able to show some signs of empathy, even if the empathy expressed is purely from an intellectual standpoint.

While working with offenders in a special group designed to address issues related to their own sexual and physical abuse, we have made several observations. First, very few of the men have ever overcome the abuse that has happened to them, nor have they even made any attempt to resolve issues related to the abuse. The abuse has been pushed down and hidden for years. For most sex offenders it is much easier to talk about the crimes they have committed against others than to talk about the abuse done to them.

The majority have not dealt with their feelings surrounding their abuse, and consequently they harbor a great deal of anger, hurt, fear, and frustration. Few are initially able to deal openly with their feelings because of a fear of becoming vulnerable to others. These individuals, despite their offending behavior, tend to experience the same syndrome (or one similar) that other victims of sex crimes experience who do not become sexually aggressive as a result of their abuse. It is important, however, to guide clients in a direction where they will not ultimately fall into a victim stance. They must not end up blaming their offending behavior on their victimization.

Most of the men report that they still possess a strong amount of hatred toward their abusers and a desire to retaliate against them. Indeed they do, as they ultimately victimize another out of anger, frustration, a desire to get their needs met, and so on. At the same time, some of the men still feel vulnerable with respect to their abusers, and if they are still in contact with the abusers, they have not been able to assert themselves enough to express their feelings or thoughts to them. However, in some cases, as mentioned earlier, there is a protectiveness on the part of the offender toward the abuser. This is especially so in those cases where the abuser is still alive and is a parent, sibling, relative, or friend. On occasion, the protectiveness is so prominent that the offender minimizes the abuse, places blame on himself for the abuse, or is reluctant to even bring it up and discuss it. In this fashion, the offender is giving power and control to the abuser. When this phenomenon occurs, it becomes extremely difficult to move the offender toward empathy and get him to recognize that his victims may not feel the same way. In some cases, the identification is so strong with the abuser that the offender is in denial regarding his own abusing behaviors.

We have found in our work that there is an effective method for dealing with these men, namely, to acknowledge that there are key emotions that must initially be addressed. These emotions, fear and anger, are the barrier behind which the rest of their feelings hide. We have found that the adult offender harbors the same feelings regarding his abuse that he experienced as a child. If the offender can confront the fear and anger and penetrate this insulating barrier, the therapeutic work becomes easier. The men begin to trust the process more, feel accepted, and become invested in understanding the origins of their feelings and frustrations.

Many of the men who were sexually abused still feel a lack of power and control in their lives, which has culminated in their attempt to overpower and control others via sexual abuse or exploitation. In many cases, the offender still feels strongly that the person (or persons) who abused him retains some control over him. We have even seen this phenomenon with men whose abusers were parents who have since passed away. The offender's offense(s) are often an anger reaction to and retaliation for his own abuse and his feeling powerless and out of control. The issue of control rings loud and clear when an offender describes his wish to have been able to control the abuser and stop the abuse while not recognizing that at the time of the abuse he was too small, too young, and too immature to have been able to control the situation.

Traditionally, males have been raised differently than females. Males are taught to brush off injury and fend for themselves. It is "manly" to fight one's own battles. Boys are taught not to complain or tell on others and that to do so is a sign of weakness. Females, on the other hand, are often raised from early childhood not to be aggressive and not to fight. They are encouraged to turn to others for assistance. A common response for males when they cannot fight for themselves or when they lose a fight is to become angry with themselves or others. As a result, the male may misdirect his anger and target another in an effort to build his self-esteem and make himself feel better. This is especially so in the case of sexual offenders.

By and large we have found that the men in our treatment program do not associate their feelings from being victimized with their abuse of others before, during, or after their crimes. As part of the minimization of their offending behavior, offenders often feel that the child benefited from the sexual experience or that they offered the child something that he or she would never have had otherwise (e.g., love, attention, understanding, gifts, etc.). Consequently, while the offender is abusing another, he is not thinking about or relating to his own sexual abuse, nor is he cognizant of the possibility that his victim is experiencing the same trauma he experienced. If the offender found his abuse to be positive in some way, he is less likely to recognize the potential harm to his victim. Sex offenders generally lack empathy for others. They report the uncanny ability to block any thoughts or feelings that they might have concerning what the victim may be going through at the time of the assault, just as they have blocked or repressed the feelings which resulted from their own abuse.

In those cases where the offenders did in fact reflect back on their own sexual victimization, they focused on what they considered to be the positive part of the experience, that is, the pleasurable aspects of touch and good sexual feelings. These men report being able to quite effectively suppress the traumatic aspects of their own victimization. Regardless of their own feelings, recall, and the like, they come into treatment with little sense of the harm they have caused their victims. It is some of these individuals that we find can become sexually aroused by their own sexual abuse.

In some cases, the offenders report such sexual urges in their daily log or discuss the arousal in a therapy group. They are clearly aware that this sexual arousal is connected to thoughts of their own sexual victimization. In other cases, when the offenders are not as in touch with their sexual arousal and sexual awareness, the arousal is first detected in the laboratory during a standard assessment procedure. The levels vary, and at times it is the stimulus materials that trigger the sexually arousing thoughts about their own victimization.

SUMMARY

It is clearly the case that the majority of sex offenders have been sexually abused themselves. In our clinical experience, we have found cases in which there appears to be a replication of the abuse done to the offender. In these cases, we speculate that there is an identification process occurring in which the offender is identifying with the abuser or the experience of being abused. One theory is that the offender is attempting to recreate the experience in order to address unresolved conflicts he has surrounding his abuse. Another is that the assault is an attempt to identify with the child and the innocence associated with being a child.

Not every child who is sexually abused will grow up to be a sexual abuser. It is generally believed at this time that only a small percentage of those children who are sexually abused will become sexual abusers. However, since clinical experience reveals that the majority of sexual abusers have themselves been sexually abused as children, there may exist, at least in certain cases, a cycle of sexual abuse. There is insufficient information available about what differences exist between the two groups. An important unanswered question is, What are the factors related to the sexual abuse of a child that places that child at risk for becoming a sexual abuser? Clinical experience supports four general observations (these have not been conclusively proved and they warrant further investigation): (1) Male sexual offenders more often than not are victimized by more than one perpetrator on separate occasions; (2) the abuse, whether by one perpetrator or several, usually occurs repeatedly over a long period of time, years in many cases; (3) the majority of these individuals receive no intervention or help after the abuse occurs; and (4) the majority have not experienced closure or resolution of their victimization. These observations are important and are guiding us in a more thorough investigation of sexual abuse.

As noted above, many children who are abused by more than one offender or experience sexual abuse for long periods of time do not grow up to be sexual abusers. The questions which then arise are these: (1) Which variables in addition to sexual abuse differentiate outcomes between victims of sexual abuse who go on to become sexually abusive and those who do not? (2) Why do sexual offenders who are not abused sexually or otherwise become offenders?

Sexual assault is a multidetermined type of behavior in our society and one for which we do not have clear answers regarding etiology, intervention, or prevention. This is especially true in the case of male victims and their susceptibility to the cycle of abuse. Further research is needed in this area before we can begin to come to grips with this problem and identify what factors related to sexual abuse predispose victims to become abusers. At this time, this author feels confident in suggesting that in some cases there is a significant link between sexual victimization and subsequent sexual abuse or aggression.

BIBLIOGRAPHY

Abel, G. G. (1986, February 12–14). Data presented at the Assessment and Treatment of Sexual Offenders Conference, Tampa, FL.

"Age 12 Consent Proposed." (1985, November 8). *Statesman's Journal* (p. 4). Salem, OR.

Bradford, J. W. (1983). Research on sex offenders: Recent trends. *Psychiatric Clinics of North America, 6*, 715–731.

Calderone, M. S. (1983). On the possible prevention of sexual problems in adolescence. *Hospital and Community Psychiatry, 34*, 528–530.

Conte, J. R., & Schuerman, J. R. (1987). Factors associated with an increased impact of child sexual abuse. *Child Abuse and Neglect, 11*, 201–211.

Cotton, D. J., & Groth, A. N. (1982). Inmate rape: Prevention and intervention. *Journal of Prison and Jail Health, 2*(1), 47–57.

Department of Health and Human Services. (1985). Preventing sexual abuse in day care programs. Seattle, WA: Author.

From homosexuality to heterosexuality. (1985).

Freeman-Longo, R. E. (1986). The impact of sexual victimization on males. *Child Abuse and Neglect, 10*, 411–414.

Freeman-Longo, R. E. (1985). Undetected recidivism of convicted sex offenders. Unpublished study.

Groth, A. N. (1979). *Men who rape: The psychology of the offender*. New York: Plenum.

Groth, A. N., & Freeman-Longo, R. E. (1987). [Sexual victimization in the histories of sexual offenders]. Ongoing study.

Jones, R. J., Gruber, K. J., & Timbers, G. D. (1981). Incidence and situation factors surrounding sexual assault against delinquent youths. *Child Abuse and Neglect, 5*, 431–440.

Papernay, D. M., & Deisher, R. W. (1983). Maltreatment of adolescents: The relationship to predisposition towards violent behavior and delinquency. *Adolescence, 18*, 499–506.

Petrovich, M., & Templer, D. I. (1984). Heterosexual molestation of children who later become rapists. *Psychological Reports, 54*, 810.

Pithers, W. D., Buell, M. M., Kashima, K. M., Cumming, G. F., & Beal, L. S. (1988). Relapse prevention of sexual aggression. *Annals of the New York Academy of Science*, 528, 244–260.

Pomeroy, J. C., Behar, D., & Stewart, M. A. (1981). Abnormal sexual behavior in pre-pubescent children. *British Journal of Psychiatry, 138*, 119–125.

Porter, E. (1986). *Treating the young male victim of sexual assault* (2nd revision). Orwell, VT: Safer Society Press.

Reinhart, M. A. (1987). Sexually abused boys. *Child Abuse and Neglect, 11*, 229–235.

Summit, R. C. (1983). The child sexual abuse accommodation syndrome. *Child Abuse and Neglect, 7*, 177–193.

VI

PUBLIC POLICY

19

Assistance to Victims and Prevention of Victimization: Recent Activities of the Council of Europe

Aglaia Tsitsoura
Head of the Division of Crime Problems,
Council of Europe, Strasbourg, France

INTRODUCTION

The need for assistance to victims during and after victimization has been strongly stressed during the last years in all countries, and various services have been created to this end.

The reasons for such developments are to be found both in the increased awareness of the difficulties met by the victims (gained through research and activities of victims' aid associations) and in the fact that in modern societies assistance to victims is not provided by the social environment (i.e., by family and friends) as often as in traditional ones.

The situation in the various countries as regards assistance is not well known, as many assistance services are private and act without a link with governmental authorities. Criteria for assistance, ways of intervention, and structures of the services vary considerably.

The Council of Europe examined assistance to victims in the framework of various of its activities: The Sixteenth Criminological Research Conference (see Mayhew [1985] and Willmow [1985]), the select committee on the relationship between the public and crime policy, and, more recently, the select committee on the victim and criminal and social policy. The latter prepared a draft recommendation on assistance to victims and prevention of victimization, which was adopted by the European Committee on Crime Problems in June 1987 and by the Committee of Ministers in the autumn of 1987 (recommendation R (87) 21).

This chapter outlines the policy regarding assistance to victims contained in the draft recommendation. It first considers the victims' needs and the nature

Aglaia Tsitsoura earned her doctorate in law at the University of Salonica, Greece, and her diplomas of specialization in criminal law and criminology at the University of Rome and at the University of Brussels. After practicing law in Salonica, in 1963 she joined the Secretariat of the Council of Europe in Strasbourg, France. At present, she is head of the Division of Crime Problems. Dr. Tsitsoura has produced various publications concerning penal and criminological issues and has participated in many criminal law and criminological conferences.

and form of the assistance to be offered. It then examines who should be offering the assistance and the need for coordination of victim services. The author also touches on the themes of promotion of victims' rights, prevention of victimization, and research and evaluation.

VICTIMS NEEDS: NATURE OF ASSISTANCE

Assistance During the Commission of the Offense

It is well known that often the public is reluctant to intervene during the commission of an offense in order to offer assistance to the victim. However, such intervention is crucial to prevent or stop the commission of offenses and to limit their consequences.

Recommendation R (83) 7 of the Council of Europe on participation of the public in crime policy recommends that governments encourage

> *the public, through an appeal for solidarity and through the provision of information on the technical facilities available and the appropriate action to be taken, to prevent offences from being committed and assist victims both during and after the perpetration of the offence. (Article 25)*

According to this provision, members of the public should give assistance to the victim within the limits of protection of their own life. They also should help the victim by alerting the competent public or private bodies (police, hospitals, etc.) which can intervene to protect or to help the victim.

Assistance After the Offense

Such assistance may take several forms, and it will vary according to the victim's needs.

Some victims may need more assistance than others, and some may need no assistance at all. Replies to a Council of Europe questionnaire concerning assistance to victims stress that the types of offenses which give rise to the greatest need of assistance to victims include sexual offenses, violence, terrorism or organized crime, burglary, and road traffic offenses.

According to the Recommendation R(87)21 on assistance to victims and prevention of victimization (Article 1), victims' needs should be ascertained by victimization surveys or other types of research.

The draft recommendation indicates the main forms of assistance after the commission of the offense (Article 4).

Emergency Help to Meet Immediate Needs

This may be medical help in the case of victims of violence, material help in the case of victims of burglary, or a shelter in the case of victims of domestic violence.

Continuing Medical, Psychological, Social, and Material Help

This help must give the victim the possibility to recover from the consequences of his or her victimization. The victim must be encouraged to overcome his or her difficulties and begin to lead a normal life as soon as possible.

Protection From Retaliation by the Offender

The need for such protection was also stressed by Recommendation R (85) 11, which concerns the position of the victim in the framework of criminal law and procedure (Article 15). Although such protection is a task for the police, the draft recommendation on assistance to victims provides that assistance services also have an important role to play in this field. For example, in offering a shelter to the victims of domestic violence, these services may protect the victim from an offender's new assault.

Advice to Prevent Future Victimization

Such advice should certainly help the victim to take the necessary measures for his or her protection. It should be given in a cautious way, so as to avoid increasing the fear of the victim.

Information on the Victim's Rights and Assistance in Connection With the Criminal Process

Such information should initially be given by the police (see Recommendation R (85) 11, Article 2). However, assistance services may also supply or complete such information and help the victim to secure his or her rights.

Assistance in Obtaining Effective Reparation of the Damage by the Offender, Payments from Insurance Companies, or Compensation by the State

Obtaining such payments may require administrative steps which the victim may be unable to take without assistance. Victim assistance services may give such help and advice as is required for rapid reparation of the damages suffered by the victim. (See the European convention on the compensation of victims of violent crime, Council of Europe, 1984.)

PERSONS OR SERVICES OFFERING ASSISTANCE

The Public in General: The Victim's Social Environment

The public in general and the victim's social environment should assist him or her not only during the commission of the offense (see "Assistance During the Commission of the Offense") but also after the victimization and until the victim recovers from the trauma.

The recommendation R(87)21 (Article 2) urges governments to

> *raise the consciousness of the public in general and of public services regarding the needs of the victim, for example, by debates, round tables and publicity campaigns and promote solidarity by the community and in particular, in the victim's family and social environment.*

It is noteworthy that families, too, must be sensitized in this field, not only because more and more family ties seem to be becoming looser, but also because in some cases (e.g., rape) the family may tend to blame the victim for exposing him- or herself to the risk of victimization, feel ashamed on the victim's account, and abstain from giving the necessary help.

Victim Assistance Services

Identification of Existing Facilities

During the recent decades, a large number of victim assistance services have been created in Council of Europe member states.

Besides the big victim assistance services existing in some countries (e.g., Weisser Ring in the Federal Republic of Germany), there are many small services assisting usually specific categories of victims (battered wives or children, elderly persons, prostitutes, homosexuals, road traffic victims, etc.). Sometimes some services (e.g., shelters) function in a very inobtrusive way, reluctant to inform the public authorities about their activities, staff, or financing.

In reply to the Council of Europe questionnaire, some governments declared they were not able to give an exhaustive picture of all services functioning in their territory.

Although authorities must respect the wish of some services to be completely independent, governments need to know about the existing facilities and the gaps existing in this field.

Thus, the recommendation (Article 3) urges governments to "identify currently existing public and private services able to provide assistance to victims, their achievements, and any deficiencies."

Creation, Development, and Support of Victim Assistance Services

The recommendation (Article 5) urges governments to

create, develop or extend support towards:
—services designed to provide assistance to victims generally;
—services for special categories of victims such as children and, when, necessary, also victims of particular offences such as rape, domestic violence, organised crime, racist violence.

Most of the services existing in the member states are private but receive government grants.

The recommendation does not enter into the details of the functioning of assistance services. Given the variety of the structures, aims, and means of these services, any overly specific regulation would impede rather than facilitate their functioning.

However, the recommendation evokes some specific problems concerning the work of these services.

Staff. In all countries, victim assistance services work widely with voluntary aid. The recommendation (Article 6) recognizes the importance of such aid and asks governments to encourage it and to support it "as necessary, by professional help for training, specific services, administrative and technical support."

Referral of victimization cases from the police to the victim assistance programs. Such referral may create serious problems regarding respect for the victim's private life. In fact, it is conceivable that some victims may not be willing to receive visits, telephone calls, or letters concerning their victimization. The need for protection of privacy is an important principle stressed in the European Convention on Human Rights and Fundamental Freedoms and in most of the recommendations of the Council of Europe. However, direct approach of victims by assistance services is important in order to secure the necessary help. The recommendation (Article 8) in a cautious way invites governments to

> *inform the public, by adequate means, of assistance services available and facilitate access by victims to these services; facilitate referral of victims by the police to victim assistance services and also direct approach to victims by such services to the extent compatible with the protection of the victim's privacy.*

Confidentiality. Victim assistance services may tend sometimes to give personal information about victims to the media or other third parties in an effort to illustrate the problems of victimization and the various measures to prevent it or to obtain reparation. However, such disclosure is a serious violation of the privacy of victims. According to the recommendation, victim assistance services should not disclose personal information without the consent of the victims concerned.

General Medical and Social Services

Such services (e.g., hospitals and child protection committees) are often called upon to give assistance to victims. The recommendation stresses the need to increase the contribution of such services by "training their personnel to be alert to the victim's needs."

COORDINATION: PROMOTION OF THE VICTIM'S RIGHTS

Victim assistance services operating on a public or private basis should coordinate activities (Article 10 of the recommendation). Such coordination may meet an obstacle in the wish for independence of certain services. However, the need to avoid duplication or inefficiency in assistance activities makes contacts and concentration between services necessary. In some countries, associations grouping a great number of services (e.g., the NAVSS in the United Kingdom) achieve such coordination.

Victim assistance services, although usually not operating in the framework of the criminal justice system, should secure coordination with the agencies of the system and with other public agencies as well. However, such coordination should not involve dependence of victim assistance services on the criminal justice system.

National organizations for the protection of the victim's rights may also have a coordinating role. Their importance is recognized by the recommendation, which asks governments to support such organizations (Article 11), for instance, by helping them financially.

PREVENTION OF VICTIMIZATION

A recommendation on the organization of crime prevention has been prepared by another Council of Europe select committee. This is the reason why the latter deals only very briefly with problems of prevention of victimization. After referring in general terms to the importance of measures of social development and of situational prevention, the recommendation deals more particularly with some specific problems:

1. The need to provide actual or potential victims with information permitting them to take the necessary prevention measures whilst refraining from unduly exacerbating feelings of fear and insecurity (Article 13).

2. The need for special prevention policies for particularly vulnerable groups (in their replies to the Council of Europe questionnaire, member states consider as particularly vulnerable old people, the handicapped, persons with low incomes, persons living alone, migrants, children, and the families of victims [in the case of murder]).

3. The need to promote involvement of potential victims in their own protection, for instance, by encouraging them to organize neighborhood prevention activities or similar programs (such activities should be done in concert with local agencies and the police, and they should never result in the creation of vigilante groups, which may create violence instead of preventing it).

RESEARCH AND EVALUATION

Research on Victimization

The efficient organization of victim assistance services requires data on (1) victimization rates, (2) victim needs, and (3) assistance services already available. The recommendation asks governments to promote victimization surveys or other types of research to ascertain the above data (Article 1).

Although controversial, victimization surveys are used in many countries to complete the data coming from criminal statistics (see, e.g., Zauberman, 1985).

Research on Mediation Experiments

Mediation experiments are mentioned by various Council of Europe member states (e.g., the Federal Republic of Germany and the United Kingdom). They are usually considered a good means of avoiding the criminal process, creating a reconciliation between the offender and the victim, and ensuring reparation of the damage.

However, it may happen that victims (and perhaps offenders as well) are subject to pressure in order to accept arrangements which run counter to their interests. The recommendation (Article 17) indicates that mediation experiments should be carefully evaluated to verify how far the interests of the victim (as well as those of the offender) are safeguarded by such experiments.

Evaluation and Monitoring of Victim Assistance Services

The results of victim assistance services should be followed constantly and evaluated so that successful services are supported and deficient ones are improved or replaced.

Evaluation of the Effectiveness of Prevention Programs

Programs for the prevention of victimization of the population as a whole or certain groups in particular should also be carefully evaluated (Article 19 of the recommendation). Such research should take account of the possibility of displacement of criminality to other areas or of modification of its forms. It should also take account of cost-benefit criteria and any changes in the quality of life (e.g., diminution of fear) provoked by these programs in the areas concerned.

CONCLUSIONS

The Recommendation R(87)21 contains some general lines of policy concerning victim assistance. Its aim is to attract the attention of governments to this important area.

Nowadays, most assistance services are the result of private initiative. However, assistance to victims should be more recognized as a national issue, and both authorities and private persons should be mobilized to provide such assistance.

BIBLIOGRAPHY

Mayhew, P. (1985). The effects of crime: The public and fear. [Report presented to the Sixteenth Criminological Research Conference]. *Council of Europe Collected Studies in Criminological Research, 23.*

Willmow, B. (1985). Implications of research on victimisation in criminal and social policy. [Report presented to the Sixteenth Criminological Research Conference]. *Council of Europe Collected Studies in Criminological Research, 23.*

Zauberman, R. (1985). Sources of information about victims and methodological problems in this field. *Council of Europe Collected Studies in Criminological Research, 23.*

20

A Federal Perspective on Victim Assistance in the United States of America

Richard B. Abell
Assistant Attorney General, Office of Justice Programs, U.S. Department of Justice, Washington, DC

Man has almost constant occasion for the help of his brethren.
Adam Smith

INTRODUCTION

This chapter reports the results of historical research into the evolution of the victim assistance movement in the United States. Evidence is presented supporting the thesis that provision of assistance to crime victims was not fully institutionalized in the United States until the efforts of the federal administration under Reagan bore fruit in the form of federal legislation, establishment of a Federal Office for Victims of Crime, and the exercise of federal leadership across the country on behalf of victims. It is argued that these developments were made possible by the existence of a growing victim movement at the state and local level. Resulting improvements in the administration of justice vis-à-vis victims and in the provision of services for victims are outlined. Despite these remarkable developments, complicated challenges in the victims' arena are foretold. The humanistic message is made clear: Human beings are in constant need of help from others.

In theory, most legal systems have long contained provisions through which victims might obtain compensation or restitution. It was not uncommon for early civilizations to require payments by offenders to their victims. References to victim compensation are found in the Code of Hammurabi, the *Iliad*, and the

Richard Bender Abell is Assistant Attorney General of the Office of Justice Programs, United States Department of Justice. He previously served as Deputy Assistant Attorney General for the Office of Justice Programs. As a former district attorney, he has worked specifically with juvenile cases, rape crisis intervention programs, and victim/witness procedures and programs. Mr. Abell is currently Chairman of the National Crime Prevention Coalition and serves as a member of the Board of Directors for the Federal Prison Industries, Inc., the National Drug Policy Enforcement Coordinating Group, and the National Drug Policy Board Coordinating Group for Drug Abuse Prevention and Health. He is also a member of the Advisory Board of the National Institute of Corrections, the Federal Coordinating Council on Juvenile Justice and Delinquency Prevention, and the Advisory Committee for the National Center for State and Local Law Enforcement Training (in Glynco, Georgia).

Old Testament. For example, in Leviticus 6:4–5, the Lord told Moses that if a soul hath sinned "and is guilty, that he shall restore that which he took violently away . . . he shall even restore it in the principal, and shall add the fifth part more thereto." In common-law countries, the victim could bring an action in tort against the offender. In many European countries, the victim could seek damages by becoming a party to criminal proceedings against the offender. But most of those provisions were almost never used and were virtually ineffective.

These systems of payment from offender to victim were gradually changed with the advent of state-controlled prosecution of offenders. Under the Anglo-American jurisprudential system of law, the state gradually assumed many of the "functions" of the victim in legal proceedings. Under this system, the state assumed the responsibility for "making the victim whole" by bringing the offender to justice. (Unfortunately, the state's assumption of responsibility also included its appropriation of all proceeds from criminal remedies to recover any losses incurred as a result of the crime.) Thus the state assumed the obligation to discover, apprehend, try, and punish the offender for the criminal offense. The victim's only recourse for physical, mental, or financial relief was the right to sue the offender in civil court for wrongs committed against the victim (Carrow, 1980; Finn & Lee, 1987; Sparks, 1982).

Tragically, the criminal justice system in the United States traditionally has been offender oriented, focusing on the apprehension, prosecution, protection, punishment, and rehabilitation of wrongdoers. Victims have always played a vital role in the system by supplying most of the information necessary for apprehension and prosecution. Yet the criminal justice system consistently has failed to accord victims the respect they deserve and that which is equal to the importance of their roles.

While scrupulously defending the rights of offenders, the system has ignored the rights of victims. Until recently, the victim of crime was regarded as little more than a witness; great care was exercised to protect the rights of criminals. The system did little to help victims recover from the financial and emotional trauma they suffered.

Instead, the American criminal justice system has devoted enormous amounts of money, time, and effort to the arguably questionable concept of "rehabilitating" criminals. The pendulum of fairness and equity has swung far too much in the direction of offenders, away from victims. However, the Judeo-Christian concept of self-responsibility for one's actions has been brought back into discussions of the nature of criminality. Students of criminology are beginning to come to the realization that criminals and noncriminals alike choose the paths they take of their own free will. Consequently, those who choose to take the wrong path should be held accountable for their actions. Thus, increased concern for victims is required to bring a balance of fairness and equity into the administration of criminal justice.

As Niccolo Machiavelli once wrote, "There is nothing more difficult to take in hand, more perilous to conduct, or more uncertain in its success, than to take the lead in the introduction of a new order of things." The federal government has now taken the lead in the introduction of new programs and activities to help victims, and, in spite of many obstacles and uncertainties, it has been very successful in finding many new and very effective ways to assist victims.

FEDERAL INACTIVITY BEFORE THE 1980s

The first comprehensive assessment of the state-of-the-art of the administration of justice in the United States was undertaken only about 20 years ago. Called the Commission on Law Enforcement and Administration of Justice, its report, *The Challenge of Crime in a Free Society*, was issued in 1967. Less than 2 of its more than 1,000 pages of analysis, suggestions, and recommendations were devoted to treatment of jurors, victims, and witnesses. Concern was expressed over facilities, compensation for witnesses, difficulties encountered by victims in recovering their stolen property, waste of police time waiting to testify, and repetitious court appearances by witnesses. On the subject of economic impact of crime on witnesses, the commission comprehended only one facet of the problem in noting that victims are often poor, like their offenders (Commission on Law Enforcement, 1967, pp. 90–91).

The first effort to set standards and goals for the administration of justice in this country likewise virtually ignored victims altogether. The administrator of the Law Enforcement Assistance Administration (LEAA)[1] appointed in 1971 the National Advisory Commission on Criminal Justice Standards and Goals. It was established "to formulate for the first time national criminal justice standards and goals for crime reduction and prevention at the State and local levels." In its report, *A National Strategy to Reduce Crime* (National Advisory Commission, 1973), the commission made almost 400 recommendations, yet not a single one addressed the needs of victims. Three focused on improved treatment of witnesses, recommending that they be called only when necessary; that they be more realistically and equitably compensated for the time and travel involved in delivering testimony (at least above the 75 cents per day then paid in the state of Alabama); and that facilities for witnesses, sometimes inadequate or nonexistent, be improved.

The Standards and Goals Advisory Commission also reiterated the observation of the Commission on Law Enforcement and Administration of Justice that "sensitivity to the needs of witnesses who are required to return to court again and again, often at considerable personal sacrifice, is usually lacking."

Nevertheless, the 1970s saw a groundswell of grass roots support for victim or witness activities. During this era, civilians began working with police to help victims of crime. The first victim service programs were established, helping victims of rape and domestic violence. The state of Wisconsin enacted the first comprehensive bill of rights for victims. And the concept of a "victim impact statement"[2] was developed and implemented. These and other state and local

[1]The LEAA was created in 1968 as the major entity in the federal government's effort to combat all types of crime. It mainly provided funds to the states (based on population size) and directly to organizations for the support of activities designed to reduce crime. In its early history, LEAA's efforts were concentrated on strengthening law enforcement, with considerable emphasis on hardware and technological approaches. LEAA was defunded in 1980.

[2]Such statements contain information—supplied by the victim and for the court's consideration—on the effects of crime on the victim. Victim impact statements are most often used by the court at the sentencing stage in order to take into account the impact of the crime on the victim (i.e., the severity of the criminal act) and thus assist the court in determining the appropriate sentence for the defendant.

activities served as the basis for the current federal administration's initiative to bring federal leadership and support to the victim movement.

FEDERAL ACTIVITIES IN THE 1980s

American society only recently has recognized the imbalance resulting from attention to the rights of offenders and neglect of the victim and has set out to make a correction in this imbalance. Therefore, this myopic approach to the administration of justice for all law-abiding citizens has been changing dramatically in the past few years. Because of President Ronald Reagan's commitment to help victims and witnesses of crime, the "forgotten party" of the criminal justice process has been brought into the proceedings. Following is a brief description in chronological order of the legal and administrative activities initiated since 1982.

On April 23, 1982, President Reagan appointed the Task Force on Victims of Crime. During 1982, the task force held hearings in six cities across the country, receiving the testimony of almost 200 witnesses. The issuance of its report (*President's Task Force on Victims of Crime*, 1982) marked a significant step in the victim movement. The recommendations of the task force—the most complete ever developed on the subject—made clear both the seriousness of the plight of crime victims and witnesses and enumerated the wide range of available reform measures. The report recommended enactment of implementing legislation to restore a balance to our criminal justice system and the establishment of needed victim and witness programs at the federal, state, and local levels. It also called for creation of the Federal Office for Victims of Crime within the Office of Justice Programs (OJP)[3] which was accomplished in 1983.

On October 12, 1982, the Federal Victim and Witness Protection Act (Public Law 97-291) became law. It is an omnibus measure enacted to enhance and protect the necessary role of crime victims and witnesses in the criminal justice process, to ensure that the federal government does all that is possible within the limits of available resources to assist victims and witnesses of crimes, and to provide a model for legislation for state and local governments. On July 9, 1983, the U.S. Department of Justice (1983) published a series of implementing guidelines setting forth procedures to be followed in responding to the needs of crime victims and witnesses. They are intended to ensure that responsible officials treat victims and witnesses fairly and with understanding. The guidelines are also intended to enhance the assistance which victims and witnesses provide in criminal cases and to assist victims in recovering from their injuries and losses to the fullest extent possible. These guidelines also reflect the view of the Department of Justice that the needs and interests of victims and witnesses have not received appropriate consideration in the federal criminal justice system.

[3]The Office for Victims of Crime (OVC) is within the OJP, which is within the U.S. Department of Justice. The OVC administers the Victims of Crime Act of 1984, including a state compensation and assistance program (a grant program providing assistance to victims and research) and a national victims resource center. The OJP is the umbrella organization within the U.S. Department of Justice which coordinates and gives overall policy direction for the anticrime and victim assistance efforts of the department. It also provides support services for the other organizational entities within it. These consist of the OVC, the Bureau of Justice Statistics, the Bureau of Justice Assistance, the National Institute of Justice, and the Office of Juvenile Justice and Delinquency Prevention.

As a follow-up to the President's Task Force Report, in 1983 the Task Force on Family Violence was established. It was charged with the responsibility of identifying the scope of the problem of family violence in the United States and of making recommendations to bring about solutions.

The task force gave priority attention to *assistance* for victims of family violence. Its proposals were prefaced by the enlightened recognition that "the assistance needs of the victims of family violence range from the most immediate need for safety and shelter to long-range needs for post-trauma counseling and therapy." Its recommendations delineated a number of steps that should be taken to address the unique needs of family violence victims (Attorney General's Task Force on Family Violence, 1984).

Another major accomplishment focusing on the needs of innocent victims and witnesses of crime was the enactment into law of the Victims of Crime Act (VOCA) of 1984 (Public Law 98-473). It was introduced in nine sessions of Congress before it passed. Signed into law in October 1984, this legislation constitutes a landmark step in the continuing national effort to make our governments, our institutions, and our communities more responsive to the needs of innocent victims of crime. This legislation was based on the recommendations of the President's Task Force on Victims of Crime. Before its enactment into law, our justice system was more interested in guaranteeing the constitutional rights of the felon than the rights of the victim. VOCA was designed to reverse that trend.

VOCA strengthened the federal government's leadership role in the victim movement by providing incentives to the states to institutionalize their victim assistance efforts. The act established a Crime Victims Fund of up to $100 million annually. The money comes from federal offenders—from fines, new penalty assessment fees, forfeited bail bonds, and criminals' literary profits—not from our innocent taxpayers. The fund may be used for three purposes: to help states support local victim assistance programs,[4] to supplement state victim compensation programs,[5] and to assist victims of federal offenders. Each state receives a base amount of $100,000 for victim assistance programs. The remaining funds are divided on the basis of each state's share of the total national population.

President Ronald Reagan is the first U.S. president to have proclaimed a "Victims' Week" in America—complete with White House ceremonies and victim participation—to draw attention yearly to victims of crime.

The U.S. Department of Justice continues to play a strong role in advancing the victim movement in America through program activities sponsored by its Office of Justice Programs. Some of this leadership has emanated from its responsibility to administer federal legislation; other activities have been undertaken at its own discretion—because of the administration's concern for victims and strong interest in restoring a proper balance of equity and fairness to the

[4]Victim assistance programs help citizens victimized by crime through a variety of activities, including emergency services, counseling, advocacy and support services, claims assistance, court-related services, and other services related to the criminal justice system. See the section "State and Local Progress" for additional details.

[5]State victim compensation programs reimburse victims of crime for the financial losses they incur as a consequence of their victimization. These may include lost wages, mental health counseling, and other emergency financial needs. Compensation, including funeral expenses, is also provided to survivors of victims.

justice process. Space only permits highlighting a few of these federal initiatives here. Some of these are ongoing; some have been completed; others are underway. Each of these initiatives is related to the three fundamental principles promulgated by the President's Task Force on Victims of Crime: (1) Victims must be protected; (2) the justice system must be responsive to victims' needs; and (3) victims need assistance to overcome the burdens imposed by crime.

- In late 1983, the National Conference of the Judiciary on the Rights of Victims of Crime was convened in the United States. Participants were selected from courts in all 50 states, the District of Columbia,[6] and Puerto Rico.[7] Their objectives were to discuss issues and problems related to the treatment of victims of crime by our criminal justice system and to consider methods that might be employed to minimize the burdens and trauma that victims experience when they participate in the adjudication process. A set of recommended practices was adopted by the conferees for promulgation throughout the states. The recommendations addressed fair treatment of victims and witnesses, victim participation, protection of victims and witnesses, and judicial education (National Conference of the Judiciary on the Rights of Victims of Crime, 1985).
- In 1984, the National Symposium on Child Molestation was also convened in the United States (Office of Justice Programs [OJP], 1984). It focused national attention on the heinous crime committed by those outside the family who sexually molest children and cause them to suffer incalculable harm. Experts were brought together to identify the most effective approaches for investigating, prosecuting, and sentencing sexual abusers, as well as helping their victims recover.
- Model statutes dealing with victims of crime have been developed for consideration by the states across America (Office for Victims of Crime, 1986). We are currently working with the states to help them implement these statutes. If enacted, these laws, for example, would
  —require that the effect of the crime on the victim be considered at the defendant's sentencing
  —open parole hearings[8]
  —permit hearsay at preliminary hearings[9]
  —limit the disclosure of victim addresses and phone numbers
  —extend the statute of limitations for offenses against children
  —reform procedures for defendants' pretrial release
  —establish guidelines for determinate sentencing
  —disclose any sex offense history of those employed in child-related positions
- Development of a statute has been commissioned to put an end to the unfair practice of forcing sexual assault victims to pay for physical examinations.

[6]The District of Columbia is the federal jurisdiction of the U.S. government. It is commonly referred to as Washington, DC.

[7]Puerto Rico is a territory of the United States.

[8]Parole is the status of official supervision, under which offenders are placed for a given period of time (normally, at least 1 year) following their release from prison.

[9]A preliminary hearing is held by the court, following formal charging of alleged offenders, to determine the specific charges for which they are to be tried and to set a date for their trial.

- Several projects have been launched to assist (1) victims of crimes committed by juveniles and (2) victims of crime who are juveniles or children. These include a national training and education program to help jurisdictions use restitution for victims as a sanction for delinquent acts.
- In 1984, the president signed into law the Missing Children's Assistance Act (Public Law 98-473), which established a special program of financial assistance to ensure the continuation of research, program development, and technical assistance regarding child victimization and the problem of missing and exploited children.
- Support has been provided to the National District Attorneys' Association (NDAA)[10] to open a national center for the prosecution of child abuse.
- A National Symposium on Sexual Assault was convened in conjunction with the U.S. Federal Bureau of Investigation (FBI).[11] It marked the first time at a national level that medical professionals were brought together with individuals working in criminal justice and social services to discuss ways to improve the treatment of victims of sexual assault.
- The National Victims Resource Center[12] has been established to provide useful information on victimization, including sources of help for victims, program models, state legislation, prevention of victimization, and the like.
- A "protocol" has been developed to improve emergency room procedures for handling sexual assault victims in order to properly collect evidence in a way that furthers the well-being of victims and strengthens the prosecution's case.
- Several new activities are underway focused on the AIDS problem. In addition to the President's National Commission on AIDS, the Department of Justice has undertaken several activities focused on the AIDS problem as related to the administration of justice. These include a committee of the department's Research and Development Board,[13] a working group on AIDS and the victims of crime, research efforts, and nationwide dissemination of justice-related information. These various efforts, and others, are addressing a variety of issues pertaining to AIDS and the justice system, including the nature and extent of AIDS, solutions to problems that arise, the impact of AIDS on the law enforcement community, implications for correctional management, prevention and disposition approaches, and accountability for transmission of AIDS in the course of criminal activity.
- A "protocol" is also being developed to assist the medical profession and other practitioners in conducting examinations (and collecting evidence) for child sexual abuse.
- On April 29, 1985, the president, by executive order, established the President's Child Safety Partnership to develop recommendations as to how child victimization could be prevented, especially through involvement of the

[10]The NDAA is the professional organization of prosecutors in the United States.

[11]The FBI is the official investigative arm of the U.S. Department of Justice. It is charged with responsibility for investigating and bringing charges for such federal offenses as crimes against public officials, transporting stolen goods across state lines, kidnapping, bank robbery, and other offenses so designated by law as federal offenses.

[12]The National Victims Resource Center is a national clearinghouse of information on victim programs and other related material.

[13]The Research and Development Board was recently established by the U.S. Attorney General to help coordinate the Department of Justice's research and program development activities.

private sector. After holding hearings in seven cities across the country and gathering other information, its report has been completed and will be submitted to the president shortly. For the first time, national attention has been directed to children as victims.

• The National Crime Prevention Council (NCPC)[14] and the Advertising Council are participants in the National Crime Prevention Campaign, which features a dog named McGruff who wears a trench coat and gives tips on how to "take a bite out of crime." This campaign works to prevent victimization.

• Since the mid-1970s, OJP's Bureau of Justice Statistics[15] has been conducting nationwide surveys of households to measure *actual* victimization.[16] These survey results fill an important void in available crime data, in that crimes not reported to the police are measured. The results are extremely valuable in adding information to our knowledge about crime in such areas as the victim-offender relationship, characteristics of personal incidents, consequences of personal victimizations, and reasons for failure to report victimizations. Information in the latter area has helped us develop programs (e.g., Neighborhood Crime Watch)[17] which increase crime reporting and thereby prevent future victimizations.

• Research on victimization is a priority for OJP's National Institute of Justice.[18] Studies funded over the past few years have addressed, among other things, the sentencing of those who sexually abuse children, innovations in prosecution of child sexual abuse, techniques for interviewing crime victims, criminal justice system responses to victim harm, effects of victim impact statements, and issues confronted by judges and prosecutors when the victim is a child. Research efforts now being conducted are examining the effects of criminal justice system

[14]The NCPC is a private nonprofit organization dedicated to preventing crime throughout the United States. It sponsors (often with federal support) such activities as public awareness and educational efforts for Americans.

[15]The Bureau of Justice Statistics is an agency of the OJP. As the statistical arm of the U.S. Department of Justice, it collects, analyzes, publishes, and disseminates statistical information on crime, victims of crime, criminal offenders, and the operations of justice systems at all levels of government. It also provides financial and technical support to state statistical and operating criminal justice agencies.

[16]These are part of the National Crime Survey (NCS), which has been conducted by the Bureau of Justice Statistics since 1973. It provides the only systematic measurement of actual (as opposed to reported) crime rates and the characteristics of crime and crime victims based on national household surveys. Measures are made on the amount of rape, robbery, assault, personal larceny, and motor vehicle theft experienced by a representative sample of the U.S. population. It provides detailed data about the characteristics of victims, victim-offender relationships, and criminal incidents, including the extent of loss or injury and whether offenses were reported to the police. The interviews are conducted at 6-month intervals in about 49,000 U.S. households, and 101,000 persons who are at least 12 years old are asked what crimes they experienced since the last interview.

[17]This is a popular type of program throughout the neighborhoods of America. In such programs, citizens are trained to identify and report crimes observed in their locality. The programs have been found to be quite effective in preventing and reducing crime. Another important and very effective program is the National Association of Town Watch. Among its many activities, this association has sponsored for the past 3 years a "national night out." This is an expression of the citizen's intent to combat crime through the participation of neighborhood watch members in patrolling their own neighborhoods or observing patrols from their lawns or lighted porches for 1 hour on a single nationally advertised night (August 11 this year).

[18]The National Institute of Justice is a major research arm of the U.S. Department of Justice. It sponsors training, education, information dissemination, and program development activities as well as research on all aspects of crime and the criminal justice system.

participation on child victims of sexual assault, the effectiveness of various reforms designed to make the criminal justice system more responsive to victims, how victim rights legislation is being carried out, and other issues.

These activities of the OJP, buttressed by federal legislation, have greatly enhanced the victim movement in the United States. Previous grass roots support for victims has been invigorated by the new federal leadership. Consequently, state and local progress over the past few years has been significant.

STATE AND LOCAL PROGRESS

Under current federal leadership, the broad category of programs known as "victim assistance" have developed and implemented a number of strategies designed to identify and address the needs of victims. These strategies are reflected in the progress made during the past several years. Some of the programs, activities, and changes that have occurred are listed below (OJP, 1986):

- Compensation to victims of crime to help pay medical bills and other crime-related expenses.
- Specific authority for courts to order criminal offenders to make restitution to their victims.
- Enactment of laws dealing with special classes of victims (e.g., children, the elderly, and sexual assault victims) who are especially vulnerable to victimization or disproportionately harmed by it.
- Enactment of comprehensive legislation recognizing a bill of rights for crime victims.[19]
- Mediation approaches to family and neighborhood disputes.
- Assistance to victims in understanding and participating in the criminal justice process.
- Victim services. The broad range of services provided by such programs have been categorized as follows:
  —Emergency services: medical care, shelter, food, security repair, financial assistance, and comfort at the scene of the crime.
  —Counseling: 24-hour hotline, crisis intervention, follow-up counseling, and mediation.
  —Advocacy and support services: personal advocacy, employer intervention, landlord intervention, property return, intimidation intervention, victim impact statements, legal or paralegal counsel, and referral.
  —Claims assistance: insurance claim aid, restitution assistance, compensation assistance, and witness fee assistance.
  —Court-related services: witness reception, court orientation, notification, witness alert, transportation, child care, and escort to court.
  —Systemwide services: public education, legislative advocacy, and training.

[19]A victim's bill of rights typically includes the right to be informed of developments in the criminal justice system processing of the case of concern to a victim, protection as a witness, notification of the disposition of the case, an opportunity to submit a victim impact statement, notification of the scheduling of proceedings, and support services.

Since 1980, when California became the first state to enact statewide funding for general victim services, at least 28 other states have made some provision for ensuring that victim services are provided at the local level.

In 1981, the U.S. Attorney's Office[20] for the District of Columbia became the first among federal prosecutors' offices to establish a victim assistance program. Now, every such office makes some effort to coordinate services in this area—as called for in the Victim Witness Protection Act of 1982.

In 1980, a total of 280 victim/witness assistance projects were identified across the country. Now there are over 1,000.

Other specific developments in providing victim services in the 1980s include the following:

- In 1982, 37 states had victim compensation programs which paid about $50 million to victims; by 1986, 43 states offered compensation to victims and their survivors. (In 1986, the total allocation to the states by the Federal Crime Victim's Fund was $65 million.)
- During the past decade, numerous national groups have been formed to assist victims as well as help prevent victimization. These include Parents of Murdered Children, Mothers Against Drunk Driving (MADD), Students Against Driving Drunk (SADD), and the National Organization for Victim Assistance (NOVA).[21]
- Astounding progress has been made in the 1980s in the area of state legislation mandating the fair treatment of crime victims (OJP, 1986). For a summary of progress early in the decade, see Table 20-1.

TODAY'S ISSUES

Although a great deal of progress has been made in victim assistance during the past seven years, new challenges face us. Society is becoming more and more complex, and the issues confronting victims ever more complicated. Consideration of some recent research results will serve to illustrate the nature of the victimization problem in America.

Seventy-four percent of a large sample of American criminals convicted of seven major felonies in state courts during 1985 were sentenced to prison or jail; the remaining 26% were given straight probation with no jail or prison time to serve. Of the 2,561 defendants convicted of homicide that year in 28 large court systems throughout the country, 84% were sentenced to prison, 1% were given jail terms, 7% received combined jail and probation sentences, and 8% were given straight probation. Of 3,126 offenders convicted of rape in the same 28 jurisdictions, 65% were sentenced to prison, 1% were sentenced to jail, 17% were given a combination of jail and probation, and 16% were sentenced to straight probation (Bureau of Justice Statistics, 1987a).

[20]The United States is divided into 94 federal jurisdictions. In each of these, a federal prosecutor (U.S. attorney) has responsibility for bringing charges against persons believed to have violated federal laws.

[21]These are national organizations, formed by the initiative of citizens, to increase public awareness of specific types of victimization, provide information on how these tragedies can be prevented, and make referrals of victims to other appropriate programs for assistance.

Table 20-1 Victim assistance reforms

Reforms	Pre-1982	As of July 1985
Enacting broad laws that include a majority of the reforms below	4	31
Requiring a victim impact statement at sentencing	8	39
Victim allocution at sentencing	3	19
Permitting victim input into key prosecutorial decisions	1	10
Opening parole hearings	6	19
Abolishing parole	5	8
Requiring that victims be notified of crucial developments in case	2	27
Keeping victim counseling records confidential	6	20
Not disclosing addresses and phone numbers of victims	0	5
Allowing hearsay at preliminary hearings	23	26
Assuring prompt property return	4	20
Protecting victims from intimidation and harassment	4	27
Providing separate and secure waiting rooms	1	17
Background checks of people who work with children for a history of sex offense convictions	1	20
Mandating restitution to victims as part of sentence	8	29
Providing funds for services to all victims of crime	7	28
Preventing criminals from profiting from the sale of their stories	14	32
Victim compensation	37	43

One-fourth of all U.S. households were touched by a crime of violence or theft in 1986,[22] the same proportion as in 1985 and well below the third of all households touched by crime in 1975. Five percent of the households in the United States had a member who was the victim of a violent crime in 1986. Five percent of all households were burglarized at least once during the year (Bureau of Justice Statistics, 1987b). However, when examining the overall numbers of reported and unreported crimes, the total amount of actual crime from 1981–1986 dropped by 18%.

These data indicate the nature and extent of criminal victimization in the United States. They also illustrate that, while there is progress being made,

[22]These offenses include burglary, auto theft, household theft, rape, robbery, or assault of household members, and personal theft—no matter where the crime occurred.

criminals are not yet being punished commensurately with the gravity of their crimes and the harm done to innocent victims. Although some significant progress has been made toward helping victims cope with their plight, the issues of today are equal in complexity to any with which we have dealt in the past.

- We have reached a high level in providing basic services for victims. These services have become highly specialized, including efforts to assist families of homicide victims. Yet we must now carry the message to the public and to generic service providers as well, because there will never be enough specialized services. Such professionals as family physicians, pediatricians, lawyers, and other practitioners must become more actively involved.
- Should there be a federal law recognizing the "right to know" of victims of rape by AIDS carriers?[23] Should such a law also address the criminal implications of transmitting AIDS to an innocent victim? Many states are currently enacting legislation to address these issues.
- The issue of accountability, liability, and immunity of custodial officials is indeed a complicated and controversial one, and it requires thoughtful attention. Premature release of offenders back into society often results in subsequent victimization. The basic question is one of determining how and under what circumstances this principle of accountability should be implemented.
- Victims can be helped more through prison industries.[24] We encourage, inter alia, deductions from inmates' wages for victims, as a class, and unrelated to any orders judges may impose.
- The President's Task Force on Victims of Crime recommended the following modification of the Sixth Amendment[25] to the Constitution of the United States: "The victim, in every criminal prosecution shall have the right to be present and to be heard at all critical stages of judicial proceedings." This modification may be required to ensure the necessary balance of fairness and equity in the administration of justice. Otherwise the pendulum may well swing back in favor of the offender while trampling the rights of the individual citizen.

When reflecting on the progress that has been made to assist and compensate victims during the past few years, Americans can take pride in what has been accomplished. Although there is so much more that needs to be done, we know and understand the depth of Mark Twain's words when he wrote that "the miracle, or the power, that elevates the few is to be found in their perseverance under the promptings of a brave, determined spirit." The progress that has been

[23]*AIDS* is the acronym for acquired immune deficiency syndrome, a fatal disease for which there is no known cure at this time.

[24]Prison industries are prison-based businesses in which inmates work and earn wages as well as develop skills. The state of Minnesota has the oldest prison industries program. It is significant that Minnesota never restricted private sector involvement in its industrial program. However, federal law restricts interstate commerce of items manufactured by inmates. Some products are exempted. Others should be.

[25]The Sixth Amendment to the U.S. Constitution provides that "in all criminal prosecutions the accused shall enjoy the right to a speedy and public trial, by an impartial jury of the State and district wherein the crime shall have been committed, which district shall have been previously ascertained by law, and to be informed of the nature and cause of the accusation; to be confronted with the witnesses against him; to have compulsory process for obtaining witnesses in his favor and to have the Assistance of Counsel for his defense."

made and will continue to be made definitely reflects the efforts of brave, determined spirits in the United States.

I conclude this chapter with a quote from Oliver Wendell Holmes: "Man's mind, once stretched by a new idea, never regains its original dimensions." As progress is made in the United States to help our innocent law-abiding citizens, there is an ever-increasing commitment that the criminal justice system will continue to see and hear the needs of victims and witnesses and will never regress to its earlier deplorable dimensions.

BIBLIOGRAPHY

Attorney General's Task Force on Family Violence. (1984). *Final report.* Washington, DC: U.S. Government Printing Office.

Bureau of Justice Statistics. (1984). *Victim/witness legislation: An overview.* Washington, DC: U.S. Department of Justice.

Bureau of Justice Statistics. (1987a). *Households touched by crime: 1986.* Washington, DC: Author.

Bureau of Justice Statistics. (1987b). News release, Washington, DC.

Carrow, D. (1980). *Crime victim compensation.* Washington, DC: U.S. Government Printing Office.

Commission on Law Enforcement and the Administration of Justice. (1967). *Task force report: The courts.* Washington, DC: U.S. Government Printing Office.

Finn, P., & Lee, N. W. B. (1987). *Serving crime victims and witnesses.* Washington, DC: U.S. Department of Justice.

Hammett, T. M. (1987). *AIDS and the law enforcement officer.* Washington, DC: U.S. Department of Justice.

McGuigan, P., & Pascale, J. S. (Eds.). (1986). *Crime and punishment in modern America.* Washington, DC: The Institute for Government and Politics.

National Advisory Commission on Criminal Justice Standards and Goals. (1973). *A national strategy to reduce crime.* Washington, DC: U.S. Government Printing Office.

National Conference of the Judiciary on the Rights of Victims of Crimes. (1985). *Statement of recommended judicial practices.* Washington, DC: U.S. Government Printing Office.

Office for Victims of Crime. (1986). *Proposed model legislation: Victims of crime.* Washington, DC: U.S. Department of Justice.

Office of Justice Programs. (1984). *Protecting our children: The fight against molestation.* Washington, DC: U.S. Department of Justice.

Office of Justice Programs. (1986). *Four years later: A report on the President's Task Force on Victims of Crime.* Washington, DC: U.S. Government Printing Office.

President's Task Force on Victims of Crime. (1982). *Final report.* Washington, DC: U.S. Government Printing Office.

Sparks, R. F. (1982). *Research on victims of crime.* Washington, DC: U.S. Department of Health and Human Services.

U.S. Department of Justice. (1983). *Guidelines for victim and witness assistance.* Unpublished manuscript.

Witonski, P. (Ed.). (1981). *The wisdom of conservatism* (Vol. 3). Mars Hill, NC: Institute for Western Values.

21

United Nations Law as a Strategic Weapon

Stanley W. Johnston
University of Melbourne, Melbourne, Australia

INTRODUCTION

The UN Declaration on Victims (1985) enjoins remedies for abuse of power. This chapter identifies three such abuses—government contempt for UN law, failure to teach about the UN, and confinement to nationality—and explores remedies. The greatest catastrophes come from the failure of nations to honor their pledge to submit to UN law. We need arms in defense of the law, but other use of force is an offense in itself and victimogenic. NATO and ANZUS commands might set up a committee to advance their treaty undertakings to develop UN law and peacekeeping, for we will arm the United Nations before disarming the nations. Children tend to accept teachers' values and leadership, and education which attenuates the centrality of the United Nations leaves them political cripples. The denial of individual access to the UN Human Rights Committee is political enslavement.

There is a political side to victimization, namely, giving one's loyalty to the losing dogma of national sovereignty, to a government which is soft on the rule of law and pursues peace and prosperity through splendid, eccentric isolation. I have visited concentration camps in four countries, on both sides of the Iron Curtain, and wondered how it could happen. But countries with nuclear weapons, and their subjects and allies, are planning for a war which will make the genocides of Stalin and Hitler look mild. People swallow the camel of ungoverned military machines and strain at the gnat of Charles Mason. History will not distinguish between communist and capitalist bombs but will know as savages all who did not support the United Nations and its law. Between war and peace, law is the missing link: We reconcile our images of peace and of power through the medium of law, and the convergence of today's military and peace movements will come in the form of UN peacekeeping and world citizenship (i.e., through individuals' direct participation in the world political order). To pretend a detachment from that consummation is to practice an awesome type of victimization. It shows neither enlightened self-interest nor care for avoidable suffering.

Stanley W. Johnston is Reader in Criminology at the University of Melbourne and editor of *For a Stronger United Nations: The Policy of the United Nations Association of Australia*. Recently, he has been appointed a Fellow of the Australian College of Education and an Associate of the Chisholm Institute of Technology.

Victimology's new *grundnorm*, the UN Declaration of Basic Principles of Justice for Victims of Crime and Abuse of Power (1985; General Assembly Resolution 40/34) enjoins "appropriate rights and remedies" for victims of abuses of political power. Part B of the declaration defines "victims" as those who suffer harm through violation of internationally recognized human rights, and it provides that states should make remedies readily available. I here examine some likely remedies. We are all victims of such abuses of power, though stoic realism stopped us complaining about it until we saw feasible remedies. Now, with institutions of the world state in place—and with the offender typically a government—it is appropriate to have recourse to the United Nations.

The League of Nations broke down, and people wonder if we can trust the UN. Compared with what? There is no alternative. The UN has lasted 43 years and is the practical path to peace. It enjoys global support and describes the common sense of human values and priorities. No other body even has that agenda. If the UN is not adaptable, we will bury it—but that might be dangerous in the nuclear age. We can place more confidence in the rule of UN law than in intergovernment alliances. Governments are often the enemy. In skimping on their pledge to submit to the UN, they are the gravest threat ever to life. The very size of their military budgets identifies them anachronistically with the Westphalian fragmentation of sovereignty. In order to save us from the schizoid nationalization of compassion, truth, law, and loyalty, victim science must broaden its political premises and offer moral leadership. Victimologists so far have picked the easy cases, the little problems. We must also work where the hurts and the needs are greatest, lest, by default, we reinforce the bad in the old order.

THE RIGHT TO DEFENSE THROUGH LAW

People have a right to peace under law (Universal Declaration of Human Rights of 1948 [UDHR], Article 28; Declaration on the Right of Peoples to Peace of 1984). Governments accept that their first purpose and responsibility is to protect "life, liberty and security of person" (UDHR, Article 3). The realization of that right depends, in turn, on individuals accepting that they are world citizens and that national affections are incidental and, when exclusive of the larger self, puerile and victimogenic. Two political axioms are self-evident. First, the UN is not a foreign affair; it is our own and best government. To see world affairs as foreign affairs is to diminish ourselves: We are part of the main. Second, peace depends on loyalty to the UN and on the enforcement of its law (Einstein, 1947/1981, p. 441).

Peace means calm or good order. It is linked with order, both as a cause and as a result. In the ceaseless dialectic of peace and conflict, just systems of law and order are a necessary, and usually sufficient, condition for peace. Social conflict is not a pathology: Dialogue, competition, and conflict are necessary for both change and stability in government. Conflict has only to be regulated to avoid destructive excesses. The challenge lies in describing and installing the means of restoring calm out of conflict. Since we will not sever national defenses for a poorly defined world state, victimology has the task of administrative definition. This requires us to strengthen the UN as the principal system for keeping the peace. Everyone needs the UN in order to fulfill his or her own objectives. The choice is between world government and peace on the one hand and world anarchy and war on the other: "As anarchy leads to war, government establishes peace, and just laws preserve it" (Adler, 1952, p. 98). As local peace depends on local government, so world peace depends on world government. And as local police forces do not prevent all crime, so the UN will not prevent all conflict.

We must identify the UN as the federal world state and declare our allegiance. Pious attitudes are not enough; peace requires a popularly supported legal structure to harmonize competing claims. We need, not the tokenism of new structures, but acceptance of the authority of the existing structure. Dreamers look for a world government yet to come, but we have had our constitutional convention, we have our government: The United Nations is the world state, and it is gradually attracting and asserting authority. The UN quietly gains authority as it imposes its will in southern Africa and as regional alliances threaten "defense" through perdition. The UN Charter has changed the political order. The UN is not a loose, optional, amphictyonic confederation but the supranational government appointed by its charter to take "preventive and enforcement action" with full governmental power. That power, and world citizenship, will be consummated as the UN progressively recognizes people personally. There is a dynamic interplay between loyalty and sovereignty (see Hobbes [1651] on the reciprocal duties of sovereign and citizen). The United Nations is healing the political fragmentation which resulted from the Westphalia Peace Treaty (1648) and which overvalues race and nation. We are now witnessing the culmination of the great revolution against Roman tyranny which was formally begun at Westphalia in 1648: the shaping of the democratic world government which recognizes individuals. Such a government is not attainable merely through international law, and it was scarcely conceived of in the rough, generally illiterate communities under Roman rule before 1648.

In those conditions, Vegetius said, "If you want peace, prepare for war." He was half right. Arms are not a diversion of resources from the economy; arms sap the economy only when they threaten law. Without armed force in aid of the civil power, the economy is very poor. *Unregulated* force is the enemy. George Shultz said, "Diplomacy not backed by military strength is ineffectual: Leverage, as well as goodwill, is required. Power and diplomacy are not alternatives; they must go together" (*The Age* [Melbourne], June 20, 1987). But arms and diplomacy combined are still not enough. When exercised outside the collective props of law, they are political weaknesses. Influence declines rapidly when it relies on power without authority. The swords of war must be converted into swords of law and justice before they can be beaten into plowshares. To set up UN criminal justice (the proven method of securing peace) will be the single greatest contribution to civilization and the economy which any of us will see. So let us update Vegetius: If you want peace, prepare for law. Will the step up—from national solipsism to the rule of law—come about only through terrifying slaughter or can an effort of enlightened political will achieve that goal? It depends partly on the quality of the science of victimology. Crises facilitate constitutional change, but we ought to be fine-tuning the UN all the time. The UN Secretariat tries to establish a context in which justice and law can prevail;

the International Law Commission works to develop and codify law (Urquhart, 1986).

The nation is not the only paradigm of state, peace, and law. After city states, feudal states, empire states, and nation states, the natural evolution of political order is now toward the world state. In this period of political spasm, there is an authority vacuum which only the UN can fill. There is no going back: We can build confidence now only through the UN. The UN will rarely confront, and thus glorify, a whole nation state. Its Code of Offences Against the Peace and Security of Mankind will divide and conquer—by making officials individually liable and by using administrative sanctions.

Upon joining the UN, a state shares sovereignty with the UN and undertakes to submit to its superior authority on the many matters within its jurisdiction (Charter Articles 2.4, 2.5, 25, 43, 45, 49, 51, and 94). And domestic jurisdiction is overridden when the UN applies enforcement measures under Chapter 7, Article 2.7. The UN has a legislature, judiciary, and executive, all of which express the general will. Its General Assembly is the supreme legislature. Embodying the distilled reason and wisdom of formally assembled humanity, its resolutions represent an historic confluence of positive law and natural law and possess an inherent authority. They are a triumph of lawmaking and of civilization, and should be taught in schools (UNGA Res 1511). Assembly resolutions themselves are now a major source of law—responsive, comprehensive, clear, and urgent. The UN is making law, but not international law between consenting states (the UN did not ask the consent of Rhodesia and South Africa before incriminating their racist regimes). Its law tends to be customary law and supranational. UN assistance in the teaching of merely international law (UNGA Res 176, 40/66) is a mistake. Talk of "law" that is between but not above nations is nonsense and a public mischief. The private treaties of international society are inferior to the positive UN law which issues from the standing public forums of the world community (Article 103).

The UN judiciary is the World Court, with its 162 parties. Articles 33 and 36 of the UN Charter set out the means of settling disputes and give preeminence to adjudication by the Court. The UN General Assembly should promote the World Court and expect those seeking election to the Security Council to submit to it. A government's failure to submit to the World Court is an abuse of power: No government is above the law. Article 38 of the World Court's Statute speaks of "civilized" nations. Who then is civilized? One thing is sure: Those who do not submit to UN law are not! In 1940, in his "blood, sweat, and tears" speech, Churchill said, "Civilization means a society based upon the opinion of civilians. It means that violence, the rule of warriors and despotic chiefs, the conditions of camps and warfare, of riot and tyranny, give place to parliaments where laws are made, and independent courts of justice in which over long periods those laws are maintained." We might repeal Paragraphs 2–5 of Article 36 of the World Court's Statute and rely on Article 94.1 of the UN Charter to bring UN members irrevocably under the compulsory jurisdiction of the World Court (cf. Article 25 of the UN Charter). The United States should repeal the insolent Connolly Amendment qualifying its submission to the World Court. It would be chaos if every government obeyed only the laws it wanted to. French and U.S. contempt for World Court judgments on UN dues and on Nicaragua discounts their solemn pledges, under the UN Charter and the NATO Treaty, to respect the law. Veto powers hardly need to operate outside the law which they control. The World Court needs jurisdiction over all actors, including litigants other than nation states (other political bodies, indigenous peoples, individuals, and corporations). Terrorism, for instance, will not cease until terrorists, too, can have their day in a fair court. The World Court should admit no reservations on its jurisdiction. It needs a criminal chamber (Statute Article 26) and should find ways to punish parties for contempt. For public relations, it should go on circuit and hear cases on site (Statute Article 22). Under Article 94.2 of the UN Charter, the Security Council should routinely enforce the decisions of the World Court. No court has its own police; it relies on the support of the executive.

As to the executive, the Secretariat is gifted and economical but far too small for its tasks. The annual UN budget (now only about $1 billion) is derisory. Since the U.S. contribution is relatively low as a percentage of GNP, U.S. bickering over UN funding is disingenuous. When a state dislikes a UN decision, that is cause for new lobbying among delegates, not for denigrating the UN. There is good reason to change the rules of voting, but that does not justify disobeying decisions made under the existing rules. The UN budget could be enlarged by having countries contribute a growing percentage of national military budgets, starting, for example, at 1%. Spending a proportion of defense budgets on defense through law is an attractive principle. But the executive council (the Security Council) must change and fulfill its responsibilities under the UN Charter (Chapters 5, 7, and 14) to enforce the decisions of the World Court, to activate its Military Staff Committee and set up a standing UN peacekeeping force, and to regulate armaments. The Security Council is in radical default of those obligations. In Articles 24, 26, 39, 43, 46, and 83, they are not mere powers. The permanent members of the Security Council are subverting, and will therefore forfeit, their historic constitutional authority. Their selective reading of the UN Charter holds us all to ransom. A remedy for that abuse of power might be for the General Assembly to seek from the World Court an advisory opinion or writ of mandamus to direct the Security Council to fulfill its duties.

The alternative to law is not justice or bliss but the brutish anarchy described by Hobbes and exemplified today by the permanent members of the UN Security Council. Those five were given privileges and powers in the expectation that they would police the world. They enjoy a nonelective seat on the council and an individual veto—two exceptions to the principle of the equality of nations. They have corresponding responsibilities. Yet with a curious view of their own interests, they have scarcely begun to discharge their preventive and enforcement functions. None of them even submits unreservedly to the jurisdiction of their own court. The Security Council must someday fulfill its responsibilities under Chapters 5, 7, and 14 of the UN Charter. The structure of the UN is adequate; it is the behavior of certain member states that leaves something to be desired. With pervasive violations of rights recognized in the common law declared by themselves in the UN, governments now kill over a million people a year and impoverish numerous others. This involves macrovictimization by governments and macrovictimity among peoples. Loyalties play a crucial part in both: Individuals, too, are responsible.

One major aim of the NATO and ANZUS alliances has yet to be systematically pursued. The preamble to the NATO Treaty (1949) asserts the parties' faith in the UN and their determination to defend the rule of law. Likewise the

ANZUS Treaty (1951) and the now defunct SEATO Treaty (1954), both of which included the United States, Australia, and New Zealand. Article 1 of the ANZUS Treaty is identical with Article 1 of the NATO Treaty:

> *The parties undertake, as set forth in the Charter of the United Nations, to settle any international disputes in which they may be involved by peaceful means in such a manner that international peace and security and justice are not endangered, and to refrain from the threat or use of force in any manner inconsistent with the purposes of the United Nations.*

Article 8 of the ANZUS Treaty envisages "the development by the United Nations of more effective means to maintain international peace and security."

But NATO and ANZUS have produced no initiatives toward defense through law. Instead, they are characterized by militarism (Suter, 1984; cf. Gibbon, 1776, p. 1). Just as we plan weapons systems on a long lead time, pushing back the frontiers of the craft, so must it be with law. In order to seize the moral high ground, the NATO and ANZUS commands should appoint committees to promote the rule of law through UN peacekeeping, step out beyond private alliances and identify themselves with public policy, and open a dialogue with peace scholars. Such committees could move to activate the UN Military Staff Committee, for UN peacekeeping will increasingly be the form taken by military action. The Military Staff Committee should publish a manual on standard equipment, procedures, training, discipline, and funding. Armed force is needed in UN preventive and enforcement action (Articles 1, 2, 5, 39–50, 53, and 94), and national force is tolerable only when it conforms with Chapters 7 and 8 of the UN Charter (i.e., as directed or approved by the UN Security Council). Sanctions reinforce law and are not just components of power politics. Since Chapter 8 of the UN Charter places legal constraints on regional alliances, those alliances could ask that UN peacekeeping be more reliable. See UNGA Res 378 on methods of involving the UN in crises and on the machinery for bringing self-defense issues before the Security Council. The task is to forge links between powerful actors and the embryonic agencies of law—in this frontier-law situation, the military must come to the aid of the sheriff. Defense academies should critically analyze UN law. NATO and ANZUS could try to wipe the slate clean on behalf of their allies. Now that Japan, West Germany, East Germany, and Italy are member states of the UN, charter references to "enemy states" are inappropriate. In order to keep the UN Charter forceful and prevent it from becoming a victim of its own history, we might now delete Article 107 and the last 98 words of Article 52 (see also Article 77(1)(b)).

NATO and ANZUS public relations must make a wider appeal. The peace preserved by the two treaty organizations will be strengthened when it is tied to law. If others fear the World Court and get offside with the UN, the loss is theirs. We lose nothing by submitting to law but rather gain by trading license for liberty. No army can stand against an idea whose time has come: Correct thinking beats military might. As Shakespeare wrote, "Twice armed is he whose quarrel is just." And as Tennyson wrote, "My strength is as the strength of ten because my heart is pure." Victory depends on the military serving the common sense and policing the world values expressed in the UN. A government which does not submit to UN law forfeits its citizens' loyalty. This may not come to judgment in a court of law, but it undermines morale and the will to win.

Legitimacy, through loyalty to the UN, is the most powerful strategic weapon against enemies abroad and at home. Policing and military action alike depend on dedication to law (Morgenthau, 1966, vol. 3, ch. 9). The Australian Defence Department observed in 1968, "The Vietnam War demonstrated that where governments are weak, administratively incompetent and unable to attract loyalties by drawing the population into effective programs for economic reform and growth, then the military force faces an almost impossible task in countering insurgency" (Dibb, 1986, p. 24). Strategic defense, therefore, is defense under UN law. The first line of defense is a stable world order and collective security under the UN. UN law is both goal and weapon. As part of the agreements required by Article 43 of the UN Charter, the profession of arms will ultimately transfer its current allegiance from 218 various political masters to a central command. As in local law and the doctrine of the just war, reasonable force may be used to police the law: The means must be proportionate to the end sought. Deterrence, fear of countervailing pain, need only be the normal fear of law. Yet general disarmament would make us vulnerable in the absence of reliable UN peacekeeping. Thus we need to arm the UN before disarming the nations.

Some governments give law a bad name. We cannot teach respect for the law of a government which does not take its own UN pledges and votes seriously. Its caprice slights the political process and provokes terrorist and criminal acts in hopeless protest (direct and indirect) at the paradox of lawlessness in government. The UN Code of Conduct for Law Enforcement Officials (1979) points out that "the law must be enforced fully with respect to any law enforcement official who commits an act of corruption, as governments cannot expect to enforce the law among their citizens if they cannot, or will not, enforce the law against their own agents and within their own agencies" (Article 7 commentary). States which do not uphold the decisions of the World Court create a crisis of loyalty, and as heresy finally overcame Church tyranny, so crime will rise until it exposes this hypocrisy and governments set a decent example. Governments generally come into line quickly because their business is law, and they know that legitimacy and loyalty depend on their abiding by law. But street demonstrators against apartheid or against weapons of mass destruction can sap the legitimacy of a careless government and army and thus in effect make law.

Whose law will law-abiding officials support in, say, apartheid South Africa—local law or UN law? Nuremberg and Article 4 of the Draft Code of Offences Against the Peace and Security of Mankind (1954) make it clear that those who oppose UN law and government are not innocent noncombatants; they are personally liable. Officers must satisfy themselves that the orders they execute are lawful; ignorance of the law is no excuse. It is ethical to rise against anarchist or criminal tyranny and unethical not to. Whilst nongovernment groups and individuals get short shrift in international law, they benefit directly from UN law on human rights and transnational corporations. So they have an interest in getting governments to support the UN.

THE RIGHT TO EDUCATION FOR PEACE

Whether or not there is an enforceable juridical right to peace under law (Dawes, 1986), there is at least a right to bigot-free education concerning peace under UN law, and we must take administrative steps to realize this right. Failure to teach about the UN is an abuse of this right. A full education is one based on the world community and world state. It will detribalize people and acculturate them to the world view alongside local peculiarities. Science, technology, the media, travel, and education all describe or use world culture (Hall, 1958, pp. 109–110). H. G. Wells said, "The future is a race between education and catastrophe." But that depends on what is taught. Social science begins with axiomatic political judgments. To ignore the world order and omit military defense leaves social defense theory fragile, partial, and eccentric. Victimology must grow up and accommodate the institutions of the world state. Ancient Athenians described those who stood aloof from public affairs as unwhole people, incomplete, or half citizens (the Greek word was *idiotes*, from which we get *idiot*). Those who do not join in the world political process today may be called idiots. National borders and regional alliances are shifting parts of the whole and are subject to change. But not so our constitutional obligations to the UN. One hundred and fifty-nine countries (98.23% of the world) are constituent members of the UN, to which they have pledged fealty. Their membership of the world body is usually older, more comprehensive, and more lasting than their regional alliances. The UN needs its Abraham Lincolns (humble and loyal leaders) in order to centralize power. Education and research are means of implementing human rights. Education about the authority and enforcement of UN law will redeem victimology from reactive epiphenomena so it can become an autonomous science, alert to and able to promote human rights.

UN statements of doctrine on this are abundant. Their very multiplicity is an indictment of teachers. The Universal Declaration of Human Rights (Article 26.2) and the Covenant on Economic, Social and Cultural Rights (1966; Article 13) provide that education shall "further the activities of the United Nations for the maintenance of peace." The UN Declaration of the Rights of the Child (1959; Article 10) provides that the child "shall be brought up in a spirit of understanding, tolerance, friendship among peoples, peace and universal brotherhood and in full consciousness that his energy and talents should be devoted to the service of his fellow men." The UN Declaration on Youth (1965) accepts that education should acquaint youth with the role of the UN in preserving and maintaining peace and promoting understanding and cooperation and that it should foster the ideals of peace, human solidarity, liberty, dignity, equality, and respect and love for humanity and its creative achievements: "Young people must become conscious of their responsibilities in the world they will be called upon to manage and should be inspired with confidence in a future of happiness for mankind." The UN urges teaching on the purposes and functions of the UN (UNGA Res 137, 176, and 1511; ECOSOC Res 748) and dissemination of UN resolutions (UNGA Res 636). See also the Declaration against Discrimination in Education (1960; Article 1(b)), the Convention on Racial Discrimination (1965; Article 7), and the Declaration on the Preparation of Societies for a Life in Peace (1978). UNESCO aims "to contribute to peace and security by promoting collaboration among the nations through education, science and culture in order to further universal respect for justice, for the rule of law and for the human rights" (UNESCO Constitution, 1945, Article 1). Since its constitution speaks of the world heritage of education, science, and culture, UNESCO could devise model global syllabi: national syllabi are notoriously biased.

The development of UN authority must be part of the routine syllabus. Where would the authority of national law be if it were not respectfully taught in the law schools? Understanding of the UN will promote interest in and support for its work. Good teachers will show independence and integrity and help students to join in the world community. Children can prepare for peace by learning civics for the normal person, the world citizen, based on the UN Charter and the Human Rights Covenants, which are rewritings of the social contract to empower individuals. Yet even universities shrink from *universitas* and commit self-maiming by denying people's full humanity. Apart from the United World Colleges, schools still victimize children by teaching them endemic conflict and turning them out as fatalistic nationals in a lawless jungle, as if wars are not within human control. Children hear little of UN political achievements. They expect a nuclear war but do nothing about it. Victims indeed! But it is no harder to teach them the truth: Remedies are available. The first step is for them to take responsibility and to retract their blind faith in leaders. In the long run, victims of the abuse of national power will be saved by taking their placc as UN citizens.

THE RIGHT TO UNITED NATIONS CITIZENSHIP

People define themselves by reference to groups and ideals. Social scientists choose some political order (usually their nation) to which they give (usually unarticulated) obeisance. The most concrete fact in the social sciences is a loyalty: We die for it. *Dulce et decorum est pro patria mori* say the scoundrels who take refuge in patriotism. Bigots mock up an enmity and then fondly say the enemy is different. But dialogue on the differences is uncritical and sterile, and such enemies have more in common with each other than either has with a world citizen. Some feel that their ego identity depends on having an enemy out there. They love their enmities more than life itself, and the race consciousness is still geared to fending off enmities sired by the accidental fragmentation of the political order. International alliances are no basis for either science or sober administration; yesterday's allies are today's enemies, and vice versa. This intraspecific hatred on command, this loyal killing by uniform, of any whom today's government calls "enemy aliens" (based on disposition which has no lasting significance) is uniquely human. We used to forgive war crimes by pretending that no one was responsible for war: The troops were under orders and the leaders above the law. But we have now changed the rules and will incriminate officials who use armed force otherwise than as ordered or approved by the UN Security Council. Itself once a step forward from the walled city state, nationalism has become an absurd tradition, an unserviceable god.

We each choose a political persona, authorize a sovereign, and invest it with legitimacy (Hobbes, 1651). Projecting the correct persona makes it easier to protect it. We respect our origins and will not forsake local roots and affections; loyalty to family and nation is desirable. Moreover, intergroup rivalry is not undesirable. The danger is to maintain a certain kind of pride in the local which disparages and repudiates participation in the world order and reduces people to political idiocy in world affairs. This latter problem, however, is soluble. To give to a nation, race, religion, or ethnic group the fierce tribal loyalties which have not found satisfaction in the family or a primary group is to distort politics.

Our common humanity is stronger than the incidental variations of tradition, language, and law that impede communication. We are aware of the pathology of loyalty which issues in genocide, but loyalty can be victimogenic long before it becomes fanatical. This pathology shows in a sectarian allegiance to nation or race which can denigrate or preclude an overriding loyalty to the larger world order embodied in the UN, make racist generalizations about members of another nation, or alienate foreigners and deny them equal protection of law. Such exclusive loyalties are divisive, belittling, and destructive. Primitive national man can scarcely imagine what it will be like to live in a world in which there are no aliens—can imagine neither the peace and security it will offer nor the wealth it will liberate.

Due in part to UN human rights procedures, there is now a rapid evolution in the interrelationships of the individual and the two states currently competing for his or her allegiance—the nation state and the world state. We are taking tangible steps toward world citizenship; the political order is not static. Nor is the criminal justice system. The role of criminal justice is to initiate and superintend the moral dialectic. In that dialectic the premises of the established order are themselves open to question. Some corrupt the criminal process by turning it into a reactionary instrument of repression, just as the Inquisition tried, in vain, to protect the Church by suppressing heresy.

World citizenship is not mere acceptance of our common humanity, genetic and cultural; nor is it mere global thinking, philanthropy, or ethics; nor cosmopolitan indifference. The question is political and legal. Citizenship is the legal link between an individual and a state under which the individual receives certain rights and protections in return for allegiance and duties. The politically mature will claim world citizenship and publish a program to achieve it. No world citizenship without world government. *Pax Romana* and the claim *civis Romanus sum* both depended on the power of Rome. Whereas some people are stateless, others are citizens of more than one state. Some state laws stop their citizens from pledging loyalty to a foreign state. But the UN is not foreign to any member state or, arguably, even to any nonmember state (UN Charter Articles 2.6, 36.2, 50, and 93.2). Practically all countries are constituent states in and under the federal world government.

Nation states currently enjoy preeminence both in UN voting and as objects of UN government. But they are not the only actors, beneficiaries, and objects of UN attention. And although peace and security are the primary business of the United Nations, they are not its only business. In this postnational age, the UN also regulates human rights, non-self-governing territories, the global commons, transnational corporations, and so on—the wide range of matters ceded to it under the UN Charter Articles 13 and 55, among others. The UN exists for peoples as well as governments, and it will keep changing the relationships of the three major protagonists—world state, nation state, and individual—until national subjects are liberated as world citizens. The status and safety of the victims of nationalism depend on giving them legal standing on human rights matters.

The administrative development of UN recognition of individuals requires, first, UN citizenship (passport, ID, etc.) for any who want it, especially stateless persons and the residents of nonmember states. The so-called human right to a nationality (see UDHR, Article 15; the Covenant on Civil and Political Rights,

Article 24; the Convention on the Reduction of Statelessness) is a contradiction in terms and would lock people forever into a national persona. (Some instruments even speak of the right to a nationality without distinction as to national origin.) That right obviously needs redefining to permit people to find their truly human right to world citizenship.

Second, the UN General Assembly should encourage timid and tyrannical governments to grant the right of individual petition to the UN under the Covenant on Civil and Political Rights (1966) and the Convention on the Elimination of Racial Discrimination (1965), two UN instruments which may assume the authority of customary law. The right is abused in simply being withheld by undemocratic governments. Where the respondent is a national government, natural justice dictates that the only appropriate remedy is impartial UN judgment achieved by that appeal procedure. The procedure is of the essence: It is the only escape from the tyranny of local opinion. No longer is a nation the final judge of a person's civil and political status. Status is determined by the UN Human Rights Committee, and victimologists might help to persuade governments to accept the jurisdiction of that committee.

Third, we should anticipate UN voting reform, further modification of national equality, (1) by giving say two votes to a member state with above average population (this would give the UN universality by facilitating admission of all the mini-states), and (2) by requiring, say, two negative votes to veto a Council resolution. The veto power is much abused. The requirement of great power unanimity has helped avoid a major war, but it could safely and profitably be modified in such a way as to lead to more sensitive drafting of resolutions. One day UN delegates may be chosen by direct election from equal electorates to a house of peoples' representatives that would sit alongside the General Assembly of unequal nations.

Fourth, there should be recognition of a peace tax and of the right to serve in the UN peacekeeping force. Personal gifts to the UN might be tax deductable, and people may have the option of paying the defense portion of their taxes to the UN instead of to the nation.

Finally, world citizenship will require individual liability under the UN criminal code.

National liberation movements aim to cut the shackles of an imperial power abroad or a dominant race or martinet at home. By contrast, the political liberation sketched here will break the chains of any exclusive sectarian loyalty and let people enjoy rights and responsibilities in direct relationship with the world state embodied in the UN. For three centuries we tried to contain the political order in nation-tight compartments. But that is quite unnatural. If the state is ever to wither away, it will be after we have grown accustomed to standing tall politically as world citizens.

BIBLIOGRAPHY

Adler, M. (1952). *Great books of the Western World* (Vol. 3). Chicago: Britannica.

Dawes, C. E. (1986). The right to peace. *Australian Law Journal 60*, pp. 156 ff.

Dibb, P. (1986). *Review of Australia's defence capabilities*. Australian Government Publishing Service.

Einstein, A. (1981). *United Nations World*, October. In O. Nathan & H. Norden (Eds.), *Einstein on peace*. New York: Avenel. (Original work published 1947)

Frost, M. (1986). *Toward a normative theory of international relations*. Cambridge: Cambridge University Press.
Gibbon, E. (1776). *The decline and fall of the Roman Empire*.
Hall, J. (1958). *Studies in jurisprudence and criminal theory*. Dobbs Ferry, NY: Oceana.
Hobbes, T. (1651). *Leviathan*.
Johnston, S. W. (1976). Instituting criminal justice in the global village. In E. C. Viano (Ed.), *Victims and society*. Arlington, VA: Visage Press.
Morgenthau, H. J. (1966). Political conditions for a force. In R. A. Falk & S. H. Mendlovitz (Eds.), *The strategy of world order*. New York: World Law Fund.
Suter, K. (1984). *ANZUS: The empty treaty*.
Urquhart, B. (1986). *The UN and international law* (Rede Lecture, 1985). Cambridge: Cambridge University Press.

22

Criminal Policy Regarding Protection of the Victim

Duygun Yarsuvat
University of Istanbul, Turkey

INTRODUCTION

This chapter offers a comparative overview of the status of the victim in the various legal systems which reflect the continental and common law traditions. Particular attention is paid to the protection of the victim according to the laws of Turkey. The author stresses the changing attitudes, thoughts, and legal provisions relative to the obligation of society and of the state toward the victim of crime and his or her survivors.

The fact that millions of people have suffered moral and physical harm caused by criminal actions of others every year has led legislators to amend existing legal systems. Besides basic crimes such as transgression of sexual freedom, crimes against property, and crimes against the physical being of persons, it has also been observed that other illegal actions, such as violations of consumer rights by misuse of power, environmental crimes, neglect of employees' rights, bribery, embezzlement, and corruption, have been causing damage suffered by innocent third parties. Furthermore, a lack of a just approach which can prevent or compensate for the undesired effects on victims has been acknowledged (Lamborn, 1983).

In view of this, almost every legal system has involved itself with revising the position of the victim within that legal system and acknowledging the victim's rights.

THE POSITION OF THE VICTIM WITHIN LEGAL SYSTEMS

In the last couple of years, the "victim" has increasingly become the focus of penal lawyers and criminologists, in parallel with the increasing number of crimes. Ever since Beccaria, penal lawyers have dealt with the perpetrator and have tried to improve the perpetrator's position within the legal system, secure

Duygun Yarsuvat completed his initial university education at the University of Istanbul, Faculty of Law. Then he continued his studies at the Institute of Mass Media, Brussels, Belgium; Princeton University; Columbia University; and the International Labor Organization in Geneva. He teaches penal law, criminology, and criminal procedure at the University of Istanbul and at Marmara University. Presently, he is serving on the committee assigned to prepare the draft of the new Turkish Criminal Code. He has also published extensively in the fields mentioned above.

his or her rights, and investigate and prevent the factors which have caused him or her to commit the criminal act. A thorough study of the international developments within the past 20 years shows that all attempts along this line concentrate on the perpetrator.

However, those who fight against crime have recently begun dealing with the victim, the long forgotten and ignored party of the crime. They have been trying to examine crime according to the victim's point of view, to find the reasons for this, and to place the victim in a more secure position within the legal framework. Especially in Continental Europe, the victimization movement has expanded significantly during the 80s, and improving the victim's position has been accepted as the primary goal of criminal policy.

With this aim in mind, some legal systems, such as those of Norway, Sweden, Austria, France, Finland, Holland, the United Kingdom, and the United States, have enacted amendments regarding compensation for damages suffered by victims.[1]

Furthermore, similar joint attempts and activities have begun at the international level. For the first time, at the Eleventh Assembly of International Penal Law in 1974, it was acknowledged that victims' damages should be compensated for by the state (Resolutions du Onzième Congres International de Droit Penal, 1974). In June 1983, the Council of Europe prepared a convention regarding compensation for damages suffered by victims of violent offenses and sent it for ratification to the member states. The adoption of a resolution on the rights of victims of crime and abuses of power by the United Nations General Assembly in 1985 has provided international recognition to victim issues.

The issues related to victimology may be summed up and studied under these headings: Developments Regarding Penal Justice, Other Procedural Principles Beyond Penal Justice, and the Role of the Victim in Crime Prevention.

DEVELOPMENTS REGARDING PENAL JUSTICE

The Victim as an Element of Penal Law

A glance at comparative law shows that in most legal systems the victim has the right to intervene within an existing lawsuit and trigger or continue penal prosecution by filing a private suit. In a few cases, such as in the United States, the victim participates in the prosecution only as a witness. Additionally, the victim may file suit in civil court and demand that his or her rights be protected because he or she suffered damages as a result of the crime.

[1]The royal decree for establishing a fund to finance the compensation of victims came into force in Norway on March 12, 1976. A similar law was enacted in Sweden in 1971 and was amended in 1974. In Austria, a code dated September 1, 1971, is in force. In France, code no. 77-5, dated January 3, 1977, came into force in March 1977, and was subject to an amendment which broadened its application in July 8, 1983. The Finnish code dealing with the same issue is dated December 1973 (no. 935). In Denmark, a draft code prepared in 1975 was acted on in 1976 and came into force on October 1, 1976. During the same year, a code aimed at compensating victims in West Germany was first applied. In Holland, a fund to finance compensation for victims was first established in the early 1970s and was enacted by the parliament on January 1, 1976. The oldest code aimed at compensating victims is found in England (1964).

However, the complex structure of penal justice makes it difficult for victims in almost all legal systems to be aware of all the rights they possess. Victims also have insufficient knowledge regarding legal and procedural steps which can help them obtain or protect those rights. Difficulties arise especially during the preliminary stages of the prosecution which take place immediately after the crime. In practice, victims are under heavy moral pressure and shock and usually cannot look after their rights. They may need not only legal but also medical and moral aid. In addition to this, some victims may require further assistance (e.g, seniors, infants, or minority groups with a language problem). Therefore, it is important to have simple procedures and provide moral assistance in addition to legal aid.

Many penal systems require the filing of a complaint by the victim to start prosecution. We refer to such crimes as "crimes for which prosecution depends on a complaint." In such cases, the victim has the right to withdraw the complaint. If the victim decides, for example, that the prosecution harms his or her social life or negatively affects his or her psychological well-being, the victim may step back from the charge. As a result of this, "prosecution depending on a complaint" can, within the current legal system actually protect the victim. This is especially true in cases where public prosecution may put the victim in an undesired and difficult position within society.

Compensating the victim for damages is not very common within existing legal systems. Usually, in case of minor crimes, the victims request self-compensation instead of punishment for the victimizers. As victims, they may not consider the preventive effects of penalties such as imprisonment. At this point we face the correlation between punishing the perpetrators and compensating the victims for damages. The most recent approach in comparative law is to make up for the damages suffered by the victim and to punish the victimizer as well.

One must point out that it is wrong to see the victim and victimizer as two characters on opposite ends of a seesaw. The rights and situation of the victim are not necessarily improved by increasing the punishment of the offender. Sometimes imposing an increased sanction upon the victimizer makes it impossible for him or her to compensate for the damages suffered by the victim as a result of the victimization (e.g., an imprisoned perpetrator cannot financially compensate a victim for damages even if willing to do so).

State Compensation for Damages

In many penal systems, new methods have been developed during the past 10 years for compensating victims. The reasons underlying compensation by the state can be found in documents and practices that are well established. Bentham argues, for example, that since the state undertakes to protect its citizens, it has to make up for the damages they have suffered simply because of the fact that it has not fulfilled its obligation to protect them (see Dönmezer-Erman, 1958).

Positivists have claimed that such compensation lies within the scope of penal justice and that the judges should by themselves or upon the request of prosecutors decide for compensation. In 1885, at the Criminal Anthropology Assembly in Rome, it was declared that protecting individuals may be achieved not only by protecting victims but also by compensating them for damages and that this is a duty imposed upon the state.

According to the classic approach, the victim may file a suit in civil court requesting compensation. In some cases, this might be achieved by administrative actions. On the other hand, the victim who is acting as an intervenor in a penal suit before a penal court may claim his or her personal rights from the same court. These are direct approaches to receive compensation.

In addition to these direct approaches, indirect approaches also exist, for example, to reprieve the sentence if the victim's damages have been recovered, to decide the sentence according to whether or not the damages have been compensated for, or to have the court decide whether or not the damages shall be paid for. However, there is no doubt that none of these approaches alone is totally sufficient.

As it is well known, in many cases the victimizers remain unknown. Especially in sexual crimes, the number of "dark figures" is very high. Even if the victimizer can be identified, his or her financial resources are usually insufficient to compensate for the victim's damages. Obviously, legal proceedings can be very long and expensive (Dönmezer, 1977).

In modern law, the idea of compensating the victim for damages is based on human rights concepts. The right to have social security is among the social rights guaranteed and protected by the state. This right also covers the obligation of the state to protect against damages and to compensate for them. Accordingly, the state undertakes to take all precautions which would serve to protect the individual (Erem, 1971; Yücel, 1967).

Looking at legal systems which studied these issues, one can establish mutual basic points, for example, establishing a fund, defining the victim, defining crimes within the scope of a compensation obligation, the amount of compensation, and the authorized office to decide for compensation (*Dedommagement des Victimes d'Infractions Penales*, 1978).

Establishing a Fund by the State in Order to Compensate for Damages Suffered by Victims

Some countries which have amended their legislature in this direction have established a special fund independent of their general budgets: Finland (1973), Holland (1976), and Sweden (1974). On the other hand, France in 1983 and Austria and Germany in 1973 have reserved a certain sum within their general budgets for this purpose.

The Victim

Almost all legal systems agree that real persons may be compensated in case they become victims as a result of a victimization, with the following two exceptions.

First, the victim's nationality is important when compensation is in question. In general, discrimination exists regarding citizens and noncitizens, and while citizens shall be compensated if they are victims, compensating noncitizens depends on whether or not their domicile is within the boundaries of the country. German, Austrian, and Belgian laws grant compensation only to victims who are citizens. In contrast, British (1964), Swedish (1974), Finnish (1973), Norwegian (1976), and Dutch (1976) legislation does not discriminate according to nationality and grants compensation no matter what the nationality of the victim.

Some countries have moved a step beyond this and have exceeded the principle of territoriality regarding penal law. According to law in these countries, even if the victimization which requires compensation has occurred in a foreign country, a citizen or resident is still allowed to receive compensation. Such is the case with Norwegian and Dutch law.

Second, special circumstances of the victim are also an important factor. The relationship between the victim and the victimizer is taken into consideration when deciding on compensation. Britain, for example, rejects compensation among relatives living in the same quarters. Austrian law refuses the right to apply for compensation if the victim has participated in the crime, has provoked the victimizer, or has shown neglect in preventing the victimization.

In comparative law, it is generally accepted that the heirs of the deceased victim, who are left without his or her support, may file a request to be compensated for the damages the victim has suffered.

Crimes Within the Scope of Compensation

Reimbursement according to comparative law generally covers crimes related to violence, such as homicide, assault and battery, sex-oriented crimes, and so on. The laws of some countries, especially the Austrian Code of 1972, allow reimbursement in cases where imprisonment exceeds 6 months and the victimizer is insane or dead or cannot be prosecuted due to a statute of limitations or the like. Similarly, the Danish Code of 1972 and the Swedish Code of 1948 state that the state shall compensate the victim if an offense against private property has been committed by someone who has escaped or been released from prison or who is an alcoholic. Additionally, those who have suffered harm while helping the police shall, according to a 1935 Swedish law, be reimbursed by the state.

Calculating the Compensation

Comparative law grants compensation only for material damage due to victimization. In contrast, the Dutch system aims to reimburse for both material and moral damages that are a direct result of offenses. However, if a victim's financial situation covers the damages suffered due to the offense, no compensation shall be awarded.

All codes covering this subject have set a maximum limit for calculating compensation to reduce the burden imposed on the state. In Norway, reimbursement may not be less than 500 NKR and not more than 100,000 NKR; in Holland, the maximum limit is 25,000 DFL for material compensation and 10,000 DFL for moral compensation. Similarly, in Finland, it may not exceed 100,000 FM. In France, commissions established under the Court of Appeals shall determine the maximum limit every year. In 1983, it was 250,000 FF (Verin, 1983).

Procedural Rules Regarding the Grant and Calculation of Compensation

Some legal systems require that victims must apply to the police as soon as possible after they have been victimized as a prerequisite for granting compensation. Accordingly, a complaint should exist (this is the case in Norway and Sweden). Finland sets a statute of limitations of 5 years. On the other hand, Holland requires an application within 6 months of the date the victimization occurred.

Authorized to decide on reimbursement are either "judicial" or "administrative" authorities. While German, French, and British systems use the former, Norwegian, Swedish, Finnish, and Austrian systems use the latter. Except in Sweden, the administrative or judicial decision to grant reimbursement is reviewable by a supreme court or authority.

Briefly, the European Convention on the Compensation of Victims of Violent Crimes contains the above mentioned rules. A thorough examination of these shows that, while the victimizer is primarily responsible for reimbursing the victim, social security institutions and the like, although not directly involved in the offense, are also responsible for compensating for the damages. In cases when such an obligation has not been fulfilled, the duty ultimately lies with the state. In this manner, a chain of responsibility is established. The convention also defines which victims may request compensation. As one can see from the title of the convention, only victims subject to physical offenses may apply for such reimbursement. However, citizens of a country which is a member of the Council of Europe may apply for compensation even if they have been victimized in another member country. Also, a noncitizen who lives permanently in a member country may exercise the same rights. The convention leaves issues such as what constitutes damages, what are the procedures, and what are the limits for reimbursement to domestic legislatures (Tsitsoura, 1983). The above mentioned convention was signed in June 1983 and left open for ratification by member countries. Turkey has signed but not yet ratified the convention.

REIMBURSING THE VICTIM ACCORDING TO OTHER SYSTEMS BESIDES PENAL JUSTICE

It is well established that it is in the social interest for legislators to impose sanctions upon the perpetrators of some acts. The victim may file suit in civil court and demand compensation for damages. Offenses which are of a financial nature allow a victim to apply to a civil court for reimbursement as well as to a penal court. In some cases, the victim files suit only in a civil court or brings an administrative action instead of going to a criminal court. One should point out that asserting one's rights in court is time-consuming and expensive. For this reason, in some legal systems, the victim may request reimbursement directly during the penal proceedings. It is hard for the victim with limited financial sources to gather all the evidence, such as witnesses' testimony, expert reports, and other documents, without incurring high costs. It is unlikely that the victim who receives no financial aid and who has limited income can make use of all these tools in civil proceedings. Furthermore, it is more favorable for the defendant to go to trial in a civil court than in a criminal court, since there is no threat of a penalty in the end.

There is no doubt that protection of the victim is not limited to judicial authorities or criminal proceedings. The modern state gives great importance to providing social and financial security. It follows that there should be a social system which can answer to every need of the victim. Social security, medical insurance, and mandatory car insurance are examples of such systems. These systems at times allow the victim to demand reimbursement without having to prove whether or not the offense was committed willfully or by negligence. On the other hand, in some countries, as a result of preferential insurance, individuals may only ask for reimbursement if the damages are a direct result of an offense they have been subject to. According to the latter insurance system, the responsibility of the victim is broader than in the former. It is the victim's duty to prove that the victimizer acted willfully. In some cases, demanding reimbursement from an insurance company may be much more difficult than seeking damages from the victimizer by filing suit in a civil court.

Recent Developments

In some systems, the conflicts between victims and victimizers are solved by the parties themselves or through the intervention of judicial authorities. It is possible, according to some legal systems, for the victim and the victimizer to come to an agreement that will be included in the final decision of the court. This method is used especially for offenses whose prosecution depends on the existence of a complaint by the victim. Release on bail may depend on whether the victim has been reimbursed or not, as per the prosecutor's request. A third system suggested by S. A. Thorvaldson, a Canadian lawyer, requires that the fine decided upon as a result of the penal proceeding be given to the victim as compensation (Thorvaldson, 1981). Another method is to have the victim and the victimizer go to an arbitrator and have him or her solve the conflict.

It has also been claimed that it is not sufficient for only the material damages suffered by the victim to be compensated for by the state: Moral damages should also be taken into consideration. Actually, moral satisfaction can only be achieved by punishing the victimizer according to justice. On the other hand, the victim deserves special consideration at a preliminary stage, even shortly after the offense has been committed. Accordingly, some legal systems now include amendments aimed at improving the victim's situation starting in the early stages of the prosecution. Such amendments require, for example, setting up contact with victims, informing victims of their rights, and mitigating the immediate consequences of offenses.

Setting up Contact with Victims

The code which has addressed this issue is the 1982 French Code. According to this code, "victim's offices" have been formed under the Ministry of Justice. The stated purpose of these offices is to protect the interest of victims prior to prosecution. The duties of these offices include seeing that support organizations for victims are formed and that other state organizations undertake to take care of victims. To ensure that victims who are facing the legal mechanism for the first time be greeted with a warm welcome and with interest and that their minimum needs are taken care of is an important part of penal policy. Some lawyers even argue that the place where victims are first brought and where the first interrogations are done should meet certain standards.

Informing Victims About Their Rights

It is a known fact that in many cases victims are unaware of their rights. Therefore, police or prosecutors should inform them of their rights and explain to them how—judicially or administratively—they can be compensated for damages. Sometimes as a result of this process it might be decided that there is no need to bring a public prosecution. Such a practice can be found in the French legal system.

Also, the duty to act as an arbitrator between the victim and the accused has been given to prosecutors by a decree of the French Ministry of Justice dated 1982. The prosecutor shall explain to the accused his or her responsibilities and ask that he or she compensate the victim for damages. This is aimed at making good the victim's damages before the prosecution actually starts (Verin, 1983).

Mitigating the Immediate Consequences of the Offense

The offense might, in some cases, leave important marks on the victim's life. The victim might have to readjust his or her life, might have to move away from home, or might suffer a loss of reputation. It has been claimed that in such cases society should help the victim. This help should be in the form of treatment and social aid. Also, in order to help the victim, the police should try to estimate the damages during their preliminary investigation.

PROTECTING THE VICTIM ACCORDING TO THE TURKISH LEGAL SYSTEM

The methods already accepted by comparative law fail to take place in the Turkish legal system. On the other hand, the approaches of the classic legal system are also to be found in Turkish law. Civil and penal actions in Turkey are very time consuming and can be quite a financial burden for the plaintiff. Also, those who lack sufficient knowledge about legal procedures find it impossible to follow court actions. For example, it is very unlikely for a woman living in a rural area to ask to be compensated for damages suffered due to an offense. When victims in Turkey decide to look after their rights and demand reimbursement, they do this according to traditional rules or apply for social security; only in limited cases will they apply to the state.

Traditional rules can be found in the Civil Code, Code of Obligations, Penal Code, and Criminal Procedure Code. Article 24 of the Civil Code deals with the right of action in cases where there is a transgression of personal rights. Article 41 of the Code of Obligations covers offenses in a broad sense, since it deals with torts. In calculating the amount and contents of the compensation, one takes Articles 43, 45, and 49 of the Code of Obligations into account.

Article 37 of the Turkish Penal Code states that the victim's right to be reimbursed continues even if the perpetrator has been sentenced. In addition to this, Article 38 allows the victim to request moral compensation. Furthermore, Article 39 gives the victim the right to request moral and material compensation from all associates. It also states that joint liability exists in case the offense has been committed by more than one person. Some articles of the Turkish Penal Code specifically state that compensation may be requested for certain violations. For example, according to Article 465, the employer is financially responsible for any negligent assault, battery, or homicide committed by his employees. This is an example of the liability without culpability defined in the Code of Obligations. Similar liabilities are imposed upon animal owners and car owners.

Article 103 of the Penal Procedure Code allows property taken away by virtue of an offense to be given back to the victim without the need for any decree. Furthermore, Article 365 states that anyone who has suffered damage due to an offense may intervene with the prosecution at any stage and request his or her personal rights.

In case of threat, violation of domicile, violation of private life, minor assault, defamation, transgression of intellectual or property rights, and unfair competition, the victim may bring a personal action according to Article 344 of the Penal Procedure Code. The Penal Code also contains indirect methods for compensating the victim. For example, by giving back the value of or the property itself that was taken away from the victim by virtue of the offense, the court may reduce the penalty imposed upon the perpetrator, according to Article 524. Article 93 of the Penal Code takes the reimbursement of the victim's damages into account for reprieving the sentence. Similarly, according to Article 4, Section 2 of Law No. 647, short-term imprisonment may be substituted for by restitution or reimbursement. Article 19 of the same law links conditional release with compensation given by the perpetrator for damages suffered.

In addition to these possibilities of compensation, social security institutions try to reimburse victims for damages suffered (e.g., Bağ-Kur, Emekli Sandiği, and Sosyal Sigortalar Kurumu). These institutions help their members financially in case of death, unemployment, and illness according to their by-laws (e.g., Bağ-Kur by-laws, Articles 41, 56, 63; Emekli Sandiği by-laws, Articles 27, 129; Social Security Code, Article 26). However, we should point out that the social security institutions mentioned above only undertake to provide reimbursement for damages caused by certain offenses and under certain circumstances. There is no broad practice.

Turkey does not yet have a system where the state reimburses the victim. Such reimbursement is only applicable in certain cases. One is for crimes committed against state officials; the other is covered by Government Decree No. 35 regarding debts of brokers.[2]

According to Law No. 2330, dated November 3, 1980, those who have the duty to protect law and order and follow-up or investigate smugglers may be compensated for damages suffered due to their duties, even if they are no longer on duty. Members of the police force, military personnel, customs officers, related judges and prosecutors, administrative personnel in charge of related operations, prison personnel, secret service personnel, and local guards are within the scope of Law No. 2330. Those who suffer damages due to violence and their dependents are entitled to compensation. The retirement alimony of those who are no longer on duty is also increased to a certain extent.

Government Decree No. 35, dated 1981, which was intended to liquidate certain brokers and prevent further damages to those who had invested money in them, is a typical example of the way in which victims are reimbursed by the state. A series of decrees signed by the government have established a fund for this purpose. Turkish administrative courts have also issued decisions which grant victims compensation by the state.

The problem of compensating for victims' damages has especially become an issue during this era when the numbers of demonstrations, riots, and unknown political murders have increased. An interesting and rare example of laws imposing liability on the state to compensate victims of riots is Law No. 6684,

[2]See Government Decree No. 35, Resmi Gazete 14.1.1982, s.17574. This application has been amended by Decree No. 38, Resmi Gazete 6.4.1982, s.17656.

dated February 28, 1956, regarding reimbursement of those who have suffered damages due to demonstrations in Istanbul and Izmir during September 6–7, 1955. This law was enacted for one specific occasion and is not applicable to damages as a result of any other similar event (Azrak, 1979).

The Administrative Supreme Court has handed down a decision regarding applications for the compensation of victims of riots according to the theory of fault of service.[3] However, in the past, the court has based its decisions on the theory of social risk.[4] Shifting the burden for damages caused by demonstrations from the individual to society is in accordance with constitutional provisions. Applying the principles of the social welfare state in the constitution forces us to come to such a conclusion.

CONCLUSION

Ostensively, the existing legal system in many countries, such as Turkey, has to be amended when it comes to the protection of victims. Developments to be found in comparative law and at the international level should be introduced into the law of those countries. The following suggestions can be made in view of the decisions reached at the Seminar on Victim Policy held in Helsinki in 1983:

1. Receive victims within the legal system. Educate the police force and judicial authorities with regard to the treatment of victims involved in the judicial system.
2. Inform victims about their rights. Supply victims with information about their legal rights and provide them with legal assistance to protect their interests.
3. Provide judicial assistance. Victims should be able to make use of judicial assistance in order to protect their interests and rights.
4. Allow victims to pursue more than one judicial proceeding. Victims should be able to pursue various proceedings—penal, civil, and administrative—and should be able to choose one of these after taking their chances of success into consideration.
5. Have victims play an important part in various proceedings. They should be allowed an active part during the proceedings.
6. Order compensation for the damages as part of the sentence. It should be established that courts decide for reimbursement as primary, secondary, or alternative punishment. Then, the burden of compensating for the victim's damages shall lie upon the perpetrator until said damages have been totally paid for.
7. Have the state compensate for the victim's damages. Existing laws should be amended so that the state shall reimburse a victim of a major offense if the offender is unknown or unable to provide reparation for the damages caused.

[3]The Turkish Supreme Court for Administrative Decisions has ruled that damage was caused by the late and inefficient action by the police forces, regarding the Kahramanmaraş, Konya, Kayseri, and TÖB riots. Daniştay 12. Dairesi 12.6.1967, 1968/140, 1968/1183; 12. Daire, 14.7.1968, 1968/2424, 1969/1911; 12. Daire 3.4.1970, 1969/3535, 1970/754.

[4]The Turkish Supreme Court for Administrative decisions ruled that it is correct to have the administration compensate for the damages without discussing its culpability. Daniştay 8. Daire, 5.6.1961, 1960/8562, 1961/2149 and D. 8. Daire 20.2.1962, 1961/2456, 1962/765.

The principles of the European convention on compensating victims of violent crimes should be reviewed and integrated into current law.

Such changes and amendments are a necessity and are required by the basic social rights of individuals. The state has the duty to support the social security of each individual by virtue of such a system, which is an expression of the social welfare state.

BIBLIOGRAPHY

Azrak, U. (1979). Sorumluluk Hukukunda yeni gelişmeler, Sempozyum III, 12–13 Mayis, Ankara.

Dedommagement des Victimes d'Infractions Penales. (1978). Strasbourg.

Dönmezer-Erman. (1958). Ceza Hukuku Dersleri, İstanbul.

Dönmezer, S. (1977). Devlet ve Suç Mağduru İlişkisi, Onar'a Armağan, İstanbul.

Erem, F. (1971). Türk Ceza Hukuku, Genel Hükümler II. Cilt, Ankara, pp. 372–373.

Lamborn, L. (1983). *Towards the United Nations Declaration on Crime, Abuses of Power, and the Rights of Victims*. Paper presented at the Ninth International Congress on Victimology, Vienna.

Resolutions du Onzième Congres International de Droit Penal. (1974). *Revue Internationale de Droit Penal*, pp. 684–688.

Thorvaldson, S. A. (1981). *Reparation by offenders: How far can we go*? Manitoba: Canadian Congress for the Prevention of Crimes.

Tsitsoura, A. (1983). *The European convention on the compensation of victims of violent crimes*. Paper presented at the Seminar on Victim Policy, Helsinki.

Verin, J. (1983). *La reparation due aux victimes d'infractions penales*. Paper presented at the Seminar on Victim Policy, Helsinki.

Yücel, M. (1967). Suçtan Zarar Gören Şahsin Korunmasi, Adalet Dergisi, n.11, s.859.

[illegible] principles of the [illegible] [illegible] should be reviewed and [illegible] into national law.

[illegible]

BIBLIOGRAPHY

[illegible]

23

Victimology in Portugal

Maria Rosa Almeida
Office of Studies and Planning, Ministry of Justice, Lisbon, Portugal

INTRODUCTION

Legislative concern about crime victims has inspired several provisions of Portuguese law. A distinctive feature of the system is that victims may be granted an active role in the proceedings. Restitution by the offender is mandatorily ordered by the sentencing court. Victims can receive part of the wages of their imprisoned offenders. However, these and other provisions intended to ease the plight of victims appear to be ineffective. Consequently, assistance to crime victims is now recognized as requiring official intervention.

The growing attention paid to victims has led to a different but related development: a crime survey program restricted to the Lisbon area. Besides obtaining information on the incidence of certain forms of crime and their circumstances, the survey also intends to gather data on victim characteristics, attitudes about crime, satisfaction with authorities, and degree of punitiveness, among other items.

THE LEGAL STATUS OF CRIME VICTIMS

Portugal is a newcomer to the field of victimology. Interest in victim research and in victim assistance programs has developed only recently. Yet Portugal has a tradition of assigning a potentially more active role in criminal procedure to victims than do some other legal systems.

In rare instances, a criminal case can only be brought to court if the victim or the victim's representative places a formal charge, in which case the public prosecutor has to accept the complainant's accusation or otherwise refrain from accusing. Private prosecution offenses are extremely rare; at present, only libel and slander fall into this class. Somewhat more frequent are consent-bound prosecutions, that is, prosecutions that can only occur if the victim reports the offense. This is the case in simple assaults, sexual crimes, theft within the family, damage, and a few other offenses. These exceptions to the mandatory nature of criminal prosecution derive mainly from the consideration that, in certain instances, the criminal justice system should respect the victim's point of view

Maria Rosa Almeida graduated in law from the University of Coimbra, Portugal, and took a diploma in criminology at the Institute of Criminology, Cambridge, United Kingdom. She is currently staff member of the Research and Planning Bureau, Ministry of Justice, has published several articles in the area of penology, and is a member of the panel in charge of the first Portuguese crime survey.

and not take action against his or her wishes. In both situations, the victim can be assigned the institutional role of assistant, which means that he or she is a party to the proceedings. The more original aspect of our legal system is that the status of assistant can also be claimed by victims of crimes in general (provided that these cause damage to individual victims) or even by any citizen in offenses of bribery and embezzlement of public money. The main goal of the law here is to encourage victims to produce their own evidence and to subject the public prosecutor's function to some measure of control.

Although assistants are entitled to bring charges different from those of the prosecutor, their procedural role is subsidiary afterwards. There is one important exception, however. In the case of private or consent-bound prosecution, they have the right to discontinue the proceedings, subject to the defendant's agreement, at any time before sentencing.

No statistical information is available on the number of victims who ask to become assistants, but it is known that they seldom make use of this possibility, either for financial or other reasons. Here, as in so many other instances, the law on the books and the law in action can be far apart! The legislative goal of involving victims more actively in criminal proceedings does not seem to have been reached. Yet, not less than 22% of the cases reaching the court stage were discontinued by complainants during 1985. Many more may have ended in the same way at earlier stages, but we do not know how often for lack of statistical information. This partial figure may be taken as a hopeful sign that a considerable number of conflicts between individuals may be solved informally. With adequate mediation, many more might possibly be diverted from the criminal justice system altogether, with fewer risks of illegitimate pressure being exerted on victims than might occur now. Devising frameworks and procedures for bringing victims and offenders together, discovering the limits to this practice, and following up its results might well be among the more promising future developments in the area of crime control.

Another instance of legislative concern regarding victims is the mandatory nature of restitution. Upon sentencing, the court shall set down a sum to be paid by the offender irrespective of any request by the victim. As it is an established fact that offenders (more exactly, convicted offenders) often lack the means to meet their financial obligations, the 1982 Criminal Code devised a provisional solution. While legislation on state compensation is not yet approved, the court can rule that the instruments of the crime or any benefits related to it which are seized by the state be assigned to the victim instead. If the victim is deprived of his or her means of subsistence as a result of the offense, the product of any fine imposed on the offender can be used for the same purpose. It is doubtful that the financial needs of victims will be met through these procedures.

Another equally well-meant and equally ineffective scheme is to assign part of the wages of imprisoned offenders to the victims. Given the token nature of prison wages, this transfer would be of little value to victims. Also expressive of the legislative attention paid to victims are the provisions of the Penal Code which subject suspended sentences, probation, and parole, at the court's discretion, to the condition that the offender pays restitution to the victim. When omission to assist someone in need was criminalized in general terms under the new Penal Code, victims were still a focus of attention. Until then, "bad samaritans" were liable to criminal prosecution only in the case of traffic offenses. At present, there is a general duty to assist others in situations of serious need, provided that this can be done without undue personal danger. It must be said that the new incrimination has been used very little so far, only two cases having led to convictions in 3 years. In the long run, criminalization of omissive behavior may perhaps contribute to shaping new values and a more sensitive public conscience.

The new Code of Penal Procedure, which came into force in January 1988, assigns a role to the victim in an area unfamiliar to our legal tradition: the suspension of proceedings. Suspension—which is devised somewhat like probation—will be admissible only for offenses punishable with imprisonment not exceeding three years, is subject to certain conditions (i.e., both defendant and assistant must agree to it), and can be made dependent on the fulfillment of certain obligations (i.e., the payment of restitution to the victim).

In our legal system, the role of victims in the procedure and their chances of having a voice and of being kept informed are tied to their position as assistants. It is not so much the victim but the victim as an assistant who is given an active although subordinate role in the proceedings. If for financial or other reasons victims rarely request to become assistants (assistants have to be represented by lawyers), the entire elaborate legislative scheme to make them parties to the proceedings proves to be of very little practical value. Nevertheless, the Portuguese system seems to have potentialities. If an effective scheme of free legal assistance is offered to some victims, the financial stumbling block may be removed. It remains to be seen whether difficulties of a different nature would not emerge, for instance, difficulties in communication arising from the social distance between citizens and courts.

THE CRIME SURVEY

The Idea

The Research and Planning Bureau at the Ministry of Justice is getting ready to conduct a crime survey. Information about victimological studies reached us from several sources. In Portugal, a faculty member at Coimbra Law School published a stimulating book on the subject (Andadre, 1980), and in 1983 a daily newspaper produced the results of a survey, including items on the incidence of some offenses and on the respondents' concern with crime. In 1986, the Training Center for Judges and Public Prosecutors made public the results of a survey on child abuse. Crime surveys carried out abroad, in the United States, The Netherlands, and Great Britain, as well as international meetings, such as the 1983 Espoo (Finland) seminar devoted to victim policy and the Sixteenth Criminological Research Conference held by the Council of Europe in 1984, drew our attention to relevant issues. Combined with this background information, a more immediate reason stimulated our interest in conducting a crime survey.

For some time, the Planning and Research Bureau had been working on a program for collecting data on crimes reported or otherwise known to the authorities. Portugal does not have yet a national system of crime statistics distinct from judicial statistics. Such information as exists is provided by different police bodies using their own classifying, counting, and recording criteria, but no information is available on offenses reported directly to prosecutors' offices. The final design of the form had to wait for the new Code of Penal Procedure to be put into execution. In the meantime, reflection on the validity of statistics as a measure of crime led us to look to crime surveys as an independent and probably more accurate measure of the incidence of crime (more exactly, of traditional crime). A panel that included members from other state departments was set up to design the survey. For some time, we made use of the invaluable assistance of Professor Geis from the University of California at Irvine.

At the beginning, the panel's main purpose was to assess the incidence and circumstances of certain offenses and to collect a few data on victims. Later, it became more victim oriented. The questionnaire comprises 76 items, of which 17 refer to criminal incidents, 18 to their factual circumstances or the processing of the case, and the remaining 41 to the demographic characteristics, reactions, and attitudes of victims.

Paying so much attention to victims is not without risks. Like much other research in criminology, surveys are not ideologically neutral. By concentrating on a few offenses which admit individual victims, they may contribute to reinforcing certain stereotypes of crime and draw away attention from the seriousness, in terms of frequency and social harm, of much nontraditional crime. This risk can be lessened only if survey reports emphasize the partial nature of the information and avoid pretending to speak of crime in general when speaking of the crime included in the reports.

The Contents

The Portuguese survey follows the common practice of dividing incidents into personal and household ones. Theft in its several forms (including burglary) is the offense most often depicted. Assault, sexual assault, and criminal damage are also offenses currently included in surveys. To these, swindles, threats, and offensive insults in their major varieties were added, because they appear to be well represented among reported offenses. If only traditional crime is considered, the relatively greater focus on offenses against persons seems justifiable in the Portuguese context, because in Portugal, contrary to the general norm, defendants are charged twice as frequently with crimes against persons as with crimes against property.

Besides assessing the incidence of the surveyed offenses, we will also try to obtain some information on their consequences and circumstances. The former will be measured in terms of personal harm or property loss; the latter, in terms of when and how the offenses were committed (e.g., weapons, existence of security devices), of the number and sex of offenders (if known), of any previous relationships between victims and perpetrators, and of the victims' decisions to chase their offenders.

As mentioned before, most items in the questionnaire deal with victims' characteristics, reactions, and attitudes. There are a vast number of things we would like to know, but we gave priority to those which could help us find answers to the following basic questions. Is victimization evenly distributed throughout the population or are certain groups (e.g., the women, the elderly, the young, those living in better [or poorer] housing) more susceptible to it? Does the experience of victimization affect some groups more deeply? How often do victims receive help? When they do, does it come mainly from primary groups? Is victimization more often the result of acts committed by strangers or by people related in some way to the victim? Is nonreporting more frequent among certain social groups or in the case of certain offenses? Does it appear related to the harm suffered by the victim or to the victim's more positive (or negative) attitude toward authorities? Is fear of crime more marked among groups with higher risk of victimization or are personal characteristics more relevant? Is concern with crime closely linked to fear of crime? Is punitiveness correlated with certain demographic characteristics? How does crime rate compare with other social problems?

Other areas of information were omitted, not because they were thought irrelevant but because they were considered too difficult to explore due to the schematic nature of the questionnaire and the need to keep it relatively short. Thus, no data were collected on victims' satisfaction with the role assigned to them in the procedure, on the problems and needs victims usually face, and on how victims could best be helped with problems. To allow victims to contribute to devising a viable assistance scheme would require lengthy interviews and discussions with victims, individually and in groups. Also left out were questions pertaining to victims' life-styles, which might be useful as empirical tests of a situational approach to crime.

The Method

The Portuguese survey will be restricted to the Greater Lisbon area, which has a population of 2.5 million. The field work is to be carried out by specialized interviewers in October 1989. Advice given by leading experts on crime surveys convinced us that more than one solution was acceptable on sampling.

Assuming the crime rate to be moderate in the Lisbon area, we initially favored the option of interviewing every adult person in a sample of 10,000 households about his or her victimization in order to maximize the number of personal incidents reported (only one person would be interviewed about household incidents). This strategy proved impossible. As interviewers were not to call at the same household more than three times and telephone interviews were not to be used, a considerable drop in numbers had to be expected, unless we were prepared to accept the less reliable procedure of using proxy respondents. Our final decision was to interview only one person, randomly selected, in every household about both personal and household victimization. In this way, we hope it will be possible to achieve reasonably accurate estimates of rare offenses and to analyze some of their characteristics.

ASSISTANCE TO VICTIMS

The emergence (or reemergence) of concern for crime victims was to a great extent brought about by feminist organizations. These organizations were concerned not so much with crime victims in general but with women victims of sexual abuse and of violence within the family. Sexual and physical abuse of women, we may suspect, epitomize the most distressful forms of victimization. Undoubtedly, another powerful factor was the influence of international declarations, in particular, two declarations adopted by the Council of Europe—the 1983 European Convention on the Compensation of Victims of Violent Crime and Recommendation NoR (55) 11 of the Committee of Ministers on the Position of the Victim in the Framework of Criminal Law and Procedure (June 18, 1985)—and the Declaration of Basic Principles of Justice for Victims of Crime and Abuse of Power, which was adopted by the United Nations General Assembly in December 1985.

On different occasions, the Portuguese Minister of Justice has issued statements on crime victims, declaring that the public powers should assume a more active role in organizing and providing assistance. Another sign that state intervention in this area is beginning to receive the attention of politicians is the fact that recently (in November 1986) the Communist Party presented a bill to Parliament on this subject (the bill has not yet been discussed). The bill proposes that permanent victim assistance hotlines be available in public prosecutors' offices; that special units for victim assistance be established in criminal police stations, staffed by specialized personnel under the supervision of public prosecutors; that crime victim aid associations be allowed to represent victims at the proceedings; and that a program of state compensation be instituted.

State compensation will be obtainable for death or physical or mental harm resulting from a criminal act, provided that in the latter situation the victim loses his or her earning capacity for at least one month and suffers a serious life disturbance entailing loss of income, inability to work, or impairment of physical or mental integrity. Only victims whose "per capita" household income does not exceed the minimum salary set by law will be entitled to compensation.

As it is, the bill is open to criticism. Because it relies so much on specialized staff, its implementation would be expensive and run the risk of increasing bureaucracy and role conflicts within criminal justice agencies. A more viable scheme would be to sensitize baseline criminal justice staff about victims' problems and to train them to provide adequate information or contact other services or organizations able to offer assistance to victims. It is also questionable whether courts, overburdened as they are, will be able to grant prompt compensation awards (it is immediately after the offense that a victim's needs are usually most acute).

Moreover, the requirement that there be a minimum of one month's loss in earning capacity and a serious disturbance in life conditions, together with the strict financial criteria adopted for selection, would appear to confirm the statement made by van Dijk (1984, p. 81) at the Espoo seminar that state compensation gives too little, too late, and to too few of the crime victims. Yet, the bill is an important beginning. Enriched as we now are by the practical experience of other countries, it is our responsibility to make victim assistance and compensation not a mere symbolic gesture but an effective device in the quest for a more just and sensitive society.

BIBLIOGRAPHY

Andrade, M. C. (1980). A vitima e o problema criminal. *Boletim da Faculdade de Direito* (Coimbra).
van Dijk, J. J. (1984). *Towards a victim policy in Europe*. Helsinki: HEUNI.

Drug Testing in the Pharmaceutical Industry: Its Faults and Its Victims

Frank J. Henry
Sociology Department, McMaster University, Hamilton, Ontario, Canada

INTRODUCTION

When a pharmaceutical company produces a new drug and secures a patent on it, the company enjoys, for a time, a monopoly on that product and the profits that accompany a monopoly position. There is, then, a constant pressure to produce new drugs, either drugs of the "me too" variety that allow a company to invade a monopoly position held by another drug manufacturer or completely new drugs. Sometimes this pressure is explicit. For example, the 3M Corporation requires its drug subsidiary, Riker, to produce 25% of its gross sales from products introduced in the previous 5 years (Braithwaite, 1984, pp. 65–66). One of the necessary steps involved in bringing a new drug to market is an investigation into its effectiveness and possible harmful side effects. This research is performed in two basic stages: Animal studies are made in the first stage, and if the results of these are favorable, the clinical stage of experimentation involving human subjects follows. I analyze the framework within which drug testing occurs and then examine a number of the methods and techniques that enable drug companies to obtain favorable results in drug testing without outright falsification—although, as will be shown, drug companies also sometimes engage in outright falsification if that is "necessary" in order to obtain approval for a drug from the Food and Drug Administration (FDA).

The pressures produced by drug companies' orientation to profit are passed on to others associated with the drug company in the testing of its products, namely, to testing laboratories and to physicians selected to do clinical trials. The testing laboratory or clinical investigator knows that unfavorable results are not likely to be welcomed by the drug company and that such results reduce the probability of repeat business. The relationship is similar to that between higher and lower executives within the corporation itself: Testing laboratories and clinical investigators certainly are not ordered to do anything illegal or

Frank Henry is an associate professor of sociology at McMaster University, Hamilton, Ontario. He received his PhD from the Catholic University of America in Washington, DC. His research has involved analysis of a wide range of empirical data: fertility, mortality, racial and ethnic discrimination, residential relocation, imprisonment as a general deterrent, the development of opinion and attitudes, and corporate crime and violence. He has published extensively in several scholarly journals.

unethical, but the pressure is there. Sometimes the profit tie, as with top management, is more direct. Dr. Stanley Jacob of the University of Oregon Medical School was hired by Research Industries Inc. to monitor the safety tests on two new drugs for bladder inflammation. When the FDA investigated irregularities in these studies, it was found that Dr. Jacob had $600,000 of Research Industries stock. According to Dr. Marcus Reidenberg, head of the division of clinical pharmacology at Cornell University Medical College, drug study monitors commonly have stock purchase plans from the company whose drugs they are studying. In addition to stock option plans, clinical investigators are well paid. In 1980, for a short-term study of patients, a physician would typically be paid $10,000; for a 100-patient study running some months, the usual fee would be $30,000 or $35,000 (McTaggart, 1980). In summary, the organization of drug testing incorporates testing laboratories and physicians who run clinical trials into the profit-oriented structure of the drug industry.

It might be thought that drug companies would be very careful in the safety testing of their products, if not because of the suffering and death that an unsafe drug can cause, at least because of the danger of being sued and having to pay huge damage claims. However, the cut into profits made by product liability and criminal suits may not be that great, and it is difficult to trace illnesses and deaths to a specific drug. In the wake of the MER/29 disaster, discussed later in this paper, it is true that Richardson-Merrell stock prices dropped for several years, but then they recovered and continued an upward climb (Braithwaite, 1984, p. 74), and the company's sales and profits continued to rise during the entire period (Silverman & Lee, 1974, pp. 92–93).

The difficulty of tracing diseases and deaths to a specific drug can be illustrated by the cases of thalidomide and clioquinol. Thalidomide is nearly 100% teratogenic if taken during the 5th to 8th week of pregnancy, when the limbs begin to form (Knightley, Evans, Potter, & Wallace, 1979, p. 91). A study made in 1949, before the advent of thalidomide, found 1 case of missing or shortened limbs in 4 million births, but in 1960 nearly every pediatric clinic in Germany had at least 1 such case (Teff & Munro, 1976, p. 5). In Hamburg there were an estimated 50 cases of phocomelia between September 1960 and October 1961 (Knightley et al., 1979, p. 97). A total of more than 25,000 children were victims of thalidomide, and there were also thousands of cases of peripheral nerrites caused by thalidomide (Teff & Munro, 1976, p. 3). Despite all this evidence, thalidomide was on the market for over 4 years until enough documentation accumulated to force its removal.

Subacute myelo-optic neuropathy (SMON) is a disease discovered in the late 1950s in Japan. As the disease develops, pain in the stomach and diarrhea are followed by paralysis of the legs and, in some cases, blindness. Over 5,000 reported cases of SMON in Japan were verified. A variety of factors were hypothesized as responsible, including a specific infectious agent considered likely to be a virus. Eventually, due to research sponsored by the Japanese government, SMON was traced to clioquinol, an antidiarrheal drug sold mainly by Ciba-Geigy. Although clioquinol is suitable only for amebic dysentery, it had been vigorously promoted for all types of diarrhea and even as a preventive. The Japanese, with their traditional concern for all types of gastrointestinal disorders, were especially susceptible to this form of promotion, and many Japanese took Entero Vioform or Mexaform daily. However, SMON showed up in at least twelve other countries as well. The main point is that it took years of research to discover the cause of this disease, and the world still might not know the cause were it not for the research program sponsored by the Japanese government in the wake of a 1967–1968 epidemic. SMON virtually disappeared from Japan after the banning of clioquinol there in 1970, but Ciba-Geigy continues its aggressive marketing of the drug in many other parts of the world (Knightley et al., 1979, pp. 244–245; Silverman, Lee, & Lydecker, 1982, pp. 44–54). These two cases show that even when a drug produces very serious side effects for a large number of victims, it is extremely difficult to trace these effects to the drug involved, and they strongly suggest that, from a profit-oriented point of view, thoroughness in drug testing is not required.

DRUG TESTING

Preclinical drug testing is based on a number of assumptions. It is generally assumed that a drug that is safe for two other species is also safe for human beings. However, reactions to drugs vary widely, and whether a drug is approved sometimes depends on the animals chosen for testing. Rats, mice, rabbits, dogs, and monkeys are widely used in drug testing.

A second assumption is that humans are approximately as sensitive to the drug being tested as the animal species used in the test. However, sensitivity to drugs varies widely by species. Humans, for example, are about 60 times as sensitive to thalidomide as mice, 100 times as sensitive as rats, and about 200 times as sensitive as dogs. A dose of one-half milligram per kilogram of body weight per day (0.5 mg/kg/day) in the critical stage of pregnancy will produce birth defects in human babies. A 100-mg/kg/day dose is necessary to produce deformities in bitch pups.

A third assumption is that a linear extrapolation of the results at high doses can be made with reasonable accuracy. For example, if 100 mg/kg/day produces a specific cancer in 1 rat among 50, it is assumed that 10 mg/kg/day will produce 1 such cancer in approximately 500 rats and that 1 mg/kg/day will cause about 1 such cancer in 5,000 rats or 5,000 people (Epstein, 1978, pp. 65–66). The reason for this assumption is that it would be expensive to use the large number of test animals required for the lower doses.

A fourth assumption is that drugs can be tested one at a time, although it is known that drugs sometimes interact synergistically to produce a greater effect (Hall, 1976, p. 66). Laboratory animals are seldom given alcohol along with tranquilizers, for example. Experimental animals were not given foods containing tyramine when the effects of MAO-inhibiting antidepressants were studied, but the cardiovascular effects of these antidepressants require tyramine as a predisposing factor. Similarly, halothane and isoniazid cause liver damage if rapidly metabolized, as would be the case if phenobarbital were taken first (Balazs, 1976).

A fifth assumption is that healthy animals in their prime that are living in an air-conditioned environment, fed a wholesome diet, and getting adequate exercise and rest can be surrogates for people of various ages and states of health living in the real world (Hall, 1976, p. 77). One difficulty with this assumption is that diseases may alter the effects of drugs. Hepatitis, for example, will alter the effect of a drug metabolized in the liver. Several classes of drugs, especially psychoactive drugs, are more toxic for a patient in a hyperthyroid state (Balazs, 1976).

The weakness of these assumptions means that even the most careful drug testing is far from perfect. The fact that a tested drug is later found to be unsafe does not ipso facto indicate carelessness or negligence in the testing. Nor does approval of such a drug by a regulatory agency necessarily indicate carelessness or negligence on the part of the agency. Since both drug companies and regulatory agencies know this, it may encourage a certain laxity in testing and approval procedures. The situation would be quite different if every unsafe drug on the market indicated a failure in drug testing, agency approval, or both.

There are a number of ways of obtaining favorable results in the preclinical safety testing of drugs without outright falsification. One way is to use too few animals in the experiment so that no statistically significant result appears. The basic procedure in testing the safety of a drug is to follow several sets of animals which are similar and which are treated the same, except that the control set is not given the drug being tested and each of the other sets is given a specific dose level of the drug. If no significant adverse effects are observed among the animals at a particular dose level, the drug is considered safe at that dose level. However, the statistical significance of an observed difference between control and noncontrol animals is directly dependent on the number of cases involved. For example, if no animals in a 20-animal control set developed cancerous livers and 1 animal in the low-dose set did, this 5% difference would be considered a chance finding (not statistically significant). However, the same 5% difference would be considered statistically significant if there were 60 animals in each set. In general, the fewer the animals used, the greater the probability that any difference will be able to be attributed to chance, (i.e., as due to something other than the drug).

It should be noted that the entire application of the statistical testing of hypotheses in the safety testing of drugs is erroneous, an inappropriate application of statistics. The basic idea of the statistical testing of hypotheses is to help guard the researcher against acceptance of a false research hypothesis when the observations supporting the hypothesis are due to chance. For this reason, the statistical orientation may be more reasonable in testing the efficacy of a drug. For example, if one set of rats is given a new tranquilizer and the other set is not, and the tranquilized set shows a certain percentage reduction in activity, a statistical test might reasonably help to eliminate chance as an explanation of this difference. In safety testing, however, the situation is reversed and the research hypothesis is that the drug has no adverse effects. Statistical testing is used not to guard against acceptance of a false research hypothesis but to make its acceptance more likely.

Perhaps the only completely adequate way to test the safety of drugs would be to run the experiments like clinical trials and test safety and efficacy together. One set of animals with a particular illness would be treated with the current drug of choice and the other set with the new drug. With a diversity of carefully matched subjects, a sufficient number of cases followed over a long enough period of time, and accurate detailed observations made of both positive and negative effects, a reasonable conclusion might be reached concerning the superiority or inferiority of the new drug. Obtaining an adequate number of experimental animals with the same disease would be only one practical difficulty with this method of testing. On a more practical level, statistical estimation, Salisburg (1981) argues, should be substituted for statistical testing of hypotheses. When a difference of 5%, for example, is tested and found to be insignificant, it is equivalent to estimating that the difference is zero. But the best estimate of the percentage difference is not zero but five. One probable effect of the use of estimation procedures rather than hypothesis testing would be the use of more adequate numbers of test animals.

Studies sometimes begin with an adequate number of test animals, but so many die from extraneous causes that the number surviving more or less assure that any observed differences will be statistically insignificant. For example, Hazelton Laboratories began the safety testing of red dye #40 for Allied Chemical with 300 rats. However, only 6 weeks into the study, an epidemic of a respiratory disease killed many of the subjects. In the end, there were only 59 animals left, and red dye #40 was reported to the FDA as nontoxic (Epstein, 1978, pp. 184–185). Most drugs produce severe adverse effects only in some circumstances, and if these effects are fairly uncommon, they can sometimes be easily hidden by reporting only average data. Griffin (1977) cites a case in which an attempt was made to hide some extreme falls in hemoglobin levels in two animals by reporting only means and standard deviations and commenting that the average hemoglobin levels were only slightly reduced following administration of the drug.

The range of doses is also crucial for adequate drug safety testing, especially when testing for carcinogenicity. If the doses are too low, too few animals will develop tumors or other adverse effects, and the differences between the control sets and the noncontrol sets will be declared insignificant. (Again it is clear that the orientation given by the statistical testing of hypotheses is basic to the obtaining of favorable results in drug safety testing.) If the dose levels are too high, many animals will die from the gross toxic effects of the drug before the tumors or other specific adverse effects of the drug have had a chance to develop (Epstein, 1978, p. 64). Since the range between too low a dose and too high a dose for many experimental animals is quite small (Salisburg, 1981), it is not difficult for an experienced technician to design an experiment in which all of the doses are either too low or too high. It is also a common practice to examine only the control animals and those in the highest-dose group (Griffin, 1977).

An example of a testing program that contained a number of the shortcomings just discussed was Upjohn's 1978 attempt to get Depo-Provera approved for marketing as a contraceptive in the United States. A letter from the FDA to Monsieur le Ministre de la Sante de la Republique populaire d'Angola explains why the animal tests were considered inadequate.

> *Safety questions raised by studies in beagle dogs showing an increased incidence of mammary tumors associated with the drug have not been resolved. Benign tumors in the dogs occurred at the human dose (on a mg/kg basis), and benign and malignant tumors occurred at 25 times the human dose over a period of three years. No intermediate doses were studied. Although the tumors at the human dose level were benign there were too few animals to ascertain the propensity for malignancy at doses lower than 25 times the human dose. Of the 4 dogs studied at this dose level only 2 survived for as long as 5 years. (Subcommittee on Commerce, Consumer and Monetary Affairs, 1978, p. 95)*

Since drugs may cause cancers in any one or more of a wide range of organs and body areas, it is necessary to do an extremely careful and thorough examination of the entire body of each test animal following sacrifice or unplanned death. But this is impossible if an animal has died and begun to decompose before the autopsy is performed, which often happens (Epstein, 1978, p. 64). When FDA pathologist Adrian Gross examined some of the raw data at Industrial Bio-Test Laboratories (IBT), he found the initials TBD on many of the animals' records: too badly decomposed (to do an autopsy). Its reports for the FDA had not included this category (Foster & Dowie, 1982).

One procedure that comes very close to outright falsification is that of using modern microsurgery in the way that G. D. Searle Company did in the safety testing of Aldactone, a diuretic prescribed for high blood pressure. Tumors were removed from test animals during their lifetimes. When the animals were sacrificed and autopsied, the pathologist could truthfully report that no tumors were found. This procedure was not reported to the FDA, only the final results were (Foster & Dowie, 1982; Searle Investigation Task Force, 1976).

If a test doesn't produce favorable results, it may be rerun. A different species or strain of animal may be used, the dose levels may be adjusted, the manner of observing or recording the data may be modified, a different pathologist may be assigned to the microscopic examinations, or some other change may be made in the protocol. Or the test may simply be rerun a number of times. Eventually, favorable results may be obtained, and these will be sent on to the drug company or the regulatory agency (Braithwaite, 1984, p. 55). "The conscious withholding of unfavorable animal or clinical data" was one of the drug company ploys condemned by Dr. James Goddard, FDA commissioner, in a speech to the Pharmaceutical Manufacturers Association (Silverman & Lee, 1974, p. 105). Unfavorable data are withheld in a number of ways. For example, Dr. Paul Lowinger made studies of drug safety for a number of companies. He learned that one of his studies had not been reported to the FDA; subsequent investigation revealed that only 9 of his 17 studies had been reported (Fuller, 1972, pp. 115–117).

A common fault in clinical trials of drugs is the manner in which the control group is selected. Ideally, each subject would be carefully matched with another subject, and then a random assignment would be made—one subject to the experimental group that is to receive the drug being tested and the other subject to the control group that is to receive a placebo or the current drug of choice. If the control group is selected in such a way that the subjects are in general less healthy or more severely affected with the disease involved, the study will be biased toward more favorable results for the new drug. This not infrequently happens.

One of the clinical trials for Searle's antidiarrheal Lomotil was run with 477 children in Argentina. All 70 subjects in the control group were in hospital, but only 31% of the experimental group. Furthermore, when those hospitalized patients who received Lomotil are compared to the hospitalized patients who did not receive Lomotil, additional evidence of bias appears: 63% of the control group were suffering severe effects of malnutrition, whereas only 1% of the experimental group were; dehydration was rated mild for only 17% of the hospitalized controls but for 42% of the hospitalized experimental group (delValle et al., 1965/1982). Similarly, in another Lomotil study of infants in India, all of the patients in the control group were in hospital but only 58% of those in the experimental groups were (Karan, Mukberjee, & Mukberjee, 1976). The research design for yet another study of Lomotil was approved in advance by the company. There was no control group (Santhanakrishnan, Raju, & Raju, 1980).

In his speech to the Pharmaceutical Manufacturers Association, Commissioner Goddard also spoke of "the deliberate choice of clinical investigators known to be more concerned about industry friendships than in developing good data" (Silverman & Lee, 1974, p. 105). Dr. Ronald Smith did a clinical study of the tranquilizer Mellaril for Sandoz that showed new ways in which Mellaril could safely be used. Smith's studies always seemed to come up with favorable results for the drugs he tested, and he soon became popular with other drug companies, including Lederle, Upjohn, and Marion Laboratories. When the FDA eventually discovered that Dr. Smith did most of his drug testing by flushing the drugs down the toilet, he was in the process of completing 12 drug tests for six different drug companies (Foster, 1982). IBT was a reliable testing company: Most of its tests produced favorable results. IBT's clients included 31 of the largest drug and chemical companies in the world. Of some 900 IBT safety tests examined by the government as of 1982, at least 80% were found to be invalid (Biometric Testing, 1979). After the investigation, IBT wrote to the major drug companies assuring them that in the future they could depend on IBT testing, because they would be subject to particularly careful scrutiny by the FDA. As a result, the companies stopped using IBT (Braithwaite, 1984, p. 82). IBT is not the only drug-testing company to have been found guilty of invalid drug testing. In 1979, Biometric Testing Incorporated was brought before a federal grand jury for falsifying reports on drugs. Two former executives pleaded guilty (Firm's Ex-aides, 1979; Stackelberg, 1982). Forty-five percent of the 350 testing laboratories and drug companies investigated by the FDA in a recent survey were found to have made significant departures from U.S. government testing guidelines (Stackelberg, 1982).

FDA studies of clinical investigators have found considerable evidence of inadequacy in their testing of drugs. A 1976 investigation of 238 clinical studies found that three-fourths of them failed to comply with one or more legal requirements (Clinard & Yeager, 1980, p. 267). Many clinical investigators did not follow study protocols and kept inadequate and inaccurate records. Of the studies checked between 1977 and 1981, 83% failed to comply with one or more U.S. regulations (Stackelberg, 1982). From 1976 to 1979, the FDA investigated 525 doctors involved in the clinical testing of drugs. Eight cases were referred to the Attorney General for criminal prosecution; 11 other doctors were permanently disqualified from further drug testing. The studies of 14 others were found to be invalid, but the doctors were not disqualified. A number of the physicians who had falsified reports were from Boston University, Columbia, Georgetown, and UCLA (McTaggart, 1980).

Bad luck does seem to dog some physicians who make clinical studies of drugs. Dr. James Scheiner of Fairfax, Virginia, had his office vandalized the night before an FDA audit of his raw data. All of his records relating to drug testing had been dumped in a whirlpool bath. The next time an audit was scheduled, Dr. Scheiner had a fire in his office, and on the third occasion, he was mugged in his office and all his records stolen (Braithwaite, 1984, p. 153). With a little trial and error, a drug company can develop a sizeable stable of clinical investigators and testing laboratories likely to produce favorable results in a high percentage of studies.

Many new drug applications submitted to the FDA are inadequate. Some are returned with requests for additional evidence of the safety and/or efficacy of the drug. However, as former FDA statistician William Weiss put it,

> *The medical officer is in an untenable position because if he were to adopt the view that an application were incomplete unless the research supporting it was properly conducted, he would pass few applications. But this would result in a major shift in FDA policy. (Mintz, 1965, p. 140).*

The FDA apparently sometimes engages in a selection process similar to that of the drug companies and testing laboratories in order to get a new drug on the market. A group of outside experts who have been hired to review the evidence regarding the safety and efficacy of a new drug may be dismissed and a new panel created. Or some members may be retained and others dismissed or transferred to other panels. For example, Dr. Donald Klein, a consultant on Abbott's payroll, was retained on a panel that was reviewing Abbott's new drug application for Cylert, whereas Dr. Mary Howell, who expressed skepticism about Cylert, was dismissed. (Eventually the whole panel was dismissed.) An investigation of the FDA led by Norman Dorsen, chair of New York University Law School, reported the following: "We found a systematic pattern of involuntary transfers and other unfavorable actions against employees who were more adversarial toward industry than management was" (Hughes & Brewin, 1979, p. 243).

Although there are, as we have seen, numerous ways of obtaining favorable results in drug testing without outright falsification, outright falsification is so widespread that slang terms for the practice exist. In Japan, it is called "making" a report; in the United States, it is called "dry labeling" or "the graphite method," meaning that pencil and paper are all that are required to make the report (Braithwaite, 1984, p. 57).

MER/29 was a drug developed in the late 1950s by Wm. S. Merrell Company, a division of Richardson-Merrell Inc., for the treatment of arteriosclerosis. It was supposed to work by inhibiting the production of cholesterol, but it was of doubtful value because there was evidence that it caused the accumulation of demonsterol, which forms deposits in the arteries just as cholesterol does. With regard to safety, the animal test results for MER/29 were quite consistent. All of the animals tested developed abnormal blood changes; abnormal blood changes in test animals are regarded as a major danger signal. Also many, if not most, of the animals, especially those given MER/29 for a longer period of time, developed eye cataracts or went blind. These results were never given to the FDA; in fact, at one point Dr. Joseph Murray, liaison officer to the FDA, specifically misinformed the agency that there had been no blood changes in the rats or monkeys tested with MER/29.

When one study with monkeys was completed and abnormal blood changes were observed, Dr. Van Mannen, director of the Biological Science Division of Wm. S. Merrell, ordered laboratory technician Beulah Jordan to falsify the reports by inventing new figures and even to include data for one wholly imaginary monkey. When Ms. Jordan protested to her immediate superior, William

King, head of the Toxicology Department, he responded, Van Mannen "is higher up. Do as he tells you and be quiet." Similarly, wholly fictitious "blood tests were reported for dead rats as if they had continued to live and to take MER/29" (*Toole v. Richardson-Merrell*, 1961, p. 404).

The promotional campaign for MER/29 was the biggest Merrell had ever launched. Cholesterol was receiving a great deal of media attention as a factor in heart disease, and so the executives of Merrell expected MER/29 to be a big profitmaker. And it did add $7 million to gross sales in its first year on the market. Despite the data on abnormal blood changes, cataracts, and blindness in laboratory animals and on hair and weight loss and increased crankiness in monkeys, MER/29 advertising stressed how completely safe it was: "virtually nontoxic and remarkably free from side effects even in prolonged clinical use" (*Toole v. Richardson-Merrell*, 1961, p. 406).

Eventually, the number of complaints reaching the FDA and the amount of adverse comment in the medical journals brought the agency to demand all of Merrell's data concerning the toxic effects of MER/29. Dr. Murray withheld some of the most damaging test materials, but forwarded the rest. The result was a meeting in November 1961 with FDA officials in Washington at which they advised Merrell that MER/29 should be withdrawn from the market. A compromise was reached eventually: MER/29 need not be withdrawn, but a strong warning letter had to be sent to the medical profession. Then in April 1962, FDA officials made a surprise visit to Merrell laboratories and took all of the records of animal experiments. In May 1962, the order banning sales of MER/29 was finally issued (*Toole v. Richardson-Merrell*, 1961, pp. 407–408). During its two years on the market, 490 cases of cataracts caused by MER/29 were reported. There is evidence that if the drug had remained on the market and patients had continued to use it, a very high percentage of them would have developed eye opacities. Allen Toole was one person who did. His eyes became opaque, and it was necessary to operate and remove the lenses of both eyes (Conklin, 1977, pp. 45–46; *Toole v. Richardson-Merrell*, 1961).

Because the entire drug industry, including the testing laboratories and the physicians selected to do clinical trials, is directed toward profit, the testing of drugs is oriented not so much to assess their efficacy and safety as to win government approval for their marketing. This orientation is evident in the basic structure of drug evaluation (which uses the procedure of the statistical testing of hypotheses to help guard against the finding of adverse effects) and in numerous techniques ranging from the slightly fraudulent to the completely dishonest. Because it is extremely difficult to connect the tragic effects that a drug may have to the drug itself, the number of victims of inadequate profit-oriented drug testing will never be known.

BIBLIOGRAPHY

Balazs, T. (1976). Assessment of the value of systemic toxicity studies in experimental animals. In M. Mehlman, R. Shapiro, and H. Blumenthal (Eds.), *New Concepts in Safety Evaluation* (pp. 141–153). New York: Wiley.

Biometric testing, ex-aides are accused of falsifying lab reports on new drugs. (1979, May 31). *Wall Street Journal*, p. 14.

Braithwaite, J. (1984). *Corporate crime in the pharmaceutical industry*. London: Routledge & Kegan Paul.

Clinard, M., & Yeager, P. (1980). *Corporate crime*. New York: The Free Press.
Conklin, J. E. (1977). *Illegal but not criminal*. Englewood Cliffs: Prentice-Hall.
delValle, A. S., et al. (1982). Diphenoxylate hydrochloride in infantile diarrhea. In C. Medawar and B. Freese (Eds.). *Drug diplomacy*. London: Social Audit. (Original work published 1965)
Epstein, S. (1978). *The politics of cancer*. San Francisco: Sierra Club Books.
Firm's ex-aides plead guilty to conspiracy to falsify drug tests. (1979, October 8). *Wall Street Journal*, p. 16.
Foster, D. (1982, June). Good marriage, bad science. *Mother Jones*, p. 49.
Foster, D., & Dowie, M. (1982, June). Poisoned research. *Mother Jones*, pp. 38–47.
Fuller, J. G. (1972). *200,000 guinea pigs: New dangers in everyday foods, drugs, and cosmetics*. New York: Putnam.
Griffin, J. P. (1977). The seven deadly sins: A U.K. view. In G. E. Paget (Ed.), *Quality control in toxicology*. Lancaster: MTP Press.
Hall, R. (1976). *Food for nought*. New York: Vintage Books.
Hughes, R., & Brewin, R. (1979). *The tranquilizing of America*. New York: Harcourt, Brace, Jovanovich.
Karan, S., Mukberjee, V., & Mukberjee, L. (1976). Assessment of safety of Lomotil in infants. *Indian Pediatrics, 13*, 295–300.
Knightley, P., Evans, H., Potter, E., & Wallace, M. (1979). *Suffer the children: The story of thalidomide*. New York: Viking Press.
McTaggart, L. (1980, December 7). Putting drug testers to the test. *New York Times Magazine*, pp. 174–180.
Mintz, M. (1965). *The therapeutic nightmare*. Boston: Houghton Mifflin.
Salisburg, D. (1981). Statistics and toxicology: An overview. In E. Gralla (Ed.), *Scientific considerations in monitoring and evaluating toxicological research* (pp. 123–136). Washington, DC: Hemisphere.
Santhanakrishnam, B. R., Raju, M., & Raju, V. B. (1980). Safety of dephenoxylate hydrochloride therapy in malnourished infants suffering with nonspecific diarrhea. *Indian Pediatrics, 16*, 909–912.
Searle Investigation Task Force. (1976, March 24). *Report of preclinical (animal) studies of G. D. Searle Company*. Memorandum to Searle Investigation Steering Committee of the Food and Drug Administration.
Silverman, M., & Lee, P. R. (1974). *Pills, profits, and politics*. Berkeley: University of California Press.
Silverman, M., Lee, P. R., & Lydecker, M. (1982). *Prescriptions for death: The drugging of the third world*. Berkeley: University of California Press.
Stackelberg, P. (1982, April 3). U.S. agency critical of tests. *Edmonton Journal*, p. A3.
Subcommittee on Commerce, Consumer and Monetary Affairs of the House Committee on Government Operations. (1978). *U.S. export of banned products*. Washington, DC: U.S. Government Printing Office.
Teff, H., & Munro, C. R. (1976). *Thalidomide: The legal aftermath*. London: Gordon & Cremonesi.
Toole v. Richardson-Merrell Inc. (1961). *California Reporter, 60*, 398–419.

25

Victimization of Drug Addicts and Human Rights

Augusto Balloni
Department of Sociology, University of Bologna, Italy

This chapter examines the societal reaction to the problem of drug addiction, which is traditionally classified as a form of criminal or deviant behavior. One of the strongest reactions to this type of deviance is the attempt to "sweep it under the rug" by assigning the task of dealing with it to professional specialists whose main responsibility is to keep it out of public view and concern. The chapter also addresses the ideological conflicts stemming from the definition of addiction as an illness, a definition which is not, however, genuinely accepted by many members of society and of the helping professions. The chapter calls for an evaluation of the ideology, treatment practices, and goals of so-called therapeutic communities. It concludes by warning about the dangers and pitfalls of behavior control techniques and by calling for the development and enforcement of an appropriate code of ethics for treatment programs.

It is believed and feared that every day a large number of people are either directly or indirectly victims of drugs. The general public is frightened and perplexed: Something has to be done. According to numerous experts, the problem is undoubtedly destined to grow unless something is done immediately. People seem to be seeking an answer and wondering what one person can do.

Politicians state that without the active efforts of everyone, the problem simply cannot be solved. The opinion of those with responsibility in the health sector and social control agencies seems to echo this.

In fact, the presence of a condition that makes people feel anxious or threatened links up first with moral indignation and then to a system of beliefs necessary to legitimate certain forms of control—matters related to the study of moral panic. In particular, laws prohibiting the use of narcotics are often used as examples of how public interest concerning a particular situation is generated

Augusto Balloni, M.D., is professor of criminology in the Faculty of Political Science, director of the Deviating and Criminal Behavior Studies Center (Ce.S.Co.De.C.), and coordinator of the research doctorate in criminology at the University of Bologna. A specialist in forensic medicine and neuropsychiatry, he is the author of numerous publications and books in the psychiatric-forensic sphere, particularly with reference to criminology. He also serves as an expert at the Bologna Surveillance Court.

This chapter is based on material first published in the preface of the book *San Patrignano: I Perchè di un Processo*, edited by the author. The various contributions to the book were prepared in the wake of the trial of the people responsible for running a community for drug addicts.

and are also used to outline the stages by means of which a "symbolic crusade" is prepared and launched.

In the context of social therapy covering the phenomenon of dependence on narcotics, indignation, worry, and panic have frequently occurred in recent years. A contribution to this state of affairs may be the fact that the so-called drug addict problem, though changing over time, is invariably placed in the province of criminality, deviation, alienation, or illness, that is, in a sphere that certainly calls for something to be done if the situation is to change.

The tendency is to avoid making comparisons with the so-called chronic social ills. With regard to solving these problems, people always wait for something to happen from above.

When we throw rubbish from our car window, we do not realize that it will form a part of the refuse cluttering the streets and polluting the environment. In the same way, when we throw elderly people, psychotics, and drug addicts into institutional "holes" where they are not seen, we feel that the problem has been solved, and we refuse to admit that abandonment of the aged and the need to cure psychotics, alcoholics, and drug addicts do exist. Our approach to solving social problems seems to be merely to make them disappear from view: *out of sight, out of mind.*

We try to arrange things so that the most urgent social problems are always far from our daily experience, unconsciously trying to keep them away from us.

When social problems like drug addiction or mental illness come to the surface, urgent in their dramatic expressiveness, we are often inclined to react as if a sewage pipe had burst. Upset and worried, we urgently call the plumber to take care of the emergency—to make the refuse flow away unseen without creating any disturbance and, above all, without vexing us.

The same attitude tends to be adopted with regard to social problems: We want to be sure the problems can be quickly removed with a minimum of personal involvement.

Despite these attitudes, social problems remain. Not least among them today is the consumption, use, and abuse of drugs by young people and the consequent need to cure them. This need to cure does, however, presuppose that we are dealing with sick persons.

Thus, on the subject of treating drug addiction, the dynamic of therapeutic intervention comes into play, as does the problem of health policy as a personal conquest, not just programmed activities.

Is this situation an illness or simply a condition of social inconvenience? Because if we are dealing with illness, it would link up with the role of the sick person. It would then be necessary to check whether this role fits the drug addict. Remember, for example, that according to Talcott Parsons (1951, pp. 436–437) there are four aspects of the institutionalized expectation system relative to the sick role:

1. There is an exemption from normal social role responsibilities. This exemption—relative to the nature and severity of the illness—must be legitimized by and in relation to the various others involved. The doctor's role is often to legitimize the illness and to protect society from malingering, thus exonerating the sick from their duties.

2. Since a sick person cannot be expected to get well solely by an act of will, he or she requires to be taken care of.
3. Being ill is seen as undesirable, so the patient has the obligation to want to get better.
4. The patient is sometimes obliged to seek technically competent help, that is, a physician with whom he or she must cooperate in the process of trying to get well.

It is here that the role of patient intertwines with that of the physician in a complementary role structure. It is evident, on the basis of the above brief remarks, that the patient's role is closely connected with the ideology of the treatment.

Is it also the same for the drug addict?

Within the sphere of heroin dependence, for example, a rather ambiguous situation arises, because the consumer of this drug "chooses" his or her behavior. In this case, can the behavior of the drug addict be considered an illness? Even though the mere fact of being sick represents deviance, it is quite different from other deviant roles—precisely because the sick person is not considered responsible for his or her condition. However, this approach is not considered valid for the drug addict, so that even the expectation that the addict will cooperate in his or her cure is problematic. There are situations when the drug addict may decide to cooperate in his or her treatment and try to get better (e.g., when methadone is used to break the habit). In such cases, however, one cannot speak of a chronic, incurable disease, as people tend to do when talking about the situation of the drug addict in general. Besides, for the latter, who is considered responsible for his or her own condition, becoming addicted is accompanied by acts held to be illegal (theft and drug pushing). This supports setting up a program of punishment to cover the entire drug-using system and to act as a deterrent. This is in contrast with the treatment ideology, which considers drug abuse as an expression of a pathological personality or of an illness.

Ideological conflicts are reflected in actual practices: Those who consider the drug addict an immoral person who acts voluntarily ask that he or she be punished. Those who instead see the use and abuse of drugs as an illness, consider the drug addict as ill, a victim of circumstance, someone to help and take care of. Between the two standpoints there are and always have been areas of institutionalized cooperation that are psychiatric-legal in nature. Thus the problem shifts and gives rise to a considerable number of cultural and ideological questions.

For those who want drug addicts punished, there is the bitter recognition that classical punishment is an ineffective deterrent and serves only to overload the control agencies and the prisons. Linked to this is the anxiety of those who are discouraged by the presumed constant increase of drug abuse. On the other hand, the claims of drug users who maintain that they act under the influence of an irrepressible need cannot be ignored, although they are weak. Ideology and therapeutic practices are therefore thrown into crisis by often unproven considerations. Physicians may think that drug addicts do not cooperate but abuse the therapeutic structures to get around obstacles, for example, by utilizing hospitalization at moments of crisis due to acute disorders or lack of supplies or to get over problems they are having with the control agencies. Those responsible for the various forms of outpatient treatment are even more worried by the fact that "their patients" may, for example, sell methadone on the black market rather than use it. Moreover, operators in both penal and medical institutions appear almost to fear drug addicts. Therefore operational plans based on compromise are adopted. They are connected with forms of social therapy and are based on the following assumptions:

1. Narcotics constitute a threat to society. The traditional therapeutic and punishment schemes are inadequate to deal with this threat.
2. The use and abuse of drugs have medical and legal implications. Thus, it is in the interest of society to identify drug addicts for whom rehabilitative treatment is the best answer. The importance and urgency of the problem makes it necessary to force treatment especially on those who have committed crimes. In such cases, social control agencies can use their power and influence to *facilitate treatment.*

Against this background, so-called therapeutic communities flourish. Their aims may be to help drug addicts, their families, and people in general to understand. They can also serve the ideology of "clearing up the streets," thus contributing to the solution of a social problem in the same way that a plumber does when he channels waste through hidden pipes. To avoid misunderstanding, when it comes to the social therapies practiced in these communities, it would be necessary to conduct an evaluation so as to have concrete verification of who benefits from belonging to a therapeutic community and who does not. If one wants to provide a realistic report, one clearly cannot limit oneself to the utilization of coercion. Coercion is too primitive a method to be a significant example of behavior control. It raises again the highly important moral problem of its utilization and the delicate question of the proper balance between personal liberty and public interest. This balance, laboriously achieved in free societies, should not be upset or destroyed by naivete or arrogance.

In the field of drug dependence, one can attempt to address the moral problem of behavior control. This links up with the search for a way to use power with justice. This is not a new subject, but then matters related to human experience are rarely new. In fact, the appropriate use of power and behavior control is rarely clear, even for those possessing a culture that guides them in deciding what is good and what is bad. This is particularly true if there is no belief in divine revelation or in natural law. Thus, the doubts remain. The correct use of power by one person trying to influence the behavior of another is really no simpler today than it was in the past, when the instruments of domination were few and crude. Ever more refined methods of social control abound, and they are spreading at such a rate that the usual instruments for directing them (e.g., laws) appear inadequate. Thus, it becomes increasingly important to know how these controls are structured, by whom they are applied, and to what end.

Techniques of behavior control may appear to be inevitably expanding, but their improper use could be disastrous. Abuses have already taken place in so-called total institutions through recourse to "shock" treatment and abuse of psychotropic drugs and psychosurgery. These considerations make it absolutely necessary that the work done and the results obtained through treatment in therapeutic communities be divulged by means of objective data. This will ensure that any self-respecting person who has power over others, even for short periods, will be guided by ethical principles in the use of that power. The most important ethical problems regarding behavior control, then, call into question the concept of liberty, which is antithetical to the concept of control. This antithesis is more marked when free will is to be guaranteed.

BIBLIOGRAPHY

Parsons, T. (1951). *The social system*. Glencoe, IL: The Free Press.

26

Increased Fear of Crime and Related Side Effects of Persuasive Communication: The Price Tag of Burglary Prevention Campaigns?

Frans Willem Winkel
Department of Social Psychology, Free University, Amsterdam, The Netherlands

INTRODUCTION

In recent years, special crime prevention departments were created within the police organization in The Netherlands. Their primary task is to persuade the public, via communication campaigns, to become actively engaged in preventing victimization. Such campaigns are predicated on the idea that the prevention of (petty) crime is not exclusively a police responsibility but a task of the police and of the public jointly. Information and advice are held to be effective means to intensify public involvement in crime prevention.

A number of authors believe that there is a price tag attached to such communication campaigns. They are conducted at the unavoidable cost of harmful side effects, such as stimulating or increasing response generalization (Winkel, 1987a), intensifying fear of crime, and inflating subjective estimates of victimization risk and the perceived negative impact of crime. Also, the efficacy of the police may be called into question.

Besides the hypothesis that burglary prevention campaigns necessarily and automatically foster fear of crime, some alternative hypotheses are formulated. A common characteristic of these alternatives is that the occurrence of increased fear and related side effects results from the conducting of communication campaigns *conditionally rather than automatically*. Two types of conditions especially are singled out: (1) those pertaining to the message and (2) those characteristic of receivers.

The entire set of hypotheses are tested in an experiment. Distinct types of receivers are exposed to various kinds of burglary prevention messages meant to exhort the public to preventive behavior. Experimental support is obtained

Frans Willem Winkel is senior lecturer in the Department of Social Psychology, Free University of Amsterdam, and research advisor to the association Mens en Recht. In 1987, two books he wrote, *Crime Prevention Campaigns* and *Intergroup Relations*, were published. A coedited book on fear of crime will appear in 1989. Dr. Winkel's research interests are psychology of law, police studies, and victim assistance programs.

only for the alternative hypotheses, among which are the message hypothesis, the effectiveness hypothesis, the orientation hypothesis, and the gender hypothesis. A final paragraph notes some implications for designing future burglary prevention campaigns in such a way that the unwanted side effects discussed here may be avoided.

THEORETICAL POINTS OF VIEW

General Fear Effects

The victimological literature contains repeated warnings to the effect that preventive communication campaigns may well call forth unwanted side effects. Garofalo and Laub (1978, p. 252), Henig and Maxfield (1978, p. 305), and, in The Netherlands, Soetenhorst-de Savornin Lohman (1982, p. 160) and Van der Vijver (1983, p. 43) are among those who insist that the spread of prevention brochures is likely to awaken and stimulate fear of crime. Psychological theories can be cited to render such warnings more plausible. I will mention two of these: (1) the theory of "fear appeals" (cf. Janis, 1987) and (2) the distinction between "crime prevention" and "victimization prevention" suggested by Cohn, Kidder, and Harvey (1978).

The most direct way to gain insight regarding the question of whether prevention campaigns occasion fear is to see how fear-instilling information actually induces fear. Fear appeals always turn out to include two moments: (1) the message refers to an "unpleasant occurrence" or pictures consequences which the receiver would find troublesome, harmful, or damaging, and (2) the message emphasizes that the receiver runs the personal risk of being confronted with unpleasant happenings of this kind. In short, the theory states that all communication, including communication on crime which in one way or another contains both of these moments, inspires fear. Since burglary prevention messages (cf. prevention campaign texts) can hardly avoid using them, such communication is fear inducing by definition. According to this theory, then, burglary prevention campaigns will automatically increase fear; in other words, the campaigns occasion general fear effects.

Effectuation of general fear is plausible also in light of Cohn's distinction between "crime prevention" and "victimization prevention." According to Cohn et al. (1978), two psychologically distinct types of reaction to crime are at issue here: In a psychological perspective *crime prevention* is active and directive, whereas *victimization prevention* is more a matter of "wait and see," more passive. Cohn et al. relate these concepts to the theory of Wortman and Brehm (1975). According to Cohn et al., crime prevention corresponds with "reactance" (active resistance), whereas victimization prevention corresponds with learned helplessness and reinforced fear of crime. Typical of the former approach are "actions which try to eliminate the breeding grounds and presumed root causes of crime" (1978, p. 287). Programs designed to stimulate job opportunities for youth represent this kind of action. Victimization prevention is its psychological converse. Cohn et al. state, "In this category we include both avoiding dangerous areas and using locks, burglar alarms, dogs and other measures which protect a home or establishment against victimization (target hardening)" (p. 288). Reactions such as these are witness to a return to a shelter-mentality: "People who prevent victimization achieve control only when they are behind their fortifications or within their safe territories" (p. 288). The chief aim of burglary prevention campaigns in The Netherlands—and in the United States and Great Britain as well—is to make potential victims render their homes more resistant to burglary. Attention is riveted on target hardening and on checking for break-in flaws. In brief, using the terminology of Cohn et al., victimization prevention reactions to burglary are being stimulated especially. According to their analysis, the result is that fear of crime comes alive and grows stronger. Burglary prevention campaigns (i.e., victimization prevention messages) produce a general fear effect.

Message Variations

It seems to me that the hypothesis regarding general fear effects can be made more precise. To do this one needs to pay attention to how the two contents ("risk" and "loss") mentioned above are filled in. Of special importance is the way in which recommendations—the package of recommended preventive measures—are presented to the receiver. In light of models of effective persuasive communication developed by, among others, Ajzen and Fishbein (1980) and Jaccard (1981), basically three variations in message are conceivable in the elaboration of these two elements. The crux of such models is that a persuasive message is successful (i.e., able to influence behavior in the desired direction) if and only if the message makes it plausible that carrying out the suggested form of behavior will be profitable for the receiver. To effectuate this goal, the sender can accentuate his or her message in three ways. The sender can (1) emphasize that execution of the desired action is to the receiver's advantage, (2) emphasize that not acting on this alternative is disadvantageous, or (3) fuse both strategies into one message by simultaneously dealing with the positive consequences of carrying out the advice and the negative consequences of disregarding it. Following Fishbein, I will refer to these three strategies as "positive," "negative," and "mixed" message strategies. Each of these meet the criterion of effectiveness, since in all three cases the message links behavior to consequences.

In the case of burglary prevention campaigns, these three strategies can be applied as well. In the positive version, the prevention advice to secure windows and lock doors would read like this: "If you close all the windows, large or small, and lock the door behind you even when your errand takes only five minutes, you make it hard for a burglar to enter your home. A locked door means increased risk for him; secured windows and doors make your house uninviting to prowling thieves. Hence, by locking the doors and closing the windows you reduce the risk of a burglary." In the negative version, disregard of the advised preventive measures is linked to loss. Leaving windows and doors unsecured is here related to increasing the risk of break-in, providing opportunity, and rendering the house an inviting prospect to burglars. In the mixed message strategy, the two formulations are alternated.

Ajzen and Fishbein (1980, p. 218) state their preference for the negative strategy, since in this way the effect aimed at (i.e., that preventive measures will indeed be taken) is pressed for the hardest. In view of the side effects, however, the question is whether we should share this preference.

In principle, the recommendations contained in the message make is possible for the receiver to control his or her feelings of fear, since the implication is that the unpleasant event will not or is less likely to occur if the advice is acted upon. In other words, the recommendations offer reassurance. The degree to which they do so obviously depends on the formulation chosen—on which type of message is used. In light of information research comparing explicit and implicit conclusions (Winkel, 1981), one may conclude that the positive version is the more reassuring. A positive message states most explicitly that behavior of the type recommended will be advantageous, that it will help reduce victimization risk. The negative formulation offers the least reassurance. All it explicitly says is that inactivity increases the risk of burglary. It seems reasonable to expect that on this score the mixed type will take an intermediate position. When we include a control group in our considerations as well, a group exposed to no message, we can assume that, in the case of negative information, fear of crime is engendered as side effect; that no side effects are called forth by a mixed message; and that a positive message will lead to a reduction of fear of crime. In sum, the message hypothesis states that experimental results regarding fear of crime will show a linear downward tendency in a pattern moving across negative information, no information, a mixed message, and positive recommendations respectively.[1]

The degree to which recommendations function as reassurance is influenced not only by the type of message but by other variables as well. Reassurance is especially likely when the receiver perceives the measures propagated as effective ones, that is, as truly preventive (cf. Rogers, 1975; Sacco & Silverman, 1982). In other words, the perceived efficacy of the recommendations appears to be an important condition in determining whether or not fear will increase in reaction to the message. The effectiveness hypothesis holds that negative communication may be expected to reinforce fear, *particularly* when the receiver believes that all these alternative behaviors will be of little or no use. When, on the other hand, they are perceived as highly effective, it is far more likely that fear will not result or that less fear will be reported. The perceived effectiveness of recommended measures can be characterized as a "receiver condition" on account of which the message elicits differential fear reactions. Some further receiver conditions that are significant in this connection will be discussed in the next paragraph.

Receiver Conditions

In the literature on mass communication, the effects of persuasive campaigns are described with increasing frequency as "the products of an interaction between characteristics of the message and characteristics of the audience" (Sacco & Silverman, 1981, p. 199; cf. Atkin, 1979; Tyler & Cook, 1984). This description

[1]Increase of fear may be termed a side effect both on the basis of the model given by Ajzen and Fishbein (1980) and on the basis of the parallel-response model of Leventhal (1970), in which fear reactions and the reactions desired are taken to be parallel (i.e., independent) reactions to the message. Either theory rejects the classic "fear drive model," in which increase of fear is held to be a necessary condition for eliciting the reaction sought (i.e., preventive behavior on the part of the receiver).

may be applied to side effects as well. Here the question becomes: What kind of receivers experience increased fear of crime when confronted with negative information, and for whom does the reaction to the message lead to reduced fear? To answer this question one needs some acquaintance with victimological research into fear of crime. A frequently recurring conclusion in victimology is, for instance, that women report greater fear than men do (cf. Riger, Gordon, & LeBailly, 1978). In view of this, one can readily hypothesize that side effects come forward especially among female receivers and not among men—or that among men one may even note reduced fear of crime.

Empirical investigation as a whole reveals a very large number of variables that may influence feelings of fear. Hence, one can formulate a good many hypotheses regarding the interaction of message and receiver. This unwieldy mass can be rendered more manageable when the relevant variables are schematized. Winkel (1987a, 1987b) distinguishes two major groups of fear-of-crime determinants. The first main category comprises the totality of variables which, in one way or another, express individual involvement with the theme of crime. The second category is composed of those variables which refer to the risk of falling victim to crime. Within the first group are three types: (1) communicative involvement, (2) victim involvement, and (3) emotional involvement. The aspects of risk, the second group, can be subdivided into (1) risk assessment, (2) risk orientation, and (3) risk protection.

Communicative involvement refers to how frequently one talks with others about crime. Such conversations may be occasioned by newspaper or television reports of crime, by one's own experience as victim, or by such experiences as told by others. In addition, the concept relates to thc degree of exposure to mass media crime reporting and to the interest in such reporting displayed by the individual. Victim involvement includes both one's own experiences (direct victimization) and indirect victimization (i.e., acquaintance with victim experiences of others nearby).

Emotional involvement comprises elements such as the degree to which one's own neighborhood is thought of as safe or unsafe, fear of crime, the expected development of the amount of future crime, and the position taken regarding the significance of crime as a social problem compared with other social issues. To avoid misunderstanding, I would point out that the concept of emotional involvement corresponds to "trait anxiety," which psychologists distinguish from "state anxiety." The degree to which a given stimulus leads to a reaction of fear (state anxiety), for example, the increase of fear as a side effect of burglary prevention communication, is assumed to depend on, among other things, the degree to which the receiver of said stimulus is a fearful person (trait anxiety) (cf. Van der Ploeg, 1980). On the whole, victimological research finds that thc more one is involved with the theme of crime, the more intense are the feelings of fear.

With respect to the risk variables, *risk assessment* refers to the perceived likelihood of becoming the victim of some crime or to the risk others believe one to run. *Risk protection* refers to the degree to which the individual relies on or has confidence in the protection offered by the police. *Risk orientation* refers to the views held by the individual concerning the controllability of the risk of becoming a victim. If this orientation is "internal," the individual believes that he or she is able to influence victimization risk. In the case of "external" orientation, the individual regards him- or herself as at the mercy of the environment: Being victimized or escaping this fate is a matter of bad luck or good luck. Victimization risk is then considered to be beyond control; one's own influence is negligible. In victimological research the guiding thread is that higher fear is accompanied by an external risk orientation, a higher risk assessment, and risk protection that tends toward the inadequate.

Interaction Effects

It stands to reason that those who are the recipients of burglary prevention messages can differ in terms of the victimological determinants sketched above. Some receivers are characterized by a low level of emotional involvement, others by a high one. Combined with the message, such variations can lead to differential fear reactions or "interaction effects." In the preceding section it was pointed out, for instance, that female receivers will show an increase of fear in reaction to a negative message, whereas this effect will not occur—in fact, the opposite effect has been known to take place—when the receivers are males. A psychologically more interesting receiver condition is risk orientation regarding victimization. This orientation is accorded a prominent place in various psychological models of feelings of fear: Fears are virtually always related to external risk orientation. The definition of fear given by Van der Wurff and Stringer (1986, p. 107) expresses this succinctly: "Fear is the simultaneous experience of a threat and the inability to counter that threat. The elements of this definition are fairly common to the literature on emotions such as fear and anxiety." In the same vein, Cohn et al. (1978) note that "we equate fear of crime with perceived loss of control" (p. 286).

In relation to risk orientation as receiver condition, then, one can obviously make a clear-cut prediction. We may assume that increased anxiety as reaction to a negative prevention message will come to light, especially among those receivers whose risk orientation is external. Internally oriented receivers either show no fear effects or may even react with a reduction of anxiety.

In line with the ideas introduced in the previous paragraph, identical interaction effects may be formulated with respect to the other two risk determinants and in relation to emotional involvement. Reinforcement of fear in reaction to negative communication is likely among receivers who assess their risk as high, among receivers who judge risk protection to be inadequate, and among receivers who are emotionally very much concerned about crime. Clear-cut predictions regarding the receiver conditions of victim involvement and communicative involvement are more difficult (cf. Winkel, 1987b).

Hypotheses

Summarizing the theoretical analysis we can state four hypotheses regarding preventive messages and fear.

The first hypothesis, referring to *general fear effects*, is that burglary prevention communication automatically elicits side effects in the sense explained. The implication of this hypothesis is that *all* individuals exposed to burglary preventive communication report greater anxiety regarding crime than do individuals who were not so exposed. Concerning related side effects, the hypothesis implies that, compared to the nonexposed, these receivers report a higher subjective victimization risk; associate victimization more with harm, loss, or damage; and express less confidence in available police protection against burglary and other forms of crime.

Alongside this hypothesis, three *conditional* ones can be formulated in which the occurrence of side effects is linked to the presence of specific message conditions or receiver conditions.

The second hypothesis, the *message hypothesis*, is an example of this. The message hypothesis states that differential fear effects occur in conjunction with the manner in which the preventive message and the recommendations are elaborated. Briefly, the occurrence of side effects depends on the type of message used. This hypothesis implies that reported fear in a general sense decreases linearly in a pattern running from negative information (−), absence of information (0), a mixed message (+/−), to positive communication (+). This pattern is observable both in the fear-of-crime reports and the side effects that relate to fear of crime.

The third is the *effectiveness hypothesis*, which predicts differential fear effects in conjunction with the effectiveness attributed to the recommended prevention measures by the receiver. The implication of this hypothesis is that negative communication leads to more intense anxiety in a general sense among receivers who experience the proffered advice as of little effect. Conversely, this side effect does not occur, or less fear is reported, among those who hold the recommended measures to be effective. As in the case of the second hypothesis, the prediction extends to fear-related side effects as well.

Fourth, an *interaction hypothesis* can be formulated, in which are predicted differential fear effects in a general sense in coherence with the presence of a number of receiver characteristics or conditions. This hypothesis consists of three parts.

1. Among female receivers, negative communication elicits related side effects, whereas such related side effects do not occur and fear in a general sense is reported less frequently among male receivers.
2. The interaction hypothesis predicts increased fear in a general sense when the receiver condition is one of high emotional involvement. Low emotional involvement implies the absence of side effects in a general sense, or leads to, among other things, less intense fears being reported by those exposed to the message compared with those not confronted with it.
3. With respect to the risk determinants, the interaction hypothesis states that general anxiety is reinforced among receivers with an external *risk orientation*. Side effects in a general sense do not occur and fewer fears become apparent within the group characterized by an internal risk orientation. Similar predictions can be made regarding the two remaining risk determinants. Fear and related side effects are expected to become visible among receivers with a high *risk assessment* and among those who find their *risk protection* inadequate. Again, low risk assessment and sufficient risk protection lead to no unwanted side effects or to reduction of fear.

THE EXPERIMENT

Procedure and Variables

The study was conducted in stages. Use was made of questionnaires. The first list of questions, which was meant to collect biographical data and relevant receiver conditions, functioned as pretest measurement prior to offering prevention information. The second questionnaire, intended to focus on relevant side effect variables, functioned as posttest measurement. Between these two, burglary preventive communication was offered to an experimental group by way of an information leaflet (see "Campaign Brochure" below).

To plan the distribution of the material, the local police assisted in the selection of neighborhoods where burglary prevention communication would seem most appropriate. The selection sought to ensure maximum correspondence between the content of the message and the characteristics of the neighborhood's housing. The aim was to preclude the possibility that receivers would reject the recommendations out of hand as irrelevant because they were poorly adapted to local housing conditions. In view of the message, the selection criteria included such things as visibility of the living room from the street, the presence of a back alley or rear entrance, absence of special provisions against burglary sometimes installed when a house is built, and the presence of a letterbox in or near the front door. These criteria led us to select neighborhoods with single-family dwellings built before or around 1970. A streetplan was drawn up for each area selected. The experimental conditions were distributed on these streets at random, as were the house numbers of those to be approached.

Eight "blind" poll takers participated in the work. They were briefed extensively, and each was given a streetplan with addresses. The test subjects were asked to respond to a survey, conducted by the Free University in cooperation with the police, on the "opinions of Dutch citizens regarding various forms of crime and regarding the possibility of preventing crime." It was stressed that such personal views are significant in connection with proposed planning of police strategy.

During the initial contact, only the first list, which was to function as premeasurement, was distributed (it was referred to as "the first part of the survey"), and people were asked to fill it out personally. Presentation of only part of the whole was justified by explaining that some past experience showed that those questioned sometimes come upon ambiguities in the questions or have difficulty answering some of them. It is better, people were told, to catch such snags quickly, since the entire list should be filled out as accurately as possible. In point of fact, the list of questions was brief and easily answered, and written answering instructions and examples were provided.

The polling crew was told to retrieve the forms as quickly as possible. During this second contact, the poll taker inquired about possible difficulties and told subjects that the distribution of the forms had gone unexpectedly well. He or she alleged to be not yet ready to present the additional survey forms. At best, these would be distributed the following day, when the area would be visited once more. Taking in the initial forms, the poll taker did leave at each residence a leaflet that he or she happened to have. The poll taker urged subjects to read it, because it would be referred to in the second questionnaire.

This second questionnaire included a prevention message and a written request to answer the questions *after* reading the brochure. On account of repeat questions regarding age, gender, educational level, and the code number entered by the poll taker, pretest and posttest data could be located.

Receiver Conditions or Characteristics

Besides a number of characteristics providing general background, such as age, marital status, family size, and perceived class level, the relevant receiver conditions were collected by means of 30 questions.

To measure emotional involvement, questions were asked concerning the perceived safety of the neighborhood (i.e., how safe or unsafe one feels in and around one's house). In addition, subjects were queried about the relative importance of crime as a social problem compared with other social issues and about what they expect in terms of future crime developments. Built into the questionnaire was the possibility of answering "yes" or "no" to questions like, "Do you think the people living here are safe in their homes when alone at night?" It was also possible to answer questions like "How safe or unsafe do you feel when walking this street at night?" by using a 7-point scale (from "very safe" to "very unsafe").

In connection with risk orientation, the subjects were given statements typical of either external or internal orientation. Examples of such assertions are "becoming or not becoming a victim of a crime depends on how lucky you are" and "whether or not you are victimized depends strictly on yourself." Agreement or disagreement with these statements could be expressed on a 7-point scale (from "complete agreement" to "complete disagreement").

Risk assessment was determined by way of asking, "How great a chance do you think you have of falling victim to some crime this coming year?" The answer could be given on a 11-point scale (from 0% [impossible] to 100% [certain]).

Subjective risk protection was ascertained by asking, "To what degree do you feel protected by the police?" This question, too, involved a 7-point scale (from "very adequate" to "very inadequate").

To measure the perceived effectiveness of recommended preventive actions, various statements were offered, together with a 7-point answering scale (from "very true" to "quite wrong"). Examples: "If people do some simple things—like closing the windows and locking the doors when they leave or installing security locks—they help prevent becoming the victims of a burglary"; "We can reduce the chance of a burglary by taking very simple measures."

Side Effect Variables

To measure the side effect variables, people were given 22 questions related to fear of crime, (subjective) victimization risk, (perceived) negative impact of victimization, and (perceived) police protection. An example of the questions regarding the first group (fear): "Please indicate to what degree your assessment of the chance that your house will be broken into makes you feel like this: . . ." These questions were arranged on a 7-point answering scale (from "very calm, safe, and confident" to "very tense, unsafe, and afraid").

To chart subjective victimization risks, subjects were asked to indicate on a scale from 0% to 100% how great a chance they or others in the house have of falling victim to some crime within 1 year. They were also asked to answer this for the next 5 years. The answer to this second type of question was given on a 5-point scale (from "much less" to "much greater"). The questions about risk ran like this: "The chance that my house will be broken into is . . . percent" and "The chance that I will become the victim of a crime inside my home is . . . percent."

The negative impact of victimization was traced in various questions concerning the perceived seriousness of the consequences of victimization. These questions included a 7-point scale ("quite harmless" to "very harmful"). Examples of impact questions: "To what extent do you experience possible burglary as a harmful, negative, or damaging event for you personally?" and "To what extent do you think that the possible consequences of a crime directed against you are unpleasant, negative, or harmful?"

Finally, perceived police protection against victimization was ascertained through questions such as, "How far do you consider yourself to be protected by the police against break-ins?" and "To what extent do you consider yourself to be protected by the police against violent crime?" These two questions were answered using a 7-point scale (from "very adequate" to "very inadequate").

Campaign Brochure

The experimental subjects were offered burglary prevention communication. Since the recommendations were formulated in three different ways, these people received either a positive message, a negative message, or a mixed message. The positive message linked positive results to carrying out recommended actions. Among such positive consequences were reduction of the chance of burglary, rendering the house unattractive as a target, reduction or removal of the opportunity for a break-in, and obstructing burglary attempts. The negative message always associated negative behavioral consequences with disregard of the measures advised. Examples: You increase the chance that your house will be broken into, you present would-be thieves with an opportunity, and so on (the formulations are "reversals" of the positive formulations). In the mixed message, positive and negative linkages alternated in such a way that half of the content consisted of references to positive consequences and half contained negative references. In view of the first hypothesis, the three types of message contained an identical introduction. Also, in every case the title page carried the symbol commonly in use for crime prevention campaigns.

Following an introduction, six burglary prevention recommendations were given. An explanation was added to each. The experimental manipulation described earlier was inserted in these explanations.

RESULTS

Sample Characteristics

The sample includes a total of 324 test subjects. The data of 16 subjects were removed, since in their case it was impossible to be sure that pretest and posttest measurements were correlated correctly (different ages or gender were reported, for instance). Approximately one-half are female (n = 160; 49.9%), the rest are male (n = 164; 50.6%). The average age is 44.15 years. With respect to education, three levels were distinguished: The lower level includes 144 subjects (44.4%), the intermediate level includes 111 subjects (34.3%), and 69 subjects (21.3%) had completed advanced schooling. As to the class level at which the subjects placed themselves, most of them (n = 182; 58.2%) felt they belonged to the lower middle class, 71 subjects (21.9%) placed themselves in the lower or higher working class, and 66 (20.4%) placed themselves in the higher middle class. The number of people who described themselves as well-to-do is negligible (n = 5; 1.5%). Most of those questioned rent the houses they occupy (n = 258; 79.6%); 66 (20.4%) own the homes they live in.

Depending on whether campaign information was offered or not, and depending on the type of message given, four groups can be distinguished. The control group, which received no burglary prevention communication, consists of 84 subjects. The positive message group comprises 78, the negative 77, and the mixed group 85. The preliminary analysis shows these four groups to be very similar with respect to the receiver conditions relevant to the interaction hypothesis.

Experimental Results

General Fear Effects

Within the complex of dependent variables, five types of side effect can be distinguished theoretically. These relate to fear of crime, estimated victimization risk, expected negative impact of victimization, and assessment of the protection against victimization provided by the police. This last category was split into two: police protection against burglary and against crimes of violence. Either case involves a single dependent variable. Among the other side effects the indices are always built up of constituent variables. The index for fear of crime comprises nine variables and possesses a reliability of α = .95. The risk index is composed of eight variables; its reliability is α = .85. The index for estimated negative impact of victimization contains three variables and has reliability of α = .90. In view of these high reliabilities, the conjoining of variables is an obvious move.

To test the hypothesis concerning general fear effects, a contrast analysis was carried out between subjects exposed to burglary prevention communication and subjects from the control group. Table 26-1 offers a summary of the relevant means and the results of the test.

Table 26-1 offers no room whatever for the speculation that burglary preventive communication leads automatically and directly to side effects of the sort intended. It appears, then, that the hypothesis of general fear effects must be rejected. Inspection of the probability levels in the table shows that, on the whole, there is no significant difference between the informed and the uninformed regarding fear of crime, estimated victimization risk, and expected negative impact. The groups do not significantly differ in their evaluation of police protection either.

Message Hypothesis

In light of the message hypothesis, rejection of the general hypothesis comes as no surprise; in fact, such rejection is explicable in terms of it. After all, to

Table 26-1 Means (*M*) and standard deviations (*SD*) of test subjects exposed or not exposed to communication, with test statistics (*t*) in contrast analysis and probability levels (*p*)

	No communication		Communication			
Side effect	*M*	*SD*	*M*	*SD*	*t*	*p*
Fear of crime	3.84	1.31	3.75	1.58	.44	.65
Subjective victimization risk	3.25	1.31	3.28	1.23	.20	.83
Estimated negative impact	3.98	1.23	3.85	1.59	.69	.49
Police protection						
Against burglary	5.17	1.43	4.90	1.43	1.55	.12
Against violence	5.20	1.42	5.04	1.41	.89	.37

test the general hypothesis the three groups that were exposed to communication were swept into the one category called "informed." Not taken into account was the possibility that increase of fear within one group was counterbalanced by fear reduction in the others. Table 26-2 reveals whether or not such neutralization actually did take place.

The means reported in Table 26-2 render it plausible that neutralization, as implied by the message hypothesis, did indeed take place. With this, we have found a fitting explanation for rejecting the hypothesis of general fear effects. It is clear from the pattern of these means that the group exposed to a negative message reports higher fear of crime, victimization risk, and negative impact and claims to feel less protected by the police than the group exposed to a positive message. This result underscores the importance of the message conditions whereby differential fear effects occur. Specifically, it appears that the manner of formulating the recommended preventive provisions influences the arising (or not arising) of harmful side effects.

The pattern of linear decrease implied by the message hypothesis is significant with respect to a majority of the side effect variables investigated when a polynomial test is carried out. Two further cases reveal a clear tendency to linear reduction. With respect to fear of crime, victimization risk, and negative impact, the pattern observed is in complete agreement with the pattern hypothetically predicted. The decrease in these instances always takes the path from negative information via no information to a mixed message and finally a positive message. Regarding police protection against burglary and violent crime, one can note at least a strong agreement between the observed pattern and the predicted pattern.

On the whole, the results reproduced in Table 26-2 amount to a confirmation of the message hypothesis. This confirmation relativizes the claimed preference for negative messages supposedly backed by the consideration that these would achieve the desired effects better. From the point of view of the side effects, this preference is not unqualifiedly justified.

Effectiveness Hypothesis

The effectiveness hypothesis expresses an interaction between message and (subjectively) perceived efficacy (α = .73). The hypothesis implies that negative communication–engendered side effects become visible particularly with persons who perceive the provisions recommended as ineffective.

Table 26-2 Means (*M*) and standard deviations (*SD*) in side effect variables of subjects in the control group and the positive, negative, and mixed message groups, with test statistics and probability levels (*p*) in the execution of a polynomial test for linearity (*F/lin*) and the deviation from linearity (*F/dev*)

	Communication											
	Negative		Absent		Mixed		Positive					
Side effect	*M*	*SD*	*M*	*SD*	*M*	*SD*	*M*	*SD*	*F/lin*	*p*	*F/dev*	*p*
Fear of crime	4.03	1.62	3.84	1.31	3.64	1.55	3.59	1.54	3.99	.02	.16	.68
Subjective victim risk	3.55	1.27	3.25	1.31	3.14	1.17	3.16	1.23	4.20	.02	.70	.50
Negative impact	4.02	1.68	3.98	1.23	3.77	1.55	3.77	1.54	1.66	.09	.16	.84
Police protection												
Burglary	5.02	1.45	5.17	1.43	4.94	1.40	4.71	1.46	2.63	.05	.86	.42
Violence	5.19	1.44	5.20	1.42	4.94	1.40	4.71	1.40	1.88	.07	.15	.85

Higher score = more side effect

Table 26-3 Means (*M*) and standard deviations (*SD*) of subjects exposed or not exposed to negative communication with high and low perceived effectiveness of the recommended preventive measures, with test statistics (*F*) belonging to the interaction term communication × effectiveness and probability levels (*p*)

	Perceived effectiveness									
	No communication				Negative communication					
	Low		High		Low		High			
Side effect	*M*	*SD*	*M*	*SD*	*M*	*SD*	*M*	*SD*	*F*	*p*
Fear of crime	4.20	1.26	3.46	1.26	4.55	1.64	3.56	1.47	.31	.26
Subjective victim risk	3.24	1.30	3.25	1.33	4.03	1.12	3.12	1.26	5.45	.01
Negative impact	4.26	1.11	3.69	1.30	4.60	1.65	3.50	1.55	1.42	.11
Police protection										
Burglary	4.86	1.61	5.51	1.14	5.45	1.19	4.63	1.56	11.22	.00
Violence	4.93	1.53	5.48	1.23	5.48	1.26	4.92	1.57	6.27	.00

Inspection of the test statistics and probability levels given in Table 26-3 makes clear that significant interaction occurs in three cases: police protection against burglary, protection against crimes of violence, and the estimation of victimization risk. An interaction tendency is visible in the case of expected negative impact of victimization. There is no significant interaction effect on fear of crime. Instead, the pattern of the reported means indicates increased fear of crime in both categories of test subjects. This increase, it should be added, is most evident among receivers who perceive effectiveness as low.

When we look at the means related to significant interaction effects, the observable pattern there always turns out to be in line with the hypothetical prediction. Receivers who experience the recommendations as hardly effective express a far more negative judgment regarding police protection. Where effectiveness is considered high, an opposite judgment is expressed: These subjects evince a growing confidence in the police protection provided. Assessment on the part of these subjects tends toward adequate risk protection.

For the estimates of victimization risk, predicted and observed patterns also agree. A higher estimate of that risk is evident among subjects belonging to the category of those who perceive effectiveness as low. Conversely, this side effect is not found among those who experience the preventive measures as effective: The estimations of these subjects, informed or not informed, are virtually identical. The pattern that corresponds to the interaction tendency also corresponds to the predictions. The subjective expectation that victimization has a seriously negative impact becomes the more pronounced among those who belong to the category "low effectiveness."

The combined results of Table 26-3 preponderantly confirm the effectiveness hypothesis. The only clear exception is the absence of the predicted interaction effect on fear of crime. One may conclude that the occurrence of side effects is determined not only by message conditions but also by receiver conditions. Testing the fourth hypothesis will provide the answer as to which other receiver conditions may be of possible significance.

Interaction Hypothesis

The fourth hypothesis is made up of five parts. Each subhypothesis predicts an interaction effect between communication and a given receiver condition. The first concerns the gender of the receiver (see Table 26-4). The prediction is that side effects become especially evident among women. Among male receivers they are not expected to occur. Two interaction effects are not reproduced in Table 26-4. These concern the differential effects on perceived police protection against burglary and against crimes of violence. The terms of interaction are significant in neither of these two cases; the calculated test scores are $F = .08$ ($p = .77$) and $F = .17$ ($p = .67$) respectively. In other words, the gender hypothesis is not confirmed for these side effect variables.

The F values and probability statistics listed do show significant interaction effects regarding fear of crime and estimated negative impact of victimization. Also, one observes an interaction tendency in relation to victimization risk. The listed means show that the observed pattern is in agreement with the prediction. Female receivers react to the message with increased fear, whereas male receivers evince fear reduction. A similar pattern is seen in expectations regarding negative impact: This expectation is reinforced in the case of female receivers

Table 26-4 Means (*M*) and standard deviations (*SD*) for male and female subjects exposed or not exposed to negative communication, for fear of crime, subjective victimization risk, and estimated negative impact, with *F* values belonging to the interaction term communication × gender and probability levels (*p*)

	No communication				Negative communication					
	Female		Male		Female		Male			
Side effect	*M*	*SD*	*M*	*SD*	*M*	*SD*	*M*	*SD*	*F*	*p*
Fear of crime	4.23	1.19	3.51	1.32	4.68	1.55	3.27	1.37	2.48	.05
Subjective victim risk	3.47	1.37	3.06	1.24	3.97	1.19	3.04	1.22	1.57	.10
Negative impact	4.32	1.19	3.70	1.20	4.47	1.53	3.14	1.41	5.63	.01

only. As far as the estimated chance of victimization is concerned, there are no differences between male receivers and the control group, whereas female receivers report greater victimization risk than women in the control group do. In brief, regarding these three side effects the gender hypothesis is confirmed.

Orientation Hypothesis

The remaining parts of the fourth hypothesis concern either risk characteristics or aspects of receiver concern about the topic of crime. Table 26-5 represents the analysis of the interaction between negative communication and risk orientation.

The crux of the orientation hypothesis is that side effects are expected to become evident in receivers whose perception of victimization is externally oriented. Within the group of subjects who hold that by and large they themselves control the risk of victimization, no side effects are expected. In two cases, analysis reveals no significant interaction. Parallel to the results above, here too no differential reactions occur in the judgments regarding police protection against burglary ($F = 0.05$, $p = .81$) or against crimes of violence ($F = .20$, $p = .65$). Differential effects are inscribed in fear of crime and in the expected negative impact of crime. In both cases, there is significant interaction. In addition, an interaction tendency is seen also in the estimated victimization risks. The pattern emerging from the listed means is in every case in agreement with the pattern predicted by the orientation hypothesis. Subjects with an external risk orientation and exposed to negative communication report higher fear of crime than comparable subjects in the control group do. When the orientation is internal, the message does not elicit this side effect; rather, a reduction of fear is realized. Among externally oriented subjects, a negative message results in an evident intensification of the expected negative impact. Again, the internally oriented do not react in this way. Finally, the externally oriented present especially high estimates of victimization risk.

The orientation hypothesis, then, is supported in the majority of the side effect variables; hence, the occurrence or nonoccurrence of side effects is dependent on the receiver's perception of the controllability of victimization risk.

Risk Characteristics

In addition to risk orientation, two further risk characteristics may be of significance, namely, risk assessment and risk protection. Concerning the protection hypothesis, a brief comment will suffice. This hypothesis is not supported by the data obtained. The rise of fear, increased subjective victimization risk, and intensification of expected negative impact occur regardless of whether subjects consider themselves adequately or inadequately protected by the police. We do note that these side effects are more pronounced among subjects experiencing insufficient protection. Taking fear of crime as representative of this, we note the following: When risk protection is deemed inadequate, the mean of fear in the control group is 4.13 ($SD = 1.18$) and in the negative communication group 4.53 ($SD = 1.63$). When risk protection is seen as adequate the mean is 3.45 ($SD = 1.40$) and 3.50 ($SD = 1.46$) respectively. There is no significant interaction effect on any of the side effect variables. In other words, perceived risk protection does not lead to differential reactions to negative communication.

Table 26-5 Means (*M*) and standard deviations (*SD*) of subjects with internal or external risk orientation, exposed or not exposed to negative communication, with test statistics (*F*) belonging to the interaction term communication × risk orientation and probability levels (*p*)

	No communication				Negative communication					
	External		Internal		External		Internal			
Side effect	*M*	*SD*	*M*	*SD*	*M*	*SD*	*M*	*SD*	*F*	*p*
Fear of crime	3.74	1.41	3.92	1.22	4.74	1.52	3.57	1.62	5.70	.00
Subjective victim risk	3.15	1.39	3.33	1.24	3.70	1.17	3.40	1.37	1.40	.11
Negative impact	3.93	1.34	4.02	1.14	4.50	1.52	3.53	1.72	5.42	.00

Relatively more support is given to the assessment hypothesis. For fear of crime, there is significant interaction between message and risk assessment ($F = 3.00, p = 0.04$). Greater fear is reported by subjects with high risk assessment who were exposed to a negative message ($M = 4.38, SD = 1.55$) than is reported by comparable subjects not so exposed ($M = 3.88, SD = 1.35$). Within the group with a low risk assessment, on the other hand, a decrease of fear of crime occurs. Among communication receivers, the mean is 3.50 ($SD = 1.61$); in the control group, it is 3.80 ($SD = 1.28$). Estimated negative impact reveals a tendency toward interaction ($F = 1.71, p = 0.09$).

In the group of subjects with a high risk assessment, negative communication makes for intensification of perceived negative impact. In the informed group, the mean is 4.32 ($SD = 1.70$); in the control group, it is 4.05 ($SD = 1.27$). In the group with a low risk assessment, negative communication tends to a reduction of estimated negative impact. The relevant means are 3.56 ($SD = 1.56$) in the negative communication group and 3.90 ($SD = 1.20$) in the control group.

In summary, with respect to the risk hypotheses (constituents of the comprehensive interaction hypothesis), the conclusion is that evident support is offered for the orientation hypothesis, the protection hypothesis is not confirmed, and there is but marginal support for the assessment hypothesis.

Table 26-6 deals with the interaction between communication and involvement characteristics (with emotional involvement as the specific receiver condition).

The Emotional Involvement Hypothesis

The subhypothesis concerning emotional involvement predicts differential reactions to communication influenced by the degree of emotional involvement with crime as phenomenon. On account of this, side effects are expected in the group whose involvement is high, whereas such effects are not expected to occur among those with low involvement. Inspection of the F values and probability levels show that this hypothesis is marginally supported at best. Only in the case of fear of crime do we ascertain a significant interaction effect. Interaction in relation to estimated negative impact and victimization risk are not significant. The pattern outlined in the listed means agrees with the pattern implied by the involvement hypothesis. Among those who are highly emotionally involved, negative communication elicits increased fear. When emotional involvement is low, this side effect does not occur; rather, the informed subjects report less fear of crime than those belonging to the control group. Evidently, emotional involvement as receiver condition is important only for the prediction of differential fear reactions in the narrow sense.

A closer look should be taken at the significant interaction effect reported in Table 26-6 between communication and emotional involvement on the one hand and the evaluation of police protection against burglary risk on the other. The pattern of the corresponding means does not agree with the predicted pattern. Subjects with high emotional involvement do not react to negative communication by trusting the police less but by trusting them more. Given that precisely in this group negative communication leads to increased fear, this result is remarkable.

An alternative explanation could be that behind the result found in these subjects lurks some sort of rationalization, in particular, problem denial. Denial would amount to an attempt to control the fears brought on by the message by

Table 26-6 Means (*M*) and standard deviations (*SD*) of subjects with high or low emotional involvement, exposed or not exposed to negative communication, with test statistics (*F*) belonging to the interaction term communication × involvement and probability levels (*p*)

	Emotional involvement									
	No communication				Negative communication					
	Low		High		Low		High			
	M	*SD*	*M*	*SD*	*M*	*SD*	*M*	*SD*	*F*	*p*
Fear of crime	3.34	1.28	4.31	1.16	3.14	1.34	4.75	1.48	2.31	.05
Subjective										
victim risk	2.81	1.20	3.66	1.28	3.11	1.22	3.91	1.22	.02	.86
Negative impact	3.45	1.18	4.48	1.07	3.26	1.39	4.64	1.66	.65	.40
Police protection										
Burglary	4.70	1.58	5.62	1.11	5.08	1.40	4.97	1.50	5.35	.02
Violence	4.70	1.58	5.60	1.13	5.02	1.46	5.32	1.42	1.40	.11

acting as if the police are well equipped to protect against burglary. That this kind of rationalization in response to being exposed to a fear-inspiring message may take place is pointed out by, among others, Mann and Janis (1982) and Rogers (1975).

There are other interactions that indicate possible traces of rationalization regarding police protection against violent crime. This may be indicated by the tendency to interaction of communication and risk assessment with perceived police protection against burglary (F = 1.70, p = 0.08) and violent crime (F = 1.40, p = .11) and the tendency to interaction of negative communication and the receiver condition of risk protection with the perceived protection against burglary (F = 1.45, p = .11). In each of these cases, confidence in available police protection is weakened in receivers who initially considered themselves adequately protected or as running little risk, whereas the opposite is the case among subjects with insufficient risk protection or high risk assessment. An example is the mean of perceived protection against burglary in subjects whose risk assessment is high. In the control group, the mean is 5.32 (SD = 1.36), whereas among those exposed to negative communication, the mean is 4.93 (SD = 1.40). In each instance mentioned, an attempt is possibly made to control elicited fears.

CONCLUSION

Victimological literature confronts us with recurrent speculations and cautions that burglary prevention communication results in the unwanted side effect of increased fear of crime. These speculations strongly suggest that such communication always and automatically leads to this side effect and to related ones in the areas of assessed victimization risk, estimated negative impact of victimization, and public confidence in available police protection against crime. The experimental results reported here underline the primitive character of this suggestion. No automatism in the relationship of fear and communication is indicated.

The hypothesis on general fear effects, which expresses this unconditional suggestion most directly, could not be bolstered by experimental support. A number of conditional hypotheses arrived at by theoretical analysis, however, were supported experimentally. The relationship between fear and communication, then, turns out to be conditional rather than automatic: Side effects become apparent if and only if certain conditions are met. These conditions are formed by both message characteristics and receiver characteristics that prove to have differential consequences. The experimental support found for the message hypothesis illustrates the significance of message conditions. Experimental support for the effectiveness hypothesis and for various parts of the interaction hypothesis illustrate the importance of receiver conditions such as the effectiveness of the preventive advice as subjectively perceived, the receiver's gender, and the receiver's risk orientation. The confirmation of the message hypothesis simultaneously offers an explanation for the rejection of the general fear hypothesis. The increase in general fear which follows upon exposure to negative communication is compensated for by the general fear reduction resulting from being exposed to positive communication.

The experimental support for the message hypothesis also provides some pointers regarding how future prevention campaigns could avoid unwanted side effects. Side effects could be kept at bay if a strategy of negative communication is avoided. Preventive messages should not exclusively link neglect of preventive recommendations and negative consequences such as increased risk of burglary.

Some have held that in terms of the effect aimed for (i.e., increased willingness to take preventive action), negative communication is preferable. This point of view, however, is one-sided. When side effects are taken into consideration, this preference becomes highly questionable. To avoid unwanted side effects, we must design messages that at least also include the positive consequences of carrying out preventive recommendations (e.g., reduction of burglary risk), as the strategy of the mixed message does.

One goal that goes beyond the mere avoidance of negative side effects is to effectuate, by means of burglary prevention communication, a decrease in fear of crime among the population. On this point, the message hypothesis suggests that future campaigns should utilize a strategy of positive communication. In a positive message, the carrying out of recommendations is linked to positive consequences, in particular, to reduction of burglary risk. In a broader sense, a positive message is most explicit in suggesting that crime, in this case, burglary, is controllable.

I consider it likely that this notion of the controllability of crime plays a crucial role in the occurrence or nonoccurrence of side effects. The experimental support given to various hypotheses regarding receiver conditions also points in this direction. First, testing the effectiveness hypothesis revealed, among other things, that side effects become apparent especially among persons who experience the measures recommended as ineffective. Negative communication clearly diminished the confidence of these subjects in available police protection against burglary and violent crime. In addition, in this group negative communication occasioned a rise in the estimated victimization risk. Among subjects who perceive the recommended preventive actions as effective, opposite effects were noted. Reinforcement of perceived control over victimization was sketched above as an important instrument in the reduction of fear.

Put more generally, these results allow us to conclude that side effects are likely to arise among receivers who consider burglary uncontrollable or virtually uncontrollable (the category of low effectiveness), whereas side effects will probably not occur among receivers who feel that burglary can be controlled (i.e., receivers characterized by a perceived high effectiveness of the recommendations). The experimental support given to the orientation hypothesis points to the key role possibly played by "controllability" as well. When this hypothesis was tested, it became clear that negative communication led to a decided increase in fear among externally oriented subjects. Receivers with an internal risk orientation do not display this side effect; rather, negative communication here led to a reduction of fear. Naturally, victimization-risk orientation is closely tied to views on the controllability of crime. Those who believe that they can do something about being victimized belong to the group who are internally oriented. In other words, within this group there is a strong conviction that crime is controllable. In contrast, this notion is underdeveloped among the externally oriented. This group conceives of victimization as a matter of bad luck.

In summary, we may conclude that the message hypothesis, the effectiveness hypothesis, and the orientation hypothesis all point in the same direction, namely, to the view that side effects are avoidable and that fear is reducible by means of communication if the campaign expressly refers to the theme of the controllability of burglary. One conceivable instrument for influencing the perceived controllability of crime is the increase of police visibility. Various experiments (cf. Winkel, 1986) have already shown that when the police are more visible and more approachable, the result is less fear of crime, lower estimates of victimization risk, less emphasis on perceived negative impact, and improved relations between the police and the public. Combined with the results described above, this would suggest that messages should be positive and preferably communicated by way of personal contacts between uniformed police officers and members of the community.

BIBLIOGRAPHY

Ajzen, J., & Fishbein, J. M. (1980). *Understanding attitudes and predicting social behavior.* Englewood Cliffs: Prentice-Hall.

Atkin, C. K. (1979). Research evidence on massmediated health communication campaigns. In D. Nimmo (Ed.), *Communication yearbook 3* (pp. 655–669). New Brunswick, NJ: Transaction Books.

Cohn, E. S., Kidder, L. H., & Harvey, J. (1978). Crime prevention vs. victimization prevention: The psychology of two different reactions. *Victimology*, *3*(3–4), 285–296.

Garofalo, J., & Laub, J. (1978). The fear of crime: Broadening our perspective. *Victimology*, *3*(3–4), 242–253.

Hening, J., & Maxfield, M. G. (1978). Reducing fear of crime: Strategies for intervention. *Victimology*, *3*(3–4), 297–313.

Jaccard, J. (1981). Attitudes and behavior: Implications of attitudes toward behavioral alternatives. *Journal of Experimental Social Psychology*, *17*, 286–307.

Janis, I. L. (1967). Effects of fear arousal on attitude change: Recent developments in theory and experimental research. In L. Berkowitz (Ed.), *Advances in experimental social psychology* (pp. 166–225). New York: Academic Press.

Leventhal, H. (1970). Findings and theory in the study of fear communications. In L. Berkowitz (Ed.), *Advances in experimental social psychology* (pp. 119–187). New York: Academic Press.

Mann, L., & Janis, I. L. (1982). Conflict theory of decision making and the expectancy-value approach. In N. T. Feather (Ed.), *Expectations and actions: Expectancy-value models in psychology* (pp. 341–365). Hillsdale, New Jersey: Erlbaum.

Riger, S., Gordon, M. T., & LeBailly, R. (1978). Women's fear of crime: From blaming to restricting the victim. *Victimology*, *3*(3–4), 274–284.

Rogers, R. W. (1975). A protection motivation theory of fear appeals and attitude change. *The Journal of Psychology*, *91*, 93–114.

Sacco, V. F., & Silverman, R. A. (1981). Selling crime prevention: The evaluation of a massmedia-campaign. *Canadian Journal of Criminology*, *23*(2), 191–203.

Sacco, V. F., & Silverman, R. A. (1982). Crime prevention through massmedia: Prospects and problems. *Journal of Criminal Justice*, *10*, 257–269.

Soetenhorst-de Savornin Lohman, J. (1982). Gevoelens van onveiligheid: Wat kan de overheid eraan doen? *Beleid en Maatschappij*, *6*, 156–162.

Tyler, T. R., & Cook, F. L. (1984). The massmedia and judgements of risk: Distinguishing impact on personal and societal level judgements. *Journal of Personality and Social Psychology*, *47*, 693–708.

van der Ploeg, H. M. (1980). Validatie van de zelfbeoordelingvragenligst [Dutch version of the Spielberger State-Trait-Anxiety Inventory]. *Nederlands Tijdschrift voor de Psychologie*, *35*, 243–249.

van der Vijver, C. D. (1983). *Laat ze het zelf maar zeggen: De bruikbaarheid van bevolkingson-*

derzoek voor de beleidsvorming van de politie. Directie Politie, Ministerie van Binnenlandse Zaken.

van der Wurff, A., & Stringer, P. (1986). De duistere wereld van de angst voor misdaad. In J. van Grumbkow, D. van Kreveld, and P. Stringer (Eds.), *Toegepaste Sociale Psychologie* (Vol. 2, pp. 101–115). Lisse: Swets en Zeitlinger.

Winkel, F. W. (1981). Beslissingen: het rechtspsychologisch perspectief. *Delikt en Delinkwent*, *11*, 506–521.

Winkel, F. W. (1987a). Response generalization in crime prevention campaigns: An experiment. *British Journal of Criminology*, *27*(2), 155–174.

Winkel, F. W. (1987b). *Politie en voorkoming misdrijven: Effecten en neveneffecten van voorlichting*. Amsterdam: Mens en Recht.

Winkel, F. W. (1988). Reducing fear of crime through police visibility: A field experiment. *Criminal Justice Policy Review*, *1*(4), 381–398.

VII

CONCLUSIONS AND RECOMMENDATIONS

27

Conclusions and Recommendations of the Fourth International Institute on Victimology

The Fourth International Institute of Victimology (NATO Advanced Research Workshop) was held in Tuscany, Italy, August 9–15, 1987, with the objective of bringing together scholars, professionals, and policy makers to:

1. conduct a critical overall review of the state of the art in victimology
2. survey the major research efforts on victimization conducted to date
3. identify and inventory major findings in the field
4. develop a comprehensive research strategy and agenda
5. demonstrate how data on victims can be useful to administrators and decision makers
6. strengthen international cooperation and communications

Task Forces were formed to achieve the objectives of the meeting as they relate to four specific areas of victimological theory and research listed in the basic preliminary document of the meeting:

1. harm and its causes
2. seeing oneself as a victim
3. claiming the victim status and role
4. receiving society's recognition and possible support

The four Task Forces worked intensely during the meeting to answer specific questions related to those four areas and to develop appropriate conclusions and recommendations. The result of their work is presented here in summary form for circulation among the international community of organizations, programs, associations, scholars, professionals, and practitioners whose work and influence can directly affect the unfolding and outcome of those four stages of the victimization process.

It is hoped that the ensuing discussion, communications, and translation into plans for collaborative action and research will substantially advance the cause of creating a violence- and victimization-free society. (For more details, see Emilio Viano, "Victimology Today: Major Issues of Research and Public Policy," Chapter 1 in this volume.)

TASK FORCE 1: HARM AND ITS CAUSES

Members: Michael Agopian, Maria Rosa Almeida, Thomas Feltes, Joseph Giovannoni, Frank Henry, Brian Hilton, Stanley Johnston, Wesley Skogan, Jock Young

The essential element for victim status is the presence of harm, suffering, or injury whose cause has traditionally been a crime.

I. Targeting of Victims

A. How are harms clustered socially and spatially?
B. How does this focus relate to social disadvantage?
C. How do harms compound in their impact?
D. Construction of a matrix of harm involving risk rates, compounding, and vulnerability.

The net result of these efforts will be the epidemiological mapping, socially and spatially, of harms, disadvantages, and their impact.

II. Weighing of Harm Inflicted by Offenders

A. Which offenders contribute the greatest victimization?
B. What are the major sources of social harm (e.g., street crime versus corporate crime)?

III. Prioritizing Resource Allocation

A. Where are resources needed the most to protect and cushion against victimization?
B. What is an appropriate matrix for this prioritizing task?

IV. A Causal Analysis of Victimization

The Task Force has identified an etiology of victimization on four levels:

A. Structural and cultural conditions that generate offenders
B. Degree of protection by formal agencies of social control
C. Degree of protection by informal agencies of social control
D. Exposure to risk by routine activities, e.g., life style and work patterns

Research must be directed into the respective causal contributions of these four levels with respect to specific harms. Previous research has tended to remain only on one level, using only one variable in the victimization equation.

V. Evaluation of the Cost-Effectiveness of Social Intervention

The effectiveness of social intervention should be evaluated:

A. In terms of specific institutions and interventions
B. In terms of cost-effectiveness by comparing different types of interventions

according to the four levels outlined under Section IV above; for example, one could evaluate the impact of juvenile delinquency control programs by comparing the cost-effectiveness of the four types of intervention:

1. Structural (e.g., by reducing youth unemployment)
2. Formal (e.g., by increasing police resources)
3. Informal (e.g., by organizing neighborhood watches)
4. Risk reduction (e.g., through target hardening)

VI. Need for Cross-National Research

A. Specificity: One must keep in mind and address the problems of generalizing across cultures
B. Range of variables: Cross-national research provides us with a wide range of variables operationalizing the four levels identified above (see IV) and the incidence of various harms

VII. Theory and Research

The Task Force calls for theoretically informed empirical research which attempts to integrate the various theoretical perspectives involved in victimology.

VIII. Secondary Victimization

The Task Force calls for the investigation of the following areas:

A. Secondary victimization as the result of the impact of the justice system and of the helping professions on the victim
B. Secondary victimization of the survivors of the victims
C. Secondary victimization of the families and relatives of the offenders
D. Secondary victimization through the displacement of criminal activities and of victimizing factors:

    1. Locally (e.g., through neighborhood crime watch displacement)
    2. Nationally or internationally (e.g., displacement of drug trafficking, hazardous working conditions, and hazardous wastes from one region or country to another)

IX. Conclusions

When it comes to victimization research in the international community, the Task Force:

A. Notes the vital role of social science research in reducing social harm and conflict
B. Underlines Article I of the North Atlantic Treaty of 1949 which advocates and addresses NATO's role in promoting respect for the rule of law and the institutions of peace
C. Urges NATO's Scientific Affairs Committee to allocate more funds for social science research and activities that will result in the reduction of social harm and the advancement of peace

TASK FORCE 2: SEEING ONESELF AS A VICTIM

Chair: Susan Edwards

Members: Prabodh Bhowmick, Robert Freeman-Longo, Fernand Goffioul, Irving Kaufman, Marcia Morgan, Vergil Williams

Seeing oneself as a victim depends first on perceiving the nature and source of the victimization (objective evaluation), and second on internalizing a perception of oneself as victim (subjective evaluation). This phenomenon occurs in a process which may begin before the occurrence of an objective act and may continue throughout an individual's attempt to claim victim status and the individual's later reception of justice and support. An individual during this process may construct and reconstruct his or her assessment of the victimization such that it may have different effects, sometimes positive, sometimes negative. The perception of the act, the harm or injury inflicted, the loss of power or exploitation experienced, may have repercussions which may be injurious or debilitating either psychologically or socially even some while after the event has occurred. Being a victim, perceiving oneself as a victim, must of necessity be examined in a social, legal, and psychological context.

First, sources of victimization, whether they be corporate, criminal, civil, natural, community, industrial, political, or acts of terrorism, whether they affect individuals in isolation or groups, are often derived from state definitions and validated in legal provisions.

They involve actions where the individual is denied power, feels a sense of injustice, is physically or psychologically harmed and humiliated. The individual may then experience loss of self-esteem, anger, rage, fear, powerlessness, and impotence. The victim response to the acts or behavior may be influenced by the severity of the source of the victimization and by society's recognition of this.

However, this often excludes many "classes" of victims who perceive a harm or injury, feel a sense of injustice and anger, and have been injured and internalize that harm. Yet, the state refuses to recognize that any harm has been done or injustice perpetrated. For example, the pharmaceutical industry refuses to recognize the harm caused by some drugs (Henry, 1987). In many societies a wife is not recognized as the victim of rape. Acts of abuse of state power and acts of terrorism are denied by the organization, group, or country that is the perpetrator.

Who defines what is a source of victimization and who are the legitimate victims involves fundamental questions of power. For example, "one person's freedom fighter is another person's terrorist" is a cliché which reflects the conflict and power implicit in such definitions.

Such forms of victimization have certain consequences, since victims have to cope not only with the original objective harm inflicted on them and its repercussions but also with a denial of harm, exploitation, or injury. This automatically has additional grave psychological consequences for individuals whose recovery may often depend on publicizing their grievances to achieve some level of validation and equilibrium.

These victims largely go unknown and are often silenced in a political process which prefers to focus attention on law and order while diverting attention away from corporate malpractice and acts of terrorism, which all reflect state power and coercion.

Most victimization analysis has therefore started out from an analysis of those "classes" of victims where the state recognizes the victimization. More typically, then, the point of focus has been on crimes like robbery, burglary, and rape by strangers. More recently attention has also been directed toward violence against women and children within the family. Within this area, however, although the state may define certain behaviors as criminal acts or acts of victimization, the perception of victims and the actual abuse of power vary from one victimization category to another. This has important consequences for the subjective perception of what has occurred.

Self-perceptions of victimization are also dependent on societal reactions, that is, on religious, cultural, political, and economic influences which involve a "reflexive" process (Schutz, 1967). Perceptions of oneself as a rape victim, for example, vary and are dependent upon country, culture, and time. In Egypt, Abou-Zeid (1966, p. 257) reminds us of the shame for all family members as a consequence of rape, so that the victim would be outcast. Religious factors have their impact too in shaping this social construction of the victim's identity. Islamic fundamentalism and the return to traditional Sharia law in certain Muslim countries result in a different societal reaction to alcohol abuse, theft, and other offenses, with the result that subjective perceptions may be more devastating in societies where the sociolegal reaction is based on retribution.

Yet the totality of the societal reaction, that is, ideologies, conceptions, and the collective attitude or consciousness toward certain sources of victimization and their victims, actually exists prior to the victimization. Society builds up models of deserving victims, real victims, undeserving victims, and illegitimate victims.

Such victimological models affect and shape the individual's response to the objective victimized. But the individual perception or response to the harm or loss inflicted is the result not only of societal reactions but also of individual personality, psychological factors, and social credibility and status. Here, the subjective perception of the act and the harm or loss inflicted are minimized or maximized in accordance with (1) personality and the ability to transcend the victimization and (2) age, gender, class, and race. Particular personality types may be less resilient to the victimization. Shock, trauma, and psychological disturbances may follow. Social credibility and status may also be impacted.

In addition, self-perception may also be influenced by the relationship of the individual to the "victimizer," whether it be an individual act of crime, a corporate act of public deceit or negligence, an act of terrorism, or a natural disaster. Turning to crime, for example, violent assault by strangers is less likely to evoke a societal response which blames the victim than domestic violence or sexual assault perpetrated by someone known to the victim.

Whether we talk of criminal acts, terrorism, or state exploitation, the victim-offender relationship has fundamental consequences for the way in which some victims perceive themselves. Victims of incest, for example, while recognizing that the act has taken place, nevertheless depend on their own perceptions when exonerating or neutralizing the behavior of the aggressor. Similarly, victims of terrorism often identify with the victimizer. Both are often a typical strategy of survival. As Sykes and Matza (1957) have shown, delinquents engage in neutralization techniques as well in an attempt to minimize the gravity of their behavior. Similarly, victims for a variety of reasons use various neutralization strategies to deny the event, or the harm, or the consequences. Victims frequently engage in such strategies as "He didn't mean it," "It was an accident," "It's not their fault," with the result that victims then turn to their own behavior, often in a self-reproaching sequence which may be damaging.

Particular criminal acts involving sex offenses often result in victims' exonerating the offenders. Self-deprecatory strategies follow. The neutralization of the offenders' actions is often further facilitated by state definitions and the response of the criminal justice process. Crimes against women involving rape, domestic violence, and sexual assault, as well as the sexual and physical abuse of both male and female children, are primary examples of this.

Finally, there are those individuals who decide not to acknowledge the act or harm. This may have negative consequences on a short- or long-term basis if the individual is repressing the experience. Supporting agencies and/or informed friends or relatives have a key role in assisting individuals toward a recognition of the act (Mendelson, 1987).

Although the role of professionals may be crucial, clinical intervention dealing with severe cases may not always be therapeutic for the victim if professional etiquette results in the setting up of another power relationship which further perpetuates and exacerbates the loss of power and control on the part of the victim.

It is important that the self-fulfilling prophecy that the victim deserves to be victimized or seeks to be is effectively confronted. Many groups, including police, courts, medical doctors, and clinicians, have to be sensitized to the consequences of the negative labeling of victims. The role of these agencies in helping victims overcome trauma is crucial.

Ideally the process of seeing oneself as a victim should be therapeutic and cathartic. It should enable the individual to recover from the original objective harm inflicted or injustice experienced. Ideological models of the victim are for the most part harmful, debilitating, and injurious. Sometimes, little that is positive emerges from seeing oneself as a victim. Support agencies try to combat the negative repercussions by helping victims toward transcendence. Thus, to see oneself as a victim becomes the first step toward survival and resolution, that is, toward the normalization of one's life and hopefully of one's personal growth.

A greater awareness of this sociopsychological mesh of self-perception can only be facilitated by providing a better understanding and identification of sources of victimization and perceptions and needs of victims by closely examining what victims say. In this respect, we propose the following recommendations.

Research Issues

1. NATO should (co-)sponsor the preparation and implementation of a cross-national survey, to be conducted in all member countries, on the experiences with crime, the perceptions of internal security, and public attitudes toward the criminal justice system.

2. Victimization surveys should address the attitudes of victims and nonvic-

tims toward various types of victims and their special needs and should explore existing stereotypes and misconceptions as well as sources of informal support among the population.

3. Victimization surveys should be supplemented by studies focusing upon the process of perceiving oneself as a victim, in particular, by means of qualitative methods like in-depth interviews and longitudinal and/or cross-cultural research.

4. Special areas of interest in the studies mentioned above should be:

- the various stages of the process, their determining factors (e.g., bodily and mental symptoms), and cues from the social environment concerning their meaning (e.g., the opinions of the perpetrators and formal agencies)
- cognitions and emotions like fear, a disturbed sense of justice, generalized suspicions, self-blame, feelings of powerlessness and humiliation, anger and rage
- the need to be helped, the need to see that justice is done, and the need to be compensated by the state, insurance, or the offender
- differences between perceptions of males and females toward both sex-specific and non-sex-specific victimization
- perceptions of children

5. There is a need for evaluation studies on victim assistance programs to pay attention to their impact upon victims' self-perception by addressing issues like:

- accessibility for various categories
- intrusion upon the victim's privacy
- stigmatizing effects
- the use of professionals or volunteers
- the establishment of self-help groups

6. There is a need for studies into the social and political roots of the victim movement and its impact upon the attitudes of the public toward crime and justice and upon criminal policies.

Policy Issues

1. Need to raise the consciousness of the public and of social institutions about victimization issues so as to

- reduce injurious stereotypes
- facilitate early identification of the possible personal problems that may be presented later

2. Need to establish easily accessible services which can assist various categories of victims in understanding and evaluating their victimization, like telephone hotlines for battered wives, children who are maltreated, and medical patients and a victim ombudsman for harassment at the work place.

3. Need to develop checklists for use by victims, their families, and victimological practitioners regarding the emergence of postvictimization symptoms which need to be addressed.

4. Need to monitor service or treatment programs for victims with a view to identifying elements which may lead to pathologizing of problems experienced by victims or other forms of undue labeling which may impede a rapid recovery from victimization experiences.

5. Need to promote a debate nationally and internationally on the political,

moral, and legal implications of exposing forms of victimization which have not been made illegal in particular countries, such as sexual exploitation and mutilation of women or boys.

TASK FORCE 3: CLAIMING VICTIM STATUS AND ROLE

Chair: Lenore Walker

Members: Christina Antonopoulou, John Evans, Eliana Gersão, Simha Landau, Malcom MacLeod, Lars Weisaeth, Frans Winkel, and Duygun Yarsuvat

I. What factors influence victims claiming victim status? There are several assumptions our group made about the benefits of claiming victim status, while recognizing there can also be harm.
   A. Prevention of further harm and new victims.
   B. Minimization of harm already experienced.
   C. Remediation of harm already experienced.
      1. Reempowerment of a victim.
      2. Education about natural reactions to unnatural events.
      3. Receive intervention specific to posttraumatic stress disorder (PTSD).
   D. Access to special programs.
   E. Assistance from judicial programs.
   F. Assistance in giving up victim status.
   G. Catch of offenders.

II. Victims claim victim status through a variety of ways which we can observe and measure. They include the following.
   A. Viewing other bodies of literature about help-seeking behavior concerning severity of trauma, history of personal efficacy, competency, and responsibility and looking at situational individual differences.
   B. Victims' perceptions about how they claim victim status can be understood through direct communication with victims and through theoretical approaches like labeling, just world, cognitive dissonance, equity, social learning, psychopathology, and external blame theories.
   C. The concept of hardiness may help explain the differential impact of victimization on victims.
   D. Victims who have adequate information are more likely to move on through the process of victimization responses to becoming survivors and coping successfully.

III. There are some questions about who takes on the victim status and for what reasons and length of time. Some victims receive primary gains from the victim role while others experience longer-term secondary gains, such as war victim pressure groups or those needing economic gains. There are other victims who do not claim victim status for fear of retaliation, refusal to upset family, shame, and lack of identification with harm. Institutional victims may balance the gains with the negative effects of claiming victim status. We need to understand more about the positive and negative components of claiming victim status.

IV. There are issues reflecting on secondary victimization causes which influence whether or not a victim claims status by a formal or informal report. Some of those causes are as follows.
   A. Informal responses from family and friends.
   B. Police role.
   C. Community responses (including issues of race, class, gender, and power issues in areas with and without social transition).
      1. Negative as well as positive effects of compensation funds.
      2. Restitution.
      3. Volunteer schemes.
      4. Mediation.
      5. Treatment for the offender, which should emphasize power and social role, not just pathology.
      6. Treatment for victim (free and voluntary).
      7. Access to legal and expert witnesses.
      8. Public humiliation of offenders (individuals and institutions).
      9. Confidentiality issues for victims.
      10. Human rights.
   D. Types of victimization.
      1. Cross-national offenses, (e.g., Chernobyl).
      2. Institutional victimization.
      3. Economic victimization.

V. Psychological reactions of victims are critical to understanding if, how, and why victims claim victim status and report offenses. Problems include the following.
   A. How to legitimize victim status when one cannot see injury.
   B. How to measure harm.
   C. Reinforcement of shame through repeated victimization or the reporting of it.
   D. Multiple victimization, prevention, and therapeutic intervention.
   E. Clean typology of victimization.
   F. Avoid blaming the victim.

VI. Who benefits when a victim reports an offense?
   A. Victim's role in the criminal justice process.
   B. Perception of impact on recidivism.
   C. Detention/containment.
   D. Retribution/punishment.
   E. Wants offender to get treatment or wants own treatment.
   F. Wants judicial assistance, including compensation funds.

VII. There are a number of recommendations, including research questions, we need to examine.
   A. A more educated community will facilitate the positive effects of claiming victim status. To begin such an education process, one should consider several approaches.
      1. Use of an educated media.
      2. Education in the schools.
      3. "Gatekeepers" in the community.
      4. Testimonials from high status people.
      5. Parenting classes to learn nonviolent behavior.

B. Specific training for professionals and paraprofessionals in the various fields, including the following. (The effectiveness of the training should be evaluated.)
   1. Legal profession (police, lawyers, judges).
   2. Mental health service providers.
   3. Medical personnel (doctors, nurses, paramedics, and medical educators).
C. Encourage better coordination between community agencies, including government and nongovernmental groups on regional, national, and international levels.
D. Change norms in society about sex roles stereotyping; deemphasize popularization of violence.
E. Special consciousness-raising about violent crimes, especially those against women and children, targeted at the following groups.
   1. Government.
   2. Unions and management.
   3. Military.
   4. Advertising.
   5. Corporations and business groups.
F. Seek to minimize the image of violence victims for entertainment and exploitation (such as the sale of products and services).
G. Seek ways to control international networks and trafficking in violence.
H. Encourage use of special techniques and legal provisions to protect child victims who are witnesses to crimes (e.g., videotape their testimony, use closed-circuit television during the trial).
I. Encourage careful protection of human rights, particularly in regard to the following.
   1. Detainees suspected of crimes.
   2. Political prisoners.
   3. Criminal convicts.
   4. Witnesses of crimes.
   5. Those wrongfully accused or convicted.
J. Strongly encourage research to answer questions raised throughout this summary and to investigate the following issues.
   1. Follow-up evaluation of victims to ascertain what is best for them.
   2. Harmful effects of different victimization rating scales and measurements of harm.
   3. Cross-national and cross-cultural differences.
   4. What are the most useful research methodologies?
      a. Research in context.
      b. Feminist scholarship.
      c. In-depth studies.
      d. Survey data.
   5. What is the impact across the life span (e.g., prospective studies)?
   6. Problems of multiple victimization.
   7. How can we coordinate the fragmented research and knowledge base across various disciplines?
   8. Whether claiming the victim status is positive or negative for:
      a. The victim?
      b. Society?

9. If so, under what specific conditions?
10. Encourage availability of funds for research.

TASK FORCE 4: RECEIVING SOCIETY'S RECOGNITION AND SUPPORT

Chair: Aglaia Tsitsoura

Members: Richard Abell, Augusto Balloni, Patricia Begin, Daniel Della Giustina, Burt Galaway, John Lea, Irene Melup, Miguel Polaino Navarrete, Jacquelien Soetenhorst

This Task Force was concerned with the social reaction to victimization expressed through assistance and support to victims, reparation of the damage, and prevention of victimization.

I. It was recognized that the victim should expect sympathy, support, and assistance from his or her close environment. This was the case in small communities where family and neighborhood ties were close. It may not be the case in vast communities, like large cities, where people live mostly in isolation. In such an environment, the victim must find recognition and support by public and private agencies, including the criminal justice system. To this end, the victim's rights should be reviewed and redefined and the necessary resources for support should be made readily available.

Collective victimization (e.g., by abuse of political or economic power) presents special problems whose solution frequently requires international cooperation.

II. Society's care for potential or actual victims should begin with adequate *information* on the dangers of victimization by crime or by accidents and on the ways to avoid it. Programs providing this type of information in schools have proved successful in some countries (e.g., the United States).

Assistance strategies should be developed as a means of prevention. However, members of the Task Force stressed that failing to adopt such strategies should not disqualify the victim from claiming his or her rights.

Information on prevention of victimization provided in schools, by the media, or by any other means should be objective and factual in order to avoid unintended effects such as the deterioration of the quality of life (e.g., fear of going out in the evening, unnecessary fear of being in public or of strangers, etc.) and the reporting of imaginary victimization. Research should examine such effects.

Information should also help actual victims locate the private or public services providing assistance and support. Finally, information should concern the victim's rights in the framework of the criminal justice system and similar procedures.

In some countries, like Canada and the United States, the organization of "Victims' Weeks" serves to disseminate useful information on victimization and to develop society's consciousness on the victim's problems and needs.

III. *Prevention* of victimization should be adequately organized in a comprehensive manner so as to avoid dispersion of efforts or other undesirable effects. For example, prevention programs should not result in a mere displacement of crime from one area to another. Equally, *assistance* services should be integrated or coordinated with existing social, mental health, and community services in order to avoid gaps or duplication of efforts.

Assistance provided through general services, like social welfare, health, or community mental health systems, is considered preferable in some countries, since it has the advantage of avoiding the labeling of the victims. However, such assistance lacks in specificity. Thus, specialized services may be necessary, at least for certain types of victims. Research should be carried out on the merits and efficiency of the various types of services (general versus specific, for all victims or only for some category of victims, professional versus voluntary, etc.) in order to obtain data for better planning and implementation.

Training of professional and of volunteer staff dealing with victims is considered necessary everywhere.

Funding of prevention and assistance efforts presents a special problem. In some countries, fines, special fees, or funds generated through deductions from the compensation prisoners receive for working in prison are utilized to support victim assistance.

In some countries (e.g., Italy and Spain), organized crime and terrorism present special problems. Specific measures for prevention and assistance are necessary, for example, providing protection from retaliation or granting a new identity and relocating the victim or the witness who reported the offense to the police or cooperated with the prosecution.

IV. Although public services should actively strive to prevent victimization and provide assistance to victims, *participation of the public* in these efforts is essential.

Associations, groups, and neighborhoods should organize prevention programs.

Volunteer work is, in all countries, the basis for assistance to victims. However, the need for professional support and involvement is also widely recognized.

The public should also be given the opportunity to collaborate in drawing up crime prevention and victim assistance policies. Members of the public and of associations should be encouraged to express their opinion on the effectiveness of measures taken and on new measures considered advisable.

V. The position of the victim in the framework of the criminal justice system varies from country to country. It is stronger in European continental countries, where the victim can participate in the criminal trial as a "partie civile." It is weaker in common law countries, where the victim is called only as a witness. In these countries, there is a trend to increase the victim's role and, in particular, to give the victim the right to make a statement on the impact of victimization on his or her life either during the preparation of the pre-sentence report or at the sentencing of the offender.

Reparation of the damage is always the responsibility of the offender. However, when the offender is not identified or is financially unable to provide reparation, the state should intervene and compensate the victim. Victim compensation programs now exist in many countries. However, their procedures and the offenses they cover vary substantially from country to country.

Mediation is a procedure bypassing the criminal justice system and thus avoiding its drawbacks (e.g., labeling, costs, delays, etc.). It provides the same rights for the victim and for the offender. However, either or both parties can be pressured to reach agreements that do not satisfy their individual interests.

Research should be carried out on the advantages and disadvantages of intervention by the criminal justice system and of parallel procedures.

VI. Criminality and consequently victimization have *international dimensions*. Victimization may also result from accidents affecting large areas that include several countries or by the circulation at the international level of dangerous substances.

Therefore, it is necessary to promote international cooperation by agreeing on common principles of prevention and assistance to victims, by adopting common strategies, and by exchanging information in this field.

International organizations have been active in this area. The Declaration of Basic Principles of Justice for Victims of Crime and Abuse of Power adopted by the General Assembly of the United Nations in 1985 affects both individual and collective victims. The application of such principles may present grave difficulties, especially in nondemocratic countries. However, the moral force of the principles, international pressure, and the support of the United Nations may promote victims' rights even in those cases.

In its more restricted area (21 member states), the Council of Europe has offered two recommendations providing common principles (1) on the position of the victim within criminal law and procedure and (2) on assistance to victims and prevention of victimization. It has also adopted a European convention on the compensation of victims of violent crimes.

International cooperation is also needed in the field of risks presented by advanced technology, in particular, by nuclear plants. People should be informed quickly and efficiently of accidents which have occurred and of the means of protection.

People victimized may not have the possibility of claiming their rights at the national level because of inadequate legislation, lack of information, inadequate communications, dictatorial regimes, and so forth. International means of recourse should be created to meet the needs of such victims.

CONCLUDING RESOLUTION

The participants of the Fourth International Institute on Victimology (NATO Advanced Research Workshop) designed to advance research and public policy in this field,

Welcoming the opportunity provided here for scientific discussion,

Gratified by the fruitful results achieved by this carefully prepared and well organized meeting of experts,

Cognizant of the need for strengthened regional and international cooperation in this sphere:

Express their appreciation to the North Atlantic Treaty Organization (NATO) and to Professor Emilio Viano for this major opportunity of advancing knowledge and informed action in this critical area,

Urge NATO and other international organizations to sponsor further initiatives of this kind, continue the support of collaborative research endeavors, and facilitate professional dialogue, training, and the continuing exchange of information in the sphere of victimology in view of its importance for the advancement of human rights, social peace and well-being, and harmonious relations among States,

Call upon other regional and international organizations and national governments actively to collaborate in implementing the recommendations made, and otherwise to help promote action oriented research, the adoption of agreed principles, and the implementation of effective policies in this field.

This concluding resolution was *adopted by acclamation* on August 14, 1987.

BIBLIOGRAPHY

Abou-Zeid, A. (1966). Honor and shame amongst the Bedouins of Egypt. In J. G. Peristiany (Ed.), *Honor and shame*. Weidenfeld and Nicholson.

Henry, F. (1987). *Violence against children: The pharmaceutical industry*. Paper presented at the Fourth International Institute of Victimology.

Mendelson, G. (1987). The concept of posttraumatic stress disorder: A review. *International Journal of Law and Psychiatry*, *10*(1), 45–62.

Schutz, A. (1967). *The phenomenology of the social world*. Evanston, IL: Northwestern University Press.

Sykes, G., & Matza, D. (1957). Techniques of neutralization: A theory of delinquency. *American Sociological Review*, *22*.

Appendix

FOURTH INTERNATIONAL INSTITUTE ON VICTIMOLOGY NATO ADVANCED RESEARCH WORKSHOP

Crime and Its Victims: International Research & Public Policy
Tuscany, Italy, August 9–15, 1987

This event was sponsored and funded by the North Atlantic Treaty Organization and by *Victimology: An International Journal*.

Participants

Richard B. Abell, Assistant Attorney General of the United States, Office of Justice Programs, Washington, D.C.
Michael Agopian, Criminal Justice Department, California State University, Long Beach
Maria Rosa Almeida, Gabinete de Estudos e Planeamento, Ministerio da Justica, Lisbon
Christina Antonopoulou, General Secretariat for Equality, Ministry to the Presidency, Athens
Patricia Begin, Policy, Programmes and Research Branch, Department of Justice, Ottawa
Augusto Balloni, Dipartimento di Sociologia, Universitá di Bologna
Prabodh Kumar Bhowmick, Faculty of Science, Calcutta University
Daniel E. della Giustina, Department of Safety and Health Studies, West Virginia University, Morgantown
Susan S. M. Edwards, Polytechnic of Central London
John L. Evans, Director General, Research and Statistics Group, Ministry of the Solicitor General, Ottawa
Thomas Feltes, Institute of Criminology, University of Heidelberg
Robert Freeman-Longo, Sex Offender Unit, Oregon State Hospital, Salem
Burt Galaway, School of Social Work, University of Minnesota, Minneapolis
Eliana Gersão, Centro de Estudos Judiciarios, Ministerio da Justica, Lisbon
Joseph Giovannoni, Sex Offender Treatment Specialist, Honolulu
Fernand Goffioul, Faculte de Medicine, Ecole de Criminologie, Universite de Liege
Frank Henry, Sociology Department, McMaster University, Hamilton, Ontario
Brian Hilton, Cranfield Institute of Technology, Royal Military College of Science, Shrivenham, Wiltshire, U.K.
Sherry Icenhower, *Victimology: An International Journal*, Arlington, Virginia; Administrator, Fourth International Institute on Victimology/NATO Advanced Research Workshop
Stanley W. Johnston, Criminology Department, University of Melbourne

Irving Kaufman, School of Social Work, Smith College, Northampton, Massachusetts
Simha Landau, Institute of Criminology, Faculty of Law, Hebrew University, Jerusalem
John Lea, Centre for Criminology, Middlesex Polytechnic, Queensway, U.K.
Malcom D. MacLeod, Department of Psychology, University of St. Andrews, Scotland
Irene Melup, Crime Prevention and Criminal Justice Branch, United Nations, New York
Marcia Morgan, Migima Designs Inc., Eugene, Oregon; Doctoral Student, Sociology, University of Oregon
Miguel Polaino Navarrete, Instituto de Criminologia, Universidad de Cordoba, Spain
Wesley G. Skogan, Center for Urban Affairs, Northwestern University, Evanston, Illinois
Jacquelien Soetenhorst, Social Faculty, University of Amsterdam
Aglaia Tsitsoura, Division of Crime Problems, Council of Europe, Strasbourg
Jan J. M. van Dijk, Research and Documentation Centre, Ministry of Justice, The Hague
Emilio Viano, School of Justice, The American University, Washington, D.C.; *Victimology: An International Journal*, Arlington, Virginia; Director of the Fourth International Institute on Victimology/NATO Advanced Research Workshop
Lenore Walker, Walker and Associates, Denver
Lars Weisaeth, Section for Disaster Psychiatry, Psychiatric Institute, University of Oslo/The Joint Medical Armed Forces Medical Services, Norway
Vergil Williams, Department of Criminal Justice, University of Alabama, Tuscaloosa
Frans W. Winkel, Faculty of Social Sciences, Social Psychology, Free University of Amsterdam
Duygun Yarsuvat, Faculty of Political Science, University of Istanbul
Jock Young, Centre for Criminology, Middlesex Polytechnic, U.K.

Index